RSF: The Russell Sage Foundation Journal of the Social Sciences

Higher Education Effectiveness

VOLUME 2 · NUMBER 1 · APRIL 2016

RSF: The Russell Sage Foundation Journal of the Social Sciences   ISSN 2377-8261

The Russell Sage Foundation

The Russell Sage Foundation, one of the oldest of America's general purpose foundations, was established in 1907 by Mrs. Margaret Olivia Sage for "the improvement of social and living conditions in the United States." The foundation seeks to fulfill this mandate by fostering the development and dissemination of knowledge about the country's political, social, and economic problems. While the foundation endeavors to assure the accuracy and objectivity of each book it publishes, the conclusions and interpretations in Russell Sage Foundation publications are those of the authors and not of the foundation, its trustees, or its staff. Publication by Russell Sage, therefore, does not imply foundation endorsement.

Board of Trustees

Sara S. McLanahan, *Chair*
Larry M. Bartels
Karen S. Cook
W. Bowman Cutter III
Sheldon H. Danziger
Kathryn Edin
Lawrence F. Katz
David Laibson
Nicholas Lemann
Martha Minow
Peter R. Orszag
Claude M. Steele
Shelley E. Taylor
Richard H. Thaler
Hirokazu Yoshikawa

Mission Statement

RSF: The Russell Sage Foundation Journal of the Social Sciences is a peer-reviewed, open-access journal of original empirical research articles by both established and emerging scholars. It is designed to promote cross-disciplinary collaborations on timely issues of interest to academics, policymakers, and the public at large. Each issue is thematic in nature and focuses on a specific research question or area of interest. The introduction to each issue will include an accessible, broad, and synthetic overview of the research question under consideration and the current thinking from the various social sciences.

RSF Journal Editorial Board

Annette Bernhardt, University of California, Berkeley
Marianne Bertrand, University of Chicago
Karen S. Cook, Stanford University
Sheldon H. Danziger, Russell Sage Foundation
Nancy Folbre, University of Massachusetts
Janet C. Gornick, The CUNY Graduate Center
John A. Ferejohn, Stanford University
Larry V. Hedges, Northwestern University
Jennifer Hochschild, Harvard University
Rucker C. Johnson, University of California, Berkeley
Douglas S. Massey, Princeton University
James Sidanius, Harvard University
Mary C. Waters, Harvard University
Bruce Western, Harvard University

Copyright © 2016 by Russell Sage Foundation. All rights reserved. Printed in the United States of America. No part of this publication may be reproduced, stored in a retrieval system, or transmitted in any form or by any means, electronic, mechanical, photocopying, recording, or otherwise, without the prior written permission of the publisher. Reproduction by the United States Government in whole or in part is permitted for any purpose.

Opinions expressed in this journal are not necessarily those of the editors, editorial board, trustees, the Russell Sage Foundation, or the Spencer Foundation.

We invite scholars to submit proposals for potential issues through the *RSF* application portal: https://rsfjournal.onlineapplicationportal.com/. Submissions should be addressed to Suzanne Nichols, Director of Publications.

To view the complete text and additional features online please go to **www.rsfjournal.org**.

Russell Sage Foundation
112 East 64th Street
New York, NY 10065

ISSN (print):   2377-8253
ISSN (electronic): 2377-8261
ISBN: 978-0-87154-992-1

The Spencer Foundation

Michael S. McPherson, *President*
Deborah Loewenberg Ball, *Chair*
Pamela Grossman, *Vice Chair*
Carl Cohn
Richard J. Murnane
Stephen W. Raudenbush
C. Cybele Raver
Mario L. Small
T. Dennis Sullivan
Mark A. Vander Ploeg

RSF: The Russell Sage Foundation
Journal of the Social Sciences

VOLUME 2 NUMBER 1
APRIL 2016

Higher Education Effectiveness

ISSUE EDITORS
Steven Brint, University of California, Riverside
Charles T. Clotfelter, Duke University

CONTENTS

Part I. Introduction

U.S. Higher Education Effectiveness **2**
Steven Brint and Charles T. Clotfelter

Overview of the Volume **38**
Steven Brint and Charles T. Clotfelter

Part II. Supply and Demand: Cost and Distributional Outcomes

The Changing Landscape of Tuition and Enrollment in American Public Higher Education **42**
Steven W. Hemelt and Dave E. Marcotte

Income and Access to Higher Education: Are High Quality Universities Becoming More or Less Elite? A Longitudinal Case Study of Admissions at UW-Madison **69**
Sara E. Dahill-Brown, John F. Witte, and Barbara Wolfe

Beyond Earnings and Social Reproduction: Can College Lead to Good Jobs Without Reproducing Social Inequalities? **90**
James E. Rosenbaum, Caitlin E. Ahearn, Janet E. Rosenbaum, and Kelly I. Becker

Part III. Policy Interventions: Incentives, Controls, and Metrics

Pricing and University Autonomy: Tuition Deregulation in Texas **112**
Jeongeun Kim and Kevin Stange

Looking Inside the Black Box of Performance Funding for Higher Education: Policy Instruments, Organizational Obstacles, and Intended and Unintended Impacts **147**
Kevin J. Dougherty, Sosanya M. Jones, Hana Lahr, Rebecca S. Natow, Lara Pheatt, and Vikash Reddy

The Promises and Pitfalls of Measuring Community College Quality **174**
Michal Kurlaender, Scott Carrell, and Jacob Jackson

Part IV. Teaching and Learning: Contexts and Practices

Aligning Science Achievement and STEM Expectations for College Success: A Comparative Study of Curricular Standardization **192**
Siqi Han and Claudia Buchmann

Evaluating Promising Practices in Undergraduate STEM Lecture Courses **212**
Lynn C. Reimer, Katerina Schenke, Tutrang Nguyen, Diane K. O'Dowd, Thurston Domina, and Mark Warschauer

PART I
Introduction

U.S. Higher Education Effectiveness

STEVEN BRINT AND CHARLES T. CLOTFELTER

This volume of *RSF* presents new evidence about higher education in the United States. As we use the term, *higher education* is synonymous with postsecondary education and includes two-year community colleges, four-year colleges, and universities that offer graduate training in addition to four-year baccalaureate degrees. As editors, we have been charged with writing an introduction that is more than a summary of the research papers to follow. Instead, we were asked to produce an overview of the key facts and themes about U.S. higher education and its effectiveness that will be important both for specialists and for readers who are new to the subject.

This volume focuses on *effectiveness*, a topic that has not been as prominent in scholarship as we believe it should be. Scholars of higher education have been principally interested in how colleges and universities work and what forces in their environments lead them to change. But most policymakers (and most of the public) do not want simply to understand institutions, but rather to know how to make them work better than they currently do. Because colleges and universities are central institutions in American society, their effectiveness should be considered a topic of national priority.

The meaning of effectiveness depends on what society expects to achieve through higher education. We begin by asking the basic questions: What are the functions of higher education in society? What does effectiveness mean in this context? And how can effectiveness be measured once it is defined? After this discussion, we briefly describe the historical development of American higher education and its current structure and challenges. We do so to set a context for the issues explored here, an analysis of the effectiveness of U.S. higher education in relation to system-level, campus-level, and classroom-level effects. This three-fold division based on the primary actors involved in effectiveness policies and practices provides a useful heuristic for dividing the topics we consider in this issue.[1] Because we believe systems-level actions will be of the great-

---

Steven Brint is distinguished professor of sociology and public policy at the University of California, Riverside. **Charles T. Clotfelter** is Z. Smith Reynolds Professor of Public Policy, professor of economics and law, and associate dean for academic programs in the Sanford School at Duke University.

We would like to thank Cynthia E. Carr, Kevin Curwin, and Sarah R. K. Yoshikawa for research assistance. Direct correspondence to: Steven Brint at brint@ucr.edu, 1100 Hinderaker Hall, UC Riverside, 900 University Avenue, Riverside, CA 92521; Charles T. Clotfelter at charles.clotfelter@duke.edu, 178 Rubenstein Hall, Sanford School of Public Policy, 201 Science Drive, Durham, NC 27708.

1. These three levels of analysis should not be considered entirely distinct from one another. Initiatives that seem to be manifest mainly on campuses or in classrooms typically have national sponsors and partisans. Moreover, national policy takes root on diverse campuses. Campuses are more and less receptive and able to realize incentives and even controls fashioned at the national level.

est interest to readers, we devote more space to issues at that level than to those at the other two levels.

Although we discuss variation among the fifty states only very briefly here, the states represent a fourth analytically distinct level of analysis, and one that many higher education scholars have embraced to investigate differences in outcomes due to state-level variation in pricing, performance incentives, and regulation. Several papers in this volume explore the consequences of state policy variation.

WHAT DO POLICYMAKERS WANT FROM HIGHER EDUCATION?

We concentrate on the most fundamental purposes of higher education as these have been formed and promoted by national policymakers, by senior leaders on college and university campuses, and by teachers in classrooms.[2]

At the system level, we will take as our primary topics those that have been the focus of policymakers since the time of the great expansion of U.S. higher education following World War II. Policymakers have focused on higher education's capacity to develop the knowledge and skills students need for professional, technical, and managerial positions. As higher education has expanded from an elite to a mass system, policymakers have taken an interest as well in whether higher education opportunities are accessible to all and fairly distributed. This topic is important not only as a measure of social mobility opportunities but also because more equal attainments are potentially a way to bring greater equality to society (Goldin and Katz 2008). Finally, policymakers and researchers alike have focused on the volume and quality of higher education's production of basic and applied research, as well as of the doctoral students who will become the next generation of scholars and scientists (see, for example, Cole 2009; Geiger 1993; National Academies 2007).[3]

In the decentralized system of U.S. higher education, campuses are natural units for analysis because the policies developed on campuses influence the achievement of both system-level and classroom-level functions. Campus-level initiatives are so numerous that some selection is necessary. We have chosen to focus on a subset of initiatives that have been embraced by many campuses and can therefore be considered national trends at the campus level: the importation of business practices, new interdisciplinary designs for research and teaching, and policies to increase undergraduate graduation rates. The adoption of modern business methods for purposes of improving the efficiency of resource allocation has been a feature of American universities for a century, and it continues to stimulate widespread interest (see, for example, Christensen and Eyring 2011). Similarly, many campuses are emphasizing interdisciplinary initiatives and other organizational designs intended to improve collaborative interactions among the faculty (see, for example, Rhoten 2003; Weingart and Stehr 2000). And programs to increase the retention and graduation rates of enrolled students are on the agenda of nearly every public university (see, for example, Association of Public and Land-Grant Universities 2015).

At the classroom level, the sole aim broadly endorsed by the faculty and the public alike is for faculty to provide instruction that contributes to students' learning. This focus is in keeping with the traditional goals of higher education and is supported by empirical studies that find better outcomes for students who

---

2. To attempt to identify and discuss all of the purposes of higher education would be a challenging task and is beyond the scope of this volume. Indeed, senior professors at the University of Chicago, an institution renowned for its commitment to teaching and learning, have been addressing freshmen each year since the 1960s on "the aims of education," and each one of these lectures takes up a different set of themes (see http://aims.uchicago.edu/page/past-speakers, accessed February 23, 2016).

3. The social benefits of higher education—its association with higher levels of community engagement, better informed citizens, more stable family structures, and reduced crime levels, to name just a few—have been underappreciated by policymakers and researchers. We will perpetuate that bias here, though we do urge further investigation of the net social benefits of higher education (for overviews, see Bowen 1977; Hout 2012; Kingston 2015).

have achieved high grades in rigorous majors (Arcidicano 2004; Murnane, Willett, and Levy 1995) or have made significant gains in analytical and critical thinking while at college (Arum and Roksa 2014). The instructional practices and technologies that contribute to student learning are therefore key topics.

Measuring Effectiveness

It follows that the term effectiveness will reflect the extent to which and the quality with which higher education achieves these expectations. A focus on effectiveness leads to questions such as the following: Are students being prepared adequately for the labor market? Is the system accessible to students from all backgrounds? How large are the gaps in success between students from different backgrounds? Is research productivity high and is it contributing to human well-being? Are universities producing well-prepared graduate students? Are the new business methods contributing to greater effectiveness in the allocation of resources? Has the emphasis on interdisciplinary collaboration led to a greater capacity to tackle key national problems? How much are students learning? To what extent are the new instructional practices and technologies contributing to student learning?

Usable metrics for assessing effectiveness remain aspiration more often than reality. For example, no exams exist that can measure student learning adequately in each of the scores of disciplines in which they can major. But social scientists do have some ways of addressing questions of effectiveness.

At the system level, tracing gains over time is the primary method for assessing effectiveness. For example, we can determine whether graduation rates are increasing over time and whether the gaps in graduation rates between more and less advantaged groups are increasing or decreasing. Similarly, we can measure the growth in research publications over time and whether research is becoming more or less concentrated in a handful of top-performing universities. In some cases, we can also compare outcomes for U.S. higher education with results found in other developed countries. Have other countries exceeded the United States in the production of baccalaureate-level graduates or in the production of research—and, if so, why? Indirect measures of quality can also be useful. Does the United States remain the leading "importer" of students from abroad? If so, this provides strong circumstantial evidence that quality levels relative to the rest of the world remain high. Variation among states can also sometimes be exploited to determine the consequences of policy interventions for national level priorities. For example, one can measure the effects on the graduation rates of underrepresented minorities of changes in state financial aid policies from need-based to merit-based criteria or the effects on graduation rates from the adoption of performance funding policies.

We have found evaluation studies at the campus level to be underdeveloped. For the most part, we are forced to rely on case studies of single-campus interventions—as well as studies that focus on the unintended consequences of these interventions. Issues related to the Hawthorne effect and selection bias loom large in campus-led studies. The same interventions have been studied across a number of campuses only in a very few instances. By contrast, at the classroom level, it is sometimes possible to compare techniques of instruction using rigorous experimental designs to investigate the conditions that contribute to student learning. In these cases, students are randomly assigned to treatment and control groups to determine the effect of an intervention such as new courseware or daily reading quizzes. A few types of interventions, such as active learning methods, have been extensively studied using common assessments in multiple institutions. However, studies of many innovations remain limited to one or a few classrooms, leading to thin research evidence in support of some innovations that have been touted for their capacity to revolutionize teaching and learning.

Ideally, one might suppose that cost-benefit analysis could be employed to make decisions about how to invest resources to improve effectiveness, but that approach would require that outcomes be valued in dollars, surely a difficult trick to pull off for example in considerations of equity and public service. More feasible is the hope of judging effectiveness by comparing the costs of alternative approaches that achieve the same outcome. For example, if the same level of learning could be achieved either by conventional lecture courses or by combining online instruction with small discussion sections, it is reasonable to judge the effectiveness of the two approaches by comparing their costs, both explicit and implicit. Empirical social science research can contribute to such an assessment and is a primary purpose of studies such as the ones included in this volume.

THE AMERICAN HIGHER EDUCATION SYSTEM AND ITS CHALLENGES

It is helpful to begin with a brief overview of the historical antecedents of the U.S. system of higher education and its current structure and problems to put the issues surrounding higher education effectiveness into context.

Historical Antecedents

In its earliest decades, American higher education was private, religious, and privileged. The first colleges were established to train ministers and educate gentlemen. They also enrolled small numbers of scholarship students who contributed to the motivational climate of the college without necessarily fitting easily into its dominant culture (Horowitz 1987). State governments followed by establishing publicly run colleges and universities, with more diverse purposes and clienteles. By 1900, still only about 725 colleges had been established, and they remained small by today's standards. Eighty-five percent of them were private. The typical private institution (the one attended by the median student) enrolled about five hundred students, and the typical public one had only about three hundred more (calculated from Snyder 1993, tables 23 and 24).

In the mid-nineteenth century, inspired both by the desire to see the benefits of education spread more widely across the population and an appreciation of the value of imparting practical knowledge, the state universities, especially those in the newer states of the Midwest and West, grew in scale. This growth was encouraged with the federal support provided by the Morrill Acts of 1862 and 1890, which gave state governments the wherewithal to build and expand public universities. The share of students attending public institutions increased sharply after 1900, rising from one-quarter to more than half by the mid-1930s (Snyder 1993, 66).[4] In addition to the vast expansion of public universities due to the Morrill Act, other institutional developments helped to increase the popularity of higher education, notably, the founding of two-year junior colleges, beginning at the turn of the twentieth century, as a means both to take pressure off universities and to respond to the aspirations for upward mobility among larger numbers of students (Brint and Karabel 1989). Another important development, the transformation of "normal schools," or teachers colleges, into comprehensive state colleges and universities offering a wide range of occupational and academic curricula in addition to preparation for teaching, began at the end of the nineteenth century and accelerated through the first half of the twentieth century (Dunham 1969). During the late nineteenth and early twentieth centuries, the development of a range of extracurricular activities, and particularly football rivalries (Riesman and Denney 1951), greatly contributed to the popularity of college in the American imagination.

The great expansion of U.S. higher education was, however, a product of the post–World War II era. At that time, leading policymakers concluded that jobs of the future would require higher level skills than before and that more young people would need to be equipped to complete college than previous generations had thought feasible. Our current system—its strengths and its challenges—is a product of this period of transition from elite to mass to nearly universal higher education (Trow 2007). The authors of the influential Truman Commission Report on higher education argued

---

4. Higher education enrollments expanded during recession periods, such as the 1870s and the 1930s, an indicator that higher education is a counter-cyclical industry; when economic times are bad, more young people consider higher education as an alternative to pursuing work, because they can try to improve their marketability with higher level credentials and because the opportunity costs are not as great (see Craig 1985).

that half of young people had the capacity to finish at least two years of college and one-third had the ability to finish the baccalaureate (U.S. Presidents Commission 1947). They also argued for a vast expansion of financial aid opportunities to allow students without economic means to achieve higher level degrees. Federal support took other forms in the twentieth century, including military-related research during World War II, the subsequent G.I. Bill (1944), which provided generous financial support for veterans to attend college, the National Defense Education Act (1957), which supported graduate students intending to become college and university professors, numerous other programs to give financial aid to students, and the direct funding of nondefense spending through agencies such as the National Science Foundation (founded in 1950) and the National Institutes of Health.

Current Size and Structure

The sector's importance can be seen in the steady growth of enrollments. In 2012, some twenty million students were enrolled, nearly a hundred times more than in 1900 and nearly ten times more than in 1950 (NCES 2014, table 303). In 1920, only 5 percent of young adults age twenty-five to twenty-nine had finished four years of college. That fraction grew to 8 percent by 1950, and escalated thereafter, reaching one-third by 2012 (table 104.20). One consequence was that post-baccalaureate credentials also became more common. Nearly twenty-five million Americans held advanced degrees (master's and above) by 2012, the combined size of the five largest American cities, and more than three million Americans held doctorates (table 104.30).

These students are enrolled in a highly tiered and multiply segmented sector of more than five thousand degree-granting institutions (Kena et al. 2015, figure 1). At the base of this structure are several hundred financially insecure, low-enrollment for-profit colleges (enrolling approximately 5 percent of all undergraduate students in 2013).[5] The ascending layers include: public two-year colleges (enrolling more than 30 percent of undergraduates); mainly private non-elite (and often religiously affiliated) baccalaureate-granting institutions (enrolling approximately 10 percent); master's-granting universities (more than 15 percent); and doctoral-granting institutions that produce comparatively little research (approximately 25 percent). The structure is capped by one small peak of the wealthiest and most selective private liberal arts colleges (enrolling fewer than 2 percent) and a larger peak composed of the nation's top research universities (enrolling approximately 6 percent).[6] The more stable and successful for-profits are found interspersed among the two-year and four-year baccalaureate-granting institutions (enrolling about 5 percent). Specialized institutions, such as art schools, business schools, and seminaries, enroll the final 2 percent of undergraduates (calculated from Association of American Universities 2015; NCES 2015b; and NCES 2015a, table 303.70). Many of the stronger institutions at each level aspire to climb higher in this structure, lending a dynamic quality to the system, with private, non-profit colleges typically hoping to do so by becoming more selective and public institutions typically hoping to do so by adding higher-level degrees (Brint, Riddle, and Hanneman 2006).

The most important structural divisions among higher educational institutions in the United States are those due to selectivity and wealth, the highest degrees offered and the level of research intensity among those offering the doctorate, and the locus of governing authority. This assertion is supported by statistical analyses indicating that institutions defined by these structural characteristics tend to cluster together and the fact that presidents tend to identify with other colleges and universities that are similar to their own in terms of these criteria (Brint, Riddle, and Hanneman

---

5. These calculations include part-time students.

6. The top liberal arts colleges are members of the all-private Consortium on Financing Higher Education (COFHE). The top research-intensive universities, both public and private, are roughly coincident with the sixty U.S. members of the Association of American Universities (AAU). The two groups overlap somewhat. Harvard, Stanford, Yale, Princeton and several other private AAU members are also members of COFHE.

2006; see also Reuf and Nag 2014). These divides also have parallels in the organization of the main higher education associations.[7]

Selectivity is defined by high levels of rejection of applicants and high yield among those relatively few who are admitted. Nearly all of the most selective institutions are also among the wealthiest (Kuh and Pascarella 2004). These include the Ivy League institutions, such as Harvard, Yale, and Princeton, and others of similar standing, such as Stanford, Chicago, and Duke. These institutions appear consistently among the highest ranked colleges and universities in publications such as *U.S. News and World Report* and *The Princeton Review*. One way scholars have illustrated this stratification among four-year colleges and universities is to rank them by their average subsidy per student (calculated as educational costs of instruction minus tuition net of grant aid). Institutions with the largest subsidies also tend to have students with the highest average SAT scores and other very strong academic credentials (Winston 1999). Stratification among four-year institutions by selectivity has increased over the last several decades, as shown by a divergence in average SATs across institutions. Factors that may have contributed to this stratification include falling costs of transportation, popularized ranking systems, and the rise of standardized testing as a cheap means of certifying the academic aptitude of applicants (Hoxby 2009).

The second form of stratification among higher education institutions is one based on the prestige of the highest degrees awarded, the doctorate being the most prestigious and the associate degree the least. Research productivity requires consideration as part of this second ranking structure, because not all doctoral-granting institutions are research intensive. Indeed, the production of research is dominated by only a few universities. The Carnegie Foundation for the Advancement of Teaching named 207, divided into "very high research" (108) and "high research" (99) institutions, that accounted for 90 percent of the papers catalogued in the Web of Science in 2010 from high-quality peer-reviewed journals and more than five hundred thousand citations. They also received 84 percent of federal funding for research (personal communication, Cynthia E. Carr). As generators of scientific discoveries and producers of technological innovations, the "very high research" universities are among the most important institutions in the country (see, for example, Cole 2009; Geiger 1993).

Where wealth, selectivity, highest degree offered and research productivity are measures of interorganizational stratification, segmentation falls most clearly along lines of control—that is, whether institutions are publicly supported, private nonprofits, or for-profits. Those institutions labeled public obtain at least a share of their funding for educational programs from appropriations from state or federal governments. (However, in many states the larger share of funding now comes from private households in the form of tuition.) Private, nonprofit colleges and universities do not receive significant state subsidies, but rather rely on a combination of tuition charges and endowment income.

Measured by enrollment, higher education in the United States is heavily dominated by public institutions. In the fall of 2012, students in public colleges and universities made up more than 70 percent of all postsecondary students. Public four-year colleges and universities enrolled 39 percent of all students, and public two-year community colleges 33 percent. Private colleges and universities, almost all of which were four-year institutions, made up 19 percent of the total, leaving 9 percent in private for-profit institutions (NCES 2013, table 303.25). Over the last four decades, each of these segments of the postsecondary world has

---

[7]. The criteria and the corresponding higher education associations are: selectivity-wealth (the Consortium for Financing Higher Education); research intensity (the American Association of Universities); control (the Association of Public and Land Grant Universities, the Association of State Colleges and Universities, the National Association of Independent Colleges); and highest degree awarded (the American Association of Community Colleges). There is one overarching association that unites the segments and strata in the system (the American Council on Education).

grown, but the most impressive rates have been in community colleges and the for-profit sector. From 1970 to 2012, enrollment in public four-year colleges and universities grew at an average rate of 1.5 percent a year, as did enrollments in private not-for-profit institutions. Far outstripping these sectors, community colleges saw enrollments increase by 2.7 percent a year, a rate that doubled enrollments every twenty-six years.

But for growth rates no sector can touch the for-profit sector, where enrollments grew by an astonishing factor of 100 over four decades, from less than 19,000 in 1970 to 1.8 million in 2012, for an average annual rate of 10.9 percent. The growth of for-profits has been fueled by their extraordinary efficiency in finding and distributing financial aid to student-consumers. With rare exceptions, they are occupationally oriented and often specialize in training for marketable degrees in such fields as computer programming, electronics technology, physical therapy, cosmetology, or specialized mechanical trades. Many provide education exclusively online, typically to working adults. For this reason, they compete mainly with community colleges (Tierney and Hentschke 2007), though some do offer four-year degrees. In addition to marketing to older adults, for-profits have focused on minority students, students from lower-income backgrounds, and former military personnel (Deming, Goldin, and Katz 2012; Ruch 2001).

The stronger for-profits work very closely with employers to determine skills required for jobs, standardize curricula to home in on valued knowledge and skills, pay close attention to the way students dress and present themselves at work, and concentrate assiduously on the placement of their graduates (Rosenbaum, Deil-Amen, and Person 2009, chapter 6). By contrast, the weaker for-profits are little more than diploma mills, charging high tuitions and leaving most graduates with heavy debt but no marketable degree. On average, these students end up with higher unemployment rates and lower earnings six years after entering programs than comparable students who entered other institutions, and they have higher debt and default rates on their student loans (Deming, Goldin, and Katz 2012). Federal investigations have led to the closing of many individual colleges and some large chains (see, for example, Kirkham 2015).[8]

A division and hierarchy of disciplinary fields crosscuts this hierarchy of institutions. A common mapping of the disciplines is based on the four-fold distinction between "hard" (quantitative) and "soft" (interpretive) fields on one dimension and "pure" (knowledge for knowledge's sake) and "applied" (occupation-related) fields on the other dimension (Becher 1989). U.S. colleges and universities were founded on the preeminence of the liberal arts as the essential disciplines for the training of judgment and character. The sciences and engineering were peripheral fields throughout the nineteenth century, because of their association with the shop floor and applied work (Geiger 2015, chapter 6). But scientific and quantitative applied fields, such as engineering, gained ground during the Great Depression (Brint et al. 2005), and at least since World War II, the pure and applied sciences have been core fields in universities (Geiger 1993, chapters 6–7). They have attracted the most external funds and many of the brightest students. On average, students graduating in quantitative fields have a marked advantage in the labor market (Carnevale, Rose, and Cheah 2011; PayScale 2014). Masters and doctorate degrees are thus particularly important for students who graduate in nonquantitative fields (Mullen, Goyette, and Soares 2003).

---

8. Among the secondary structural influences on organizational identity and behavior, the size of institutions is most worthy of mention. Not only can larger institutions take advantage of economies of scale and name recognition, they may have an advantage in terms of adaptability, seen, for example, in the capacity to form faculty groups to pursue new research opportunities. Smaller institutions must market themselves in relation to some special features of their environments or, most often, the assertion of higher value of small classes for intense, high-quality, and more personalized educational experiences. As illustration, a study comparing selective institutions in the early 1990s showed that undergraduate courses in history at Harvard had an average class size of 140, but at Carleton College, history classes averaged just thirty-two students (Clotfelter 1996, 242, 245).

U.S. Higher Education in Comparative Perspective

Compared with other highly developed countries, the United States has more higher education institutions relative to its population. In 2012, using one global accounting of institutions, the United States had roughly eighty-five universities per hundred thousand population, a ratio that exceeded other developed countries, including Canada (fifty-four), France (forty-three), Germany (thirty-five), and Britain (thirty-three), and far exceeded the comparable ratios of China (seven) and India (two). The large number of U.S. colleges and universities is accounted for by the unusual role of small, private, not-for-profit institutions in the higher education ecology. Although about two-thirds of students attend public institutions, private not-for-profit institutions are very nearly as numerous as public institutions. Student enrollments in private colleges and universities can range from fewer than one hundred to more than thirty thousand, but their average size is just two thousand. By contrast, public universities rarely fall below five thousand students and can enroll as many as sixty thousand on a single campus.

As a percentage of its gross domestic product (GDP), the United States spends some 2.7 percent on higher education, a markedly higher share than the 1.6 percent average among the countries of the Organization for Economic Cooperation and Development, or OECD (OECD 2014, 239). Higher education is less completely financed by public monies in the United States than in many other countries, and consequently the private household contribution is larger. Indeed, public policy with respect to the financing of undergraduate education in the United States begins with the assumption that most students and their families will pay a good share of the total cost of education, an expectation that sets the United States apart from many other countries. Households provide a larger proportion of higher education funding in Chile and Colombia, but the United States is in the next rank, together with Japan, Korea, and the United Kingdom, with households accounting for more than 40 percent of the total. By contrast, household funding represents less than 5 percent of the total in much of Northern Europe (OECD 2014, 239–40).

One justification for this assignment of cost burdens is the sizable personal economic benefit that is associated with obtaining a college degree, as discussed in a following section. Yet it is clear that the financial burden of attendance, even at public institutions, is an impediment for students from low-income families. Accordingly, it has been the practice for many institutions as well as governments to subsidize such students. For students attending public institutions, this assistance is largely in the form of cross-subsidies made possible by tapping other sources of funding. Chief among the subsidies from government are the appropriations that public colleges and universities receive from state and local government. In 2012, these amounted to $72 billion (Palmer 2015). In 2011 public institutions received on average 23 percent of their revenue from state and local governments and 19 percent from tuition. Private institutions, by contrast, received about 29 percent from tuition and another 26 percent from investment returns (NCES 2012, tables 402, 405).[9] Two-thirds of all college students receive some form of financial aid; roughly half receive aid in the form of a grant and about 40 percent receive it in the form of loans (NCES 2010, table 386).

Is the Current Structure Sustainable?

Perhaps the most vexing trend related to the accessibility of U.S. higher education has been the stagnation in financial support from state governments, especially so since it came at a time of rising enrollments. Between 1991 and 2008, total state appropriations for higher education increased by 13 percent, and total public enrollments grew by 23 percent. In the two years after 2008, appropriations actually declined, falling by 7 percent in inflation-adjusted terms, while enrollment increased by another eight percent (NCES 2012, table 404; 2013, table 303.25).

Private, nonprofit colleges face a different set of financial challenges. These institutions

---

9. Total revenues include income from auxiliaries, hospitals, and independent operations.

feel the pressure to keep tuition levels high as a signal of the high quality of the education they offer, including small classes and a community-like environment. But to attract enough students to make their enrollment targets, they typically resort to discounting tuition for many students by way of "merit" scholarships. There are simply not enough students who prefer small liberal arts colleges to charge the "sticker price" to all but the neediest students. Many liberal arts colleges now offer tuition discounts to up to 80 percent of their students. The resulting negative impact on net revenues has led to operating budgets that are very tight in many cases (NACUBO 2014).

In apparent response to these and other pressures, colleges and universities have increased their reliance on part-time and nontenure-track faculty (Ehrenberg 2012, 199). Nationwide, the percentage of faculty that is full time fell from almost four-fifths in 1970 to half in 2007 (Ehrenberg 2012, 194, citing Snyder and Dillow 2010, tables 249 and 253). The percentage of faculty not on the tenure track increased from 19 percent to 37 percent in 2007 (Ehrenberg 2012, 194). Perhaps reflecting these shifts, expenditures on instruction have grown more slowly over the past two decades than those on student services, research, and other support services. Between 1987 and 2008, the real annual rate of growth in public and private two- and four-year institutions was 1.1 percent, versus 1.6 percent for academic support and institutional support, 2.2 percent for student services, and 2.6 percent for research (Ehrenberg 2012, 204).

Even with declining relative costs for instruction, prices have continued to increase. Over the last three decades, average sticker price at private nonprofit colleges and universities has increased at a rate 3.5 percentage points faster than inflation, and the same rate has applied to community colleges as well. For four-year public institutions, tuition increases have exceeded inflation by an average of 5.1 percentage points (Ehrenberg 2012, 193; see also Baum and Ma 2014). To be sure, these increases in sticker price tuition, featured so prominently in news coverage, exaggerate the increase in the actual cost to students and their families net of financial aid. Not only can students defray the cost with grants and loans, they often enjoy an additional cost reduction when colleges provide additional relief in the form of financial aid provided by institutions themselves. In an effort to attract desirable students, most private colleges and some public institutions have increasingly offered institutional aid, often packaged as named scholarships. Such assistance ends up being equivalent to a price discount. To return some tuition dollars to enroll students from the bottom half of the income distribution, higher charges were required for those families who campus financial aid officers determined could afford them (Clotfelter 1996; Ehrenberg 2000).

One principal culprit for price increases has been the rising real cost of inputs, especially faculty salaries. To remain competitive, the leading private colleges and universities, in particular, have had to pay premium salaries to professors who are in high demand. These increases have trickled down to those public universities attempting to keep pace. Real faculty salaries have increased in recent years, after a period of decline during the 1970s, though the rate of increase has not been equal in private and public institutions. Start-up costs for newly hired faculty in the natural sciences also increased markedly. A second reason costs increased in many institutions was growth in the size of faculties at many institutions. This growth was accompanied by a reduction in teaching loads and the hiring of more nonregular faculty (Clotfelter 1996). Third, administrative costs were also a contributing factor. Part of this increase could be attributed to expanding requirements for reporting and recordkeeping, and part was due to the costs associated with the purchase of computer equipment. Consumer demand for services also encouraged staff growth. Student affairs budgets grew markedly; these budgets supported student clubs, campus arts and entertainment events, fitness centers, health and counseling centers, dorm renovations, food courts, and the rest of the amenities residential college students expected to balance the time they spent on study. Campuses also continuously added staff to a range of offices required to maintain donor and constituency relations, regulatory compliance, and economic development opportunities (Ehrenberg 2012). No doubt empire building among administrators has also contributed at least a small amount to the growth of the managerial stratum.

Why these salary increases could not be mitigated through labor-saving measures, as in some business services, may be due to a deeper problem faced by colleges and universities, the so-called cost disease (Baumol and Bowen 1966). To the extent that the operation of these institutions is like that of an orchestra, wholly wedded to a technology of operation devoid of opportunities to achieve labor-saving efficiencies, the argument goes, costs are forced to rise as long as the cost of workers rises. If these institutions are actually motivated to expand their budgets, then it is natural they would seek any and all opportunities to raise tuition. This viewpoint could be seen as the tuition corollary of Howard Bowen's dictum (1980), to the effect that universities attempt to raise all the money they can and they spend everything they raise. Such an instinct might be driven simply by mission-related ambition, a virtually unbounded desire on the part of top administrators to improve the quality of their institutions—by offering new programs, by hiring more famous professors, and by attracting more talented students—combined with their inability or unwillingness to eliminate anything.[10]

Higher tuition brought more borrowing to pay for college. Student loans were a backbone of the postwar expansion, but the average student owed relatively little. At the end of the 1970s, no public college in the country charged more than $2,500 in annual tuition for in-state tuition. By the mid-2010s, with tuition and residence halls approaching $30,000 per year in public universities and double that in the leading privates, the average private college student could expect to leave with a degree and a $30,000 student debt. Those who attended public universities were on average only a little better off. This was a tough way to begin adult life, and opinion polls showed that most Americans doubted the need for such increases. Muckraking books like *Generation Debt* (Kamenetz 2006) and *The Student Loan Scam* (Collinge 2009) stirred debate about whether college was worth the cost and how it could be made more affordable. In 2010, student debt, then approaching one trillion dollars, exceeded credit card debt as the second largest category of debt in the country (behind mortgages). Nevertheless, most students appear to accept debt as the inevitable price of a degree that remains a very good investment over the course of a lifetime, particularly given the virtual disappearance of good jobs open to those with only a high school degree (see, for example, Rotondi 2015).

We now turn to a discussion of the primary systems-level expectations of U.S higher education, as identified by postwar policymakers, and the evidence of the effectiveness of U.S. colleges and universities in relation to these expectations.

HUMAN CAPITAL DEVELOPMENT AND LINKS TO THE LABOR MARKET

A primary goal of postwar policymakers was to expand higher education to ensure human capital development to meet the changing occupational needs of an increasingly knowledge-based society. We therefore first take up the issue of human capital development and the connection of higher education institutions to desirable positions in the labor market.

The College Earnings Advantage

Few facts speak more persuasively to the importance of postsecondary education than the substantially higher incomes enjoyed by college graduates than by those with less education. In 2012, for example, among men with full-time year round employment, those with

---

10. Some observers have taken a decidedly skeptical view of cost increases as a natural outgrowth of the objectives of colleges and universities. More nefariously, such a tendency could lead administrators to take advantage of increases in government supported student aid, for example, to raise tuition, as argued by William Bennett (1987). Stephanie Cellini and Claudia Goldin (2012) provide evidence that for-profit colleges act this way, finding that those whose students are eligible for federal financial aid charge 78 percent more in tuition than those not eligible to provide federal aid, an amount close to the value of that aid.

at least four years of college earned an average of nearly $35,000 more than those who had just a high school diploma. For women, the comparable earnings advantage was over $23,000 (Autor 2014, 844). Economists invoke supply and demand to explain this college earnings advantage. College-educated workers earn more than high school graduates, the model posits, because employers' demand for these college graduates is strong, relative to the number of such workers available to be hired. Demand is strong because employers value skilled workers and because such workers are relatively scarce.

Over the last three decades, the earnings advantage for college graduates has grown. The reasons for this growth are the subject of ongoing debate, but many economists would place considerable emphasis on changes that have occurred in the American economy. Knowledge-intensive industries, such as business services and education, have grown at the expense of manufacturing, and all industries have seen increases in the need for educated workers able to use computers and adapt to a wider range of job demands (see, for example, Clotfelter et al. 1991, 64–69; Freeman 1976). As the unionized manufacturing sector has declined, the labor market for less educated workers has virtually collapsed, with low-income jobs replacing the bulk of middle-income jobs that did not at one time require postsecondary credentials (see, for example, Bernhardt et al. 2001). Thus, despite an increasing supply of college graduates, the demand for them has grown even faster. The consequence of these changes has been a doubling of the college earnings advantage for men, which increased in constant 2012 dollars from approximately $17,500 in 1979 to nearly $35,000 in 2012 (Autor 2014, 844).

To find out what portion of the college earnings advantage can be attributed to attending college, rather than unmeasured personal characteristics, researchers must somehow remove the influence of unmeasured personal characteristics that might cause college-goers to differ systematically from those who do not go. Such selection bias would imply that differences in average earnings overstate the true effect of going to college, and overcoming this bias has proven to be a formidable challenge for researchers.[11]

Human Capital Development or Signaling?
Granted that at least some of the observed differences in earnings associated with postsecondary training are related to attending college, what explains it? Economic doctrine says that wages reflect differences in workers' productive value, a proposition accepted by many scholars in addition to most economists. But the question remains, what explains the statistical association between productive value and postsecondary training? Social scientists offer two principal answers: human capital and signaling. A third explanation—that those with higher education degrees form a status group whose members choose one another without serious regard to productivity—is less well known, but worth noting.

Human Capital
Perhaps the most common explanation to the question is that colleges and universities carry out the same basic function as K–12 schools: they arm students with skills that will make them productive workers, allowing them to benefit personally from the result. Society at large benefits as well, in the form of a tangibly higher standard of living. Job-relevant knowledge may be quite specific, such as accounting

---

11. One noteworthy study to produce estimates arguably free of selection bias compared the earnings of white men who barely qualified to attend their state's flagship university with those who barely fell short. All of these applicants, those just above the cutoff and those just below, arguably were very similar, except for which side of the line they fell on. But the side they landed on turned out to be highly important. As it turned out, those who got in later earned 20 percent more than those who had to settle for a lesser university (Hoekstra 2009). Another type of evidence that where one goes to college makes a difference in the labor market comes from an audit study comparing employers' willingness to interview fictional job applicants. For jobs in business, for example, purported graduates of an online college were 22 percent less likely to get a call back than those whose resumes listed a degree from a nonselective brick and mortar college (Deming, Goldin, and Katz 2013).

practices, or it could be more general cognitive skills that make educated workers more productive, such as skills in understanding data or written expression (Becker 1964). For some, human capital also denotes socioemotional skills that students learn in college, such as how to interact with people from different backgrounds or how to participate in problem-solving groups. The cognitive skill development is very important in some disciplines, but for most students it seems likely that academic development is less important as a source of human capital than persistence and the willingness to delay gratification, traits that reveal themselves as students do or do not listen to lectures, take notes, work on assignments, and pass tests. The characteristics of study, work discipline, and deference to authority that these repeated behaviors foster may, for most students, be the primary productivity advantages associated with a college education.

Human capital is a broad concept, and it is not surprising that most economists have not attempted to measure it directly and have instead taken educational attainment as an acceptable proxy measure. However, this identification introduces a proven-by-fiat quality to the argument by equating the accumulation of skills gained during college with educational attainment, rather than with the qualities developed themselves. Over the last decade social scientists have measured the cognitive component of human capital more precisely by looking at students' scores on tests of cognitive skills (Hanushek and Woessmann 2011, 160–90). However, better measurement does not solve a fundamental objection to human capital theory: if those who go to college were already more skilled before they enrolled in college than those who did not, at least a portion of the earnings advantage they enjoy cannot rightly be attributed to college. This leads to a second explanation: signaling.

Signaling

An alternative to the human capital explanation for the higher earnings enjoyed by college graduates focuses on the informational content that simply possessing a college degree carries. Like the human capital view, this explanation accepts the essential accuracy of the neoclassical economics model of competitive labor markets and its implication that more productive workers will be more valuable to employers, holding constant their supply. Where the signaling explanation diverges from the human capital view comes down to what, exactly, the contribution of college is. In the signaling view of the labor market, most of the skills or attributes that will be valuable to employers are already instilled by the time students have finished high school. All that is necessary is to identify those most richly endowed with those abilities. In the signaling explanation, that is the primary function of college—to identify and certify talent (Spence 1973). Those who have prestigious educational credentials can advance to the head of labor queues, even if they have not developed human capital during their college years, provided that the reputational strength of the degree is stronger than the reputational strength of alternative degrees. Moreover, the signal may be more about adaptability and trainability than about job-relevant skills per se (Thurow 1972). In this explanation, any learning that occurs is incidental to, not the result of, college. The essential function of college is to certify, not to instill. Studies suggesting that not much learning is occurring in college lend weight to the signaling model (see, for example, Arum and Roksa 2011; OECD 2013).

It is likely that one of these explanations may be more relevant for particular students—or that both are relevant in different measures. A student may learn to interact well with people from a wide variety of backgrounds by attending college (a noncognitive form of human capital development) and to improve writing skills while gaining benefits from the signaling quality of the college attended. The two viewpoints of human capital and signaling can be combined in whatever proportions the facts appear to support, allocating to each some portion of the observed college earnings advantage (Bills 2003).

Status Group Preferences

Some who write about the rise of job allocation by educational credentials are skeptical of the association assumed by economists between educational credentials and productivity. For these skeptics, hiring based on educational credentials is a way to ration opportunity and simplify employers' choice in a market in which many people (including many people without degrees) could do jobs if they were given proper training. Credentials are treated as valid because they are a convenient and relatively efficient way for employers to limit applicant pools, not because they develop or certify skills (Berg 1971; Collins 1979).

Taking this view one step further, some sociologists have argued that higher education credentials signal kinship with the culture of employers more than anything else. In this view, employers choose the highly educated over the less educated because they remind them of themselves. Thus, the highly educated form a kind of "pseudo-ethnic group" whose members, like those of any other status group, recognize one another based on a common social evaluation of honor and a common lifestyle (Collins 1977, chapter 3). The highly educated are thought to speak, present themselves, and dress in ways similar to their employers. For example, they do not have visible tattoos, use profane language in public, or record loud music on their answering machines. They tend to be deferential to authority and able to interact well in management-led work groups. For those who focus on status group preferences, the economic benefit, if there is one, comes from the greater ease of understanding and the lesser friction created by those who share this culture. Pay is based on admittance to the authority structure rather than skills that boost the productivity of the firm.[12]

Some obvious problems exist in relation to this more critical perspective on the college wage premium. It is not clear why many employers would want to pay a hefty premium simply for being able to associate with people who are similar to themselves, if someone less expensive could perform the job just as well— or how employers willing to do so could stay in business. At the same time, the number of shared qualities and outlooks found among highly educated people is indeed impressive. They include high correlations between educational attainment and behaviors such as healthy diet and exercise practices, higher levels of book reading, lower levels of television watching, comparatively liberal attitudes on social issues, and less frequent church attendance (see Brint and Proctor 2011). Employers' presumption of competence based on the "cultural kinship" of the highly educated cannot be ruled out as one advantage that college graduates bring to the labor market. Indeed, studies examining race, gender, and college quality have shown that co-membership preferences are common in hiring decisions (see, for example, Deming, Goldin, and Katz 2013; Rivera 2012).

Is Human Capital Development Lagging?

Compared with the rest of the developed world, the United States is behind in producing young adults who hold postsecondary degrees. A generation ago, the share of Americans with college degrees was one of the highest in the developed world. Since then, many countries have surpassed the United States. Whereas the United States has the highest rate of attainment of postsecondary degrees for fifty-five- to sixty-four-year-olds among thirty OECD countries, its twenty-five- to thirty-four-year-olds ranked only tenth (OECD 2014, table A1.4a). Additional slippage is evident when we look at the most recent generation.[13]

Findings on more direct measures of human capital development during the college

---

12. From status group closure it is a short step to the more politically loaded idea of social reproduction (Bourdieu and Passeron 1977; Bowles and Gintis 1976). According to those who hold this view, by choosing one another for high positions, members of the same social class maintain control over those who lack credentials while legitimizing their power on the basis of the presumed economic value of higher education credentials and the presumed openness of the competition for them.

13. In recent comparisons looking at first-time degree completion across the OECD, the United States ranked twelfth at the tertiary B (or associate's degree) level and was tied for seventeenth at the tertiary A (or baccalaureate degree) level.

years are arguably even more discouraging.[14] In 2003, the National Assessment of Adult Literacy found that only about one in three college graduates could draw accurate inferences from two editorials with contrasting content or could accurately read a three-variable graph relating age, exercise, and blood pressure (Kutner et al. 2007). A 2011 study found that the average college student attended class and hit the books for more than forty hours per week in the 1960s but just twenty-seven in 2003 (Babcock and Marks 2011). Some have suggested that better tools for information retrieval permitted students to study less, but an obvious implication is that college faculty may have adjusted to lower student interest in study by reducing requirements. Richard Arum and Josipa Roksa (2011) find that only about half of students made significant gains on a test of critical thinking between the beginning of freshman and the middle of sophomore year. A year later, with senior data in hand, they concluded that more than a third of college students failed to make significant gains on critical thinking between freshman and senior years (Arum, Roksa, and Cho 2011). Those students who failed to make significant gains on the critical thinking test had shorter reading and writing assignments in their courses. These students were most likely to be found in less selective institutions and occupationally oriented majors (Arum and Roksa 2011).

Regardless of field, cognitive skill level matters in the labor market (Hanushek and Woessmann 2011, 160-8). In addition, labor market returns vary greatly depending on the field of study. By mid-career, students who graduate in some engineering specializations, such as petroleum engineering, are earning on average two to three times as much as those who graduate in many of the human services fields, such as teaching and child welfare services (Carnevale, Rose, and Cheah 2011; PayScale 2014). In statistical studies that control for input characteristics, such as students' grades and test scores and their socioeconomic backgrounds, differences in returns to fields of study show much stronger net relationships to earnings than the selectivity of the institution attended or students' grade point averages (see, for example, Arcidicano 2004; Brewer, Eide, and Ehrenberg 1999; James et al. 1989). These findings raise the question of whether comparisons by educational attainment are the right ones to make for analyses of human capital development or whether fields of study are the more appropriate bases for comparison, at least for adults who complete postsecondary programs.

Given the labor market advantages held by graduates in many science, technology, engineering, and mathematics (STEM) fields, it is not surprising that a final source of concern over human capital development is the unchanging share of American college students who complete degrees in these fields. STEM fields are a national priority area because of their contribution to economic growth (see, for example, National Academies 2007, 1). The stagnation in STEM degrees is associated with high rates of attrition among college students who start out majoring in a STEM field, only to switch majors, often because of difficulty passing introductory mathematics and science courses (327). Weaknesses in science literacy start early. The recent Program for International Student Assessment (PISA) international test of science knowledge indicated that average scores for American fifteen-year-olds were lower than those of students in all but four of twenty-four participating countries. American students also showed great variability in their scores around this average, producing a higher standard deviation than all but three of the participating countries (see Han and Buchmann, this volume).

---

14. To be sure, complaints about partying and insufficient seriousness on the part of college students are nothing new. In the 1925 film *The Freshman*, comic star Harold Lloyd poked fun at the subservience of studiousness to the frenzy over football. In his 1928 book, Robert Angell describes students' academic orientation this way: "A small minority are sincerely interested in all their academic work; a larger minority do not put their hearts into any of it; while the great mass are genuinely intent upon only a few of their subjects, commonly the more practical ones, and apathetic toward the rest" (2).

ACCESS, COMPLETION, AND EQUITY

We now turn to a second major interest of national higher education policymakers, the provision of opportunities for upward social mobility. Although the quality of higher education can no longer be assumed and fields of study matter greatly for outcomes in the labor market, college degrees nevertheless remain a key foundation for labor market success, as evidence on the college degree premium attests. For this reason, the distribution of opportunity to attend and graduate from college is a key issue for policymakers and scholars alike.

Disproportional representation of affluent students has been a characteristic of American colleges beginning in the colonial period. Despite the rise of public higher education, this bias in favor of the moneyed and professional classes continued to exist for a century after the first Morrill Act (see, for example, Angell 1928), and it continues today in an only slightly attenuated form. Consequently, American higher education has been regularly criticized for its contributions to the perpetuation of inequality. In so far as greater equality of access and completion are system-level measures of effectiveness, these criticisms amount to a fundamental challenge to the U.S. system's promise of equal opportunity for all.

Rates of college enrollment have been rising over time, but rates for those from low-income families have lagged well behind those for children of the affluent. Moreover, gaps in entry by family income quartiles have grown over time. For a sample drawn from 1961 to 1964 birth cohorts, postsecondary entry rates were 58 percent in the top quartile, 38 percent in the second quartile, 32 percent in the third, and 19 percent in the bottom quartile (Bailey and Dynarski 2011, figure 6.2). But for a sample drawn from the 1979 to 1982 birth cohorts, postsecondary entry rates were 80 percent in the top quartile, 60 percent in the third quartile, 47 percent in the second, and only 29 percent in the lowest income quartile. This is a top-to-bottom gap of more than 50 percent for the later birth cohorts compared with the 40 percent gap for the earlier birth cohorts.

Gaps in college completion by family income are greater than gaps in college entry. Among students in the 1979 to 1982 birth cohorts, for example, the share from the lowest income quartile who had completed four years of college was just 9 percent, representing a third of those who had ever enrolled. For those from the top income group, the corresponding rate of completion was 54 percent, representing two-thirds of those who had ever enrolled (Bailey and Dynarski 2011, tables 6.2 and 6.3). Comparing cohorts born in the early 1960s and the early 1980s, Martha Bailey and Susan Dynarski (2011) show increases in college completion in all income quartiles for those born later, but also an increasing gap in the rate of increase in the bottom two as compared to the top two quartiles of family income.

By contrast, gaps in access by race-ethnicity have narrowed over time, although gaps in graduation remain large. Between 1995 and 2009, for example, freshman college enrollment more than doubled for Hispanics, and increased by 73 percent for African Americans but only 15 percent for whites (Carnevale and Strohl 2013). Among 2004 high school graduates who enrolled in postsecondary institutions immediately following high school graduation, racial-ethnic gaps were not large: 73 percent of Hispanic high school graduates enrolled in college, 76 percent of blacks, 82 percent of whites, and 90 percent of Asians (Ross et al. 2012, 170). However, minorities enrolled mainly in open-access two- and four-year colleges (particularly community colleges and for-profits), and whites and Asians enrolled disproportionately in colleges and universities that select among applicants (Carnevale and Strohl 2013). Even for those who initially entered a four-year college graduation rates have varied sharply by racial-ethnic identity. Nearly 70 percent of Asian American and Pacific Islander students who entered a four-year college in 2007 completed within six years, compared with 58 percent of white students, 46 percent of Hispanic, and 39 percent of African American (NCES 2014, table 326.10).

Notably, the long-standing gender inequalities within higher education have reversed, favoring women rather than men outside of a few fields largely found in the physical sciences and engineering disciplines but including also philosophy and economics. Women are more numerous than men at every degree level in higher education. They are more likely to complete degrees. Their grades are higher, and they are more likely to win academic honors. Graduate education, even in prestigious fields such as business, law and medicine, has become more gender balanced and in nonquantitative fields women are more numerous (NCES 2014, table 303.60). To explain women's better performance on average than men's, researchers have emphasized the greater propensity of women to focus conscientiously on their studies and particularly their greater dependence on educational credentials to compete in labor markets dominated by men (see DiPrete and Buchmann 2013).

Why is the dropout rate so much higher for low-income and underrepresented minority students? One set of explanations focuses on the students and examines the factors such as inadequate academic readiness or financial resources that may slow or derail their academic progress. Undoubtedly, academic preparation is on average lower among students from the bottom quartiles of the income distribution. Social scientists have documented the advantages of social class for students from affluent families relative to their counterparts. Children of college graduates hear on average two to three times as many different words per day than the children of high school graduates. They are read to at night and are encouraged to begin reading and counting for themselves earlier than children from low-income families. They watch less television. They tend more often to live in stable and well-ordered households and communities, allowing them to fit more easily into orderly, rule-bound settings such as schools. Their families are also much more likely to place them in activities that are educationally and socially enriching, such as attending museums and concerts, traveling abroad, and participation in afterschool developmental activities supervised by adults, such as music or tennis lessons. By contrast, children from lower-income families are more likely to spend time with friends in activities that are not educationally advantageous. (For an overview of these educational attainment based differences on groups of otherwise similar students, see Attewell and Lavin 2007, chapter 6.) Annette Lareau (2002) calls this pattern of middle- and upper-middle class parenting "concerted cultivation." In later grades, children from affluent backgrounds often have access to tutors when they are struggling in a class and to test prep options prior to taking college admissions tests.

Despite extensive efforts to provide financial assistance to needy students, the financial resources available to low-income students do not always meet their full financial need, placing greater stress on their families to identify resources for college completion. Many low-income families are loan-averse and encourage their children to work to put themselves through college, a choice that can greatly lengthen time to degree and may lead to non-completion if work interferes too much with study. The research evidence suggests that when students work more than fifteen to twenty hours per week, it tends to be very difficult for them to keep their grades up (Pascarella and Terenzini 2005, 399–402; King and Bannon 2002).

A second set of explanations looks at the types of institutions in which lower-income and underrepresented minority students are disproportionately represented. Completion rates in public community colleges and historically black colleges and universities, where most minority students enroll, are very low. These are typically colleges and universities with limited resources, meaning low-paid instructors and modest counseling and other student services. Only one-fifth who enter these institutions leave with a degree in three years (NCES 2014, table 326.20), and minorities are less likely to graduate than others (Dougherty and Kienzl 2006). Transfer rates from two-year to four-year colleges are also low. Fewer than 25 percent of entering community college students transfer to a four-year college (Dougherty and Kienzl 2006). Most of those who enter community colleges and become stuck in remedial programs are from minority racial-ethnic backgrounds (Attewell et al. 2006; Bahr 2010).

In a study seeking to explain the decline in college completion rates, John Bound, Michael Lovenheim, and Sarah Turner (2010) compared two cohorts of high school graduates, from the high school graduating classes of 1972 and 1988. The percentage of these students who completed four years of college within eight years declined from 50.5 percent to 45.9 percent (135). These declines were concentrated in two sectors enrolling a large portion of all students: two-year colleges and less selective four-year public institutions. Declines in academic preparation were a major part of the explanation for declining graduation rates in community colleges. But in the case of four-year institutions, the authors blame characteristics of the institutions themselves—and in particular overcrowded classrooms and too few course offerings—for most of the overall decline in graduation rates.

Because of the close connection between educational attainment and lifetime earnings, such disparities in college completion portend limited economic opportunities for those already at the bottom of the economic ladder and continued economic stratification in the country as a whole. Contributing to these long-standing gaps in educational attainment, budget cuts and tuition increases in the last decade have increased at a particularly high rate in public institutions, the institutions that serve most students of modest means. Efforts by donors and colleges themselves to raise completion rates for disadvantaged groups have had more than a modicum of success in some notable cases. However, they have not yet found ways to match the impact of these deeply rooted systemic obstacles to equity in access and completion.

PRODUCTION OF RESEARCH AND NEW DOCTORATES

We now turn to the third major function of higher education in the United States: universities are centrally involved in the production of new knowledge and prepare the next generation of scientists and scholars. The new knowledge they produce enriches culture, contributes to new technologies and economic growth, and changes the way organizations work (Baker 2014).

By most measures, the research quality of American higher education is very high in comparison with that offered in other countries. U.S. research universities dominate the top rungs in global rankings. In Shanghai Jiao Tong University's ranking of the world's top research universities, American universities occupy sixteen of the top twenty spots (CWCU 2014). In *The Times* of London's ranking, they account for fifteen of the top twenty (Times Higher Education 2015). Moreover, the United States continues to be the destination of choice for international students, hosting nearly nine hundred thousand international students in the 2013–2014 school year, double the number of international students studying in the United Kingdom, the second leading host country (International Institute of Education 2014).

One way to measure the growth in knowledge production is to examine how many papers are published in scientific journals over time. This growth has been nothing short of spectacular. Many think of the immediate post–World War II period as a golden age of the American research university, but calculations indicate that more recent decades better deserve the appellation "golden age." Whereas some 140,000 papers appeared in the Web of Science between 1951 and 1970, the number jumped to just over five million between 1971 and 1990, and then nearly doubled again to more than nine million between 1991 and 2010 (personal correspondence, Cynthia Carr). This phenomenal record of growth can be explained by an ever-increasing number of researchers, greater research intensity in universities, the rise of new specialty areas, and perhaps especially by the development of new journals.

Within this rapidly expanding universe of scientific papers, the U.S. global share has been declining over the last three decades as other countries and regions have developed the academic work force and infrastructure to support expanded research activity. The U.S. share dropped from 38 percent in 1973 to 28 percent in 2003, according to National Science Foundation researchers (Javits et al. 2010). Using slightly different measures, British Royal Society researchers found a further decline to 21 percent between 2004 and 2008 (The Royal Society 2011). Concurrently, the share of papers from European and East Asian universities rose, China making the largest gains (The Royal Society 2011). However, the United States remains, by one measure, the leader in the top 1 percent of most-cited papers, producing half of the world's share in 2012; no other country has yet reached 20 percent (United Kingdom Department of Business Innovation and Skills 2014).

In spite of the growth of research and researchers, the idea of a postindustrial society dominated by highly educated "knowledge workers" (Bell 1973) has not yet come to pass; many industries outside the "knowledge sector" remain important as employers and generators of national income (Brint 2001, 2015). Yet it is clear that industries populated disproportionately by people with advanced degrees are among the fastest-growing contributors to GDP. If we use the criterion of 5 percent of employees holding master's level or higher degrees for identifying the knowledge sector, the sector is vast, including such industries as agricultural services, mass-media industries, chemicals, plastics, pharmaceuticals, computers and electronic equipment, scientific instruments, banking, accounting, consulting and other business services, medical services and hospitals, educational services (obviously including colleges and universities), legal services, and nearly all of government (Brint 2001; see also Powell and Snellman 2004). The knowledge sector, so defined, accounted for 43 percent of GDP by 2010 (Brint 2015). Economic geographers have shown that regions of robust economic growth are those with high proportions of educated workers, regions such as Silicon Valley, Hollywood, and Wall Street. These regions show strong spillover effects on the salaries and wages of workers outside the knowledge sector because higher incomes there drive higher incomes for services in their regions (Moretti 2013).

The production of knowledge workers has altered the landscape of innovation by amplifying the level of scientific talent working outside of universities. Research universities are responsible for just half of basic research and only a fraction of applied research (National Science Board 2014, chapter 4). Many of the most important inventions of the period, from the Internet and GPS to the birth control pill and the pacemaker, were developed in government laboratories and private corporations by university-trained Ph.D.'s, sometimes but not always building on basic research conducted in universities (see, for example, Issacson 2014). Universities retain an important role in basic research, and they are almost certainly the most potent creators of conceptual structures that become influential in organizational practice and public discourse. Yet institutions outside universities are also producing sophisticated conceptual knowledge structures that have a life independent of universities or are brought into universities to test and refine (Collins, Evans, and Gorman 2007; Powell and Snellman 2004). Rather than university domination, the United States is moving toward a society in which knowledge production becomes characteristic of many institutional domains.

The university retains a monopoly on the production of future scientists and scholars through its authority to grant the doctorate degree. Doctorate degree production increased by 150 percent between 1970–1971 and 2011–2012. Today, U.S. universities produce nearly three times as many doctorates a year (170,000) than they did in 1970–1971 (65,000) (NCES 2014, table 318.20). The United States retains a global educational influence through the strength of its graduate programs. In recent years, nearly 30 percent of all doctorates awarded by American universities have gone to students holding temporary student visas (Bound et al. 2014, 18).

This does not mean that the U.S. system for producing doctoral-level scientists and scholars is without significant problems. Graduate students in the humanities and social sciences average seven to eight years from admission to doctorate. About half of doctorates in these fields do not complete and of those who do complete about half do not obtain academic jobs (Ehrenberg et al. 2009, chapter 11). Most who do not complete obtain professional or managerial jobs, but quite a few are in lower-paid capacities (Ehrenberg et al. 2009). Doctorate production in the natural sciences and engineering does not take quite as long, but for those pursuing academic careers the doctorate is often merely the preliminary to a lengthy apprenticeship (for as many as five or more years) as a postdoctoral scholar before a faculty position becomes a feasible objective (Powell 2015). Postdoctoral scholars accumulate coauthored papers but less frequently gain the autonomy to launch their own independent research careers. Their salaries are low and rarely include robust benefit packages (National Academy of Sciences 2014). The rise of non-tenure track faculty has made securing a tenure-track position far more competitive than before (Schuster and Finkelstein 2006). Fortunately, many more positions exist for doctoral-level natural scientists and engineers outside of academe, and the majority of doctoral degree holders in these fields make careers in industry or government agencies rather than academe (National Science Foundation 2013, table 46). Two large and unresolved problems are the adequacy of funding for doctoral students and the quality of professional development opportunities for doctoral students who will not succeed in obtaining academic jobs or are not interested in obtaining them (Bok 2013, chap. 11).

POLICIES TO IMPROVE SYSTEM-LEVEL EFFECTIVENESS

This section examines the role of the federal government and the major philanthropic foundations in maintaining and improving system-level effectiveness. Federal higher education policy has been fundamental in two areas: financial aid and research funding. In recent years, major private foundations have also been centrally involved in the development of accountability mechanisms and in the promulgation of a college completion agenda.[15]

Financial Aid Policy

Scholars and policymakers have long recognized that financial constraints discourage many would-be college graduates from even enrolling in college, let alone finishing. These constraints limit the effectiveness of the higher education system. In addition to financial constraints, low-income students may also be handicapped in college-going by ignorance regarding the application process, sources of aid, and the steps needed to take advantage of such aid.

A primary role for national and state governments therefore has been to provide financial aid to support students whose lack of financial resources would otherwise prevent them from attending college. The programs explicitly aim to alleviate the financial burden of attending college include federal grants to low-income students, commonly referred to as Pell Grants, (amounting to $34 billion in 2014), state-funded scholarships including both need-based and merit scholarships, ($9 billion), federal student loans ($96 billion), federal work-study ($1 billion), and other federal programs such as those supporting veterans, military academies, and minority-serving institutions ($15 billion) (College Board 2014). In addition to these programs are a number of tax provisions that reduce the cost of making donations or specifically subsidize the cost of college attendance. Provisions in the federal personal income tax to subsidize college attendance include two tax credits, a deduction for college tuition, and a provision by which parents can claim their college-going children as dependents up to age twenty-four. The tax code also provides for tax-subsidized college savings accounts. All together, these provisions have a budgetary cost equal to about a third of the Pell Grant program, or about $11 billion (Deming and Dynarski 2009, 2–3).

There are reasons to believe that financial aid expenditures at this level are not keeping up with increases in unmet need. Unmet need can be defined as the gap between college costs

---

15. Foundations have played an important institution-building role from the earliest years of the twentieth century. In particular, the Ford, Pew, Lumina and Gates Foundations developed standard curricular units (the so-called Carnegie unit), encouraged higher levels of quality in medical education and other professions, made college teaching a more secure occupation by funding the original retirement plans, greatly aided the development of community colleges, led internationalization efforts, and fostered the diversification of the student body.

and what students have to pay after accounting for the students' expected family contribution, grants and scholarships, and any other aid that does not need to be repaid (Saunders 2015). Bridget Long and Erin Riley (2007) found substantial increases in unmet need from the 1995–1996 school year to the 2003–2004 school year for all full-time, full-year undergraduates. Moreover, these increases in unmet need affected low-income students more than other students. For example, they found that low-income students attending a public four-year college experienced a 59 percent increase in unmet need. High levels of unmet need persisted through the early 2010s (Saunders 2015). It is difficult to disentangle the effects of unmet need from other factors that affect retention and completion, such as academic preparation. However, unmet need is certainly one cause of the lower retention and completion rates of lower-income and underrepresented minority students. Serge Herzog (2005), for example, found that students in four-year public university with $1,000 in unmet need had drop-out and transfer-out odds of 7 to 10 percent above those of student with no unmet need. Students with unmet need work longer hours to pay for college and are more likely to attend part time. Longer work hours, in turn, lead to higher dropout rates among otherwise similar students, and part-time status is also correlated with lower rates of college completion (see, for example, Attewell, Heil, and Reisel 2012).

A recent review of statistical studies of the effect of financial aid policies observed that the availability of the two largest federal programs, Pell Grants and Stafford Loans, do not affect the probability that low-income students will enroll in college. In contrast, the merit aid programs that have been established in more than a dozen states do exhibit measurable positive effects on enrollments (Deming and Dynarski 2009). The explanation for this difference in effectiveness is that the paperwork required to apply for federal aid is daunting, especially for applicants whose parents have limited education. By contrast, state merit aid programs have simple requirements, and state education systems typically assume the burden of getting necessary information to colleges automatically. A policy option at the federal level would be to simplify the application process for aid. In one experiment, a national tax assistance company assisted customers with their children's financial aid applications, resulting in an increase in college enrollment rates (Deming and Dynarski 2009).[16]

Accountability and Quality Assurance

By the 1980s, international competition and the increasing number of students entering higher education with lower levels of academic preparation heightened worries about the quality of academic programs (National Governors Association 1986). The Pew and Ford Foundations were notable among the many philanthropies funding the regional accrediting agencies to develop approaches to assessment of student learning outcomes. In 1989, federal regulations first required accrediting organizations to examine student learning outcomes as a condition of recognition. By 2001, ten states, concentrated in the Midwest and the South, had experimented with or adopted standardized testing at the college level to assess student learning, but most of the regional accreditation agencies decided to allow colleges and universities themselves to determine how best to assess student learning outcomes. In 2006, a national commission formed by then-Secretary of Education Margaret Spellings issued a report calling for "a robust culture of accountability and transparency" and urging institutions to develop "new performance benchmarks designed to measure and improve productivity and efficiency" (Commission on the Future of Higher Education 2006, 14, 19, 20).

Assessment of student learning outcomes has had a mixed record, one that has not fully satisfied federal higher education officials. A

---

16. In these and other studies of the effectiveness of various financial aid policies, it is necessary for researchers to overcome selection effects, the tendency of those applying for aid to be systematically different from those who do not apply for aid. One study that explicitly deals with that source of bias relies on the results of a random control experiment in Nebraska (Angrist et al. 2014). The authors find that increased financial aid boosted both enrollment and completion.

report on accountability in higher education released in 2009 (Kuh and Ikenberry) revealed that more than 90 percent of respondents from two- and four-year institutions said they were engaged in institution-level assessments of student learning. Most were using survey instruments, such as the National Survey of Student Engagement, for this purpose, though nearly two in five respondents were using standardized tests of general knowledge and skill, such as the Collegiate Learning Assessment. Most confirmed that accreditation was the primary driver of their interest in assessment.[17] However, on campuses assessment of student learning outcomes often remained surface-level, treated as a matter of compliance rather than as a deeper commitment. Many departments went through the motions of assessing student learning outcomes without using results to improve program performance (Kuh and Ikenberry 2009).

Engineering was an exception to this mixed record. Its professional accrediting organization issued a report in 2000 requiring schools to publish detailed educational objectives, to design a curriculum that ensured achievement of these objectives, and to put in place a system for using results of assessments to improve the effectiveness of the program. In addition, it established specific outcome criteria that all engineering graduates were, in theory, required to demonstrate (Accreditation Board for Engineering and Technology 2000). A follow-up report showed that these recommendations produced real change in how courses were taught. More than half of faculty surveyed reported that they had increased their use of active learning methods, such as group work, design projects, case studies, and application exercises, due to the new requirements for accreditation. A comparison of 1994 and 2004 engineering graduates showed small but significant self-reported gains in technical abilities, such as the application of mathematics and science to engineering problems. Students also self-reported sizable increases in their ability to work in teams, to understand professional ethics, to understand contemporary issues and to demonstrate global cultural awareness (Lattuca, Terenzini, and Volkwein 2006).

College Completion

The postwar federal policy emphasis on increasing access for less advantaged groups assumed the opportunity to attend college would lead to improvement in outcomes. However, rates of baccalaureate attainment declined, leading foundations of the early twenty-first century to focus on college completion as a necessary complement to improved access. The Lumina Foundation set the goal of 60 percent of all Americans with credentials, associate degrees, and baccalaureate degrees by 2025. To promote wider access and faster completion at lower cost, the Gates Foundation invested heavily in experiments in which online modules replaced courses and students demonstrated competency by achieving a passing grade on an online exam. It also invested in the development of Massive Open Online Courses (MOOCs) and new adaptive learning technologies. This Lumina-Gates completion push was embraced by President Obama, who, in a 2010 speech, proclaimed the goal of regaining by the year 2020 the world lead in the production of higher level credentials.

The results of this effort have as yet not yielded changes in graduation rates as large as advocates had hoped. Nationally, the proportion of students who entered college and graduated within four and six years increased in both cases by more than 5 percent for the cohorts entering in 1996 and those entering in 2007. Yet four-year graduation remains under 40 percent and six-year graduation remains under 60 percent (NCES 2014, table 326.10). Constraints on seats and courses, financial aid availability, and student academic preparation

---

[17]. At the program level, four of five respondents said they were assessing student learning outcomes in at least one program, and here portfolios dominated. Extending the reach of assessment, the American Association of Colleges & Universities, also supported by the major philanthropies, successfully lobbied for the inclusion of the "core competencies" of analytical and critical thinking, information literacy, quantitative reasoning, oral communication, and written expression as campus-wide assessment components in the Western region (Western Association of Schools and Colleges 2013).

have conspired to keep the college completion movement from achieving its goals.

Research Policy

Research policy is perhaps a misnomer for the decentralized advocacy and negotiation that occurs between scientists, funding agencies, Congress, the president, and the various advisory and advocacy groups whose efforts eventually result in apppropriations and national science and engineering initiatives. This network of contending parties eventually produces federal budget appropriations that provide nearly two-thirds of nondefense spending on university research. Colleges and universities' self-financing of research has played a larger role over time and is now up to nearly 20 percent of the total (National Science Foundation 2013).[18]

International competition has been a major driver of research policy since the days of Sputnik in the 1950s. In the 1970s, the rise of Japan and the decline of American manufacturing triggered new competitiveness policies. One of these was the Bayh-Dole Act of 1980, which allowed universities greater leeway in patenting and licensing of commercially viable products, therapies, and technologies. Bayh-Dole accelerated trends in university patenting and licensing that were already developing in the 1970s (Mowery et al. 2001; Stephan 2012) by allowing all universities to profit from the patenting and licensing of discoveries made by their researchers. The Act achieved its aim of contributing to the rapid increase of university-based patents and licenses yielding income. The income earned by universities increased by approximately 2.5 times in constant dollars between 1981 and 2008 (calculated from Loise and Stevens 2010). However, earnings data are highly skewed by a few "big hits," and a majority of university technology transfer offices run in the red (Loise and Stevens 2010)

Concerns about American competitiveness also stimulated the influential National Academy of Sciences report of the mid-2000s, *Rising Above the Gathering Storm* (National Academies 2007). The report noted a shortage of high school math and science teachers, the need for pipeline programs to increase STEM enrollments in college, and a restrictive immigration system that prevented researchers trained outside the United States from seeking employment in the United States. It also advocated a reinvestment in basic research to reverse trends toward larger shares going to applied research and urged a stronger research and development tax credit to encourage private investment in innovation. Several of the recommendations of the report were incorporated into the America COMPETES Act of 2007, reauthorized by Congress in 2010.[19] Nevertheless, the educational infrastructure for producing the STEM workforce remains underdeveloped, and immigration policy has not been overhauled. A recent study by the Information Technology and Innovation Foundation found that the United States ranked twenty-seventh in the world in the size of its R&D tax incentives (Stewart, Warda, and Atkinson 2012).

ORGANIZATIONAL EFFECTIVENESS

We now turn to campus-level initiatives to improve higher education effectiveness. We focus on three developments that are prevalent on campuses across the country: importing corporate business models into university administration; a trend toward interdisciplinary organization; and increased interest in "student success," defined as undergraduate retention and graduation.

Imported Business Practices

For more than a century, university trustees and administrators have looked to the corporate sector for practices that can improve the efficiency and effectiveness of their operations.

---

18. The United States spends at 2.8 percent a comparatively high proportion of GDP on R&D. A 2013 study by the World Bank showed that only six of seventy-seven countries reporting in 2011 or 2012 spent a higher proportion of GDP on R&D (World Bank 2013).

19. The 2015 reauthorization ran into opposition from the scientific community and the Democratic Party for its efforts to roll back funding on climate change, to reduce funding for several scientific directorates, and to increase the administrative burden on researchers (National Science Foundation 2015; White House 2015).

At the turn of the twentieth century, the maverick economist Thorstein Veblen disparaged such efforts as inimical to scholarship. The Veblenian tradition of suspicion has lived on, with critics warning against excessive business influence in universities. In recent decades, this influence has been described as "academic capitalism" (Slaughter and Leslie 1997), the "corporatization" of academic life (Tuchman 2009; Washburn 2005), and the rise of the "market-model" university (Engel and Dangerfield 1998; Kirp 2003).

Functions with revenue-generating potential receive special attention because of their centrality to institutional stability. Support staffs for admissions, fund-raising, government and community relations, and research are typically among the largest on campus and the most carefully administered. These units frequently rely on consultants to help managers to improve performance (Coopers & Lybrand 1995). Campuses have engaged in efforts to "brand" themselves in the marketplace to improve their competitive position (Kirp 2003) and commercialized intercollegiate sports play an important role in these branding efforts, often across a national audience (Clotfelter 2011).

One controversial strategy to audit professorial productivity was briefly adopted and then abandoned in Texas. This audit rated professors' productivity using metrics such as number of students taught and external research funding (Berrett 2011). The pushback from university supporters led to abandonment of this effort, and other states have been reluctant to impose such audits. However, many campuses have adopted other ostensibly more efficient management policies pioneered by business corporations. These strategies include "lean" staffing with greater centralization of control and greater reliance on computerized systems and metrics to guide work processes (see, for example, Womack and Jones 2003). They also include responsibility-centered management (RCM), also known as Incentive-Based Budgeting Systems (IBBS), a popular budget model in which colleges and departments are rewarded for increasing student credit hours, majors, and sometimes also graduation rates, while central administration retains funds for common core functions, such as the library, as a kind of tax on "revenue-generating" units (Whalen 1991; Lang 1999).

Clearly quite a bit of faddism is evident in university administrators' efforts to mimic trends in corporate management, leading to short life spans for many new management practices (Birnbaum 2001). Some with longer-lasting support have checkered histories. Although lean management models can improve efficiency, notably in administratively bloated units, studies of corporations indicate that the substitution of technology for staff and the centralization and clustering of functions can also reduce the effectiveness of operations when staff numbers decline below a critical threshold or when staff motivation declines due to overwork (Amabile and Conti 1999; Cameron 1994; Cascio 1993). Responsibility-centered management has the potential to improve the efficiency of budgeting "by clarifying and making more visible institutions, investment patterns, budgets, cross-subsidies, management stregnths and weaknesses, and operational values" (Hearn et al. 2006, 312). It also has well-known unintended consequences, including the stimulation of inefficient competition across schools and departments for student credit hours and pressures for reducing mission-critical central functions such as libraries and community activities, which are supported by taxing the "revenue-generating" units (Adams 1997; Meisinger 1994).

Certain legal and economic features of colleges and universities make the analogy with private firms one that can be easily pushed too far. Unlike the specialized research institutions in Europe, American state universities serve several major objectives: broad-based undergraduate education, pragmatically oriented professional training, basic research in arts and sciences, and applied research and outreach to industry and farm (Goldin and Katz 1999, 45). The contribution of positive externalities to economy and society, as well as the public service activities of higher education institutions, justify their nonprofit status.[20] Because no single metric of performance exists

---

20. Because of these activities, colleges and universities, like all non-profit organizations, enjoy exemptions from

in colleges and universities comparable to market share or profitability, higher education management is more about balancing many important goals than about maximizing one or two key indicators. The use of bottom-line measures can consequently be a poor fit for the university environment.

Moreover, certain features of the employment situation of the professional staff also mark universities as distinctive from business firms. As James Coleman (1973) notes, one of the distinguishing marks of universities is that their central group of employees are not really employees in the usual sense, but are rather semiautonomous professionals, some of whom may feel only a minimal attachment to their employer. The market for faculty, particularly those at the top of their respective disciplines, is very much a national market. Probably the single most distinctive characteristic of these faculty positions, however, is the institution of tenure, a virtually iron-clad guarantee of permanent employment to those faculty who survive what can be a most demanding probationary period.[21] These features of the employment situation support a governance structure that is in most cases still better described as a "dual structure," involving spheres of faculty authority and influence, than as "managerial control" (Apkarian et al. 2014).

Interdisciplinary Designs

Departmental organization has been the backbone of the American colleges and organizations since the early twentieth century (Abbott 2002). But the rise of interdisciplinary forms of academic organization threatens this dominance.[22] Since the 1980s, many requests for proposals from research funding agencies have required submission by interdisciplinary rather than discipline-only teams. Institutions too have perceived the benefit of fostering cross-disciplinary collaborations. Some of the leading justifications for interdisciplinary organization, such as the alleged "siloed" quality of the disciplines, are suspect, given the permeability of disciplines to new methods and concepts (Jacobs 2013). Nevertheless, interdisciplinary curricula (Brint et al. 2009), interdisciplinary cluster hiring (Sa 2008; Urban Universities 2015), and campus-wide interdisciplinary initiatives (Brint 2005; Sa 2008) have all been on the rise in American colleges and universities since the 1980s.

In spite of their decidedly mixed record of success (see, for example, Geiger and Sa 2008, 167; Rhoten 2003, 2004; Hollingsworth and Hollingsworth 2000), interdisciplinary initiatives have retained a reputation for superiority in problem solving and breakthrough research, and these objectives have great appeal to the people who provide financial contributions and political support for universities. Moreover, the introduction of project-based collaborative learning environments has been identified by some sociologists as a way to reproduce the work environments found in the more dynamic and innovative sectors of the economy, such as Internet services and biotechnology firms (see, for example, Vallas and Kleinman 2007), with the hope that they may lead to similar levels of creativity in the academic setting.

Quite apart from their capacity to raise the profile of universities by leveraging existing strengths across fields, interdisciplinary initiatives play to the skills of administrators in pull-

---

the federal income tax. Most donations to universities are deductible in calculating the personal income tax, the corporate income tax, and the estate tax. Private foundations, a noteworthy beneficiary of the tax laws, also provided support to universities. At the local level, universities both public and private are exempted from paying most property taxes.

21. The practical implications of tenure for academic governance deepened in 1994, when mandatory retirement for faculty was outlawed (Hammond and Morgan 1991, xi).

22. Concerted federal commitments to interdisciplinary date from the arrival of Ernest Bloch at the National Science Foundation in the mid-1980s. Coming from an industrial research background, Bloch emphasized that pathbreaking research and development typically requires the collaborative work of many types of disciplinary specialists. Insurgent ethnic, gender, and non-Western cultural studies movements of the 1970s and 1980s had their own reasons for favoring interdisciplinarity as a way of linking advocates to like-minded colleagues in neighboring disciplines, thereby escaping the traditional reproductive tendencies of departmental structures.

ing together resources to pursue large-scale initiatives, placing them in a more central position in academic decision-making (Brint 2005). They also have natural constituencies among those in the sciences who are responsive to the priorities of granting agencies and those in the humanities and social sciences who see interdisciplinarity as a way to foster faculty diversity (Brint 2005; Urban Universities 2015). If only for these reasons, interdisciplinary designs that deemphasize departmental organization are unlikely to recede in importance soon.

Student Success Programs

It has been clear at least since the 1980s that aspects of the campus environment can make a difference for the retention and graduation of "at-risk" college students. For example, students who live and work on campus tend to be better integrated into campus life than otherwise similar students who live and work off campus, and they are therefore more likely to persist to graduation (Astin 1984). Prodded by the major philanthropic foundations and the federal government, campuses have over the last decade taken a more systematic approach to improving their retention and graduation rates. Because first-generation and low-income students often come to college less prepared academically, these interventions often focus on such students. Efforts to increase retention and graduation rates are now frequently referred to as "student success programs."

Unfortunately, evaluations of programs to increase retention and graduation rates often fail to take into account unmeasured motivational differences between students who do and do not sign up for programs, thus preventing robust program evaluation that controls for student motivation. The outcomes of interventions are also influenced by variation in the commitment, competence, and resources of staff, as well as by differences in program design and implementation. In one of the few strong studies of student success programs, Eric Bettinger and Rachel Baker (2014) used experimental methods to assess the impact of an intensive series of coaching and counseling interventions with high-need college students. They found a statistically significant increase in persistence and degree completion for students in the treatment group, supporting survey results indicating that high-need students benefit disproportionately from more regular contact with advisers (see Klepfer and Hull 2012). Until findings relevant to other promising academic support programs can be corroborated in multiple sites using rigorous methods, campuses will lack convincing evidence to guide design and implementation of these programs.[23]

CLASSROOM EFFECTIVENESS

We now examine the final level in our analysis of higher education effectiveness, the classroom. Educators have long recognized that traditional lecture halls are not conducive environments for learning (see, for example, Barzun 1968). This is true because many instructors are not compelling lecturers and because the traditional lecture format invites student passivity. Student attention frequently wavers in most large lecture classes (Bunce, Flens, and Neiles 2010). Nevertheless, economic realities require that many introductory courses and even advanced courses in some majors be taught in lecture halls. Fortunately, some new instructional techniques show promise in creating more effective learning environments.

Active and Experiential Learning

Active learning techniques seek to increase student participation in order to improve learning outcomes. In addition to such staples as presentations, demonstrations, debates, and project reports, active learning advocates have called for breaking large classes into smaller groups to work on questions collectively and

---

23. Persuasive multisite studies using random assignment techniques do not exist in support of most interventions often judged by higher education scholars to be effective in improving retention and graduation rates. These interventions include learning communities; pre-matriculation summer programs; athletic advising models applied to at-risk students; and timely data updates to advisers about students who are failing to achieve critical grades or take gateway courses on schedule for graduation.

then to report out results to the entire class (Mazur 1997). Some reformers adopted electronic "clicker" technology to take instantaneous polls among students to test for understanding and to solicit opinion on discussion questions posed by the instructor. Minilectures combined with problem-based small group breakouts have been carefully studied. Based on results of pre- and post-semester concept inventory tests, the studies show a pattern of significantly improved learning relative to prior term traditional lecture courses (see, for example, Hake 1998; Prince 2004).

As opposed to active learning, experiential learning involves "hands-on" activities undertaken in nonclassroom environments, including field work, observations, interviews, internships, and "service learning" opportunities in community organizations (DeAngelo et al. 2007). Although researchers have often found higher levels of student engagement due to experiential learning activities (Kuh et al. 2008), some studies have found that engagement scores are not strongly correlated with improved performance on tests of analytical and critical thinking (Carini, Kuh, and Klein 2006). The upshot of this research is that efforts to increase engagement are not as closely connected to learning outcomes as many believe.

One reason is that student-centered approaches alone cannot make up for the declines in study time and reading completion that have been observed in every discipline, among every demographic group, and at every type of institution since the 1960s (Babcock and Marks 2011). Improved in-class accountability mechanisms are consequently a valuable complement to student-centered teaching, if the goal is increased student learning. A notable experimental study showed that daily online reading quizzes significantly improved student performance on final exams, while reducing achievement gaps between students from high- and low-income backgrounds (Pennebaker, Gosling, and Ferrell 2013). Similarly, longer reading and writing assignments have been associated with gains in analytical and critical thinking among otherwise similar students (Arum and Roksa 2011).

Instructional Technologies

Online instruction has grown steadily. By 2012, nearly seven million students had taken at least one course online, representing one-third of college students overall (Allen and Seaman 2013). Online courses have many advantages. They can educate larger numbers of students, using engaging multimedia content, and potentially at a fraction of the cost of face-to-face instruction. They are convenient because students are not required to attend class at specified days and times. It is no wonder that lectures are seen by many technology enthusiasts as emblematic of an industry hanging onto an outmoded nineteenth-century technology, and consequently missing opportunities to increase students' learning while cutting costs.

Online courses suffer from extremely high dropout rates compared with face-to-face courses. Moreover, the prevailing wisdom, based on meta-analysis of hundreds of studies, is that hybrid instruction is preferable in so far as it can provide both the convenience of learning basic materials online and time for indepth questioning and feedback in face-to-face sessions (Means et al. 2009). This evidence has led to an increase in "flipped classrooms," in which lectures are viewed prior to class and class time is used for solving problems or discussing texts.

Online courses appear to work best for mature professionals who are pursuing higher level degrees or advanced certification. Regardless of age, academically well-prepared students can fare well in a fully online environment. However, several studies have suggested that younger students, male students, and particularly those who are less prepared for academic work do not tend to fare as well in fully online environments (see, for example, Xu and Jaggars 2011). Less experienced students may need the reinforcement that comes from seeing others attending and participating in learning, much as those who go to gyms may need to see others sweating to want to do the same.

Serious questions have also been raised about the distributional consequences of online higher education. A widely circulated open letter by a San Jose State philosophy professors responding to the introduction of MOOCs in their department questioned whether lectures geared to the cultural reference sets of elite students were appropriate to the predominantly first-generation students they taught. They also questioned whether online courses were more suitable for the production of technicians working alone or under the direction of others than higher-level professionals and managers whose work requires well-developed interpersonal skills and the capacity to build social networks (San Jose State University 2013).

Adaptive learning technologies (also known as courseware and intelligent tutoring systems) are another technological approach to improve learning. These technologies are used to assess difficulties that learners are having in mastering ideas and, based on these assessments, to provide individualized tutorials to help students bridge their learning gaps.[24] Adaptive learning software has the clear advantage over human instructors of being infinitely patient. When a student fails to understand a particular concept, the software begins teaching the concept again and can continue indefinitely until the concept is learned. In more sophisticated software programs, students are exposed to multiple ways of thinking about a concept or problem, an approach that is clearly advantageous when the first explanation does not work. In well-controlled experiments, researchers have shown significant improvements in students' classroom engagement and course grades following the adoption of adaptive learning technologies (Dori and Belcher 2005; Lovett, Meyer, and Thille 2008; Twigg 2003).[25] Of the technological approaches to improve higher education effectiveness, adaptive learning technologies are clearly one of the more promising.

CONCLUSION

Higher education is a central sector in American society. The effectiveness of colleges and universities is consequently a national priority concern. We have argued that higher education effectiveness can be evaluated at four levels of analysis: systems, state, campus, and classroom. We have focused on three of those levels here for the most part, leaving aside variation in state policies.

Our overview yields a mixed scorecard on efforts to improve higher education effectiveness. The system looks very good when labor market and research outcomes are assessed, but labor market outcomes appear to have as much or more to do with the interpretation of degrees as signals of talent and trainability as with any measurable human capital contributions they reflect. In disciplines and institutions where it is lacking, a renewed focus on transmitting subject matter knowledge and core cognitive competencies is warrented. When equity issues are in the foreground, research indicates that U.S. progress has stalled, particularly for lower-income students. State subsidies to public institutions have been declining in recent decades and financial aid has not kept pace with need. A high priority in national policy must therefore be to reverse these declines. We also observe persistent difficulties in the financing and professional development of doctoral students, in the latter case particularly for those who are unlikely to obtain academic jobs.

The most popular campus-level innovations are imported business practices, interdisciplinary designs, and programs to boost graduation rates. Each of these has created bandwagon effects among university administrators, but so far none has as yet shown a consistent

---

24. One example is Virginia Tech's Math Emporium, which was an early and influential model of adaptive learning software tailored to address the individual student's learning gaps. In the Math Emporium, students learn course concepts, complete practice problems, and take assigned tests at a self-paced rate. Built-in assessment programs allow faculty members to monitor each student's progress and to intervene as problems arose (Truelove 1999).

25. Adaptive learning software represents just one approach to the use of technology to enhance student learning. Other approaches include, for example, online simulations, online video demonstrations, and calibrated peer review of writing assignments. More than a hundred interactive simulations are now available in open source from the University of Colorado's PhET Interactive Simulations (Weiman, Adams, and Perkins 2008).

or replicable record of improving effectiveness in the areas they address. By contrast, many classroom-level innovations in instructional practices and technologies show promising results, with the proviso that student-centered teaching has proven to be no panacea without an equal level of student accountability for learning.

Although the scorecard is mixed, the attention to effectiveness is welcome. Perhaps the most important consequence of higher education's growing concern with effectiveness is that it can lead in the direction of policies that contribute to better system-level outcomes—and toward institutions that will eventually be capable of using well-researched and scalable practices for the benefit of their students, their faculties, and their communities.

REFERENCES

Abbott, Andrew. 2002. *The Chaos of Disciplines*. Chicago: University of Chicago Press.

Accreditation Board for Engineering and Technology. 2000. *Criteria for Accrediting Engineering*. Baltimore, Md.: ABET.

Adams, E. M. 1997. "Rationality in the Academy: Why Responsibility Center Budgeting Is a Wrong Step Down a Wrong Road." *Change* 29(5): 58–61.

Allen, I. Elaine, and Jeff Seaman. 2013. "Changing Course: Ten Years of Tracking Online Education in the United States." Babson Park, Mass.: Babson Survey Research Group and Quahog Research Group. Accessed December 17, 2015. http://www.onlinelearningsurvey.com/reports/changingcourse.pdf.

Amabile, Teresa M., and Regina Conti. 1999. "Changes in the Work Environment for Creativity During Downsizing." *Academy of Management Journal* 42(6): 630–40.

Angell, Robert Cooley. 1928. *The Campus: A Study of Contemporary Undergraduate Life in the American University*. New York: Appleton and Co.

Angrist, Joshua, David Autor, Sally Hudson, and Amanda Pallais. 2014. "Leveling Up: Early Results from a Randomized Evaluation of Post-Secondary Aid." *NBER* working paper no. 20800. Cambridge, Mass.: National Bureau of Economic Research.

Apkarian, Jacob, Kerry Mulligan, Matthew B. Rotondi, and Steven Brint. 2014. "Who Governs? Academic Decision-Making in U.S. Four-Year Colleges and Universities, 2000–2012." *Tertiary Education and Management* 20(2): 1–14.

Arcidicano, Peter. 2004. "Ability Sorting and the Returns to the College Major." *Journal of Econometrics* 121(1–2): 343–75.

Arum, Richard, and Josipa Roksa. 2011. *Academically Adrift: Limited Learning on College Campuses*. Chicago: University of Chicago Press.

———. 2014. *Aspiring Adults Adrift*. Chicago: University of Chicago Press.

Arum, Richard, Josipa Roksa, and Esther Cho. 2011. *Improving Undergraduate Learning: Findings and Policy Recommendations from the SSRC-CLA Project*. New York: Social Science Research Council.

Association of American Universities. 2010. "AAU Membership Policy." Accessed December 17, 2015. https://www.aau.edu/WorkArea/DownloadAsset.aspx?id=10972.

———. 2015. "By the Numbers." Accessed December 17, 2015. http://www.aau.edu/uploadedFiles?About_AAU/AAu_Data/AAU_BytheNumbers_2015._8.5x11_HR.pdf.

Association of Public and Land-Grant Universities. 2015. "Project Degree Completion." Accessed December 17, 2015. http://www.aplu.org/projects-and-initiatives/project-degree-completion/.

Astin, Alexander W. 1984. "Student Involvement: A Developmental Theory." *Journal of Colleges Student Personnel* 25(4): 297–308.

Attewell, Paul, Scott Heil, and Liza Reisel. 2012. "What Is Academic Momentum? And Does It Matter?" *Educational Evaluation and Policy Analysis* 34(1): 27–44.

Attewell, Paul, and David E. Lavin. 2007. *Passing the Torch: Does Higher Education Pay for the Disadvantaged and Pay Off Across the Generations?* New York: Russell Sage Foundation.

Attewell, Paul, David E. Lavin, Thurston Domina, and Tania Levey. 2006. "New Evidence on College Remediation." *Journal of Higher Education* 77(5): 886–924.

Autor, David H. 2014. "Skills, Education and the Rise of Earnings Inequality Among the 'Other 99 Percent.'" *Science* 344(6186): 843–51.

Babcock, Philip, and Mindy Marks. 2011. "The Falling Time Cost of College: Evidence from Half a Century of Time Use Data." *Review of Economics and Statistics* 93(2): 468–78.

Bahr, Peter Riley. 2010. "Preparing the Underprepared: An Analysis of Racial Disparities in Postsecondary Mathematics Remediation." *Journal of Higher Education* 81(2): 209–37.

Bailey, Martha, and Susan Dynarski. 2011. "Inequality in Postsecondary Attainment." In *Wither Opportunity? Rising Inequality, Schools, and Children's Life Chances*, edited by Greg Duncan and Richard Murnane. New York: Russell Sage Foundation.

Baker, David P. 2014. *The Schooled Society: The Educational Transformation of Global Culture*. Stanford, Calif.: Stanford University Press.

Barzun, Jacques. 1968. *The American University: How It Runs, Where It Is Going*. Chicago: University of Chicago Press.

Baum, Sandy, and Jennifer Ma. 2014. *Trends in College Pricing 2013*. Princeton, N.J.: The College Board.

Baumol, William, and William G. Bowen. 1966. *Performing Arts, The Economic Dilemma: A Study of Problems Common to Theater, Opera, Music, and Dance*. New York: Twentieth Century Fund.

Becher, Tony. 1989. *Academic Tribes and Territories: Intellectual Enquiry and the Cultures of Discipline*. Buckingham, UK: SRHE and Open University Press.

Becker, Gary S. 1964. *Human Capital: A Theoretical and Empirical Analysis, with Special Reference to Education*. New York: Columbia University Press.

Bell, Daniel. 1973. *The Coming of Post-Industrial Society: An Essay in Social Forecasting*. New York: Basic Books.

Bennett, William J. 1987. "Our Greedy Colleges." *New York Times*, February 8, p. A7.

Berg, Ivar. 1971. *Education and Jobs: The Great Training Robbery*. Boston, Mass.: Beacon Press.

Bernhardt, Annette, Martina Morris, Mark Handcock, and Marc Scott. 2001. *Divergent Paths: Economic Mobility in the New American Labor Market*. New York: Russell Sage Foundation.

Berrett, Dan. 2011. "The Wrong Kind of Accountability?" *Inside Higher Ed*, May 10. Accessed December 17, 2015. https://www.insidehighered.com/news/2011/05/10/texas_faculty_and_president_criticize_regents_measurement_of_professors.

Bettinger, Eric P., and Rachel Baker. 2014. "The Effects of Student Coaching: An Evaluation of a Randomized Experiment in Student Advising." *Educational Evaluation and Policy Analysis* 36(1): 3–19.

Bills, David. 2003. "Credentials, Signals, and Screens: Explaining the Relationship between Schooling and Job Assignment." *Review of Educational Research* 73(4): 441–69.

Birnbaum, Robert. 2001. *Management Fads in Higher Education: Where They Come From, What They Do, Why They Fail*. New York: John Wiley & Sons.

Bok, Derek. 2013. *Higher Education in America*. Princeton, N.J.: Princeton University Press.

Bound, John, Murat Demirci, Gaurav Khanna, and Sarah Turner. 2014. "Finishing Degrees and Finding Jobs: U.S. Higher Education and the Flow of Foreign IT Workers." *NBER* working paper no. 20505. Cambridge, Mass.: National Bureau of Economic Research.

Bound, John, Michael F. Lovenheim, and Sarah Turner. 2010. "Why Have College Completion Rates Declined? An Analysis of Changing Student Preparation and Collegiate Resources." *American Economic Journal: Applied Economics* 2(3): 129–57.

Bourdieu, Pierre, and Jean-Claude Passeron. 1977. *Reproduction in Economy, Society and Culture*. Beverly Hills, Calif.: Sage Publications.

Bowen, Howard E. 1977. *Investment in Learning: The Individual and Social Benefits of American Higher Education*. San Francisco: Jossey-Bass.

———. 1980. *The Costs of Higher Education*. San Francisco: Jossey-Bass.

Bowles, Samuel, and Herbert J. Gintis. 1976. *Schooling in a Capitalist Society*. New York: Basic Books.

Brewer, Dominic J., Eric R. Eide, and Ronald G. Ehrenberg. 1999. "Does It Pay to Attend an Elite Private College? Cross-Cohort Evidence on the Effects of College Type on Earnings." *Journal of Human Resources* 34(1): 104–23.

Brint, Steven. 2001. "Professionals and the 'Knowledge Economy': Rethinking the Theory of Post-Industrial Society." *Current Sociology* 49(1): 101–32.

———. 2005. "Creating the Future: The 'New Directions' at American Research Universities." *Minerva* 43(1): 23–50.

———. 2015. "Professional Responsibility in an Age of Experts and Large Organizations." In *Professional Responsibility*, edited by Douglas E. Mitchell and Robert K. Ream. London: Springer.

Brint, Steven, and Jerome Karabel. 1989. *The Diverted Dream: Community Colleges and the Promise of Educational Opportunity in America, 1900–1985*. New York: Oxford University Press.

Brint, Steven, and Kristopher Proctor. 2011. "Middle-Class Respectability in 21st Century America: Work and Lifestyle in the Professional-Managerial Stratum." In *Thrift and Thriving in America: Capitalism and Moral Order from the Puritans to the Present*, edited by Joshua Y. Yates and James Davison Hunter. New York: Oxford University Press.

Brint, Steven, Mark Riddle, and Robert A. Hanneman. 2006. "Reference Sets, Identities, and Aspirations in a Complex Organizational Field: The Case of American Four-Year Colleges and Universities." *Sociology of Education* 79(3): 126–40.

Brint, Steven, Lori Turk-Bicakci, Kristopher Proctor, and Scott Patrick Murphy. 2009. "Expanding the Social Frame of Knowledge: The Growth and Distribution of Interdisciplinary Degree-Granting Programs in American Colleges and Universities, 1975–2000." *Review of Higher Education* 32(2): 155–83.

Brint, Steven, Lori Turk-Bicakci, Mark Riddle, and Charles S. Levy. 2005. "From the Liberal to the Practical Arts in American Colleges and Universities: Organizational Analysis and Curricular Change." *Journal of Higher Education* 76(2): 151–80.

Bunce, Diane M., Elizabeth A. Flens, and Kelly Y. Neiles. 2010. "How Long Can Students Pay Attention in Class? A Study of Student Attention Decline Using Clickers." *Journal of Chemical Education* 87(12): 1438–43.

Cameron, Kim S. 1994. "Strategies for Successful Organizational Downsizing." *Human Resources Management* 33(2): 189–211.

Carini, Robert M., George D. Kuh, and Stephen P. Klein. 2006. "Student Engagement and Student Learning: Testing the Linkages." *Research in Higher Education* 47(1): 1–32.

Carnevale, Anthony, Stephen J. Rose, and Ben Cheah. 2011. *The College Payoff*. Washington, D.C.: Georgetown University, Center for Education and Work.

Carnevale, Anthony, and Jeff Strohl. 2013. *Separate and Unequal: How Higher Education Reinforces the Intergenerational Reproduction of White Racial Privilege*. Washington, D.C.: Georgetown University, Center for Education and Work.

Cascio, Wayne F. 1993. "Downsizing: What Do We Know? What Have We Learned?" *The Executive* 7(1): 95–104.

Cellini, Stephanie Riegg, and Claudia Goldin. 2012. "Does Federal Student Aid Raise Tuition? New Evidence on For-Profit Colleges." *NBER* working paper no. 17827. Cambridge, Mass.: National Bureau of Economic Research.

Center for World Class Universities (CWCU). 2014. "Academic Rankings of World Universities 2014." Accessed December 17, 2015. http://www.shanghairanking.com/ARWU2014.html.

Christensen, Clayton M., and Henry J. Eyring. 2011. *The Innovative University: Changing the DNA of Higher Education from the Inside Out*. San Francisco: Jossey-Bass.

Clotfelter, Charles T. 1996. *Buying the Best: Cost Escalation in Elite Higher Education*. Princeton, N.J.: Princeton University Press.

———. 2011. *Big-Time Sports in American Universities*. Cambridge: Cambridge University Press.

Clotfelter, Charles T., Ronald G. Ehrenberg, Malcolm Getz, and John J. Siegfried. 1991. *Economic Challenges in Higher Education*. Chicago: University of Chicago Press.

Cole, Jonathan R. 2009. *The Great American University: Its Rise to Preeminence, Its Indispensable National Role, Why It Must be Protected*. New York: Perseus Books.

Coleman, James S. 1973. "The University and Society's New Demands Upon It." In *Content and Context*, edited by Carl Kaysen. New York: McGraw-Hill.

College Board. 2014. "Trends in Student Aid 2014." New York: The College Board. Accessed December 17, 2015. http://trends.collegeboard.org/sites/default/files/2014-trends-student-aid-final-web.pdf.

Collinge, Alan. 2009. *The Student Loan Scam: The Most Oppressive Debt in U.S. History and How We Can Fight It*. Boston, Mass.: Beacon Press.

Collins, Harry, Robert Evans, and Michael E. Gorman. 2007. "Trading Zones and Interactional Expertise." *Studies in History and Philosophy of Science* 38(4): 657–66.

Collins, Randall. 1977. *Conflict Sociology*. New York: Academic Press.

———. 1979. *The Credential Society*. New York: Academic Press.

Commission on the Future of Higher Education. 2006. *A Test of Leadership: Charting the Future of U.S. Higher Education*. Washington: U.S. Department of Education. Accessed December 18,

2015. http://www2.ed.gov/about/bdscomm/list/hiedfuture/reports/final-report.pdf.

Coopers & Lybrand. 1995. *Reinventing the University: Managing and Financing Institutions of Higher Education.* New York: John Wiley & Sons.

Craig, John E. 1985. "The Expansion of Education." *Review of Research in Education* 9: 151–213.

DeAngelo, Linda, Sylvia Hurtado, John H. Prior, Kimberly R. Nelly, Jose Luis Santos, and William S. Korn. 2007. *American College Teacher: National Norms for the 2007–2008 HERI Faculty Survey.* Los Angeles: University of California, Higher Education Research Institute.

Deming, David, and Susan Dynarski. 2009. "Into College, Out of Poverty? Policies to Increase the Postsecondary Attainment of the Poor." *NBER* working paper no. 15387. Cambridge, Mass.: National Bureau of Economic Research.

Deming, David J., Claudia Goldin, and Lawrence F. Katz. 2012. "The For-Profit Postsecondary School Sector: Nimble Critters or Agile Predators?" *Journal of Economic Perspectives* 26(1): 139–64.

———. 2013. "For-Profit Colleges." *The Future of Children* 23(1): 137–63.

DiPrete, Thomas A., and Claudia Buchmann. 2013. *The Rise of Women: The Growing Gender Gap in Education and What It Means for American Schools.* New York: Russell Sage Foundation.

Dori, Yehudit Judy, and John Belcher. 2005. "How Does Technology-Enabled Active Learning Affect Undergraduate Students' Understanding of Electromagnetism Concepts?" *Journal of the Learning Sciences* 14(2): 243–79.

Dougherty, Kevin J., and Gregory S. Kienzl. 2006. "It's Not Enough to Get Through the Open Door: Inequalities in Social Background in Transfer from Community Colleges to Four-Year Colleges." *Teacher's College Record* 108(3): 452–87.

Dunham, Edgar Alden. 1969. *Colleges of the Forgotten Americans: A Profile of State Colleges and Regional Universities.* New York: McGraw-Hill.

Ehrenberg, Ronald G. 2000. *Tuition Rising: Why College Costs So Much.* Cambridge, Mass.: Harvard University Press.

———. 2012. "American Higher Education in Transition." *Journal of Economic Perspectives* 26(1): 193–216.

Ehrenberg, Ronald G., Harriet Zuckerman, Jeffrey A. Groen, and Sharon M. Brucker. 2009. *Educating Scholars: Doctoral Education in the Humanities.* Princeton, N.J.: Princeton University Press.

Engel, James, and Anthony Dangerfield. 1998. "The Market-Model University: Humanities in the Age of Money." *Harvard Magazine.* Accessed December 17, 2015. http://www.harvardmagazine.com/1998/05/forum.html.

Freeman, Richard. 1976. *The OverEducated American.* New York: Academic Press.

Geiger, Roger L. 1993. *Research and Relevant Knowledge: American Universities Since World War II.* New York: Oxford University Press.

———. 2015. The *History of American Higher Education: Learning and Culture from the Founding to World War II.* Princeton, N.J.: Princeton University Press.

Geiger, Roger L., and Creso Sa. 2008. *Tapping the Riches of Science: Universities and the Promise of Economic Growth.* Cambridge, Mass.: Harvard University Press.

Goldin, Claudia, and Lawrence F. Katz. 1999. "The Shaping of Higher Education: The Formative Years in the United States, 1890 to 1940." *Journal of Economic Perspectives* 13(1): 37–62.

———. 2008. *The Race Between Education and Technology.* Cambridge, Mass.: The Belknap Press of Harvard University Press.

Hake, Robert R. 1998. "Interactive-Engagement Versus Traditional Methods: A Six-Thousand Student Survey of Mechanics Test Data for Introductory Physics Courses." *American Journal of Physics* 66(1): 64–74.

Hammond, Brett P., and Harriet P. Morgan. 1991. *Ending Mandatory Retirement for Tenured Faculty: The Consequences for Higher Education.* Washington, D.C.: National Academy Press.

Hanushek, Eric A., and Ludger Woessmann. 2011. "The Economics of International Differences in Educational Achievement." In *The Handbook of the Economics of Education, vol. 3,* edited by Eric A. Hanushek, Stephen Machin, and Ludger Woessmann. London: Elsevier.

Hearn, James C., Darrell R. Lewis, Lincoln Kallsen, Janet M. Holdsworth, and Lisa M. Jones. 2006. "'Incentives for Managed Growth': A Case Study of Incentives-Based Planning and Budgeting in a Large Public University." *Journal of Higher Education* 77(2): 286–316.

Herzog, Serge. 2005. "Measuring Determinants of Student Retention vs. Dropout/Stopout vs.

Transfer: A First-to-Second Year Analysis of New Freshmen." *Research in Higher Education* 46(8): 883–928.

Hoekstra, Mark, 2009. "The Effect of Attending the Flagship State University on Earnings: A Discontinuity-Based Approach." *Review of Economics and Statistics* 91(4): 717–24.

Hollingsworth, J. Rogers, and Ellen J. Hollingsworth. 2000. "Major Discoveries in Biomedical Research Organizations: Perspectives on Interdisciplinarity, Nurturing Leadership, Integrated Structures and Cultures." In *Practicing Interdisciplinarity*, edited by Peter Weingart and Nico Stehr. Toronto: University of Toronto Press.

Horowitz, Helen Lefkowitz. 1987. *Campus Life: Undergraduate Cultures from the Eighteenth Century to Today.* New York: Alfred A. Knopf.

Hout, Michael. 2012. "Social and Economic Returns to College Education in the United States." *American Annual Review of Sociology* 38: 379–400.

Hoxby, Caroline M. 2009. "The Changing Selectivity of American Colleges." *Journal of Economic Perspectives* 23(1): 1–25.

International Institute of Education. 2014. *The 2014 Open Doors Report on International Educational Exchange.* New York: International Institute of Education.

Issacson, Walter. 2014. *The Innovators: How a Group of Hackers, Geniuses and Geeks Created the Digital Revolution.* New York: Simon & Schuster.

Jacobs, Jerry A. 2013. *In Defense of the Disciplines: Interdisciplinarity and Specialization in the Research University.* Chicago: University of Chicago Press.

James, Estelle, Nabeel Alasalam, Joseph C. Conaty, and Duc-Le To. 1989. "College Quality and Future Earnings: Where Should You Send Your Child to College?" *American Economic Review* 79(2): 247–52.

Javits, Harold, Teresa Grimes, Alan Rapoport, Robert Bell, Ron Fecso, and Rolf Lehming. 2010. *U.S. Academic Scientific Publishing.* Working paper SRS 11-201. Arlington, Va.: National Science Foundation, Division of Science Resources Services.

Kamenetz, Anya. 2006. *Generation Debt.* New York: Penguin Group.

Kena, Grace, Lauren Musu-Gillette, Jennifer Robinson, Xiaolei Wang, Amy Rathbun, Jijun Zhang, Sidney Wilkinson-Flicker, Amy Barmer, and Erin Dunlop Velez. 2015. *The Condition of Education.* NCES 2015-144. Washington: U.S. Department of Education. Accessed December 17, 2015. http://nces.ed.gov/pubs2015/2015144.pdf.

King, Tracey, and Ellynne Bannon. 2002. *At What Cost? The Price that Working Students Pay for a College Education.* Washington: U.S. Public Interest Research Group.

Kingston, Paul W. 2015. "Questionable Promises: College for Many More." Unpublished paper. Department of Sociology, University of Virginia.

Kirkham, Chris. 2015. "Corinthian Closing Its Last Schools; 10,000 CA Students Displaced." *Los Angeles Times*, April 27, 2015, p. 1.

Kirp, David L. 2003. *Shakespeare, Einstein, and the Bottom Line: The Marketing of Higher Education.* Cambridge, Mass.: Harvard University Press.

Klepfer, Kasey, and Jim Hull. 2012. 2012. *High School Rigor and Good Advice: Setting Up Students to Succeed.* Washington, D.C.: Center for Public Education.

Kuh, George D., Ty M. Cruce, Rick Shoup, Jillian Kinzie, and Robert M. Gonyea. 2008. "Unmasking the Effects of Student Engagement on First-Year College Grades and Persistence." *Journal of Higher Education* 79(5): 540–63.

Kuh, George D., and Stanley O. Ikenberry. 2009. *More Than You Think, Less Than We Need: Learning Outcomes Assessment in American Higher Education.* Champaign, Ill.: National Institute for Learning Outcomes Assessment.

Kuh, George D., and Ernest T. Pascarella. 2004. "What Does Institutional Selectivity Tell Us About Educational Quality?" *Change* 36(5): 52–58.

Kutner, Mark, Elizabeth Greenberg, Ying Jin, Bridget Boyle, Yung-chen Hsu, and Eric Dunleavy. 2007. *Literacy in Everyday Life: Results for the 2003 National Assessment of Adult Literacy.* NCES 2007-480. Washington: National Center for Education Statistics.

Lang, Daniel W. 1999. "Responsibility Centre Budgeting and Responsibility Centre Management in Theory and Practice." *Higher Education Management* 11(3): 81–111.

Lareau, Annette. 2002. "Invisible Inequality: Social Class and Child Raising in Black Families and White Families." *American Sociological Review* 67(5): 747–76.

Lattuca, Lisa R., Patrick T. Terenzini, and J. Fredericks Volkwein. 2006. *Engineering Change: A Study of the Impact of EC 2000*. Baltimore, Md.: ABET.

Loise, Vicki, and Ashley J. Stevens. 2010. "The Bayh-Dole Act Turns 30." Accessed December 17, 2015. http://www.bu.edu/otd/files/2011/02/The_Bayh-Dole_Act_Turns_30.pdf.

Long, Bridget Terry, and Erin Riley. 2007. "Financial Aid: A Broken Bridge to College Access?" *Harvard Educational Review* 77(1): 39–63.

Lovett, Marsha, Oded Meyer, and Candace Thille. 2008. "The Open Learning Initiative: Measuring the Effectiveness of the OLI Statistics Course in Accelerating Student Learning." *Journal of Interactive Media in Education*. Accessed December 18, 2015. https://oli.cmu.edu/wp-oli/wp-content/uploads/2012/05/Lovett_2008_Statistics_Accelerated_Learning_Study.pdf.

Mazur, Eric. 1997. *Peer Instruction: A User's Manual*. Upper Saddle River, N.J.: Prentice-Hall.

Means, Barbara, Yukie Toyama, Robert Murphy, Marianne Bakia, and Karla Jones. 2009. *Evaluation of Evidence-Based Practices in Online Learning: A Meta-Analysis and Review of Online Learning Studies*. Washington: U.S. Department of Education.

Meisinger, Richard J., Jr. 1994. *College and University Budgeting: An Introduction for Faculty and Academic Administrators*. Washington, D.C.: National Association of College and University Business Officers.

Moretti, Enric. 2013. *The New Geography of Jobs*. New York: Houghton Mifflin Harcourt.

Mowery, David, Richard R. Nelson, Bhaven N. Sampat, and Arvids A. Ziedonis. 2001. "The Growth of Patenting and Licensing by U.S. Universities: An Assessment of the Effects of the Bayh-Dole Act of 1980." *Research Policy* 30(1): 99–119.

Mullen, Ann L., Kimberly A. Goyette, and Joseph A. Soares. 2003. "Who Goes to Graduate School? Social and Academic Correlates of Educational Continuation After College." *Sociology of Education* 76(2): 143–69.

Murnane, Richard, John Willett, and Frank Levy. 1995. "The Growing Importance of Cognitive Skills in Wage Determination." *Review of Economics and Statistics* 77(2): 251–66.

National Academies Committee on Prospering in the Global Economy of the 21st Century (National Academies). 2007. *Rising Above the Gathering Storm: Energizing and Employing American for a Brighter Economic Future*. Washington, D.C.: National Academies Press.

National Academy of Sciences. 2014. *The Postdoctoral Experience Revisited*. Washington, D.C.: National Academies Press.

National Association of College and University Business Officers (NACUBO). 2014. *NACUBO Tuition Discounting Study*. Washington, D.C.: NACUBO.

National Center for Education Statistics (NCES). 2010. "List of 2010 Digest Tables." Washington: U.S. Department of Education. Accessed December 18, 2015. https://nces.ed.gov/programs/digest/2010menu_tables.asp.

———. 2012. "List of 2012 Digest Tables." Washington: U.S. Department of Education. Accessed December 18, 2015. https://nces.ed.gov/programs/digest/2012menu_tables.asp.

———. 2013. "List of 2013 Digest Tables." Washington: U.S. Department of Education. Accessed December 18, 2015. https://nces.ed.gov/programs/digest/2013menu_tables.asp.

———. 2014. "List of 2014 Digest Tables." Washington: U.S. Department of Education. Accessed December 18, 2015. https://nces.ed.gov/programs/digest/2014menu_tables.asp.

———. 2015a. "List of 2015 Digest Tables." Washington: U.S. Department of Education. Accessed December 18, 2015. https://nces.ed.gov/programs/digest/2015menu_tables.asp.

———. 2015b. "Integrated Post-Secondary Education Data System (IPEDS)." Washington, D.C.: U.S. Department of Education. Accessed December 18, 2015. https://nces.ed.gov/ipeds.

National Governors Association. 1986. *A Time for Results: The Governors' Report on Education*. Washington, D.C.: National Governors Association.

National Science Board. 2014. *Science and Engineering Indicators 2014*. Washington, D.C.: National Science Board.

National Science Foundation. 2013. "Science and Engineering Doctorates: Data Tables." Accessed December 17, 2015. http://www.nsf.gov/statistics/sed/2013/data-tables.cfm.

———. 2015. "America COMPETES Reauthorization Act of 2015 (H.R. 1806): Impact on the National Science Foundation." Accessed December 17, 2015. http://www.nsf.gov/about/congress/114/hr1806_impact.jsp.

Obama, Barack. 2010. "Remarks by the President on

Higher Education and the Economy at the University of Texas Austin." Washington, D.C.: The White House, Office of the Press Secretary. Accessed December 17, 2015. http://www.whitehouse.gov/the-press-office/2010/08/09/remarks-president-higher-education-and-economy-university-texas-austin.

Organization for Economic Cooperation and Development (OECD). 2013. *OECD Skills Outlook 2013: First Results for the Survey of Adult Skills.* Paris: OECD Publishing. Accessed December 18, 2015. http://dx.doi.org/10.1787/9789264204256-en.

———. 2014. *Education at a Glance: OECD Indicators.* Paris: OECD Publishing. Accessed December 17, 2015. http://www.oecd.org/education/eag.htm.

Palmer, James. 2015. "Grapevine Compilation of State Fiscal Support for Higher Education Results for Fiscal Year 2012–2013." Boulder, Colo.: State Higher Education Executive Officers. Accessed December 17, 2015. http://www.sheeo.org/resources/publications/grapevine-compilation-state-fiscal-support-higher-education-results-fiscal.

Pascarella, Earnest T., and Patrick T. Terenzini. 2005. *How College Affects Students: A Third Decade of Research,* vol. 2. San Francisco: Jossey-Bass.

PayScale. 2014. "2013–14 PayScale College Salary Report." Accessed December 18, 2015. http://www.payscale.com/college-salary-report-2014/majors-that-pay-you-back.

Pennebaker, James W., Samuel D. Gosling, and Jason D. Ferrell. 2013. "Daily Online Testing in Large Classes: Boosting College Performance While Reducing Achievement Gaps." *PLoS ONE* 8(11): 1–6. Accessed December 17, 2015. http://journals.plos.org/plosone/article?id=10.1371/journal.pone.0079774.

Powell, Kendall. 2015. "The Future of the Postdoc." *Nature,* April 7. Accessed December 18, 2015. http://www.nature.com/news/the-future-of-the-postdoc-1.17253#/postdoc/.

Powell, Walter W., and Kaisa Snellman. 2004. "The Knowledge Economy." *Annual Review of Sociology* 30: 199–220.

Prince, Michael. 2004. "Does Active Learning Work?" *Journal of Engineering Education* 93(3): 223–31.

Reuf, Martin, and Manish Nag. 2014. "The Classification of Organizational Forms: Theory and Application to the Field of Higher Education." In *Remaking College: The Changing Ecology of Higher Education,* edited by Michael W. Kirst and Mitchell L. Stevens. Stanford, Calif.: Stanford University Press.

Rhoten, Diane. 2003. *A Multi-Methods Analysis of the Social and Technical Conditions for Interdisciplinary Collaboration.* Final Report. BCS-0129573. Washington, D.C.: National Science Foundation.

———. 2004. "Interdisciplinary Research: Trend or Transition." *Items and Issues* (Spring/Summer): 6–11.

Riesman, David, and Reuel Denney. 1951."Football in America: A Study in Cultural Diffusion." *America Quarterly* 3(4): 309–25.

Rivera, Lauren A. 2012. "Hiring as Cultural Matching: The Case of Elite Professional Service Firms." *American Sociological Review* 77(6): 999–1022.

Rosenbaum, James A., Regina Deil-Amen, and Ann Person. 2009. *After Admission: From College Access to College Success.* New York: Russell Sage Foundation.

Ross, Terris, Grace Kena, Amy Rathbun, Angelina KewalRamani, Jijun Zhang, Paul Kristapovich, and Eileen Manning. 2012. *Higher Education: Gaps in Access and Persistence Study.* NCES 2012-046. Washington: U.S. Department of Education. Accessed December 18, 2015. https://nces.ed.gov/pubs2012/2012046.pdf.

Rotondi, Matthew Baron. 2015. *Making Meaning of Student Debt: How Undergraduate Students Make Sense of Their Student Loan and Credit Card Debt.* Ph.D. diss. Department of Sociology, University of California, Riverside.

The Royal Society. 2011. *Knowledge, Networks, and Nations: Global Scientific Collaboration in the 21st Century.* Policy Document no. 03/11. London: The Royal Society. Accessed December 17, 2015. https://royalsociety.org/topics-policy/projects/knowledge-networks-nations/report/.

Ruch, Richard S. 2001. *Higher Ed, Inc.: The Rise of the For-Profit University.* Baltimore, Md.: Johns Hopkins University Press.

Sa, Creso. 2008. "Interdisciplinary Strategies in U.S. Research Universities." *Higher Education* 55(5): 537–52.

San Jose State University. 2013. "An Open Letter to Michael Sandel from the Department of Philosophy, San Jose State University." *Chronicle of Higher Education,* May 2. Accessed December 18,

2015. http://chronicle.com/article/The-Document-Open-Letter-From/138937/.

Saunders, Katherine. 2015. "Barriers to Success: Unmet Financial Need for Low-Income Students of Color at Community Colleges." Washington, D.C.: CLASP. Accessed December 17, 2015. http://www.clasp.org/resources-and-publications/publication-1/Barriers-to-Success-Unmet-Financial-Need-for-Low-Income-Students-of-Color.pdf/.

Schuster, Jack H., and Martin J. Finkelstein. 2006. *The American Faculty: The Restructuring of Academic Work and Careers*. Baltimore, Md.: Johns Hopkins University Press.

Slaughter, Sheila, and Larry L. Leslie. 1997. *Academic Capitalism*. Baltimore, Md.: Johns Hopkins University Press.

Snyder, Thomas D. 1993. *120 Years of American Education: A Statistical Portrait*. Washington: U.S. Department of Education.

Snyder, Thomas D., and Sally A. Dillow. 2010. *Digest of Education Statistics 2010*. Washington: National Center for Education Statistics.

Spence, Michael. 1973. "Job Market Signaling." *Quarterly Journal of Economics* 87(3): 355–74.

Stephan, Paula. 2012. *How Economics Shapes Science*. Cambridge, Mass.: Harvard University Press.

Stewart, Luke A., Jacek Warda, and Robert D. Atkinson. 2012. "We're #27!: The United States Lags Far Behind in R&D Tax Incentive Generosity." Washington, D.C.: Information Technology and Innovation Foundation. Accessed December 17, 2015. http://www2.itif.org/2012-were-27-b-index-tax.pdf.

Thurow, Lester. 1972. "Education and Economic Equality." *The Public Interest* 28 (Summer): 66–81.

Tierney, William G., and Guilbert C. Hentschke. 2007. *New Players, Different Game: Understanding the Rise of For-Profit Colleges and Universities*. Baltimore, Md.: Johns Hopkins University Press.

Times Higher Education. 2015. "World University Rankings 2014-15." Accessed December 18, 2015. https://www.timeshighereducation.com/world-university-rankings/2015/world-ranking#!/page/0/length/25.

Trow, Martin. 2007. "Reflections on the Transition from Elite to Mass to Universal Access: Forms and Phases of Higher Education in Modern Societies Since WWII." In *International Handbook of Higher Education*, edited by James J. F. Forrest and Philip Altbach. Dordrecht: Springer. Accessed December 18, 2015. http://escholarship.org/uc/item/96p3s213.

Truelove, Susan. 1999. "Math Emporium Revolutionizes University's Introductory Math Program." *VirginiaTech Math Emporium*. Accessed December 17, 2015. http://www.emporium.vt.edu/emporium/generalinterest/article561999.html.

Tuchman, Gaye. 2009. *Wannabe U: Inside the Corporate University*. Chicago: University of Chicago Press.

Twigg, Carol. 2003. "Improving Quality and Reducing Cost: Designs for Effective Learning." *Change* 35(4): 22–29.

United Kingdom Department of Business Innovation and Skills. 2014. "UK Share of Highly Cited Articles." BIS Performance Indicators. Accessed December 18, 2015. https://www.gov.uk/government/uploads/system/uploads/attachment_data/file/310544/bis-performance-indicators-uk-share-highly-cited-academic-articles-april-2014.pdf.

Urban Universities for HEALTH (Urban Universities). 2015. "Cluster Hiring for Diversity and Institutional Climate." Washington, D.C.: Urban Universities for HEALTH. Accessed December 18, 2015. http://urbanuniversitiesforhealth.org/media/documents/Faculty_Cluster_Hiring_Report.pdf.

U.S. Presidents Commission. 1947. *Higher Education for American Democracy*. Washington: Government Printing Office.

Vallas, Steven P. and Daniel L. Kleinman. 2007. "Contradiction, Convergence, and the Knowledge Economy: The Confluence of Academic and Commercial Biotechnology." *Socioeconomic Review* 6(2): 1–29.

Washburn, Jennifer. 2005. *University, Inc.: The Corporate Corruption of Higher Education*. New York: Basic Books.

Weiman, Carl E., Wendy K. Adams, and Katherine K. Perkins. 2008. "PhET: Simulations That Enhance Learning." *Science* 322(5902): 682–83. Accessed December 18, 2015. http://www.sciencemag.org/content/322/5902/682.full.pdf.

Weingart, Peter, and Nico Stehr, eds. 2000. *Practicing Interdisciplinarity*. Toronto: University of Toronto Press.

Western Association of Schools and Colleges (WASC). 2013. *Accreditation Handbook*. Alameda, Calif.: WASC. Accessed December 17, 2015. http://www.wascsenior.org/resources/handbook-accreditation-2013.

Whalen, Edward L. 1991. *Responsibility Center Budgeting: An Approach to Decentralized Management for Higher Education.* Bloomington: Indiana University Press.

The White House. 2015. "Statement of Administration Policy H.R. 1806—America COMPETES Reauthorization Act of 2015." Washington, D.C.: Office of Management and Budget, Executive Office of the President. Accessed December 18, 2015. http://www.whitehouse.gov/sites/default/files/omb/legislative/sap/114/saphr1806r_20150518.pdf.

Winston, Gordon. 1999. "Subsidies, Hierarchies and Peers: The Awkward Economics of Higher Education." *Journal of Economic Perspectives* 13(1): 13–36.

Womack, James, and Daniel T. Jones. 2003. *Lean Thinking: Banish Waste and Create Wealth in Your Corporation.* New York: The Free Press.

World Bank. 2013. "Research and Development Expenditure (% of GDP)." Accessed December 18, 2015. http://data.worldbank.org/indicator/GB.XPD.SSDV.GD.ZS.

Xu, Di, and Shanna Smith Jaggars. 2011. "Online and Hybrid Course Enrollment and Performance in Washington State Community and Technical Colleges." *CCRC* working paper no. 31. New York: Columbia University, Community College Research Center. Accessed December 17, 2015. http://ccrc.tc.columbia.edu/publications/online-hybrid-courses-washington.html.

Overview of the Volume

STEVEN BRINT AND CHARLES T. CLOTFELTER

The chapters in this volume add new empirical evidence and new thinking to issues of system-level, campus-level, and classroom-level effectiveness. They were chosen by the editors from among sixty-two proposals submitted to the Russell Sage Foundation. Our choices were based on the quality of the data and analyses.

The papers concerned with system-level issues address both market and regulatory influences on institutional behavior. On the market side, they focus on the consequences of tuition increases (Dahill-Brown et al., Hemelt and Marcotte) and price deregulation (Kim and Stange). On the regulatory side, one of the papers focuses on performance funding, a state policy to improve accountability for outcomes (Dougherty et al.). The other system-level paper examines the value of sub-baccalaureate credentials as compared to college attendance without completion on a range of student outcomes (Rosenbaum et al.). The single campus-level paper focuses on variation in retention and degree production across California community colleges (Kurlaender, Carrell, and Jackson) with current proposals for institutional performance ratings, promoted by the Obama administration among others, in mind. The classroom-level paper focuses on how well the National Academy's "promising instructional practices" perform when examined relative to traditional methods (Reimer et al.). The penultimate paper in the volume provides a broader context for understanding national concerns about the production of STEM baccalaureates by examining the performance of American high school students compared to their peers in other countries (Han and Buchmann).

One of the most prominent trends in public financing of higher education in the last decade is the marked decline in state support from state governments. As noted, real per student appropriations declined in the aftermath of the Great Recession in 2008. To make up for these cuts, states and their universities have opted to raise tuition levels. Between the 2004–2005 and 2014–2015 school years, the inflation-adjusted tuition and fees at public four-year institutions increased on average by 3.5 percent a year, faster than that of private four-year and two-year institutions (2.2 and 2.5 percent, respectively) (College Board 2015). Such tuition hikes were more pronounced in some states than others. In their paper, Steven Hemelt and David Marcotte seek to determine what effect these tuition hikes had on students' choices about where to apply and attend. They ask whether students reacted to higher tuition by choosing two-year colleges, out-of-state institutions, or private institutions, over public four-year universities in their own states, and they show that tuition increases lead many students to choose lower-priced alternatives.

In light of the important role that higher education plays in shaping the structure of opportunity and the distribution of income, few issues have more urgency in debates over domestic public policy than the incomes of students who enroll in the country's heavily subsidized public flagship universities. As noted, many commentators have argued that public four-year universities, in particular elite public universities, are increasingly serving an affluent clientele. Whether there have been changes in the income profile of students attending these universities is hard to establish, however, because comparable data on the family income of entering students is difficult if not impossible to locate. Surveys are subject to error, and detailed data from financial aid applications cover only some students. In their paper, Sara Dahill-Brown, John Witte, and Barbara Wolfe develop a new measure, based on census block data, and they apply it over thirty-six years for Wisconsin's flagship institution, the University of Wisconsin, Madison, showing an increase in upper-income students applying to the state flagship university.

An idea that has long been a pet policy proposal among economists is tuition rates differentiated according to marginal costs (see, for example, Berg and Hoenack 1987; Karelis 1989). In 2003, in a burst of deregulatory zeal, Texas gave its universities the flexibility to set tuition levels, and to raise them at different rates across programs. Jae-on Kim and Kevin Stange examine what universities in Texas chose to do with this newly found flexibility. In particular, they compare changes across universities and between programs within them, showing that deregulation has led to higher costs of attendance in high-demand fields that tend to be well-remunerated in the labor market.

In an effort to improve the effectiveness of public higher education and rationalize the allocation of funds across competing institutions, more than half of the fifty U.S. states have turned to some form of "performance funding." Under this approach, annual appropriations would be apportioned according to objective, measurable criteria, rewarding institutions that improve persistence and graduation rates, for example. To see how these systems have operated in the real world of state budgetary and institutional decision making, Kevin Dougherty and his colleagues use qualitative research methods, including numerous interviews with state budget and university administrators. They explore both the responsiveness of university administrators to performance funding and some unintended consequences, such as stricter regulation of admitted students to boost graduation rates.

In the college-for-all system, students are encouraged to finish baccalaureate degrees. But only a minority of those who begin postsecondary education finish in six years, and underrepresented minorities finish at much lower rates. James Rosenbaum and his colleagues raise the question of whether this push to encourage as many students as possible to complete four-year degrees is rational for the country or for students themselves. They compare students who have "some college" attendance but have not finished their degrees with those who have finished subbaccalaureate degrees, including credentials. They find that on a wide range of economic and job satisfaction measures, holders of subbaccalaureate credentials outperform those who start but do not complete four-year colleges. Rosenbaum and his colleagues provide evidence for a change in national policy to publicize the value of subbaccalaureate credentials, particularly for students who have low chances of completing college due to limited financial means or weak levels of academic preparation.

President Barack Obama and many state governors have proposed rating colleges' institutional performance using metrics such as graduation rates, affordability, and accessibility to low-income students. Many institutional rating systems fail to take into account the characteristics of students who enter the colleges and universities under consideration. These "input characteristics" include students' socio-demographic backgrounds and high school records. Using data from all 128 California community colleges, Michal Kurlaender, Scott Carrell, and Jacob Jackson show the extent to which failures to control for input characteristics skew quality rankings. By correcting for these input characteristics, they establish that community colleges may move by as many as forty ranks in outcome measures, such as retention and graduation, compared to ratings that do not control for students' input characteristics.

The National Academy of Sciences has promoted what it terms "promising practices" in STEM education. These include instructional practices that help students "think like a scientist," active learning opportunities, and frequent formative and summative assessments. Using data from a large number of STEM classrooms at a major research university and focusing on the same students who took multiple classes, Lynn Reimer and her colleagues examine the effectiveness of these promising practices relative to traditional instructional practices. They find little evidence that these practices matter greatly for most students, but find some evidence that they matter more for low-income, first-generation, and underrepresented students, precisely the students whose completion rates in science will need to increase if the United States is to remain competitive with other developed countries.

More than half who begin college science, technology, engineering, and math (STEM) curricula nationwide fail to complete their degrees. These statistics have led to many efforts to improve students' performance and learning experience in STEM through such innovations as mandatory learning communities, mandatory group tutoring sessions, intensive advising, early research exposure, career workshops and instructional innovations such as those described in the introduction to this volume. However, the largest part of the problem precedes enrollment in college. Siqi Han and Claudia Buchmann show that U.S. students score low in both science interest and science performance on standardized international tests. Standard deviations are also much higher for American students than for students in most of the developed world. Han and Buchmann investigate whether standardized science curricula matter for students' performance on these tests, controlling for individual-level and country-level characteristics. They find evidence that standardization has a modest net effect on mean science scores, suggesting that a rigorous common core curriculum in secondary school science would contribute to higher STEM baccalaureate degree production.

REFERENCES

Berg, David J., and Stephen A. Hoenack. 1987. "The Concept of Cost-Related Tuition and Its Implementation at the University of Minnesota." *Journal of Higher Education* 58(3): 276–305.

College Board. 2015. "Trends in Student Aid 2015." New York: The College Board. Accessed December 17, 2015. http://trends.collegeboard.org/college-pricing/figures-tables/average-rates-growth-published-charges-decade.

Karelis, Charles. 1989. "Price as a Lever for Reform: Separate Checks vs. Flat Tuition Pricing." *Change* 21(2): 20–28.

PART II
Supply and Demand: Cost and Distributional Outcomes

The Changing Landscape of Tuition and Enrollment in American Public Higher Education

STEVEN W. HEMELT AND DAVE E. MARCOTTE

The costs of public higher education have risen dramatically in recent years, causing anger among students and concern among policymakers worried about falling college completion rates. In this paper, we explore how public tuition costs affect postsecondary enrollment choices. We examine changes over time in the enrollment decisions of students in states where tuition and fees at public four-year institutions increased rapidly, compared with changes for observationally similar students in states with more modest tuition increases. Using student-level data on twelfth graders in 1992 and 2004 linked to institution-level data, we find a relative decline in the likelihood of attending an in-state public four-year institution among high school graduates from states where public tuition costs increased substantially over this period. Students in states where public tuition increased the most were considerably more likely to enroll in a public two-year college than their counterparts in states that adopted more modest increases. We explore heterogeneity in this pattern of substitution between institutions of varying selectivity and control and for students in policy-relevant socio-demographic subgroups, including those in different parts of the twelfth-grade achievement distribution. Generally, large tuition increases at public four-year colleges have weakened the propensity of high school graduates to enroll in such institutions in their state, and increased their likelihood of enrollment in less prestigious in-state public colleges, out-of-state public institutions, or private universities. These effects are most pronounced among students from families of low socioeconomic status, and nonelite students who perform below the 90th percentile on twelfth-grade math tests.

Keywords: tuition costs, postsecondary enrollment, public universities

The costs of higher education are rising, and rising fast, raising widespread concerns about student debt and a possible higher education "bubble" (see, for example, *The Economist* 2011; Reilly 2011; Surowiecki 2011). Preceding this recent consternation was concern among analysts and policymakers that rising costs would prompt prospective students to forego college

Steven W. Hemelt is assistant professor of public policy at the University of North Carolina at Chapel Hill. **Dave E. Marcotte** is professor of public policy and director of the Washington Institute for Public Affairs Research at American University in Washington, D.C.

We thank Sandy Korenman, Marv Mandell, Dahlia Remler, Diane Schanzenbach, and Kevin Stange for helpful comments and conversations. We are also grateful to participants at the Fall 2011 meetings of the Association for Public Policy Analysis and Management (APPAM) in Washington, D.C., and seminars at UMBC, University of Michigan, Baruch, and the Russell Sage Foundation (RSF) conference on higher education effectiveness. Feng Ze Han provided helpful research assistance. All sample sizes are rounded to the nearest ten to comply with IES/NCES restricted-use data reporting standards. Direct correspondence to: Steven W. Hemelt, hemelt@email.unc.edu, University of North Carolina at Chapel Hill, Department of Public Policy, 131 S. Columbia St., Chapel Hill, NC 27599. Dave E. Marcotte, marcotte@american.edu, American University, Department of Public Administration and Policy, School of Public Affairs, 4400 Massachusetts Ave., Washington, D.C. 20016.

and current students to drop out. Recent empirical evidence from studies of enrollment demand and student persistence makes clear that these are well-founded concerns (on enrollment, see Hemelt and Marcotte 2011; on persistence, see Dynarski 2008; Bettinger 2004). Further, as costs increased between 1970 and 1999, the completion rate for those entering college declined by more than 25 percent (Turner 2004).

In this paper we examine a mechanism through which college costs might affect educational attainment and the relatively slow growth in college graduation rates. Shifts in where students enroll may help explain the decline of college completion rates. John Bound, Michael Lovenheim, and Sarah Turner's (2010) examination of factors underlying the decline between the 1970s and early 1990s suggests that a compositional shift toward community college enrollment played a key role. The authors further suggest that institutional rather than student characteristics play the most important role. It is clear that even among four-year colleges, graduation rates vary widely by institution type—from 84 percent at private research universities, to 60 percent at public research universities, to only 37 percent among public institutions that do not award doctorate degrees (Turner 2004).[1] In this paper, we examine whether and how price changes in public higher education have resulted in shifts for some students toward the sorts of public institutions where persistence and other measures of academic support lag, and shifts in enrollment away from state public colleges for other students.

At the core of our analyses are comparisons of postsecondary enrollment decisions of observationally identical students graduating from high school in the same state in different decades. We examine the enrollment decisions of students in states where in-state public tuition prices increased rapidly, compared with observationally identical students in states with more modest tuition price changes. To do this, we pool data on cohorts from the National Education Longitudinal Survey (NELS:88) and the Education Longitudinal Survey (ELS:2002), along with data from the Integrated Postsecondary Education Data System (IPEDS) and the Delta Cost Project on the public postsecondary educational systems in states where students in these surveys completed high school. Of course, states' decisions about financing and the costs of public higher education are surely related to other factors relevant for understanding college attendance and completion. To develop a clearer assessment of the tuition effects themselves, we use a variety of strategies and implement several checks to limit and assess the role of potential confounding changes in state economies and education systems.

BACKGROUND AND LITERATURE REVIEW

Large increases in tuition at state universities have become common (Hemelt and Marcotte 2011). Some of these have been severe enough to spark outrage among students or the public at large, as was the case in California in 2009 (O'Leary 2009; Lewin and Cathcart 2009; Friend 2010). Weak economic conditions and declining general revenue support from state legislatures have put substantial pressure on public college and university administrators and their governing boards to increase tuition (Koshal and Koshal 2000; Rizzo and Ehrenberg 2003; Archibald and Feldman 2011). The results of such pressures are made clear in figure 1. Over the past twenty years, the share of revenue at public four-year colleges accounted for by net tuition (that is, tuition after financial aid is applied) has increased from about 15 percent to nearly 30 percent and the relative contribution of state appropriations has been nearly halved, from about 65 percent to 35 percent.

---

1. Further, among public four-year institutions, graduation rates vary substantially by selectivity. Using detailed information on students in the 1999 entering cohort at public four-year colleges in Maryland, Virginia, Ohio, and North Carolina, William Bowen, Matthew Chingos, and Michael McPherson report that six-year graduation rates range from 86 percent at the most selective, flagship public institutions, to 51 percent at lower-tier four-year public colleges in these state systems (2009, 193). These disparities remain even after the authors control for differences in the characteristics of incoming students.

Figure 1. Compositional Changes in Revenue at Public Universities

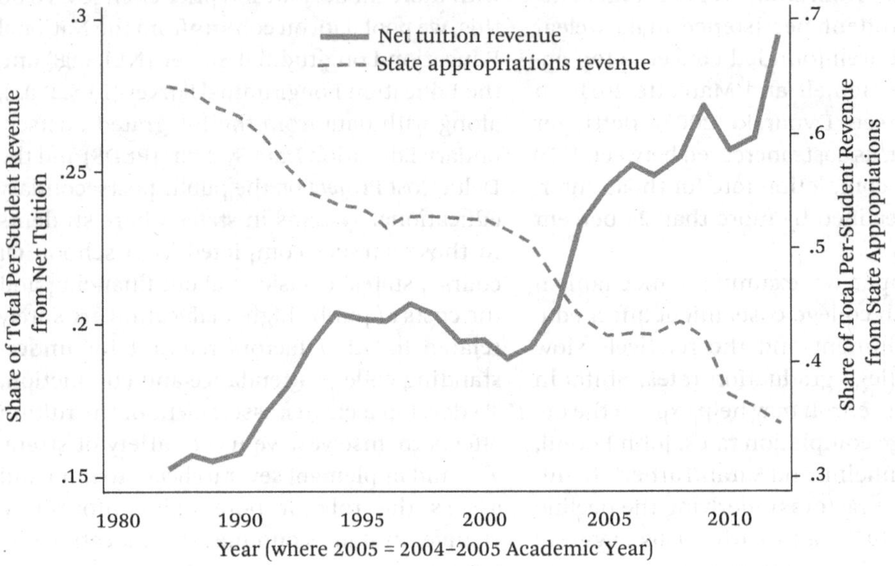

Source: Authors' calculations.
Notes: Sample limited to public four-year institutions appearing between 1987 and 2012 that reported basic enrollment and finance information to the Integrated Postsecondary Education Data System (IPEDS). Revenues accounted for by net tuition and state appropriations are expressed per full-time-equivalent (FTE) student in 2010 dollars (using the Consumer Price Index (CPI)). Net tuition excludes Pell, federal, state, and local grants but includes all tuition paid out of pocket by students and their families or via loans. Total revenue includes the sum of tuition; federal, state, and local appropriations, grants, and contracts; affiliated entities, private gifts, grants, and contracts; investment return; and endowment earnings.

An obvious concern is whether rising costs and shifts in the distribution of the burden of these increases are making higher education less affordable. If so, the recent period of fast-rising tuition may have the effect of limiting educational attainment in the aggregate. Steven Hemelt and Dave Marcotte (2011) update the literature on the relationship between tuition and enrollment, in response to the large tuition increases of the last decade (for a more extensive review, see Leslie and Brinkman 1987; Heller 1997). Among the central findings of that paper was that enrollment was most sensitive to tuition at top-ranked, flagship schools, and research-intensive universities, not at lower-ranked schools within state systems that typically serve students who might be most price sensitive. One explanation for this pattern has to do with compositional shifts in enrollment. As top-ranked, selective public universities become relatively expensive, some prospective and current students may choose private colleges or public colleges out of their home states, even as other students substitute down within their states' public higher education systems into less expensive, but lower-tier public universities. While these enrollment responses to relative price changes are straightforward predictions of consumer theory, no work has been done to test how the decisions of college-bound high school students have changed as the prices of enrollment have shifted dramatically in the last decades.

A clearer sense of how student enrollment decisions are being shaped by price setting policies is important not just to understand implications on aggregate enrollment in public higher education. Public institutions enroll the vast majority of students in American higher education, and relative price changes could result in substantial shifts across institutions, or enrollment intensity within institutions. Using information on high school graduates from 1972, 1982, and 1992, Bridget Terry Long (2004) finds that the role of college costs has fallen in terms of access to college, but still remains an important determinant of where to enroll conditional on going to college at all, especially for low-income students.

Shifts in where students enroll may play a role in helping us understand why college completion rates have declined, even as enrollment rates have risen. Bound, Lovenheim, and Turner (2010) examine initial enrollment decisions of students from the National Longitudinal Survey 1972 cohort and National Education Longitudinal Study 1988 (NELS:88) cohort, and find important shifts toward community college enrollment. They find that "student observables explain virtually none of the observed cross-cohort shifts in initial school choice" (142). Rather, supply side characteristics play the most important role. We aim to provide insight into how much of these shifts were due to relative price changes.

Our primary aim is to contribute to the understanding of how public college and university tuition policies affect college enrollment decisions, recognizing that students' decisions are embedded in a structure determined by the state in which they reside. That the vast majority of postsecondary enrollment is in public two- and four-year colleges suggests that the primary choice set for many students is the public institutions in their home states (Snyder and Dillow 2011). Further, most private colleges have limited reach, even if their prices are not tied to residency. Much of our understanding of the influence of cost and distance on enrollment decisions comes from variation within cross-sections. We extend this work by pooling cross-sections and embedding the institutions students choose from in a framework determined by where the student lives, public colleges in the same state grouped separately from private colleges and public colleges in other states.

To understand how changes in tuition policy affect college enrollment, we compare enrollment decisions of graduating high school seniors from the NELS:88 and the ELS:2002. These cohorts mainly graduated high school in 1992 and 2004, respectively.[2] The NELS:88 and ELS:2002 cohorts straddle a period of substantial tuition increases, and the data offer rich sets of controls to develop comparisons. We compare the college-going decisions of observationally equivalent students across cohorts in states that see different intertemporal patterns of tuition costs at public colleges and universities.

We estimate effects of relative tuition on enrollment choices using *changes* in enrollment decisions for observationally comparable students within the same state—comparing changes for students in states that have seen large tuition increases over and above changes for students in states with more modest price changes. Our identifying assumption is that states that adopt a sharp increase in tuition are not experiencing changes in other characteristics of their postsecondary institutions that are contemporaneous to tuition increases, nor are they experiencing different trends in the characteristics of students entering postsecondary education. Although we cannot test all possible threats to our identifying assumption, we conduct several relevant falsification and specification tests.

DATA

We combine data from several different sources to create a data set of pooled cross-sections with information on students and how their college-going decisions changed over a bit more than a decade. We use data from the National Education Longitudinal Survey on twelfth-grade students in 1992 and data from the Education Longitudinal Survey to characterize twelfth graders in 2004. These two cohorts of students straddle a period during which the financial landscape changed for many states, driving tuition at public colleges and universities upward. We then merge in data from the Delta Cost Project, the Integrated Postsecondary Education System, and Barron's Profiles of American Colleges on a variety of institutional characteristics, including

---

2. The NELS:88 and ELS:2002 are described in more detail in the following section.

tuition costs, enrollment, selectivity, and financial endowments. Below, we describe key features of these different data sets.

Institution-Level Data

IPEDS is a collection of interrelated surveys conducted annually by the National Center for Education Statistics (NCES). IPEDS gathers information from every college, university, and technical and vocational institution that participates in federal student financial aid programs (such as Stafford Loans and Pell Grants). Institutions that participate in these programs must report data on enrollments, program completions, graduation rates, faculty and staff, finances, institutional prices, and student financial aid. IPEDS has collected data from institutions since 1986, but reporting standards, variable definitions, and accounting practices have varied over time. The Delta Cost Project is an initiative that seeks to address such intertemporal issues that complicate longitudinal analyses. The Delta Cost Project developed a version of the IPEDS data better suited to longitudinal analyses, especially analyses that incorporate financial data.[3] From the Delta Cost data, we use information on tuition and fees, financial aid, and enrollment.

To group institutions, we use information on level (four-year, two-year or less) and control (public or private) to form sectors of institutions (for example, four-year public). Finally, we use Barron's data to stratify institutions by selectivity.

Student-Level Data

We use student-level data from both the NELS:88, which follows the high school class of 1992, and the ELS:2002, which tracks students finishing high school in 2004. Both of these detailed data sets survey students, schools, parents, teachers, and provide information on family and community life. These surveys include information about students' prior achievement, college plans, and college enrollment decisions. From both surveys, we extract demographic information on twelfth-grade students, including race and ethnicity, educational attainment levels of the students' parents, family income, number of siblings, and math test scores. We extract variables that describe the representative cross-section of twelfth graders in both surveys.

Related to college-going decisions, we use information on whether the student attended college within two years of graduating from high school, whether the student attended an in- or out-of-state college, as well as information about application and acceptance. A student responding to the ELS survey could list up to twenty colleges and universities to which she applied and indicate whether she was accepted; whereas students responding to the NELS could only list up to two schools to which they had applied (and whether they were accepted), as well as a third school which they attended (if different from the other two to which they only applied).

Analytic Sample

We limit our sample in a number of ways. At the student level, we restrict our sample to students who were in twelfth grade in 1992 and 2004, and successfully graduated from high school (that is, received a regular high school diploma). At the institution level, we include all colleges and universities for which the IPEDS reports basic information in both the 1992–1993 and 2004–2005 academic years. Our final sample includes about 23,300 students. When we focus solely on college-going choices conditional on enrollment, the sample drops to about 18,300 students and 2,800 institutions (for more about sample restrictions, see the appendix).

EMPIRICAL APPROACH

To understand how changing tuition policies affect students' decisions about enrollment, we model changes in the likelihood of attending college, as well as the type of college chosen, conditional on attendance. In both cases, we include individual student and family characteristics and policy variables affecting the cost of attendance. In particular, we include

---

3. For more information on the background and contents of the Delta Cost data, please see http://www.deltacostproject.org (accessed February 23, 2016).

Table 1. Classification of States by Magnitude of Public Tuition Growth

Group	N(States)	Names of States	Mean Change in Public Tuition	
			2010 Dollars	Percentage
Low	12	CO, DC, FL, GA, LA, MS, NV, NY, UT, VA, WV, WY	$1,072	41.2%
Moderate	26	AL, AK, AZ, AR, CA, CT, DE, HI, ID, KS, KY, ME, MA, MI, MT, NE, NM, NC, ND, OK, OR, RI, SD, TN, VT, WA	$2,117	68.0%
High	13	IL, IN, IA, MD, MN, MO, NH, NJ, OH, PA, SC, TX, WI	$3,336	86.8%

Source: Authors' calculations.
Notes: Average changes in tuition costs are calculated using real, enrollment-weighted in-state tuition and fees as reported by public four-year postsecondary institutions in the IPEDS/Delta Cost data.

measures of the cost of attending college in the school year after which a student finishes high school (that is, 1992–1993 and 2004–2005).

Modeling Enrollment

To distinguish between different public tuition and fee policies, we group states into three types based on their patterns of tuition growth at four-year colleges and universities. Specifically, we calculate changes in average, enrollment-weighted real tuition and fee prices (in 2010 dollars) at public four-year colleges and universities by state between the NELS and ELS periods. We then group states according to whether the growth in their real tuition and fee costs was low, moderate, or high. We determine these groupings using the 25th and 75th percentiles of the national distribution of states' average, real enrollment-weighted tuition changes at public four-year institutions. These groups are summarized in table 1. States in the low tuition-growth category include Georgia, New York, and Colorado, where the average change in public tuition costs was small (less than $1,563). The moderate category includes states such as Alabama, Michigan, and California, where real annual tuition and fee costs at public four-year institutions increased between $1,563 and $2,717, or an enrollment-weighted average of about $2,100 over the period. The states in the group with the largest increases between 1992 and 2004 include Illinois, New Jersey, and Texas, where real tuition increases were more than $2,717, with average increases of just over $3,300.

We estimate the effect of moderate and large increases in the costs of public four-year higher education in a student's home state in a difference-in-differences framework. Using the pooled NELS and ELS data, we estimate changes in enrollment decisions over time for students living in states that adopt moderate and large tuition increases between the survey years, over and above the enrollment changes we observe for comparable students in states with more modest changes in the costs of public higher education. Specifically, our difference-in-differences models take the following form:

$$Y_{isc} = \alpha + \theta T_{isc} + \gamma Aid_{isc} + \beta_1 ELS_{isc} + \beta_2(ELS * Mod)_{isc} + \beta_3(ELS * Large)_{isc} + \varphi X_{isc} + \delta_s + \varepsilon_{isc} \quad (1)$$

Here, i indexes students, s states, and c denotes whether student i is a member of the NELS:88 or ELS:2002 cohort. Y_{isc} is a binary outcome denoting whether a student attended college within two years of high school graduation; then, conditional on enrollment, Y_{isc} becomes an indicator for whether a student enrolled in a particular type of college (for example, in-state, four-year public institution). T_{isc} is a vector of tuition cost measures: specifically, it includes the enrollment-weighted average real tuition and fees (in 2010 dollars) for four-year public institutions in the student's home state, in each time period, as well as enrollment-weighted average real tuition and fees at potential substitutes in the student's home state: public two-year colleges and private nonprofit four-year institutions. Aid_{isc} is a vector of controls that measures the enrollment-weighted average, real amount of Pell Grant and institutional grant aid made available to students in a given state, year, and institutional sector (that is, public four-year, public two-year, or private four-year).[4]

We are particularly interested in the effect of large tuition increases on students' decisions, and use distinctions between students living in states that implement large real price changes for four-year colleges to establish treatment groups; changes for students living in states with modest tuition changes serve as a baseline. In model (1), we include state fixed effects (δ_s) to capture state-specific differences in the likelihood of college-going that are persistent over time, and *not* due to large shifts in four-year public tuition prices (that is, difficult-to-measure aspects of higher education culture or support). We then interact dummies indicating groups of states that experienced moderate (Mod_{isc}) or large ($Large_{isc}$) increases in public four-year tuition costs (between 1992 and 2004) with the indicator for the ELS cohort (2004 high school graduates) to identify the difference-in-differences estimate of interest. So, β_3 captures the change in the likelihood of college enrollment between 1992 and 2004 among observationally identical students in states where public four-year institutions adopted large increases in tuition costs, net of changes in the probability of college enrollment experienced by observationally comparable high school graduates in states that saw more modest increases in public four-year tuition costs over the same period. Note that β_2 and β_3 pick up enrollment responses over and above what one would expect from the linear response due to the price change.

It is important to be clear that our definitions of large, moderate, and small tuition changes over this period are arbitrary. Our decision about how to make these distinctions was guided by the goal of transparency—and led to the focus on 75th and 25th percentiles for defining fast and slow tuition-growth states. We settle on this clear way of modeling nonlinear relationships between tuition growth and college enrollment because it establishes obvious comparisons for policy purposes. Our estimates provide insights into the college matriculation behavior of students graduating in states adopting notably different postsecondary tuition policies.

In addition, we control for a range of individual student characteristics (X_{isc}), including race, ethnicity, family makeup, parental education levels, and twelfth-grade math test scores. Finally, we cluster standard errors at the state level in all models to allow for arbitrary correlation of error terms between students within states across cohorts.[5]

We also explore potential heterogeneity in any results for three subgroups: students from families of low socioeconomic status (SES),[6] students whose parents did not attend college, and African American students. Further, we estimate the impact of tuition increases on students of different ability groups. In particular, we compare very high ability students to average and below average ability students. High-performing students are less likely to be affected by tuition increases because they have a larger choice set of colleges and are more likely to receive merit-based aid.

---

4. These sets of controls help us to isolate the impacts of large changes in public, four-year tuition costs by holding constant changes in attendance costs (and need-based aid available) at competing sectors of institutions in a student's home state.

5. We also weight all models by the survey-specific weights included in the NELS/ELS in order to account for each survey's design and sampling procedure. Unweighted estimates are very similar and are available from authors upon request.

6. The NELS:88 and ELS:2002 surveys contain measures of students' SES. These measures are a function of family income, parental educational attainment, and parental occupation.

Modeling Choices

We conduct the bulk of our analyses via a series of separate difference-in-differences models with different, binary outcomes (attend college, attend an in-state public four-year college). We then extend this intuition to a nested logit model in which we can simultaneously model various outcomes. This setup recognizes college choices are embedded in groups defined by state of residence. The choice sets available to a student vary depending on the public higher education system in her home state, as well as more traditional factors such as distance and likelihood of admission. The most common approach for dealing with a choice model of this type is to assume the individual taste preference is independently and identically distributed, so the probability of a student choosing a particular school can be estimated as a conditional logit. However, a limitation of conditional logit is the need to invoke the independence of irrelevant alternatives (IIA) assumption that the trade-off between any two options will not be affected by the availability of or changes in a third option (Train 2009). This would imply that changes in tuition at a moderately selective four-year public university in a student's home state alters the likelihood a student will attend community college in a way that is proportionate to changes in the likelihood a student attends an out-of-state private liberal arts college or research university. Clearly, this assumption is questionable.

To deal with this, we extend the empirical framework to recognize that any student faced with the decision of choosing among colleges is confronted with cost schedules for different institutions that are a direct function of the state of residence. So, the relative costs of comparable students can look different, solely as a function of state of residence. We group colleges into more homogeneous types (such as selective in-state public four-year colleges or highly selective out-of-state private four-year colleges). This grouping strategy has both conceptual and empirical advantages. Conceptually, grouping accommodates the ways in which students think about their college choices. Grouping has the empirical advantage that it allows us to relax the IIA assumption in an intuitively appealing way: The nested logit approach assumes that changes in costs or attributes of a college within a group has one effect on the likelihood of attending other colleges in the same group, but another effect on the likelihood of attending colleges in a different nest.

We incorporate additional information into the data set we use to estimate the nested logit model. We use Barron's rankings data to group colleges by level, control, and selectivity. We also estimate the likelihood of acceptance (for each college group and student) as a function of math test scores and student-level demographics (that is, gender, race, ethnicity) using information from the ELS and NELS surveys on students' first two college applications (and subsequent admission outcomes). We include the probability of admission (to each group of colleges) as a covariate in our multinomial model (along with enrollment-weighted tuition and fee costs).

RESULTS

To begin understanding these data and changing patterns of postsecondary enrollment, consider the cross-tab of postsecondary enrollment decisions for the high school class of 1992 from the NELS:88 and the class of 2004 from the ELS:2002, presented in table 2. In the top panel, we present mean enrollment decisions for the full NELS and ELS samples of students graduating high school in 1992 and 2004, respectively. In general, differences are small and expected between the groups. The proportion of students enrolling in some form of postsecondary study increased from 74 percent to 80 percent between the two cohorts. This reflects the continued trend toward postsecondary study generally.

In the middle and bottom panels of table 2, we present patterns of enrollment in states that saw, respectively, the slowest and fastest growth in tuition and fees charged at public four-year colleges and universities. Total enrollment increased the most in states with the largest tuition increases. This suggests that these states may have experienced population or economic growth that led to increased demand for higher education, and hence price increases. It may also reflect differences in

Table 2. Postsecondary Enrollment Among High School Graduates

Postsecondary Enrollment	Class of 1992 (NELS:88)	Class of 2004 (ELS:2002)
Full samples		
Enrolled (yes/no)	0.736	0.804
Enrolled in public two-year college	0.243	0.274
Enrolled in public four-year college	0.269	0.326
Enrolled in private college	0.137	0.145
	N=12,090	N=11,220
Students in slow tuition-growth states		
Enrolled (yes/no)	0.758	0.804
Enrolled in public two-year college	0.255	0.253
Enrolled in public four-year college	0.291	0.350
Enrolled in private college	0.143	0.139
	N=2,550	N=2,710
Students in fast tuition-growth states		
Enrolled (yes/no)	0.715	0.811
Enrolled in public two-year college	0.198	0.254
Enrolled in public four-year college	0.284	0.318
Enrolled in private college	0.142	0.173
	N=4,850	N=4,190

Source: Authors' calculations.
Notes: Slow tuition-growth = change in real tuition at public four-years < $1,563; fast tuition-growth = change in real tuition at public four-years > $2,717; college enrollment is captured within two years of high school graduation.

quality between institutions within these states. Importantly, enrollment appears to have shifted toward public two-year and private colleges in states adopting large tuition increases at public four-year colleges, suggesting some substitution.

Table 3 presents select descriptive statistics on all students, and then separately for populations of students in fast and slow tuition-growth states. Differences are minimal between the NELS and ELS samples. Students in the class of 2004 had more highly educated parents than those in the class of 1992, on average. For example, in the NELS:88 sample, 10 percent of students had a mother who completed "some college," whereas the corresponding figure for the ELS:2002 sample is 34 percent. This increase occurred alongside a decrease in the share of mothers who were high school dropouts between 1992 and 2004 and an increase in the percentage earning a college degree. The same trends appear when examining changes in average educational attainment of respondents' fathers between the two survey periods. Such differences are expected.

Comparing the characteristics of students in fast tuition-growth states to those in states that experienced slower growth in tuition at public four-year institutions gives us a sense of how high school graduates and their families have changed over time. Overall, differences in average characteristics are minimal. For both the classes of 1992 and 2004, slow tuition-growth states have slightly higher proportions of minority students (African American, Asian, and Hispanic) than fast tuition-growth states do. More students in states with slow tuition growth (across both high school classes) have mothers who have completed some college. Across periods, we see similar changes in these descriptive statistics for both slow and fast public tuition-growth states.

Table 3. Select Descriptive Statistics on Students

	All Students		Students in Slow Tuition-Growth States		Students in Fast Tuition-Growth States	
Variable	Mean	Standard Deviation	Mean	Standard Deviation	Mean	Standard Deviation
Class of 1992 (NELS:88)	N=8,530		N=1,700		N=3,550	
Female	0.50	0.50	0.52	0.50	0.50	0.50
Black	0.11	0.32	0.17	0.37	0.10	0.30
Hispanic	0.09	0.28	0.07	0.25	0.07	0.26
Asian	0.04	0.19	0.03	0.18	0.02	0.15
Other	0.01	0.10	0.01	0.09	0.01	0.07
Math score	49.44	14.10	49.60	13.92	50.17	13.92
Mother's education level						
High school graduate	0.51	0.50	0.48	0.50	0.54	0.50
Some college	0.10	0.30	0.12	0.32	0.08	0.28
College graduate	0.15	0.36	0.16	0.36	0.15	0.36
Postgraduate	0.10	0.30	0.11	0.31	0.10	0.30
Class of 2004 (ELS:2002)	N=11,220		N=2,700		N=4,190	
Female	0.52	0.50	0.52	0.50	0.51	0.50
Black	0.13	0.33	0.19	0.39	0.11	0.31
Hispanic	0.14	0.35	0.12	0.33	0.12	0.33
Asian	0.05	0.21	0.04	0.19	0.03	0.18
Other	0.05	0.22	0.04	0.20	0.04	0.20
Math score	51.54	13.84	51.77	13.45	51.86	13.81
Mother's education level						
High school graduate	0.27	0.44	0.25	0.43	0.30	0.46
Some college	0.34	0.48	0.36	0.48	0.34	0.47
College graduate	0.18	0.39	0.19	0.39	0.19	0.39
Postgraduate	0.09	0.29	0.10	0.31	0.09	0.28

Source: Authors' calculations.

Notes: All means are weighted means, using the survey-specific weights from the NELS (or ELS) as weights to account for each survey's design and sampling procedure. Descriptive statistics are presented for observations with non-missing values. In the regressions that follow, we use indicator variables to control for observations with missing covariate information.

Multivariate Regression Results: Difference-in-Differences

To consider the impacts of large changes in the costs of attending a public four-year college or university, we turn to estimates from equation 1 presented in table 4. Columns 1, 2, and 3 display results from linear probability models of any postsecondary enrollment among all high school graduates in our samples. The remaining columns present models of college attendance at in-state public institutions among those enrolling in college. Across columns 1, 2, and 3, we progress from a model that uses cross-state variation without any indicators for large increases in public four-year tuition costs, to a model with state fixed effects, to our preferred specification that includes both state fixed effects and indicators to capture impacts on enrollment behavior of moderate and large tuition increases.

The differences between the results in columns 1 through 3 make clear the importance of using within-state variation to understand the relationship between tuition and college

Table 4. Impacts of Tuition Increases on Student Enrollment Decisions

	Sample: All Students				Sample: College Enrollees			
	Attend College	Attend College	Attend College	Attend Public College in State	Attend Public College in State	Attend Public College in State	Attend Public Two-Year College in State	Attend Public Four-Year College in State
Independent Variables	(1)	(2)	(3)	(4)	(5)	(6)	(7)	(8)
Real four-year public tuition and fees (average cost; per $1,000)	0.005 (0.006)	0.019*** (0.007)	0.025* (0.013)	−0.017* (0.010)	0.001 (0.010)	−0.037* (0.021)	−0.117*** (0.027)	0.080** (0.032)
Real two-year public tuition and fees (average cost; per $1,000)	−0.004 (0.007)	−0.003 (0.016)	−0.005 (0.015)	−0.030** (0.013)	−0.023 (0.027)	−0.038 (0.026)	−0.092*** (0.029)	0.055* (0.030)
Real four-year private nonprofit tuition and fees (average cost; per $1,000)	0.001 (0.002)	0.002 (0.006)	0.003 (0.006)	−0.006 (0.004)	−0.009 (0.009)	−0.011 (0.008)	−0.011 (0.010)	−0.000 (0.009)
2004	0.190*** (0.026)	0.151*** (0.052)	0.163*** (0.058)	0.112*** (0.038)	0.071 (0.069)	0.114 (0.072)	0.120 (0.089)	−0.006 (0.077)
Moderate four-year public tuition change*2004			−0.037* (0.020)			0.071** (0.033)	0.184*** (0.040)	−0.113** (0.052)
Large four-year public tuition change*2004			−0.019 (0.038)			0.113** (0.055)	0.388*** (0.076)	−0.274*** (0.081)
Include state fixed effects?	No	Yes	Yes	No	Yes	Yes	Yes	Yes
Outcome mean	0.787	0.787	0.787	0.636	0.636	0.636	0.297	0.339
N	23310	23310	23310	18340	18340	18340	18340	18340
R^2	0.140	0.147	0.147	0.060	0.081	0.081	0.151	0.073

Source: Authors' calculations.

Notes: All models include controls for student race, ethnicity, twelfth-grade math test scores, mother's and father's education levels, family makeup, and average Pell Grants and institutional grant aid available to students from four-year publics, two-year publics, and four-year private nonprofits within their home states. Robust standard errors clustered at the state level appear in parentheses.

*$p < .1$; **$p < .05$; ***$p < .01$

attendance: We see no relationship between tuition and enrollment in column 1, but a significant positive relationship between tuition and enrollment growth within states (in column 2). This is consistent with the possibility that postsecondary enrollment demand was increasing in states where tuition was rising the most. Yet column 3 presents evidence that, after conditioning on a direct, linear effect, states with the most rapid increases in public tuition costs between 1992 and 2004 saw (small) decreases in the likelihood of college enrollment. The point estimate for students in states that experienced moderate increases in public four-year tuition is negative and weakly significant, whereas for students in states with the largest increases it is negative and insignificant. Collectively, we interpret these results as suggesting that large increases in public, four-year tuition costs over this period slightly dampened the propensity of students (in those states) to pursue postsecondary education. Yet, relative to the overall increase in college-going likelihood between cohorts (that is, an increase of about 16 percentage points), any such negative effects are quite small.

In the remaining columns in table 4, we present results on the relationship between large public tuition increases and student enrollment at in-state public institutions, conditional on attending college. Among college-going students, changes in the likelihood of attending an in-state public institution between 1992 and 2004 were different in states where tuition costs increased substantially and those with smaller cost increases. Specifically, we estimate a relative increase in the propensity to attend in-state public colleges in states where tuition prices rose drastically compared to states with small real price changes (column 6).[7] Yet the results in columns 7 and 8 illustrate that this relative increase in attendance at in-state public institutions was due to an increased enrollment at public two-year colleges—along with a substitution away from in-state public four-year colleges.

To make these patterns clearer, in figure 2 we graph changes in enrollment probabilities implied by the estimated coefficients from table 4. The three groups of bars depict changes in the probability of enrolling in any in-state public college or university (column 6), any in-state public two-year college (column 7), and any in-state public four-year college or university (column 8). Each bar represents the predicted change in enrollment probability due to an increase in public four-year tuition costs of a particular magnitude.[8] The first panel (three bars) illustrates a moderate decline in the likelihood students enrolled in public postsecondary institutions in states where public tuition grew most slowly. Enrollment in states where tuition growth was larger saw no such decline. This is consistent with the possibility that postsecondary enrollment demand was increasing in states where tuition was rising the most.

The next two panels of figure 2 illustrate that in states where tuition increased the least, students shifted away from enrollment in two-year colleges, and toward enrollment in four-year colleges. Conditional on attending college, the likelihood of attending a two-year public college fell by about 0.12 in these states, while the likelihood of attending a four-year public college or university increased by about 0.08. In states with larger tuition increases, we see no similar increase in the propensity to enroll in public four-year postsecondary education.

Together, these results suggest that states where public higher education costs increased substantially between 1992 and 2004 have strong and relatively inelastic demand for public higher education. Nevertheless, these large increases in public four-year tuition costs appreciably affected college choice, pushing students away from four-year institutions and toward two-year colleges.

Estimates by Institutional Selectivity

We next consider the relationship between large increases in tuition for public higher ed-

---

7. Because the preferred models all include state fixed effects, these estimates are net of time-invariant unobserved differences between states.

8. We sum the product of the observed change in real tuition (at the group mean) and the coefficient on the continuous measure of tuition costs plus the coefficient on any relevant group indicator (moderate or large).

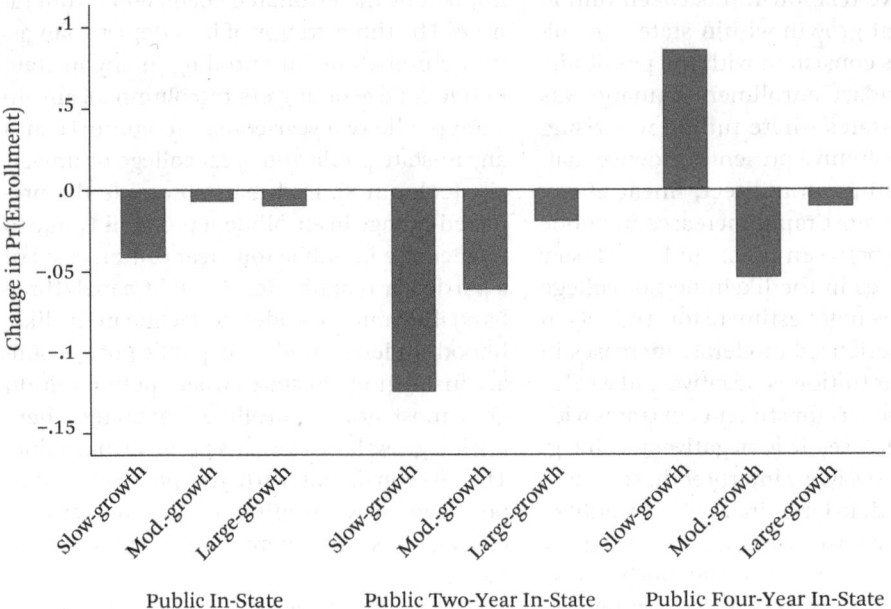

Figure 2. Changes in Public Higher Education Choices by Public Four-Year Tuition-Growth Group, 1992–2004

Source: Authors' calculations.
Notes: Sample is limited to college enrollees. Each bar sums the product of the observed change in real tuition (at the group mean) and the coefficient on the continuous measure of tuition costs plus the coefficient on any relevant group indicator (that is, moderate or large).

ucation and enrollment at postsecondary institutions with different levels of selectivity. We use Barron's data on the selectivity of colleges and universities to categorize all institutions attended by students in our sample.[9] The Barron's rankings range from less competitive to most competitive and are a function of the percentage of applicants admitted and the average academic preparation and aptitude of admitted students. Those institutions that are not ranked are classified below the less competitive group as noncompetitive.[10] We group the six Barron's categories into three slightly broader categories: highly selective (includes most competitive and highly competitive schools), selective (includes very competitive and competitive schools), and least selective (includes less competitive and noncompetitive schools).

In figure 3, we present results from a series of models in which we estimate the difference-in-differences comparisons of changes in the likelihood of enrolling in various types of postsecondary institutions for students in states where public four-year tuition grew rapidly between 1992 and 2004. Each bar captures the full effect of the mean change in public four-year tuition costs for high-growth states (combining the linear and nonlinear coefficients, as in figure 2). The estimates in figure 3 make it clear that students in states experiencing large increases in public four-year tuition costs over this period are less likely to attend selective (and highly selective) in-state public four-year institutions, but more likely to attend selective private institutions (both in-state and out-of-state). Further, the pattern illustrated here is

9. We are grateful to Ozan Jaquette and Michael Bastedo for sharing these Barron's data.

10. For example, institutions rated as most competitive generally admit less than 33 percent of applicants and have median ACT scores of 29 or higher. Less competitive institutions admit 85 percent (or more) of applicants and have median ACT scores of 21 or lower. Community colleges fall into this category.

Figure 3. Enrollment Changes After Large Public Four-Year Tuition Increases, 1992–2004

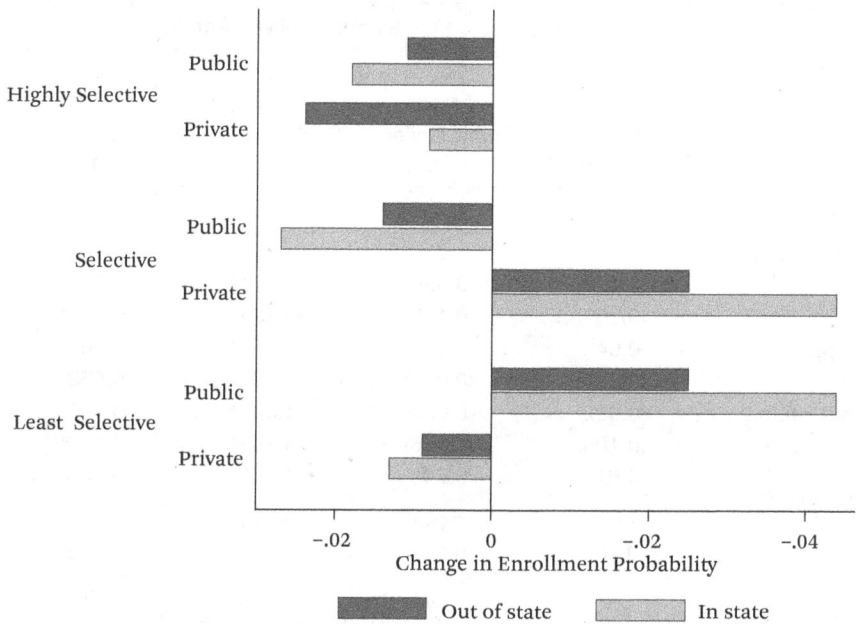

Source: Authors' calculations.
Notes: Sample is limited to college enrollees. Bars capture full enrollment effects (linear + non-linear) of large increases in public, four-year tuition costs. See text for definitions of selectivity categories.

suggestive of vertical substitution downward to less and nonselective public institutions (such as community colleges).

Differences by Demographic Subgroups of Students

Although table 4 and figures 2 and 3 provide estimates of average enrollment effects in response to large changes in tuition, we know that student subgroups vary in their price sensitivity (Long 2004). In table 5, we estimate our preferred difference-in-differences specification for three subgroups of particular interest to policymakers: low-SES families,[11] parents did not attend college, and African American. For each subgroup, we estimate our preferred models for the decision about whether to attend college, and then decisions about type of postsecondary institution, conditional on enrollment. The results in table 5 can be compared directly with those in table 4.

For students from low-SES and first-generation college families we find patterns similar to those among all students, only more pronounced. That is, large increases in public higher education tuition have no effect on the likelihood of attending college for these groups, but have larger effects on decisions about where to enroll. These findings suggest that the substitution away from four-year public universities toward two-year colleges, in states where public four-year tuition grew the most, is largely driven by impacts on the initial enrollment decisions of students from families of low socioeconomic status and first-generation college students.

Differences by Student Ability

We next consider whether the relationship between cost and enrollment in public higher education differs for students of varying academic achievement levels. We define ability us-

---

11. We categorize students from families of low socioeconomic status if the value of the family's SES variable (measured in twelfth grade) is at or below the 25th percentile.

Table 5. Impacts of Tuition Increases on Enrollment by Demographic Subgroups of Students

	Sample: College Enrollees			
	Attend College	Attend Public College in State	Attend Two-Year Public College in State	Attend Four-Year Public College in State
Independent Variables	(1)	(2)	(3)	(4)
Students from low-SES families				
2004	0.125	0.350**	0.421**	−0.070
	(0.108)	(0.145)	(0.164)	(0.110)
Moderate four-year public tuition change*2004	−0.048	0.074	0.161*	−0.087
	(0.054)	(0.085)	(0.088)	(0.069)
Large four-year public tuition change*2004	0.012	0.024	0.325*	−0.301**
	(0.100)	(0.146)	(0.166)	(0.122)
Outcome mean	0.613	0.708	0.425	0.283
N	5630	3450	3450	3450
R^2	0.168	0.069	0.140	0.133
Independent Variables	(5)	(6)	(7)	(8)
Students whose parents did not attend college				
2004	0.163	0.401***	0.289**	0.111
	(0.111)	(0.124)	(0.130)	(0.124)
Moderate four-year public tuition change*2004	0.059	0.215***	0.244***	−0.029
	(0.044)	(0.066)	(0.074)	(0.081)
Large four-year public tuition change*2004	0.133	0.341***	0.446***	−0.105
	(0.081)	(0.118)	(0.135)	(0.133)
Outcome mean	0.663	0.710	0.407	0.303
N	7520	4990	4990	4990
R^2	0.156	0.059	0.143	0.132
Independent Variables	(9)	(10)	(11)	(12)
African American students				
2004	0.242	0.234	0.109	0.125
	(0.205)	(0.222)	(0.274)	(0.258)
Moderate four-year public tuition change*2004	0.029	−0.049	−0.011	−0.038
	(0.067)	(0.088)	(0.082)	(0.115)
Large four-year public tuition change*2004	0.265	−0.162	0.002	−0.164
	(0.160)	(0.220)	(0.218)	(0.288)
Outcome mean	0.742	0.616	0.294	0.323
N	2540	1880	1880	1880
R^2	0.179	0.106	0.165	0.162

Source: Authors' calculations.

Notes: All models include state fixed effects, controls for linear changes in tuition costs at four-year publics, two-year publics, and four-year private nonprofits in students' home states, and controls for student race, ethnicity, twelfth grade math test scores, mother's and father's education levels, family income and makeup, and average Pell Grant and institutional grant aid available to students from four-year publics, two-year publics, and four-year private nonprofits within their home states. Robust standard errors clustered at the state level appear in parentheses.

*$p < .1$; **$p < .05$; ***$p < .01$

ing twelfth-grade math scores and examine distributions of students' math scores by cohort (that is, NELS separately from ELS).[12] We then group students into four different ability groups that we expect to respond differently to changes in costs at four-year public colleges in a state: elite students, in the top 10 percent; high-performing students, in the top 33 percent but not the elite group; average-performing students, between 33 and 67 percent; and low-performing students, in the bottom 33 percent.

In table 6, we provide descriptive statistics for background characteristics of students as well as ranges of SAT scores for the postsecondary institutions students in each ability group report attending. Elite students are likely to score better on entrance exams and report attending colleges with higher-performing peers. As a consequence, these students are likely to gain admission and have the means to attend a wider range of colleges. We expect students in this group to be less affected by tuition at public four-year institutions.

High-performing students are likely to be of the type to gain admission to the most selective public four-year colleges in their home states, but less likely than elite students to qualify for admission to top-tier universities nationally. Low-performing students, on the other hand, are unlikely to qualify for admission to selective public universities in their home states. Rather, these students are more likely to be admissible at less selective or open enrollment institutions, which are also relatively inexpensive. Note that 97 percent of elite students enroll in college within two years of high school graduation, versus 83 percent of average performers and 54 percent of low performers.

In table 6, for each student group we present separate estimates of the impact of large tuition changes at public four-year colleges on the likelihood of attending college and (conditional on attending college) of enrolling in any public in-state college, a public two-year in-state college, and a public four-year in-state college. Several patterns emerge from table 6.

Most strikingly, we see different effects of large public tuition increases on the college choices of high-performing and on average-performing students. High performers in states that experienced the largest increases in public four-year tuition costs are substantially less like to attend an in-state public college, especially a four-year institution. Auxiliary regressions for which outcomes measure attendance at in-state, out-of-state, public, and private institutions of particular selectivity levels (based on Barron's data) reveal that high performers exposed to such public tuition increases instead opt for selective private institutions out of state.[13] Average-performing students exposed to the largest public tuition increases were less likely to attend an in-state public four-year institution (relative to their average-performing counterparts in states with more modest tuition increases); but, unlike their higher-performing peers, average performers in these high tuition-growth states were substantially more likely to attend an in-state public two-year college. Complementary regressions on attendance at institutions of varying types and selectivity levels confirm that this effect for average performers is driven by increased attendance at lower-ranked in-state public institutions.

At the extremes of the student ability distribution, we see less evidence of such substitution in college choices. Among elite students, some evidence shows that those in states that adopted large increases in public tuition opted to instead enroll in out-of-state private four-year institutions. Yet, among elite performers, college enrollment (along the extensive margin) grew fastest in states that adopted the largest hikes in public four-year tuition costs between 1992 and 2004. This is not surprising because the demand for higher education among elite students likely is most inelastic. Among low-performing students, exposure to large increases in public four-year tuition costs resulted in an increased likelihood of attending an in-state college. Auxiliary regressions using Barron's selectivity data reveal that, for

---

12. We use the math score variable from the ELS created specifically to be used in conjunction with the math scores in NELS to examine cross-cohort changes in math performance (NELS-equated).

13. Results from all auxiliary regressions are available from the authors on request.

Table 6. Impacts of Tuition Increases on Enrollment by Student Academic Preparation

Student Subgroup		Independent Variables	Attend College (1)	Attend Public College in State (2)	Attend Two-Year Public College in State (3)	Attend Four-Year Public College in State (4)
Elite students (at or above 90th percentile)						
Characteristics:		2004	0.077	-0.406*	-0.008	-0.399*
			(0.086)	(0.213)	(0.098)	(0.231)
Student:		Moderate public tuition change*2004	0.024	-0.205*	-0.053	-0.153
Percent black	2		(0.029)	(0.114)	(0.042)	(0.120)
Percent Hispanic	4	Large public tuition change*2004	0.106**	-0.120	0.107	-0.226
Percent Asian	21		(0.045)	(0.177)	(0.078)	(0.186)
Percent going to college	97					
College:		N	2160	2100	2100	2100
SAT 25th percentile–math	568	R^2	0.131	0.182	0.100	0.127
SAT 75th percentile–math	670					
SAT 25th percentile–verbal	550					
SAT 75th percentile–verbal	655					
High-performing students (67th–90th percentile)						
Characteristics:		2004	0.049	-0.038	0.129	-0.168
			(0.059)	(0.125)	(0.116)	(0.119)
Student:		Moderate public tuition change*2004	-0.063**	-0.137***	0.017	-0.155***
Percent black	5		(0.031)	(0.043)	(0.045)	(0.049)
Percent Hispanic	8	Large public tuition change*2004	-0.109**	-0.226**	0.131	-0.357***
Percent Asian	10		(0.052)	(0.095)	(0.092)	(0.093)
Percent going to college	93					
College:		N	4910	4550	4550	4550
SAT 25th percentile–math	519	R^2	0.087	0.134	0.144	0.080
SAT 75th percentile–math	625					
SAT 25th percentile–verbal	509					
SAT 75th percentile–verbal	615					

Average-performing students (33rd–67th percentile)

Characteristics:			2004	0.228***	0.185*	0.201*	−0.016
				(0.074)	(0.095)	(0.118)	(0.141)
Student:			Moderate public tuition change*2004	−0.009	0.163***	0.274***	−0.111*
Percent black	9			(0.035)	(0.049)	(0.064)	(0.063)
Percent Hispanic	12		Large public tuition change*2004	0.018	0.209**	0.475***	−0.266**
Percent Asian	8			(0.058)	(0.083)	(0.129)	(0.115)
Percent going to college	83						
College:			N	7110	5920	5920	5920
SAT 25th percentile–math	486		R^2	0.112	0.085	0.144	0.089
SAT 75th percentile–math	595						
SAT 25th percentile–verbal	480						
SAT 75th percentile–verbal	588						

Low-performing students (below 33rd percentile)

Characteristics:			2004	0.025	0.268	0.300**	−0.032
				(0.080)	(0.166)	(0.141)	(0.131)
Student:			Moderate public tuition change*2004	−0.050	0.173*	0.161*	0.013
Percent black	20			(0.044)	(0.098)	(0.087)	(0.067)
Percent Hispanic	19		Large public tuition change*2004	0.029	0.231	0.341**	−0.110
Percent Asian	6			(0.079)	(0.178)	(0.164)	(0.109)
Percent going to college	61						
College:			N	6740	4110	4110	4110
SAT 25th percentile–math	447		R^2	0.148	0.076	0.119	0.117
SAT 75th percentile–math	559						
SAT 25th percentile–verbal	446						
SAT 75th percentile–verbal	557						

Source: Authors' calculations.

Notes: All models include state fixed effects, controls for linear changes in tuition costs at four-year publics, two-year publics, and four-year private nonprofits in students' home states, controls for student race, ethnicity, twelfth grade math test scores, mother's and father's education levels, family income and makeup, and average Pell Grants and institutional grant aid available to students from four-year publics, two-year publics, and four-year private nonprofits within their home states. Robust standard errors clustered at the state level appear in parentheses.

*$p < .1$; **$p < .05$; ***$p < .01$

Figure 4. Nested Model of College Choice

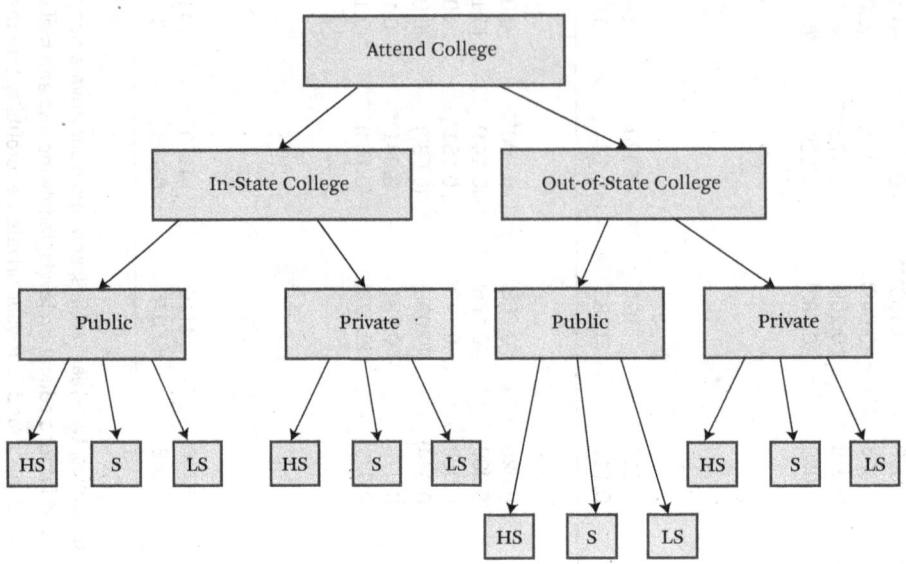

Source: Authors' compilation.
Notes: HS = highly selective; S = selective; and LS = less selective. All selectivity categorizations are based on Barron's rankings data. See text for detailed discussion of these groupings.

low performers, this increased likelihood is driven by substitution away from moderately selective in-state four-year public institutions toward nonselective ones (such as community colleges).

The different impacts of large increases in public tuition costs across the ability or performance distributions of high school graduates underscore the degree to which shifts in state-level tuition policies affect enrollment decisions of both well-prepared but modestly resourced students as well as more poorly prepared high school graduates.

Nested Logit Results
Rather than modeling enrollment decisions in a series of binary choices, as in tables 4 through 6, we turn next to our nested logit model, which treats the decision among colleges of various types as multinomial. We estimate the effects of tuition and fee price changes at public four-year colleges on a student's decision about whether to attend an in-state public college, or whether to attend a private college or a public college out-of-state and colleges of various selectivity levels. In figure 4, we illustrate the nesting structure into which we group colleges.

In table 7, we summarize the results from the nested logit analysis, presenting parameter estimates for the key policy variables, interacted with cohort, to set up the same difference-in-differences interpretation. The base against which all college choices are compared is enrollment in selective, public institutions in a student's home state. To this base, the estimates compare the likelihood of enrolling in various other types of colleges. The results in table 7 largely conform to the patterns we observe in our series of binary models: students in states adopting relatively large increases in public four-year tuition costs between 1992 and 2004 are more likely to substitute "down" to less selective public colleges, and "out" to selective private and public universities out of state (relative to their counterparts who experienced more modest tuition increases). Relative to the results from our binary models, the nested logit findings emphasize the substitution to out-of-state public and private universi-

Table 7. Nested Logit Results of Impact of Public Tuition Increases on College Choice

Independent Variables	Private, In-State	Private, Out-of-State	Public, In-State	Public, Out-of-state
A. Less/nonselective institutions	(1)	(2)	(3)	(4)
2004	−1.187***	−0.788	−0.843***	−1.158***
	(0.179)	(0.484)	(0.165)	(0.213)
Moderate four-year public tuition	−0.025	0.037	0.082	0.224
change*2004	(0.211)	(0.658)	(0.228)	(0.446)
Large four-year public tuition	0.181	0.412	0.435	0.741**
change*2004	(0.261)	(0.713)	(0.297)	(0.336)
Outcome mean	0.27	0.02	0.33	0.02
B. Selective institutions	(5)	(6)	(7)	(8)
2004	−0.379	−0.641***		−0.476***
	(0.280)	(0.165)		(0.173)
Moderate four-year public tuition	−0.028	0.257	BASE	0.576**
change*2004	(0.368)	(0.318)		(0.286)
Large four-year public tuition	0.525	1.077***		0.757**
change*2004	(0.359)	(0.370)		(0.385)
Outcome mean	0.05	0.03	0.16	0.03
C. Highly selective institutions	(9)	(10)	(11)	(12)
2004	0.724	0.434	−0.202	0.216
	(1.062)	(0.698)	(0.677)	(1.190)
Moderate four-year public tuition	1.431***	0.760*	0.464	4.371***
change*2004	(0.531)	(0.439)	(0.806)	(1.190)
Large four-year public tuition	2.504***	1.270**	−0.305	20.454***
change*2004	(0.824)	(0.502)	(0.691)	(2.011)
Outcome mean	0.01	0.03	0.05	0.01

Source: Authors' calculations.
Notes: N = 119,610; figure 4 depicts the selectivity based nests of postsecondary institutions used in the nested logit model. See text for details about grouping institutions into selectivity categories. The nested logit model includes two alternative-specific covariates: enrollment-weighted, real tuition and fees, and the probability of admission. We model the probability of admission to each selectivity nest of institutions using supplemental data from the NLES:88 and ELS:2002 surveys that capture students' postsecondary application and acceptance outcomes. In auxiliary regressions, we model acceptance as a function of students' math test scores, demographic characteristics, survey (NELS or ELS), and state fixed effects. We then predict admission probabilities for all students for all nests and use this linear prediction as an alternative-specific covariate in the nested logit model. In addition, within the nested logit college-type equations that model attendance, we include the same set of student-level covariates as in all earlier tables. Robust standard errors clustered at the state level appear in parentheses.
*$p < .1$; **$p < .05$; ***$p < .01$

ties that are selective or highly selective in response to large increases in public tuition costs in a student's home state.

VALIDITY AND ROBUSTNESS CHECKS

For both the nested logit and linear probability models, the identifying variation comes from within-state changes in the postsecondary enrollment decisions of students in states that saw rapid growth in public tuition costs between 1992 and 2004, over and above changes for observationally identical students in other states. This difference-in-differences strategy limits many potential threats to internal validity, but threats remain. Perhaps most important is the possibility that states with the most rapid increases in tuition saw unusual changes in the quality of higher education. If so, then sorting out whether the changes we observe are a price response rather than a behavioral change due to the attributes of a state's colleges is more difficult.

As a first way to assess the importance of this threat, we exploit the fact that some states have tuition reciprocity agreements that permit students in other states to pay their home state's tuition. If students who see larger price changes because of reciprocity agreements exhibit the largest enrollment declines, this provides some assurance that price is the principal motivation for the decline. As a second way to rule out the possibility that enrollment shifts were due to simultaneous changes in institutional quality, we examine changes in other indicators of the quality of public colleges and universities in states with large or small increases in tuition costs.

Tuition Reciprocity Agreements and Student Price Response

The state of Minnesota has reciprocity agreements with three surrounding states: Wisconsin, North Dakota, and South Dakota.[14] Although most reciprocity agreements have substantial conditions or limitations, those between Minnesota and these three states permit a student from the other state to attend its public postsecondary education institutions and pay the same tuition as at a comparable home-state institution (DesJardins 1999; Rayburn 2011).[15] Unlike almost all other reciprocity agreements, Minnesota's arrangements are not limited to students in particular majors. These states are also interesting because they saw quite different rates of tuition growth over the period in which we observe students in both states in our analytic sample: Minnesota's public four-year tuition grew the fastest, placing it in our top category with Wisconsin. Yet students in South Dakota and North Dakota saw more modest increases in public four-year tuition costs that placed those states in our middle group (average increase of between $1,600 and $2,700). Therefore, if price changes affect enrollment decisions, we would expect a relative decrease in the number of students from Minnesota enrolling in Minnesota's best four-year colleges, since they bear the full cost of the larger tuition increase. Because North and South Dakota students did not see the tuition costs of attending Minnesota's colleges rise as much, we should see a smaller enrollment response.

To examine the enrollment decisions of students from Minnesota, South Dakota, and North Dakota in response to these price shifts, we estimate difference-in-differences models similar in intuition to those throughout the paper, which take the following shape:

$$Y_{MN_{isc}} = \alpha + \theta T_{isc} + \gamma Aid_{isc} + \beta_1 MN_{student_{isc}} + \beta_2 ELS_{isc} + \beta_3 (ELS * MN_{student})_{isc} + \varphi X_{isc} + \varepsilon_{isc} \quad (2)$$

where the outcome is a measure of attendance at a public college in Minnesota for student i, from state s, in cohort c. For this exercise, we limit the sample to students in our NELS-ELS sample whose home state is Minnesota, South Dakota, or North Dakota. We present results from these models in table 8.

As the coefficients on the Minnesota student indicator illustrate, over this time, students from Minnesota were about 32 percentage points more likely to attend a public four-year institution in Minnesota than their counterparts in North Dakota and South Dakota. Yet the relative change in the propensity of Minnesota students to attend Minnesota's four-year colleges declined by about 19 percentage points over observationally identical

---

14. These are state-specific agreements. For example, Wisconsin and South Dakota do not have a tuition reciprocity agreement.

15. Reciprocity agreements are of two types: tangential and consortium. Tangential agreements involve two states and are agreed on bilaterally for a set period. Consortium agreements are entered into by several states and administered by a common board.

Table 8. Tuition Reciprocity and Student Enrollment Decisions

Independent Variables	Attend MN Public College (1)	Attend MN Four-Year Public College (2)
MN student	0.183	0.317**
	(0.167)	(0.154)
2004	0.653***	0.402***
	(0.087)	(0.077)
MN student*2004	−0.159	−0.192**
	(0.102)	(0.089)
N	450	450
R^2	0.237	0.149

Source: Authors' calculations.
Notes: Models include all student-level covariates reported in tables 3 through 6. Robust standard errors appear in parentheses.
*$p < .1$; **$p < .05$; ***$p < .01$

students in the Dakotas. This relative decline in the likelihood of Minnesota students enrolling in Minnesota's four-year public colleges is consistent with predictions from consumer theory. It also suggests the declining propensity of Minnesota students to attend public colleges in their home state was not driven by a decline in the quality of these schools, given that North and South Dakotans (the reference group) did not show a similar distaste for Minnesota's colleges.

Trends in Higher Education Spending

As another way to test for unmeasured shifts in the quality of four-year public institutions, we examine trends in student services expenditures and research expenditures at public four-year research institutions and at public four-year master's universities. We use these measures to assess contemporaneous changes in the characteristics of colleges and universities in states with rapid public tuition growth.

In figure 5 we present time series of student services and research expenditures per full-time equivalent student (FTE) from 1986 to 2007 at public four-year institutions. Expenditures on student services include costs associated with admissions, registrar activities, and activities whose primary purpose is to contribute to students' emotional and physical well-being and to their intellectual, cultural, and social development outside the context of the formal instructional program (for example, cultural events, student newspapers, intramural athletics, and student organizations). Each panel includes separate time series for states with the fastest and slowest growth in tuition.

In both panels of figure 5, we see sizeable increases in spending between 1992 and 2004 (the solid vertical lines). Yet, in neither case does any evidence indicate that such expenditures changed differentially across states that adopted large versus small increases in public tuition in ways that would explain our main results. For example, trends in student services expenditures (per FTE) in high tuition-growth states did not decline between 1992 and 2004 while such expenditures rose in low tuition-growth states. These trends do not suggest that changes in other attributes of public institutions in high tuition-growth states dissuaded students from attending.

Changes in Cohort Size and Quality

To assess whether the enrollment shifts we see are potentially a result of relative changes in the quantity or quality of students entering postsecondary education in states where tuition grew fastest, we conduct two tests. First, we examine trends in the stock of high school graduates across our groups of states (as a basic proxy for higher education demand).[16] Second, we consider whether treatment and control states saw different changes in average SAT scores (verbal and math) or eighth grade NAEP math scores during the years that closely match our NELS and ELS cohorts of high school graduates. We calculate standardized changes in these average scores by state and

---

16. Data on counts of high school graduates by state come from the Common Core of Data (CCD): http://nces.ed.gov/ccd/tables/ESSIN_Task5_f2.asp (accessed February 23, 2016).

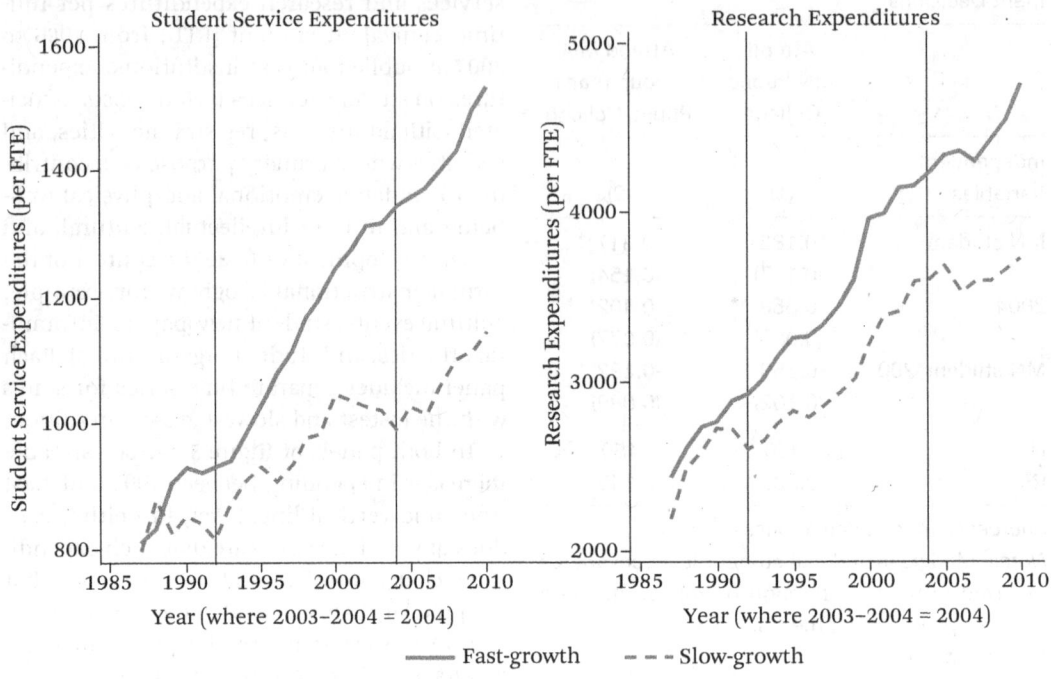

Figure 5. Expenditures at Public Four-Year Institutions by Public Four-Year Tuition-Growth Group

Source: Authors' calculations based on data from the Delta Cost Project.
Note: Expenditures are measured in 2010 dollars (using CPI-U).

by level of public tuition growth: changes in SAT scores are between 1994 and 2004; and changes in eighth grade NAEP math scores are between 1990 and 2000. Recall that on-time graduation for the NELS cohort was 1992, and for the ELS cohort was 2004.

In figure 6, we present trends in the number of high school graduates across groups of states with different levels of public tuition growth. These trends show no evidence that states adopting large increases in public four-year tuition costs produced differentially rapid or slow growth in the number of public high school graduates, compared to states adopting more modest increases in public four-year tuition costs over the same period. Insofar as stocks of public high school graduates are an adequate proxy for general higher education demand in a state, these trends suggest a similar evolution of demand across both groups of states.

Because demand for higher education (and specifically different types of postsecondary institutions) is a function of both the quantity of potential entrants and the quality of those students in a given year, we use figure 7 to explore differences in test score changes by levels of public tuition growth. It is clear that in states with the largest increases in public postsecondary tuition, NAEP math scores grew significantly faster than in states with more modest increases. Similarly, we see faster growth in SAT math scores, but not verbal, in states where tuition increased the most. The relative increase in the quality of high school students in states with large tuition increases suggests that the relative decline in enrollment growth in the most selective public colleges and universities in these states was not due to declining student quality. If anything, these states saw increases in student quality as measured by NAEP and SAT scores. So, other things equal, one would expect relative growth in demand for the most research-intensive and selective postsecondary institutions in these states.

None of these tests is ironclad, but together

Figure 6. High School Graduates by Public Four-Year Tuition-Growth Group

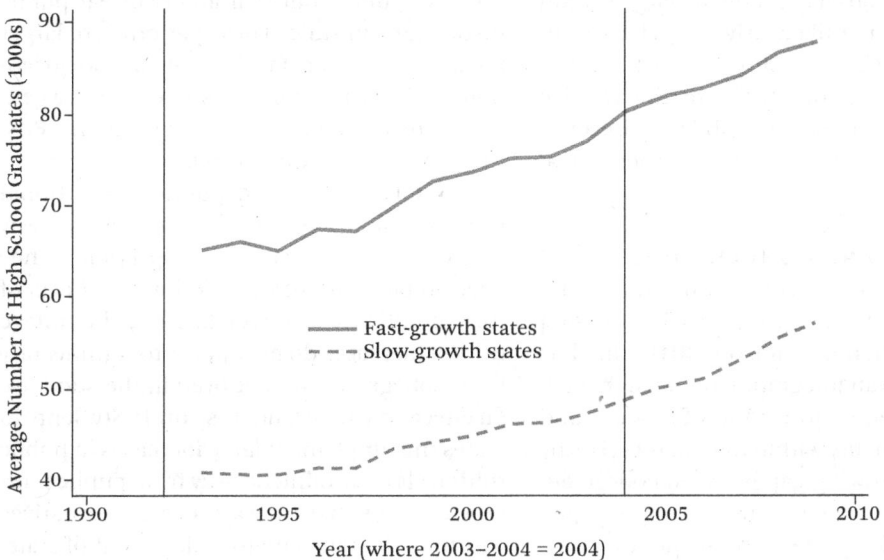

Source: Authors' calculations based on data from the Common Core of Data and the National Center for Education Statistics.

Figure 7. Changes in Average Test Scores Between NELS and ELS by Public Four-Year Tuition-Growth Group

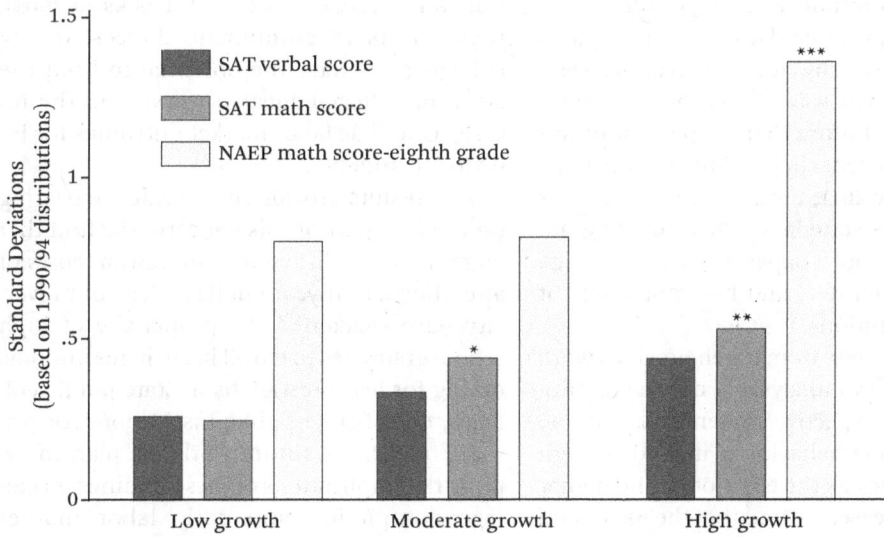

Source: Authors' calculations.
Notes: All changes in scores are standardized off of their earliest distributions: Changes in SAT scores are between 1994 and 2004. Changes in NAEP eighth-grade math scores are between 1990 and 2000. Average changes for moderate and high tuition-growth states are compared with test score changes observed in low-growth states.
N(SAT) = 51; N(NAEP) = 30
*$p < .1$; **$p < .05$; ***$p < .01$

they provide some assurance that the enrollment shifts we observe following large tuition increases were not likely driven by changes in relative cohort size or quality of students entering higher education, shifts in the relative quality of different states' public postsecondary systems themselves, or other particular features of a state.

DISCUSSION AND CONCLUSIONS

The rising costs of college continue to capture media attention and provoke wide-ranging public discussion (Abramson 2011). This has coincided with an integration of the higher education market, stratification of student and institutional quality within that market (Hoxby 2009), and a growing gap between college enrollment and completion rates. In this paper, we attempt to integrate these themes by studying a likely mechanism for at least some of these trends: rising tuition costs of public colleges and universities on student decisions about whether and where to enroll in college. We do so by comparing the early college experiences of observationally identical high school graduates before and after a period during which the financial landscape of most states changed substantially, and tuition at four-year public institutions soared. Because public institutions enroll more than 80 percent of undergraduate students in the United States (Snyder and Dillow 2011, table 2), we also exploit the fact that the state in which a student graduates high school shapes both the college prices she encounters and her choice sets of potential institutions.

Our paper differs from much previous work in that our unit of analysis is not the institution, but the prospective student. We examine the college-going behavior of individual high school graduates as the costs of public higher education increase. We find that the likelihood of attending an in-state public four-year college or university declined between 1992 and 2004 for high school graduates in states where tuition costs increased substantially during the period, compared with students in states where tuition changed more modestly. At the same time, students in states with particularly large increases in public four-year tuition costs were substantially more likely to enroll in less selective public four-year and two-year public institutions in state. These patterns are larger for students from families of low socioeconomic status and nonelite students more generally (those not in the top 10 percent on NELS/ELS math and reading tests).

As state boards and public institutional leaders look to tuition-setting policy as a way to offset declining state appropriations, they need to be aware of the enrollment effects of tuition policies. Although large public college tuition increases do not appear to significantly limit college enrollment overall, they do have an effect on where students enroll. Students in states that implement large increases in public tuition shift enrollment away from public four-year colleges, both toward other alternatives within their state, and to colleges out of state. Given the large and robust literature on the impact of college quality on college completion rates and on employment outcomes (Behrman, Rosenzweig, and Taubman 1996; Black and Smith 2004; Brewer, Eide, and Ehrenberg 1999; Bowen, Chingos, and McPherson 2009; Dale and Krueger 2002, 2011; Hoekstra 2009), these shifts in enrollment choices among college-goers have the potential to limit the stock of college-educated workers in the future, as well as labor market outcomes for individual students.

Our results provide some evidence bearing on the first part of this concern: We find that large increases in the in-state tuition costs of attending a four-year public college or university have weakened the propensity of high school graduates to enroll in such institutions, opting for less prestigious in-state public colleges, out-of-state public institutions, or private colleges. In future work, we plan to explore the implications of these findings on college completion and early labor market outcomes. Nonetheless, the current results make clear that state policies affecting the cost of public higher education help shape where students decide to pursue postsecondary education. Any efforts by policymakers to improve rates of degree completion need to recognize the potential role of composition in shaping aggregate rates of completion.

APPENDIX: DATA AND SAMPLE RESTRICTIONS

ELS:2002

We extract variables from both the student- and institution-level files. From the student-level file, we identify the cross-sectional, nationally representative group of students in twelfth grade in 2004 (that is, from the first follow-up). Within this group, we further restrict to high school graduates.

Using information in the student-level file on the first postsecondary institution attended by college-going high school graduates, we match additional information (by student and order of postsecondary institution attendance) from the student-institution-level file.

```
***** SAMPLE RESTRICTIONS;
** Restriction #1: Keep if 2004
12th-grade cohort member (identified
either in F1 or F2);
keep if G12COHRT > 0 ;
** Restriction #2: Keep only HS
graduates (i.e., regular grads, not
GED completers);
keep if F2F1HSST == 1 | F2F1HSST ==
2   /* Regular high school diploma
by (or before) summer 2004 */;
/* Text from NCES Codebook: "For
example, G12COHRT=1 used with F1QWT
generates estimates for a nationally
representative, cross-sectional
population of the 2004 spring-term
senior class. G12CHORT>0 used with
F2F1WT generates estimates for a
nationally representative panel of
the spring-term senior class,
including F1 nonrespondents." */;
```

NELS:88

We extract variables from both the student- and institution-level files. From the student-level file, we identify the cross-sectional, nationally representative group of students in twelfth grade in 1992. Within this group, we further restrict to high school graduates.

```
*** sample restrictions;
*** Restriction 1: Keep if 1992 12-
grad cohort member;
*** Restriction 2: Keep only those
earning HS diploma, NOT a GED;
keep if hsstat == 1;
```

REFERENCES

Abramson, Larry. 2011. "Why Does College Cost So Much?" *NPR Education*, October 19, 2011. Accessed December 14, 2015. http://www.npr.org/2011/10/19/141505658/why-is-college-so-expensive.

Archibald, Robert B., and David H. Feldman. 2011. *Why Does College Cost So Much?* New York: Oxford University Press.

Behrman, Jere R., Mark R. Rosenzweig, and Paul Taubman. 1996. "College Choice and Wages: Estimates Using Data on Female Twins." *Review of Economics and Statistics* 78(4): 672–84.

Bettinger, Eric P. 2004. "How Financial Aid Affects Persistence." In *College Choices: The Economics of Where to Go, When to Go, and How to Pay for It*, edited by Caroline N. Hoxby. Cambridge, Mass.: National Bureau of Economic Research.

Black, Dan A., and Jeffrey A. Smith. 2004. "How Robust Is the Evidence on the Effects of College Quality? Evidence from Matching." *Journal of Econometrics* 121(1–2): 99–124.

Bound, John, Michael Lovenheim, and Sarah Turner. 2010. "Why Have College Completion Rates Declined?: An Analysis of Changing Student Preparation and Collegiate Resources." *American Economic Journal: Applied Economics* 2(3): 29–57.

Bowen, William G., Matthew M. Chingos, and Michael S. McPherson. 2009. *Crossing the Finish Line: Completing College at America's Public Universities*. Princeton, N.J.: Princeton University Press.

Brewer, Dominic J., Eric R. Eide, and Ronald G. Ehrenberg. 1999. "Does It Pay to Attend an Elite Private College? Cross-Cohort Evidence on the Effects of College Type on Earnings." *Journal of Human Resources* 34(1): 104–23.

Dale, Stacy, and Alan B. Krueger. 2002. "Estimating the Payoff to Attending a More Selective College: An Application of Selection on Observables and Unobservables." *Quarterly Journal of Economics* 117(4): 1491–527.

———. 2011. "Estimating the Return to College Selectivity over the Career Using Administrative Earnings Data." *NBER* working paper no. 17159. Cambridge, Mass.: National Bureau of Economic Research.

DesJardins, Stephen L. 1999. "Simulating the Enrollment Effects of Changes in the Tuition Reciprocity Agreement Between Minnesota and Wisconsin." *Research in Higher Education* 40(6): 705–16.

Dynarski, Susan. 2008. "Building the Stock of College-Educated Labor." *Journal of Human Resources* 43(3): 576–610.

The Economist. 2011. "Higher Education: The Latest Bubble?" April 13, 2011. Accessed February 19, 2016. http://www.economist.com/blogs/schumpeter/2011/04/higher_education.

Friend, Tad. 2010. "Protest Studies: The State Is Broke, and Berkeley Is in Revolt." *The New Yorker* 85(43)(January 4): 22–28.

Heller, Donald E. 1997. "Student Price Response in Higher Education: An Update to Leslie and Brinkman." *Journal of Higher Education* 68(6): 624–59.

Hemelt, Steven W., and Dave E. Marcotte. 2011. "The Impact of Tuition Increases on Enrollment at Public Colleges and Universities." *Educational Evaluation and Policy Analysis* 33(4): 435–57.

"Higher Education: The Latest Bubble." *Schumpeter*, April 13, 2011. Accessed December 14, 2015. http://www.economist.com/blogs/schumpeter/2011/04/higher_education.

Hoekstra, Mark L. 2009. "The Effect of Attending the Flagship State University on Earnings: A Discontinuity-Based Approach." *Review of Economics and Statistics* 91(4): 717–24.

Hoxby, Caroline M. 2009. "The Changing Selectivity of American Colleges." *Journal of Economic Perspectives* 23(4): 95–118.

Koshal, Rajindar, and Manjulika Koshal. 2000. "State Appropriation and Higher Education Tuition: What Is the Relationship?" *Education Economics* 8(1): 81–89.

Leslie, Larry L., and Paul T. Brinkman. 1987. "Student Price Response in Higher Education: The Student Demand Studies." *Journal of Higher Education* 58(2): 181–201.

Lewin, Tamar, and Rebecca Cathcart. 2009. "Regents Raise College Tuition for California by 32 Percent." *New York Times*, November 19, p. A26. Accessed December 14, 2015. http://www.nytimes.com/2009/11/20/education/20tuition.html.

Long, Briget Terry. 2004. "How Have College Decision Changed over Time? An Application of the Conditional Logistic Choice Model." *Journal of Econometrics* 121(1–2): 271–96.

O'Leary, Kevin. 2009. "California's Crisis Hits Its Prized Universities." *Time*, July 18. Accessed December 14, 2015. http://www.time.com/time/nation/article/0,8599,1911455,00.html.

Rayburn, Jack. 2011. "Tuition Reciprocity Data Overview." St. Paul: Minnesota Office of Higher Education. Last modified April 22, 2011. Accessed December 14, 2015. http://www.ohe.state.mn.us/pdf/reciprocitydataoverview2011.pdf.

Reilly, Peter J. 2011. "When Will the Education Bubble Explode," *Forbes*, November 2. Accessed December 14, 2015, http://www.forbes.com/sites/peterjreilly/2011/11/02/when-will-the-education-bubble-explode.

Rizzo, Michael J., and Ronald G. Ehrenberg. 2003. "Resident and Nonresident Tuition and Enrollment at Flagship State Universities." *NBER* working paper no. 9916. Cambridge, Mass.: National Bureau of Economic Research.

Snyder, Thomas D., and Sally A. Dillow. 2011. *Digest of Education Statistics 2010*. NCES 2011-015. Washington: U.S. Department of Education, National Center for Education Statistics. Accessed December 14, 2015. http://nces.ed.gov/pubs2011/2011015.pdf.

Surowiecki, James. 2011. "Debt by Degrees." *The New Yorker*, November 21. Accessed December 14, 2015, http://www.newyorker.com/magazine/2011/11/21/debt-by-degrees

Train, Kenneth E. 2009. *Discrete Choice Methods with Simulation*, 2nd ed. New York: Cambridge University Press.

Turner, Sarah E. 2004. "Going to College and Finishing College: Explaining Different Educational Outcomes." In *College Choices: The Economics of Where to Go, When to Go, and How to Pay for It*, edited by Caroline M. Hoxby. Cambridge, Mass.: National Bureau of Economic Research.

Income and Access to Higher Education: Are High Quality Universities Becoming More or Less Elite? A Longitudinal Case Study of Admissions at UW-Madison

SARA E. DAHILL-BROWN, JOHN F. WITTE, AND BARBARA WOLFE

Has access to selective postsecondary schools expanded or contracted? Evaluating this question has proven a difficult task because data are limited, particularly with regard to family income. We complement previous work and provide a replicable model of institutional analysis. This paper presents a detailed, quantitative assessment of admissions at the University of Wisconsin-Madison, an elite flagship public university—the type that is supposed to offer excellent opportunities to students from all backgrounds. We use an innovative measure of family income to compare applicant, admissions, and enrollment trends for low-income and minority students from 1972 to 2007. The unique aspects of this study include the more reliable measure of income and the ability to look at the full process from applications, admissions, and matriculations (demand and supply), not generally available in national datasets.

Keywords: higher education, admission, college access, income, college application

Evidence suggests that access to higher education in the United States has beome more stratified in recent decades, with a growing concentration of wealthy students attending the most selective of colleges and access to the best institutions of higher learning increasingly constrained for low-income college hopefuls (Bailey and Dynarski 2011; Bowen, Kurzweil, and Tobin 2005; Carnevale and Rose 2004; Khadaroo 2008). Several hypotheses have been advanced to explain this broad phenomenon: that low-income students are underprepared academically (Haycock, Lynch, and Engle 2010); that low-income students are systematically "undermatching"—not applying to selective institutions for which they are qualified (Hoxby and Avery 2013); and that low-income students have made substantial gains in their academic preparation but that these gains pale in comparison with those made by high-income students, contributing to a disadvantage in the admissions processes at selective institutions (Bastedo and Jaquette 2011). Institutions of higher learning vary, however, even selective institutions, in the extent to which low-income students are represented in the student body (Leonhardt 2015). We believe that universities, systems, and researchers can benefit from investigating whether low-income students are missing from their applicant pools, likely to be excluded as a result of admissions policies, or failing to matriculate, and

Sara E. Dahill-Brown is assistant professor of politics and international affairs at Wake Forest University. **John F. Witte** is professor emeritus of public affairs and political science at the University of Wisconsin-Madison. **Barbara Wolfe** is professor of economics and population health sciences at the University of Wisconsin-Madison.

Direct correspondence to: Sara Dahill-Brown at dahillse@wfu.edu, Department of Politics and International Affairs, Wake Forest University, P.O. Box 7568, Winston-Salem, NC 27109; John F. Witte at witte@lafollette.wisc.edu, 7418 Cedar Creek Trail, Madison, WI 53717; Barbara Wolfe at bwolfe@wisc.edu, 204 Observatory Hill Office Bldg., 1225 Observatory Dr., Madison, WI 53706.

how access and representation at these different points of the college-going process has evolved over time. These questions of over-time change in the college-going process may be especially important to investigate at more selective four-year institutions because these institutions may also offer low-SES and underrepresented minority students the highest rates of return and the best prospects for economic mobility (Dale and Krueger 2002; Hoxby 1998, 2009; Zhang 2005).

However, these questions have historically been challenging to answer at micro levels, where they might provide actionable intelligence. Colleges and universities typically lack accurate data on the family income of applicants and either maintain income data only for the subset of their enrolled students who apply for financial aid or by surveying their students upon entry. Data from the Integrated Postsecondary Education System (IPEDS), which gathers records across institutions of higher learning, are similarly limited. The longitudinal surveys supported by the National Center for Education Statistics (NCES) include detailed family income data for the sample of youth in their surveys, and can therefore be used to address aggregate questions about access and attainment; these surveys, though, are administered to cohorts periodically and so will miss dynamics of over-time change and will not provide large enough samples for institution-specific analyses.

In this paper, we present a technique for using census data to generate an unbiased estimate of family income for all applicants. We demonstrate the utility of this measure by presenting a detailed trend analysis from 1972 to 2007 of the applicant pool and admissions process at the University of Wisconsin-Madison (UW-Madison.)

As one of the largest and most prominent elite public universities in the United States, a profile of access at UW-Madison may be of interest to higher education scholars and practitioners and residents of Wisconsin, but serves primarily to illustrate the utility of our measurement and its potential to support similar analyses at other colleges and universities. Using this measure, we are able to conclude that the proportional representation of those from the lowest income quintile among applicants changed little between 1972 and 2007 and that those from the second-lowest income quintile declined. Over the same period, the increase in representation of those from the top two income quintiles among applicants is notable, fueled in large part by applicants from outside Wisconsin. In the admission process, we find evidence of increasing consideration granted to economically disadvantaged applicants, though rather than expand the representation among admitted students, these considerations serve to counter the increasing weight of high school grades and standardized test scores, generating an admitted pool that closely reflects the applicants in terms of income distribution. Using yield rates to estimate the income distribution among enrollees between 1988 and 2007 suggests that some of the increase in applications from wealthy students is likely offset during matriculation.

STRATIFIED ACCESS TO POSTSECONDARY EDUCATION

In broad terms, studies demonstrate that college enrollment rates have risen for applicants from all backgrounds. A steadily increasing proportion of high school graduates have attended college since the end of World War II; approximately 68 percent of recent high school graduates enrolled in some form of higher education by the fall after graduation, up from 50 percent of recent high school graduates in 1975 (BLS 2015). On average, students are also graduating from high school at higher rates and are better prepared for college than in the past (Fry 2014; Bastedo and Jaquette 2011). Many selective colleges and universities have explicitly sought to increase enrollments among low-income and underrepresented minority students through affirmative action, targeted recruitment, state-sponsored merit aid, scholarships, and free-tuition programs (Alon and Tienda 2007, 487–88; Astin and Osegura 2004). At the same time, diversity training for faculty and tutoring services for students, among other institutional programs, have been implemented to support low-income, first-generation, and minority students on campus.

Persistent Challenges for Low-Income Students

Yet, even though total enrollment rates have risen both for children from low- and high-income families, large achievement and enrollment gaps persist between low-income students and their more advantaged peers as well as between African American, Hispanic, and white students (Terenzini, Cabrera, and Bernal 2001; Timpane and Hauptman 2004, Reardon and Galindo 2009; Snyder and Dillow 2012). Approximately 50 percent of high school graduates from the bottom income quintile enroll in two- or four-year postsecondary institutions in the year following their graduation—up from 35 percent in 1975—compared with upward of 80 percent for high school graduates from the top income quintile—up from 64 percent in 1975 (Khadaroo 2008; Snyder and Dillow 2012). This suggests a persistent overall enrollment gap of around 30 percentage points.

Postsecondary enrollment gains for children from low-income families also seem to have occurred primarily at two-year institutions, where these students are least likely to be successful (Engle and Tinto 2008; Pallais and Turner 2006). Therefore, although college-going has increased among all groups, recent studies suggest the gaps in enrollment at high quality four-year schools between the highest and lowest income groups may actually have also increased (Bailey and Dynarski 2011; Ellwood and Kane 2005; Kane 2003).

In what is, perhaps, the most comprehensive study to date, Alexander Astin and Leticia Oseguera (2004) study access to the top 10 percent of institutions of higher learning from 1985 to 2000, which is determined by the mean SAT score of the institutions' entering freshman classes in 1999. The authors use data from the Cooperative Institutional Research Program's (CIRP) entering Freshman Survey, an annual instrument administered for four decades. At the beginning of each school year, about "400,000 freshmen from more than 700 institutions complete a comprehensive questionnaire that asks about basic demographic and biographical information, values, self-concept, attitudes, and educational plans" (2004, 324). The authors find that over this interval, the income level of entering freshman in these top-tier colleges has increased but are unable to identify whether the change can be tied to applicants' self-selection or to shifting admissions preferences.

Philippe Belley and Lance Lochner (2007) and Martha Bailey and Susan Dynarski (2011) use the National Longitudinal Study of Youth (NLSY) cohorts drawn in 1979 and 1997, and find that income effects on the probability of college attendance increased substantially between the two cohorts. Bailey and Dynarski also find that the probability of attending college increased across all quintiles but that the greatest increase was in the highest quintiles. Large increases in college attendance among females in the highest quartile accounted for much of the difference.[1] Using the Mellon Foundation's College and Beyond data, William Bowen, Martin Kurzweil, and Eugene Tobin estimate that students in the bottom quartile of family income make up only 11 percent of enrollments at elite colleges (2005, 98). Analyzing IPEDS data, Kati Haycock and Danette Gerald find that even as the proportion of college enrollees receiving Pell Grants increased between 1992 and 2003, the proportion of students receiving Pell Grants at flagship public universities had fallen (2006, 7).

Looking Beyond Direct Effects of Income

Many reasons have been proffered to explain this stratification. First is that low-income students are underprepared academically by a floundering public school system, though even those who note this emphasize that well-prepared low-income students are nonetheless underrepresented among college freshman (Haycock, Lynch, and Engle 2010). Second, although many high school students are applying to more universities as they face greater competition (Clinedinst, Hurley, and Hawkins 2011; Pryor et al. 2007), Caroline Hoxby and Christopher Avery (2013) find that the vast majority of high-achieving low-income high school students do not apply to any selective,

---

1. These two studies also address measures of persistence and completion of college by family income at baseline or when the potential student was between fifteen and eighteen.

four-year institutions and are thus "undermatching." Failing to adequately match economically disadvantaged students with appropriately rigorous postsecondary schools has broad societal and economic consequences (Roderick, Coca, and Nagaoka 2011).

Third, as the number of capable applicants has skyrocketed, institutional capacity at elite colleges and universities has not grown apace, and competition for limited seats has grown fiercer (Karabel 2005; Lemann 1999; see also Alon and Tienda 2007, 489). Students from low-income families often find themselves with fewer opportunities to practice for entrance exams, and are less prepared to write essays and solicit recommendations. Many argue that increased reliance on standardized tests for admissions decisions is "incompatible with the goal of increasing the representation of people of color or poor people" (Zwick 2007, 422; Rooney 1998).[2] Measures of academic merit are likely to reflect investments by the family including special SAT (originally Scholastic Achievement Test) and ACT (originally American College Testing) prep courses, the ability to choose better schools that offer more AP (Advanced Placement) courses, hire tutors, a richer home environment in terms of reading materials, and attendance at special summer programs. And though these measures predict potential college success (Bridgeman, Pollack, and Burton 2004; Burton and Ramist 2001; see also Zwick 2007, 421), they may also mask true potential (Bowen, Bok, and Shulman 1998). Michael Bastedo and Ozan Jaquette (2011) find that even though low-income students have increased their academic preparedness for college on average, high-income students have managed to make larger academic gains, preserving their advantage.

Institutional Analyses and Difficulties in Measuring Applicant Family Income

In addition to the multiple explanations offered for the increased stratification of postsecondary education, it is also important to acknowledge the wide variation across institutions of higher learning, even among selective institutions, in the extent to which low-income students are represented in the student body; more than 30 percent of enrolled students receive Pell Grants at three campuses in the University of California system (Leonhardt 2015). Because different levels of and explanations for the underrepresentation of low-income students would suggest different action steps for colleges and universities, we believe that universities, systems, and researchers would benefit from conducting close case studies of access at their own institutions. They should investigate whether low-income students are missing from their applicant pools, likely to be excluded as a result of admissions policies, or failing to matriculate once admitted, and how access and representation at these different points of the college-going process has evolved over time. However, studies of income effects on access to elite postsecondary institutions are characterized by a number of notable data limitations.

First, the longitudinal surveys supported by NCES (such as NLSY and National Education Longitudinal Survey, or NELS) cannot be easily adapted for institutional analyses. They include detailed, validated, family income data for the nationally representative samples of youth included their surveys, and can be used to address aggregate questions about access from application to attainment, but would not include large enough samples attending specific institutions. Further, because the surveys are administered irregularly, they do not allow for close tracking of over-time changes and should not be substituted for detailed trend data (Kane 2003, 89; Alon and Tienda 2007, 488).

Second, colleges and universities typically lack accurate data on the family income of applicants and either maintain only income data for the subset of their enrolled students who apply for financial aid or that supplied by surveying their students on entry. The Free Application for Federal Student Aid requires extensive data on family's income and assets, but

---

2. Philippe Belley and Lance Lochner (2007) include the AFQT score, a measure of IQ in their analysis, rather than score on the SAT or ACT. They find those in higher quartiles of the AFQT are more likely to attend college by age twenty but that the pattern does not appear to steepen over time.

these data are only available for those who request such aid. This limits the population that can be studied to enrolled students who request financial aid. In the 1999–2000 school year, for example, approximately one-third of students attending college full time failed to apply for financial aid, and approximately 850,000 who failed to apply would likely have been Pell eligible (King 2004). In addition, these applications have only been used since 1992, limiting the period that could be covered for historical analysis. Data from the IPEDS, which gathers records across institutions of higher learning, are similarly limited.

Surveys used to supplement these institutional sources of data are also limited instruments for measuring student economic status, income levels, and financial aid receipts. The most common sources for supplementing measures of family income are student responses to survey questions administered during ACT and SAT examinations as well as during the CIRP Freshmen survey. For a number of reasons, these responses can be woefully, sometimes systematically, inaccurate; most students simply do not have accurate information on family income and wealth (Olivas 1986; Trusheim 1994; Smith and McCann 1998; Gonyea 2005). To enable in depth institutional analyses, a new approach is needed.

OUR STUDY

We consider the issue of access to higher education, particularly for low-income students, by presenting a detailed analysis of admissions at UW-Madison, a major public university and the kind of school that is supposed to offer excellent educational opportunities to students from all backgrounds—over more than three decades.

Our data, though limited to one institution, offer several contributions to the existing body of scholarship on access to high quality higher education. First, we take a unique approach to obtain an unbiased measure of family income for more than 90 percent of applicants in the sample. This measure allows us to investigate the correlation between income and merit and to compare the influence of low-income status with that of minority status on admission. Second, the data are longitudinal and cover a substantial period during which higher education and the national economy experienced dramatic changes, and therefore facilitate not just measurement of change between two points in time, but the description of dynamics. Third, detailed data are available for applicants, as well as admitted students.

Measuring Applicant Income Through Matching

Obtaining a valid, reliable measure of applicant family income is at the center of our analysis. We use U.S. Census data at the block level to estimate family income for all applicants to UW-Madison from 1972 through 2007 who are residents of the United States and report a valid address in their application file. These measures are based upon reported income data for approximately 1,200 individuals (600 households) at the census block level. With our large sample of applicants, and this smallest of the census units, this method promises to estimate family income imperfectly but with less bias and greater reliability than student self-reports (Olivas 1986). When this measure of applicant income is included in regression models, coefficients theoretically reflect the combined effect of contextual (neighborhood) and individual-level income factors, but should serve as a more valid method for drawing inferences about income than self-reports (on using aggregate data as a proxy, see Geronimus, Bound, and Neidert 1996; Smith, Ben-Shiomo, and Hart 1999). For each applicant with a home residence in the fifty states, we used the Applied Population Lab at UW-Madison to match prospective students' home addresses as reported on their initial application to a census block.[3] Blocks are the smallest geographic and population group available from the census. They are "bounded on all sides by visible features, such as streets, roads, streams, and railroad tracks, and by nonvisible boundaries, such as selected property lines and city, township, school district, and county limits and . . . roads. Generally, census blocks are small in area" (U.S. Census Bureau 2010).

---

3. Addresses were provided to the population lab with a randomly generated ID to protect privacy.

They are thus small geographic units within census tracts, which are designed to be homogeneous.[4]

Once a student had been matched to a particular census block, we merged into our original applicant files, median family income for that block.[5] We use the 1980, 1990, and 2000 censuses. Applicants between 1972 and 1980 are matched only to the 1980 data. Applicants between 1981 and 1989 are matched to their census block for both the 1980 and 1990 Census data. We match 1990 applicants only to the 1990 Census. Applicants between 1991 and 1999, are matched to both 1990 and 2000 data, and applicants from 2000 on are matched only to the 2000 data. We convert all incomes into 2009 dollars and interpolate incomes for those with two block matches (applicants from 1981 to 1989 and from 1991 to 1999). We are able to match more than 90 percent of all U.S. resident applicants by this procedure. That is, we obtain an imputed measure of family income for more than 90 percent of all U.S. applicants to UW-Madison from 1972 to 2007 based on census block data.[6] The lowest percentage of matches occurred in the first year, 1972 and again in 1987, for which we matched 87 percent of the applicants. Once applicants are matched to census block income, geographic information is stripped from the dataset to protect the privacy of the applicants. We preserve an indicator identifying residence status: out-of-state residents face the highest rates of tuition and until December of 2012 could make up no more than 25 percent of new freshmen at UW-Madison. Minnesota residents are not counted as out-of-state residents and pay tuition that is only slightly higher than Wisconsin residents. For this reason, we analyze applicants as a total population but control for residency status.[7]

ANALYSIS

Descriptive indicators in this analysis relate to the size, geographic composition, absolute and relative income, racial and ethnic diversity, and level of academic preparation of the applicant pool over three decades. We believe this descriptive project is an important one. We cannot understand the dynamics that contribute to inclusion or exclusion, nor assess the impact of admissions policies on access for disadvantaged students without first identifying the students who choose to apply in the first place. We estimate logistic regressions to identify the effects of these characteristics on admission.

Our research focuses on applicants to a single institution of higher learning, but one that increasingly draws students from throughout the United States. Figure 1 illustrates the changing residency patterns of applicants from 1972 to 2007. Three trends are worth noting. First, the proportion of applicants from Wisconsin has declined—from approximately 70 percent in 1972 to just over 40 percent in

---

4. Census tracts are themselves defined as "small, relatively permanent statistical subdivisions of a county or equivalent entity that are updated by local participants prior to each decennial census as part of the Census Bureau's Participant Statistical Areas Program," population sizes ranging from 1,200 to 8,000 (U.S. Census Bureau 2010).

5. Data on income in 1999 are derived from answers to long-form questionnaire items 31 and 32, which were asked of a sample of the population fifteen years old and older. Total income is the sum of the amounts reported separately for wage or salary income; net self-employment income; interest, dividends, or net rental or royalty income or income from estates and trusts; social security or railroad retirement income; Supplemental Security Income (SSI); public assistance or welfare payments; retirement, survivor, or disability pensions; and all other income. See: http://www.census.gov/prod/cen2000/phc-2-a.pdf (accessed February 17, 2015).

6. Yearly matching rates and all other results are available on request in a document containing supplementary tables that correspond with the analysis, figures, and discussion in this paper.

7. Even in the most recent years of our study, the students from states other than Wisconsin and Minnesota are distributed well across the country, with the notable exception of Illinois, who apply in large numbers each year and regularly make up 15 percent of the applicant pool. At their peak presence, applicants from relatively wealthy states like New York and California make up only 5.4 and 3.7 percent of the applicant pool respectively.

Figure 1. Total Applicants and Proportion by Residence, 1972–2007

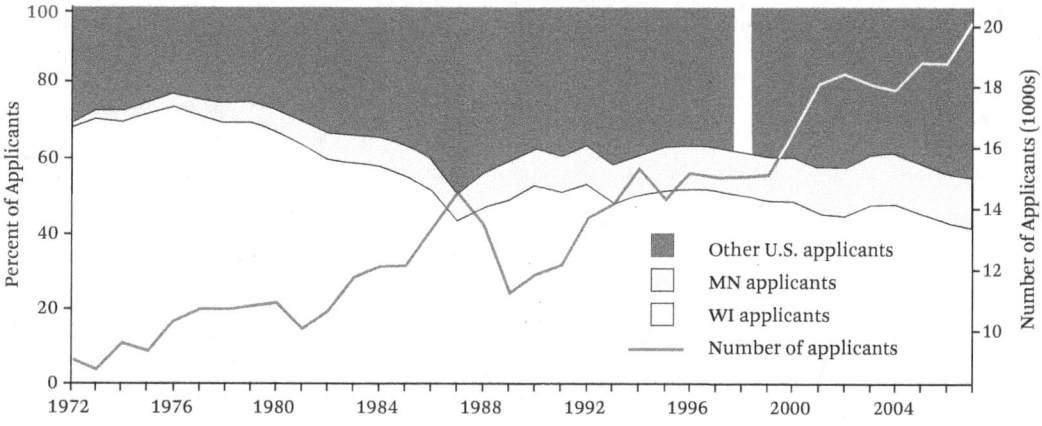

Source: Authors' compilation.

2007. Second, as at other colleges and universities, the increase in the total number of applicants for a roughly steady number of first-year spaces has been considerable, from just over nine thousand in 1972 to just over twenty thousand in 2007. Third, the rising number of applicants results primarily from an increase in applications from out-of-state students. This third factor mirrors other findings (Hoxby 2009) suggesting that privileged students now apply broadly to increase their odds of admission to at least one high quality institution.

Income Among Applicants

Applicant median family income (in 2009 U.S. dollars) appears to have increased in real terms over the thirty-six years of our study across all residency groups (figure 2). However, differences by residency are substantial and the gap between groups is widening. The estimated median income for applicants from Wisconsin increased by 20 percent between 1972 and 2007, from $67,560 to $81,097. In contrast, the median income of Minnesota applicants increased by 35 percent, from $80,112 to $108,335 and by 51 percent for out-of-state residents, from $86,955 to $131,106. This reflects, in part, a slower rate of real income growth in Wisconsin than in Minnesota and the nation as a whole.

Absolute real income therefore should not be our only metric for assessing change. Trends in real income may differ from those revealed by relative income, the ratio of applicant median family income to the relevant populations' median family income. We identify the comparisons by computing a median family income from census data for Wisconsin, Minnesota, and other U.S. states. For each of these three geographies, to identify the most accurate comparison group, we compute the median income for families that include at least one child between the ages of fifteen and twenty-four, and in which the head of household is younger than sixty-five. Excluding childless homes, and homes in which heads of households are sixty-five or older produces higher estimates of the median family income than when these two groups are included. We were unable to condition on these factors when imputing income for applicants in census blocks, suggesting that our estimate of family income for applicants may be slightly biased down, though residential sorting should make this small. We compare applicants with this median family income based on their reported state of residence, and plot those ratios over time in figure 3. Combined, these constraints yield a comparison with the potential to underestimate relative income of the applicant pool, providing a conservative estimate of disparities between applicants and the universe of possible applicants.

The median income of applicants from Wisconsin closely reflects the median family income for the state; the relative ratio ranges from a minimum of 0.97 in 1981 to a high of

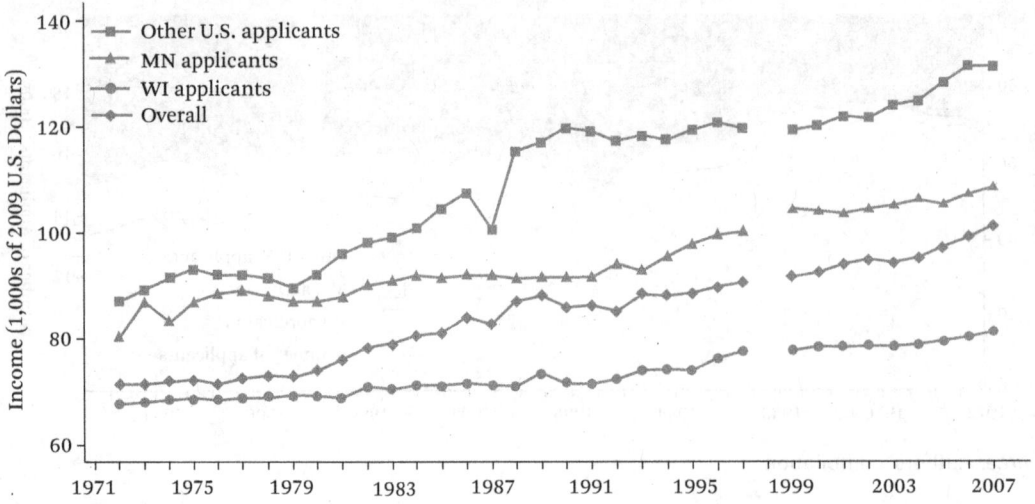

Figure 2. Real Median Family Income of Applicants, 1972–2007 (2009 dollars)

Source: Authors' compilation.

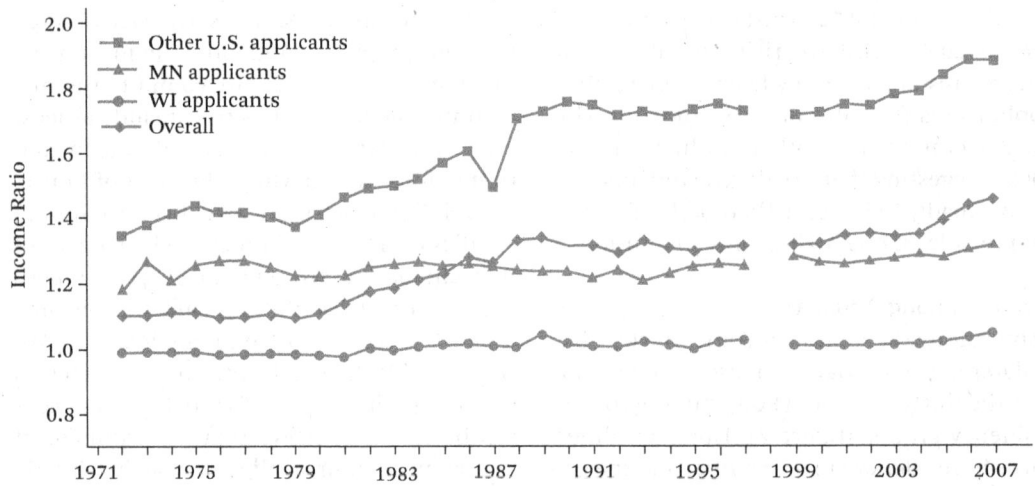

Figure 3. Family Income of Applicants to State Median Income, 1972–2007 (2009 dollars)

Source: Authors' compilation.

1.05 in 2007. The median income of applicants in Minnesota is slightly higher than for the state; the relative ratio ranges from a minimum of 1.18 in 1972 to a maximum of 1.32 in 2007. By this measure, Wisconsin and Minnesota applicants, relative to the population in their states, have remained at similar income levels over the period of study, using calculated median family income as the comparison. On the other hand, out-of-state applicants have a much higher relative median income. The median applicant from other states comes from families earning at least 1.35 times the median family income in the United States in 1972, and by 2007 the median relative income had risen to nearly twice the national median (a ratio of 1.88). More and more out-of-state applicants seem to come from a higher income strata, though relative median income for both Minnesota and Wisconsin applicants were at maximum values in the last year of our data.

Several recent reports and studies have doc-

Figure 4. All Applicants by Family Income Quintile, 1972–2007

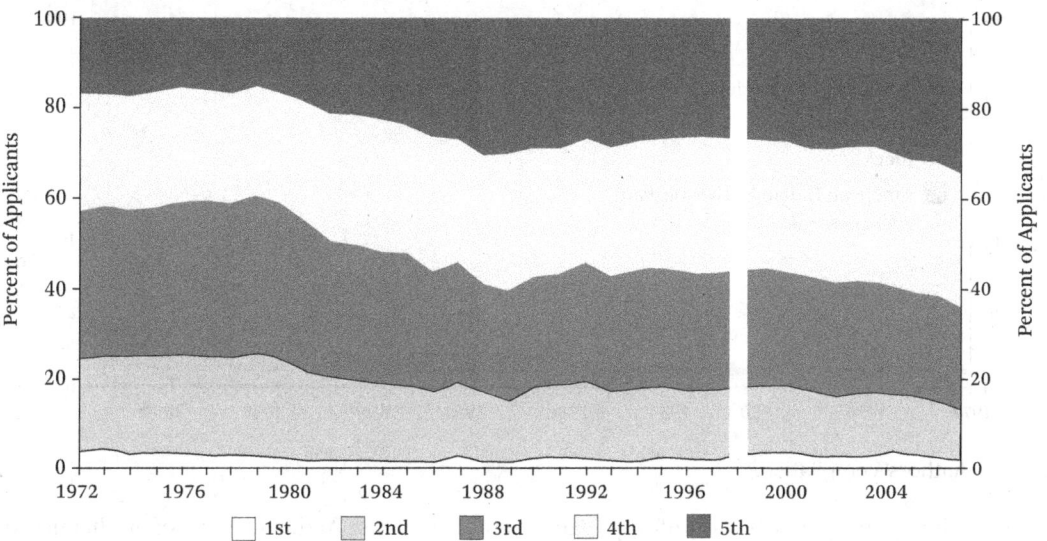

Source: Authors' compilation.

umented an increase in residential segregation by income (Bischoff and Reardon 2014; Fry and Taylor 2012). Because this increased sorting suggests that our measure of applicant income is likely to be more precise in the later years of our study, but noisier early on, we also investigate the distribution of applicant family income by treating the data as a categorical indicator. Although this produces an estimate that is less precise and may not perfectly correct for segregation, it should be a more consistent operationalization over time. In figure 4, we present the proportion of UW-Madison applicants by income quintiles. As with relative income, quintile determinations are made by comparing the student's estimated family income with the family income distribution for households that include at least one child between fifteen and twenty-four and in which the head of household is sixty-five or younger. Again, this has the potential effect of understating the representation of applicants from high-income groups and overstating the representation of low-income applicants.

This measure suggests that only a tiny proportion of applicants have ever come from the bottom income quintile; averaging 2.9 percent across years, peaking at 4.9 percent during 1973 and reaching a low point of 1.8 in 1988. In the 1970s and 1980s, applicants appear to have come primarily from middle-income families, and their representation has declined dramatically. Applicants from the second-lowest income quintile constituted 20 percent or more of the applicant pool until 1982, and by the last year of the study only 11.5 percent. Applicants from the middle quintile similarly declined from 30 percent or more through 1983 to 22.4 percent by 2007, still a representation greater than the percentage of the population. Conversely, applicants from the top two income quintiles increased from 42.6 to 64.1 percent, the majority of that increase occurring at the very top of the income distribution. In every year from 1983 onward, the majority of applicants to this public university come from families in the top two quintiles of the income distribution. Both the stagnant representation of the lowest-income applicants and the declining representation of middle-income applicants are striking.

Figure 4 must be interpreted with an eye toward figure 1. Both the Minnesota and out-of-state applicant pools are weighted much more heavily toward the top two income quintiles than that for Wisconsin residents. The distribution of in-state applicants is different than the distribution for these groups, and Wisconsin resident applicants must be the majority of the incoming freshman classes. None-

Figure 5. Proportion of Applicants by Race and Ethnicity, 1972–2007

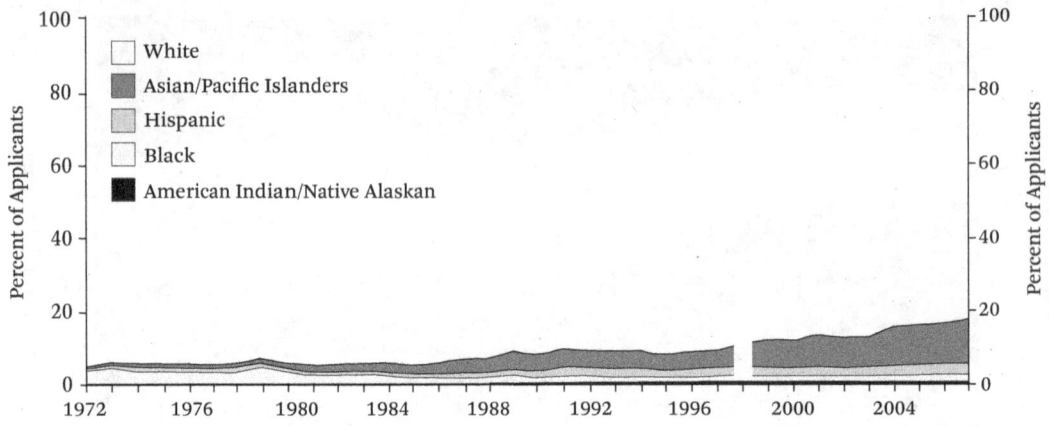

Source: Authors' compilation.

theless, the in-state distribution of applicant income yields a more muted, but similar story to the one figure 4 suggests. Representation of the top two income quintiles has increased among in-state applicants from 31.3 to 39.5 percent. The middle income quintile is consistently overrepresented, upward of 35 percent of Wisconsin applicants coming from this group in all but a few years, though this groups' presence is no longer the 40 percent it was the early years of the series.

The bottom two quintiles are substantially underrepresented even for the in-state group. In 1972, 4.274 percent of applicants from Wisconsin came from the lowest income quintile. In 2007, after rising briefly in the early 2000s, this proportion was essentially unchanged: 4.0 percent of Wisconsin applicants—just 335 applicants—were from the lowest income quintile. Applicants from the second-lowest income quintile declined steadily from 25.9 percent in 1972 to 20.7 percent in 2007. By 2007, students from the poorest 40 percent of families in the state had declined to less than 25 percent.

Racial and Ethnic Diversity and Income

To the extent that membership in a historically underrepresented minority group correlates with lower levels of family income, the racial composition of UW-Madison applicants over time is relevant to our question of how access has evolved; we describe the diversity of the applicant pool below. Figure 5 shows a considerable increase in the diversity of applicants to the university over the thirty-six years of this study. However, that increase is almost entirely due to a sharp rise in the proportion of applicants who identify as Asian. The proportion of Hispanics in the applicant pool increases some from 0.5 to 3.0 percent. For Native Americans, representation remains very small, shifting from 0.2 percent to 0.5 percent. The proportion of the African American applicants actually declines. In 1972, 356 African Americans sought admission, 3.9 percent of the pool. In 2007, despite the applicant pool having more than doubled, the number was 508, just 2.5 percent of the total. Unlike median family income, minorities are not better represented among applicants.

Comparing the applicants coming from families in Wisconsin with demographics for the state's college-age population (fifteen to twenty-five), it is possible to more critically assess the racial and ethnic composition of the applicant pool. We find a stark discrepancy that grows over time. In 1972, 2.3 percent of applicants residing in Wisconsin identified as black, versus 3.4 percent of the fifteen to twenty-five population. By 2007, 7.8 percent of that population identified as black, but only 3.1 percent of Wisconsin applicants did. The magnitude by which African Americans are underrepresented has grown, which is especially striking given rising high school graduation rates for African American students in Wisconsin during these years (Snyder and Dillow 2012).

Overlap between membership in an underrepresented minority and low-income status is also less than it was in the 1970s. (We investigated this overlap by pooling applicants in five-year increments to compensate for small sample sizes). From 1972 through 1976, 39.1 percent of black applicants and 37.5 percent of Hispanic applicants were in the lowest quintile of the income distribution. From 2002 to 2007, only 22.2 percent of black applicants and 7.0 percent of Hispanic applicants were. Racial and ethnic diversity appears to be an increasingly poor proxy for economic disadvantage.

Academic Achievement and Income

Unsurprisingly, we also find that the applicant pool has become increasingly academically competitive. The average SAT score of applicants rose from 1082 to 1274, though the proportion of applicants taking the SAT declined from 43.4 to 33.1 percent. Perhaps more impressively, the average ACT score of applicants has also steadily risen from 23.6 to 27.3 even as the percentage of applicants who report taking the ACT increased from 38.7 to 81.0. Average high school rank among applicants also climbed from 107.8 to 65.9, though the percentage of students reporting a high school rank declined from 95.7 to 64.1.

Using simple, bivariate regression predicting ACT from estimated family income, we find a small, positive relationship in the applicant pool between scores on admissions tests and our estimate of family income. Higher scores are related to higher family incomes; the two are statistically significantly associated with one another in each year from 1972 through 2007. However, the relationship between the two measures within the population of applicants is quite small in the early years of the data; Pearson's correlation coefficient only reaches 0.087 in 1972 and does not consistently exceed 0.100 until after 1997. The size of the correlation coefficient has strengthened, suggesting a progressively tighter relationship between income and measures of academic merit. The correlation coefficient between ACT and income reaches 0.220 by 2007; this is unlikely to be an artifact of increased rates of ACT test-taking given that the percentage of applicants taking the ACT does not fluctuate substantially after 1990. The applicant pool to this public university is, without question, increasingly elite in terms of academic merit. Like other high-quality institutions, UW-Madison now confronts a glut of highly qualified applicants for whom it does not have adequate space, and those students with the highest incomes are increasingly likely to also be better qualified according to these measures of merit.

Modeling Admission During Increasing Selectivity: 1972 to 2007

We demonstrate that the applicant pool has doubled in size, primarily as a result of increased demand from outside Wisconsin. Regardless of residency, the proportion of the lowest-income students in the applicant pool has remained stagnant while that of middle-income applicants has declined. The racial and ethnic diversity of the applicant pool has increased, but not with regard to the most disadvantaged group, African Americans. Status as an underrepresented minority is increasingly unlikely to be associated with membership in the lowest income quintiles. The level of academic merit in the applicant pool has increased, as merit seems to have become more closely linked with economic status. Ultimately, admission officials must make decisions based on the applications they receive, and they do not receive many from low-income students. But perhaps the pool of admitted students is more representative than the pool of applicants. Some previous work casts doubt on this hypothesis, showing that income and related factors like legacy preference may serve to further limit access for low-income and underrepresented groups (Kahlenberg 2010).

The first important trend is a predictable but dramatic increase in selectivity. Admission to UW-Madison has become much more competitive. Except for in 1975 and 1976, through the mid-1980s, nearly 90 percent of those who applied were admitted. However, since the mid-1980s, the proportion of applicants admitted has declined steadily, 63.6 percent for the final year in our data. This is undoubtedly explained by the dramatic increase in applicants, which has far outstripped space available for first-year students.

To understand how income, achievement,

Figure 6. Predicted Probability of Admission by Income Quintile, Selected Years

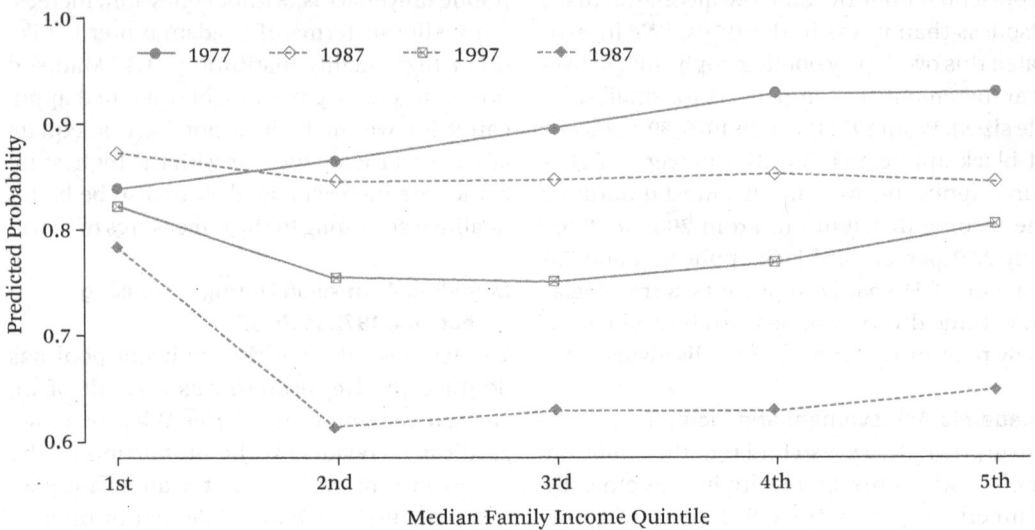

Source: Authors' compilation.

race, and other individual-level variables affect the admission process in this increasingly competitive environment, we estimate a series of logistic regressions, one for each year, in which acceptance is the dependent variable. That is, we model the following equation for each year and compare effects across applicant cohorts:

$$A_i = \beta Y_i + \gamma L_i + \delta P_i + \lambda X_i + \alpha + \varepsilon$$

where A is acceptance of individual i modeled as a function of that individual's characteristics. Y indicates a vector of dummy variables denoting family income quintile (the middle income quintile serves as the reference category in models); L indicates a vector of dummy variables denoting the applicant's geographic location (Wisconsin, Minnesota, or other); P represents a vector of measures describing an applicant's performance as captured by ACT and SAT scores, and high school rank; X describes a vector of other characteristics including age, gender, race-ethnicity; and α represents the constant. β, γ, δ and λ indicate the effects for each of these variables and are estimated separately for each year. Pseudo R squareds suggest models explain roughly 30 percent of the variance in acceptance in most years. For ease of interpretation and to facilitate cross-year comparisons, we present effects in terms of changes in probability of admission.

Income Effects

Is it more or less difficult now for low- and middle-income applicants to gain admission to UW-Madison? We find that the effect of applicant income on admission, after controlling for other individual-level factors, has changed considerably over time. Figure 6 illustrates the differences in the probability of acceptance by the income quintile for selected years. In the early period, holding all other variables constant, applicants from the lower and middle income quintiles are less likely to be admitted, and those from the upper quintiles are more likely. These effects are statistically significant only in some years and are generally small, though moving from the poorest to the most elite income quintile is occasionally substantial, from 83 percent to 93 percent probability of admission in 1977. In the middle years of our series, illustrated by 1987, the effect of applicant income quintile dissipates; membership in the lowest and highest income quintiles does not produce significantly different probabilities of admission relative to applicants from the middle quintile. In later years, from the mid-1990s on, applicants in the low-

Figure 7. Effect of Membership in the First Income Quintile Versus the Fifth, 1972–2007

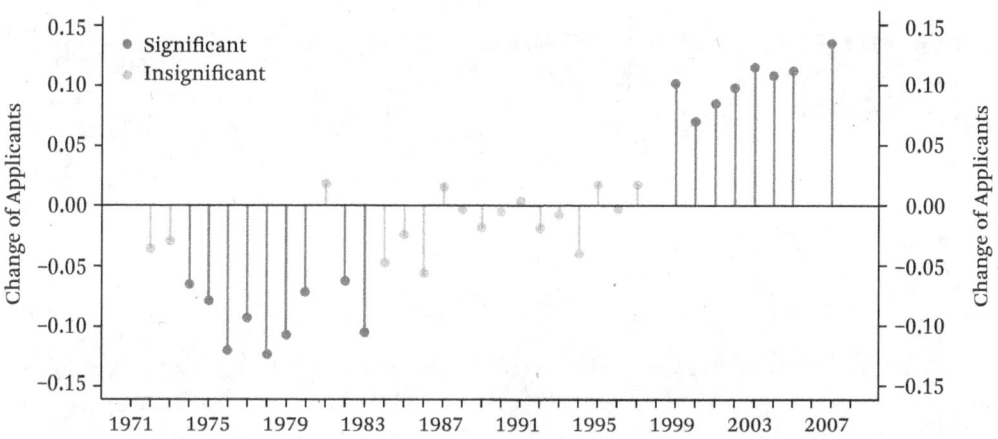

Source: Authors' compilation.

est income quintile are statistically significantly more likely to obtain admission relative to applicants from other income quintiles. This effect is large, consistent, and represents an increase in the probability of admission of between 10 and 15 percentage points, depending on the comparison quintile.

However, from 2004 to 2007, students in the highest income group were also statistically significantly more likely to obtain admission than those from the middle quintiles, though the effect was modest. These models suggest that applicants from both the lowest and highest income groups are somewhat more likely to be accepted, holding all other measures constant. In considering how this might affect access, we emphasize that applicants from the highest income quintile are far more numerous than those from the lowest.

Figure 7 illustrates further the difference in the probabilities of admission for students from the first (lowest) to the fifth (highest) income quintiles, again controlling for other observed characteristics. This figure presents the ratio of admissions for the lowest and highest quintiles. It is apparent that in the earliest years, that difference favored those in the highest quintile of the U.S. population for admission. From 1984 to 1997, differences are not significant between the lowest and highest income quintiles. However, since 1999, the advantages of the poorest students in gaining acceptance are considerable, compared with those from the richest households. Holding other factors constant, applicants from the bottom income quintile are significantly less likely than those from the top to earn admission in the early years of the data series and significantly more likely in the later years.

We find in this analysis that access for the lowest-income students does not appear to be explicitly limited at UW-Madison as a result of the admission process. In support of these results, the median family income for the rejected and admitted groups of students is roughly equivalent in most years and the distribution of incomes for admitted students (see figure 8) is nearly identical to that for applicants.

We also used our models to test whether traditionally underrepresented minority status is significant in the admissions process. As was true of low-income students, African American and Hispanic students do not apply in large numbers, but are statistically significantly more likely to be admitted when they do, in the later years of the study period. Holding all other factors constant, including income, the change in predicted probability of admission for applicants from these groups is significant and substantial from 1986 onward, as illustrated by figure 9. This effect manifests much earlier than the effect for the lowest-income applicants, and the magnitude is generally

Figure 8. All Admitted Students by Family Income Quintile, 1972–2007

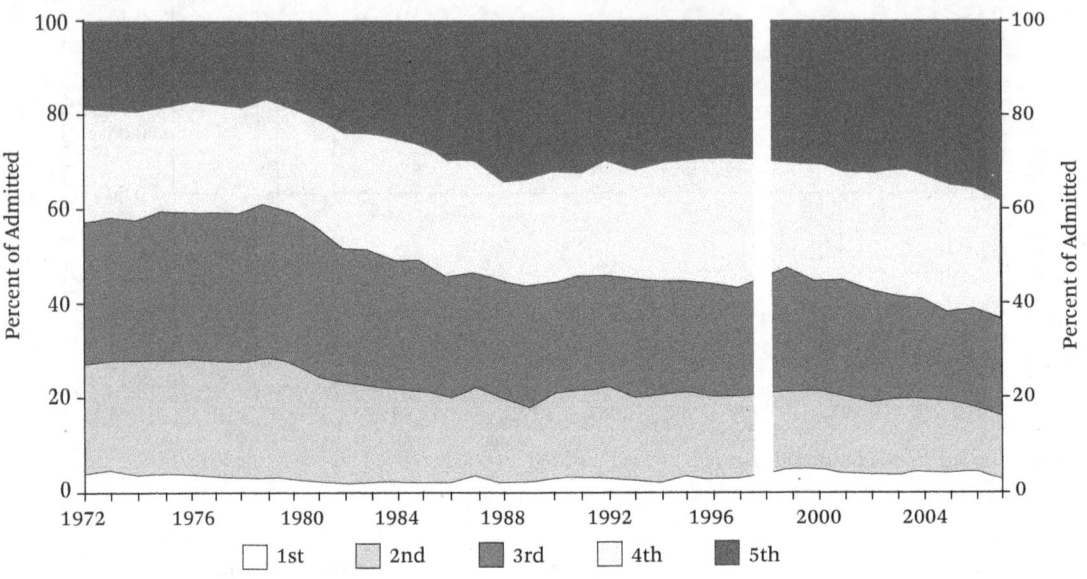

Source: Authors' compilation.

Figure 9. Effect of Identification as African American, 1972–2007

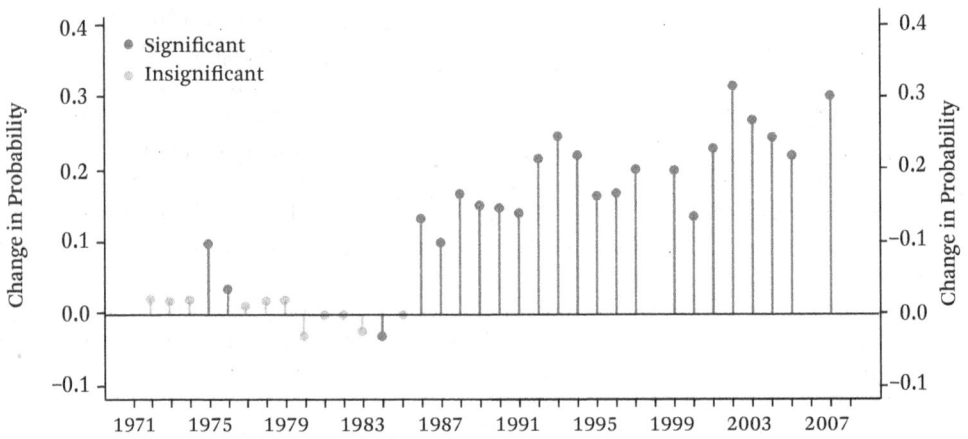

Source: Authors' compilation.

larger. The change in predicted probability of admission ranges between 0.15 and 0.30 in most years. As noted, the decreasing overlap between membership in a disadvantaged minority group and low-income status means that any admissions preference that improves access based on one category of demographic membership is no longer as likely to also improve access based on the other.

Academic Merit Effects

With the exception of the last few years of our series, which saw a small but significant increase, stratification of access by income or race-ethnicity does not appear to be increasing as a result of direct income effects on admissions decisions. However, we cannot assert that the admissions process does not privilege wealthier applicants, given the well-docu-

Figure 10. Predicted Probability of Admission, 1972 and 2007

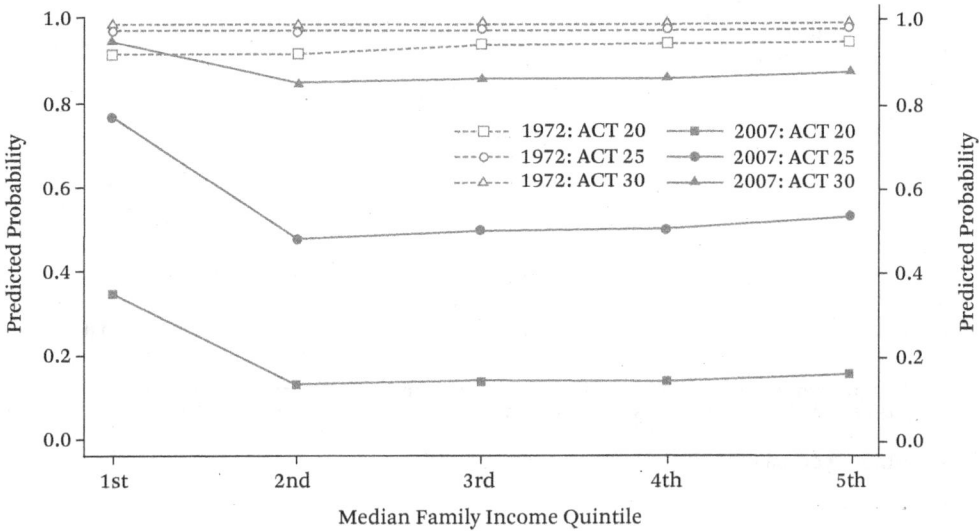

Source: Authors' compilation.

mented, positive relationship between family income and academic performance, the increase in reliance on test scores by high-quality four-year colleges and universities, and the significant effect of membership in the highest income quintile in the last years of our admission data. During the same period, when the negative effects of membership in the lowest income quintile disappeared and then reversed, the effect of achievement measures on the probability of acceptance increased. Our clearest evidence for that is presented in figure 10, which contrasts the probability of admission for the first and last years in the study: 1972 and 2007. The probabilities are broken down by income quintile (as in figure 7), but also by the student's score on the ACT admissions test. Neither income nor ACT score has a substantial effect on admission in 1972. Going from an ACT score of 20 to 30 improves the chances of admission by less than 10 percentage points.

However, by 2007, the admissions process changes considerably. The effect of applicant test score in our models is substantial and statistically significant, students across all income groups having a greater chance of acceptance as test scores increase. The difference in the predicted probability of admission, holding all other variables at their model means, jumps from less than 15 to 87 percent, more than 70 percentage points for students scoring 30 on the ACT over those scoring 20 (holding all other variables at model means). A comparison of the effect of a 10 point increase in ACT score (from 20 to 30) is plotted in figure 11.

The increase in the weight of academic merit is dramatic, and the rise of standardized test scores as the primary factor determining acceptance roughly corresponds with the beginning of significant effects for low-income and minority students. Given both this increasing emphasis on college entrance exams and the steadily rising correlation between test scores and family income, considering low-income and minority status during admission may have become necessary to prevent access from being further constrained. On the other hand, the relationship between income, test scores, and admission is not entirely clear. The applicant pool as whole is academically elite. This may result from low-achieving high school students opting out of the application process. If those who opt out are also disproportionately members of the lowest income quintile, then we are unlikely to see a strong relationship between income and achievement within the applicant pool. Similarly, possible selection dynamics make it unclear whether the increasing correlation between income and

Figure 11. Effect of ACT Score Change from 20 to 30, 1972–2007

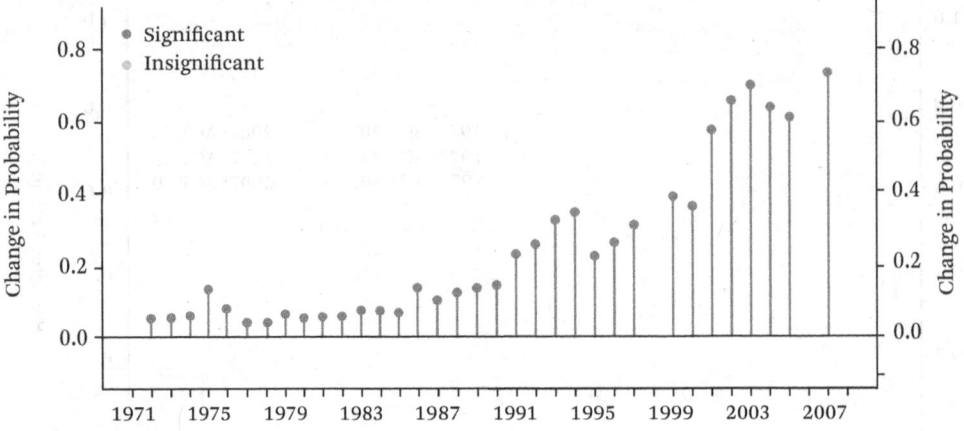

Source: Authors' compilation.

ACT signals an intensifying relationship between income and precollege achievement, or is simply a by-product of greater participation in ACT testing among applicants. Because the correlation between income and ACT increases well after the initial increase in rates of ACT taking, we believe that the first explanation, a closer relationship between precollege achievement and family income is more likely.

Estimating Income Distribution of Enrolled Students

We conduct one final analysis to estimate how the distribution of income among applicants and admitted students is likely to translate into the distribution of income among enrollees. Although we are unable to track applicants across the entire period to matriculation, UW-Madison has routinely published yield rates based on residency back to 1989. Using these yield rates, and a breakdown of the income distribution of admitted students by residency, we estimated the distribution of income among enrollees (see figure 12). Because yield rates are higher for Wisconsin residents (typically 60 to 65 percent versus 40 to 45 for Minnesota residents and 20 to 25 percent for residents of other states), the estimated income distribution for enrollees that emerges is less skewed than the distribution for either applicants or admitted students. However, it still suggests that well over 50 percent of enrollees are likely to be from the top two quintiles. This figure further suggests that the narrowing of access for those from the third quintile of family income may be less of a concern at UW-Madison than the application or admission data suggest but that access may have narrowed for those from the second income quintile and expanded only marginally for those from the lowest part of the distribution. Yields are likely to be somewhat higher for students from the lowest income quintiles, but even a 100 percent yield of admitted applicants from the bottom two income quintiles of our sample would only mean that they composed 31.8 percent of newly enrolled freshman in 2007.[8]

DISCUSSION AND CONCLUSIONS

A major advantage of this study is that we analyze the entire admissions process from application to admission to enrollment and do so over several decades. That is seldom the case with national databases such as NLSY, NELS, or High School and Beyond. Many of our insights flow from describing this process over many years. The picture that emerges from this analysis suggests a slow but steady accumulation of opportunities for students at the top of the income distribution, a small decrease in

---

8. The most recent of these reports are available at https://apir.wisc.edu/students-admissions.htm (accessed December 14, 2015).

Figure 12. Enrollees by Family Income (Estimated), 1989–2007

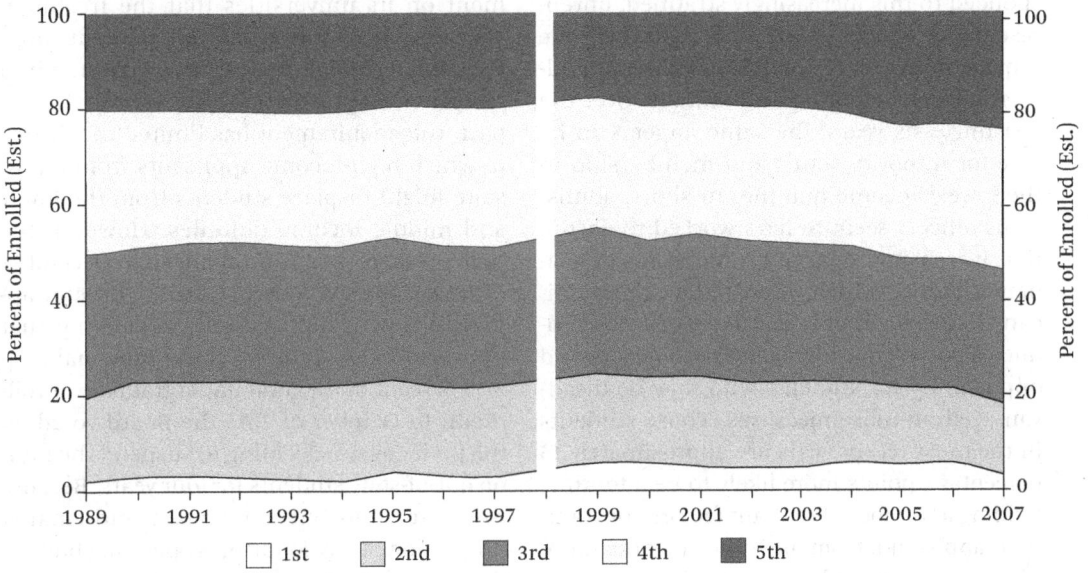

Source: Authors' compilation.

the access afforded to those in the middle (especially those falling between the 20th and 40th percentiles for family income), and small improvements in access for the poorest, though they remain grossly underrepresented. UW-Madison, and possibly other elite, flagship public universities more broadly, are likely confronting a substantially more elite applicant pool than they were several decades ago.

As academic merit rises, a higher proportion of applicants hail from the top two income quintiles; this proportion is more substantial when we focus on out-of-state applicants, but the finding holds even when we focus exclusively on Wisconsin residents. The inverse holds when we consider the bottom two income quintiles. A smaller proportion of applicants are from these two groups. Again, the decline is more extreme when out-of-state applicants are considered, but is also true of Wisconsin residents. The shrinkage in representation of low-income applicants occurs almost entirely as a result of diminished representation of students from the second-lowest income quintile. Students from families in the very bottom of the income quintile constitute the smallest proportion of the applicant pool, but their representation has been by and large constant. This picture differs from the one we imagined. Access seems to be improving for those at the top, not at the expense necessarily of those at the very bottom, who remain most underrepresented, but rather at the gradual expense of those in the middle, the second and third income quintiles. Perhaps decades of burgeoning income inequality and labor market polarization trump decades of K–12 policy interventions designed to reduce the impact of economic inequality (for example, Reardon 2011).

Also very concerning is that, even as the state, and the nation have become more racially and ethnically diverse, the presence of traditionally disadvantaged minority groups in the applicant pool at the University of Wisconsin—Hispanics, African Americans, and Native Americans—has not grown apace. African Americans in particular, when compared against the state and national populations, are less well represented among applicants than they were in the 1970s. Given the statistically significant and in some cases sizeable advantage that has been accorded to this group of applicants since 1986, the declining representation of minority applicants is particularly striking.

The admission process seems to have responded to this increasingly stratified, unrepresentative applicant pool. First, although the impact of test scores on the likelihood of admission has increased substantially over the last thirty-six years, the same appears to be true for minority status and membership in the lowest income quintile. In short, admissions officers seem to have worked to ensure that increasing reliance on measures of academic merit—which often reflect the applicants' socioeconomic status—does not produce a corresponding decrease in access and opportunity for students who may be disadvantaged on those measures. Those students in the most recent years are approximately 15 percentage points more likely to be admitted, holding a number of relevant factors constant, than applicants from any other income quintile. This difference holds across varying levels of merit measured by ACT scores. But admissions officers can only do so much given the applicant pools they now confront each year. Significant or substantive differences are minimal between the applicants and the admitted students in terms of median family income in real, relative, or distributional terms. In short, inequalities in the applicant pool are closely replicated in the admitted pool. Perhaps admissions preferences for traditionally marginalized groups or recognition of lower yields simply prevent more egregious inequalities among admitted students.

As noted, the matriculation process, in which Wisconsin residents and disadvantaged students are more likely to enroll after being accepted dampens but does not obviate the effect of an elite, unrepresentative pool of applicants. For students at the top, access has slightly improved; for those in the middle, it has slightly narrowed; and for those at the very bottom, it remains limited.

Since 2007, admissions reports indicate a modest increase in the racial and ethnic diversity among applicants, but other changes suggest that economic pressures may continue to expand access for the wealthy. The Wisconsin university system has long imposed a requirement on its universities that the freshman class be no more than 25 percent non-Wisconsin residents who are not covered by a reciprocity agreement (Minnesota). In the past, this requirement has limited the degree to which high-income applicants from out of state might displace students from the lower and middle income quintiles. However, the policy was reviewed and changed in December of 2012 as the UW-System Board of Regents approved a new, higher limit, stipulating that nonreciprocity students could now make up 27.5 percent of the total undergraduate enrollment. In October of 2015 the Board voted on the policy again, deciding to suspend the limit on out-of-state students for four years. Because the state contributes a smaller and smaller proportion of UW-Madison's operating budget, the university administration naturally considers alternative ways of raising revenues, and the many wealthy applicants offer a quick, attractive alternative.[9] In fact, although the board of regents raised the cap on nonreciprocity students only after the 2012–2013 school year, international students and domestic nonresidents have made up more than 25 percent of new freshman in every year since 2004, the same year in which we identified a statistically significant, positive effect of membership in the top income quintile. Given the distribution of income among these applicants, the raised cap will likely further increase representation of those from higher income families.

This research is a single case study that we believe creates a unique and replicable methodology. It has considerable advantages of longitudinal analysis of a complete university admissions process using an income measure we believe is superior to self-reported income, especially those based on student responses concerning family income. But as a single case study, it has its own considerable limitations in terms of generalizability. Given the enormous variation in types of colleges and universities across the country, we are not certain

---

9. State funds accounted for 33 percent of UW-Madison's revenues in 1990 and just 17 percent in the 2013–2014 school year. See UW-Madison *Data Digest* by school year at https://apir.wisc.edu/datadigest.htm (accessed December 14, 2015).

that conventional notions of generalizability, such as from samples to populations or generalizations from random field trials, apply. Therefore, what we hope is that this study is replicated by other and varying types of colleges and universities from small publics to financially marginal privates to other large state universities and to elite wealthy private schools. All these types of colleges should have the data necessary to replicate this approach and we would be very willing to share our methods and analytical tools.

REFERENCES

Alon, Sigal, and Marta Tienda. 2007. "Diversity, Opportunity, and the Shifting Meritocracy in Higher Education." *American Sociological Review* 72(4): 487–511.

Astin, Alexander, and Leticia Osegura. 2004. "The Declining 'Equity' of American Higher Education." *Review of Higher Education* 27(3): 321–41.

Bailey, Martha J., and Susan M. Dynarski. 2011. "Inequality in Postsecondary Education." In *Whither Opportunity?: Rising Inequality, Schools, and Children's Life Chances*, edited by Greg J. Duncan and Richard J. Murnane. New York: Russell Sage Foundation.

Bastedo, Michael N., and Ozan Jaquette. 2011. "Running in Place: Low-Income Students and the Dynamics of Higher Education Stratification." *Educational Evaluation and Policy Analysis* 33(3): 318–38.

Belley, Philippe, and Lance Lochner. 2007. "The Changing Role of Family Income and Ability in Determining Educational Achievement." *NBER* working paper no. 13527. Cambridge, Mass.: National Bureau of Economic Research.

Bischoff, Kendra, and Sean Reardon. 2014. "Residential Segregation by Income, 1970–2009." In *Diversity and Disparities: America Enters a New Century*, edited by John Logan. New York: Russell Sage Foundation.

Bowen, William G., Derek Curtis Bok, and James Lawrence Shulman. 1998. *The Shape of the River: Long-Term Consequences of Considering Race in College and University Admissions*. Princeton, N.J.: Princeton University Press.

Bowen, William G., Martin Kurzwell, and Eugene Tobin. 2005. *Equity and Excellence in American Higher Education*. Charlottesville: University of Virginia Press.

Bridgeman, Brent, Judy Pollack, and Nancy Burton. 2004. "Understanding What SAT Reasoning Test Scores Add to High School Grades: A Straightforward Approach." College Board research report no. 2004–4. New York: College Entrance Examination Board.

Bureau of Labor Statistics (BLS). 2015. "College Enrollment and Work Activity of High School Graduates News Release." Washington: U.S. Department of Labor. Accessed December 14, 2015. http://www.bls.gov/news.release/archives/hsgec_04162015.htm.

Burton, Nancy, and Leonard Ramist. 2001. "Predicting Success in College: SAT Studies of Classes Graduating Since 1980." College Board research report no. 2001–2. New York: College Entrance Examination Board.

Carnevale, Anthony, and Stephen Rose. 2004. "Socioeconomic Status, Race/Ethnicity, and Selective College Admissions." In *America's Untapped Resource: Low-Income Students in Higher Education*, edited by Richard Kahlenberg. Ann Arbor, Mich.: Century Foundation Press.

Clinedinst, Melissa E., Sarah F. Hurley, and David A. Hawkins. 2011. "2011 State of College Admission." Arlington, Va.: National Association for College Admission Counseling. Accessed December 14, 2015. http://www.thecollegesolution.com/wp-content/uploads/2011/10/NACAC-report.pdf.

Dale, Stacy B., and Alan B. Krueger. 2002. "Estimating the Payoff to Attending a More Selective College." *Quarterly Journal of Economics* 117(4): 1491–527.

Ellwood, David, and Thomas Kane. 2005. "Who Is Getting a College Education? Family Background and the Growing Gaps in Enrollment." In *Securing the Future: Investing in Children from Birth to College*, edited by Susan Danziger and Jane Waldfogel. New York: Russell Sage Foundation.

Engle, Jennifer, and Vincent Tinto. 2008. *Moving Beyond Access: College Success for Low-Income, First-Generation College Students*. Washington, D.C.: The Pell Institute for the Study of Opportunity in Higher Education.

Fry, Richard. 2014. "U.S. High School Dropout Rate Reaches Record Low, Driven by Improvements among Hispanics, Blacks." *FactTank*, October 2. Accessed December 14, 2015. http://www.pewresearch.org/fact-tank/2014/10/02/u-s-high-school-dropout-rate-reaches-record-low-driven-by-improvements-among-hispanics-blacks/.

Fry, Richard, and Paul Taylor. 2012. "The Rise of Residential Segregation by Income." Washington, D.C.: Pew Research Center. Accessed December 14, 2015. http://www.pewsocialtrends.org/files/2012/08/Rise-of-Residential-Income-Segregation-2012.2.pdf.

Geronimus, Arline T., John Bound, and Lisa Neidert. 1996. "On the Validity of Using Census Geocode Characteristics to Proxy Individual Socioeconomic Characteristics." *Journal of the American Statistical Association* 91(434): 529–37.

Gonyea, Robert M. 2005. "Self-Reported Data in Institutional Research: Review and Recommendations." *New Direction for Institutional Research* 127(1): 73–89.

Haycock, Kati, and Danette Gerald. 2006. "Engines of Inequality: Diminishing Equity in the Nation's Premier Public Universities." Washington, D.C.: The Education Trust. Accessed December 14, 2015. https://edtrust.org/resource/engines-of-inequality-diminishing-equity-in-the-nations-premier-public-universities/.

Haycock, Kati, Mary Lynch, and Jennifer Engle. 2010. "Opportunity Adrift: Our Flagship Universities Are Straying from Their Public Mission." Washington, D.C.: The Education Trust. Accessed February 23, 2016. https://edtrust.org/resource/19453/.

Hoxby, Caroline M. 1998. *The Return to Attending a More Selective College: 1960 to the Present*. Unpublished manuscript. Department of Economics, Harvard University.

———. 2009. "The Changing Selectivity of American Colleges." *Journal of Economic Perspectives* 23(4): 95–118.

Hoxby, Caroline M., and Christopher Avery. 2013. "The Missing 'One-Offs': The Hidden Supply of High-Achieving, Low-Income Students." *Brookings Papers on Economic Activity* 2013(1): 1–65.

Kahlenberg, Richard D. 2010. *Affirmative Action for the Rich: Legacy Preferences in College Admissions*. New York: Century Foundation Press.

Kane, Thomas. 2003. *The Price of Admission: Rethinking How Americans Pay for College*. Washington, D.C.: Brookings Institution Press.

Karabel, Jerome. 2005. *The Chosen: The Hidden History of Admission and Exclusion at Harvard, Yale, and Princeton*. New York: Houghton Mifflin Harcourt.

Khadaroo, Stacy Teicher. 2008. "Too Few Low-Income Students? Pressure Mounts on Colleges to Reduce Barriers for that Pool of Talent." *Christian Science Monitor*, August 7.

King, Jacqueline E. 2004. "Missed Opportunities: Students Who Do Not Apply for Financial Aid." ACE issue brief. Washington, D.C.: American Council on Education Center for Policy Analysis.

Leonhardt, David. 2015. "Top Colleges Doing the Most for Low-Income Students." *New York Times*, September 16. Accessed December 14, 2015. http://www.nytimes.com/interactive/2015/09/17/upshot/top-colleges-doing-the-most-for-low-income-students.html.

Lemann, Nicholas. 1999. *The Big Test: The Secret History of the American Meritocracy*. New York: Farrar, Straus and Giroux.

Olivas, Michael A. 1986. "Financial Aid and Self-Reports by Disadvantaged Students: The Importance of Being Earnest." *Research in Higher Education* 25(3): 245–52.

Pallais, Amanda, and Sarah Turner. 2006 "Opportunities for Low-Income Students at Top Colleges and Universities: Policy Initiatives and the Distribution of Students." *National Tax Journal* 59(2): 357–86.

Pryor, John H., Sylvia Hurtado, Victor B. Saenz, Jose Luis Santos, and William S. Korn. 2007. *The American Freshman: Forty Year Trends, 1966–2006*. Los Angeles: Higher Education Research Institute.

Reardon, Sean F. 2011. "The Widening Academic Achievement Gap between the Rich and the Poor: New Evidence and Possible Explanations." In *Whither Opportunity?: Rising Inequality, Schools, and Children's Life Chances*, edited by Greg J. Duncan and Richard J. Murnane. New York: Russell Sage Foundation.

Reardon, Sean F., and Claudia Galindo. 2009. "The Hispanic-White Achievement Gap in Math and Reading in the Elementary Grades." *American Educational Research Journal* 46(3): 853–91.

Roderick, Melissa, Vanessa Coca, and Jenny Nagaoka. 2011. "Potholes on the Road to College: High School Effects in Shaping Urban Students' Participation in College Application, Four-Year College Enrollment, and College Match." *Sociology of Education* 84(3): 178–211.

Rooney, Charles, with Bob Schaeffer. 1998. *Test Scores Do Not Equal Merit: Enhancing Equity and Excellence in College Admissions by Deemphasizing SAT and ACT Results. Cambridge, Mass.: Fair Test and the National Center for Fair and Open Testing.

Smith, George Davey, Yoav Ben-Shiomo, and Carole Hart. 1999. "Re: 'Use of Census-Based Aggregate Variables to Proxy for Socioeconomic Group: Evidence from National Samples'." *American Journal of Epidemiology* 150(9): 996–97.

Smith, Kris M., and Claudia W. McCann. 1998. "The Validity of Students' Self-Reported Family Incomes. AIR 1998 Annual Forum Paper." Paper presented at the 38th Annual Forum of the Association for Institutional Research. Minneapolis, Minn. (May 17–20, 1998).

Snyder, Thomas D., and Sally A. Dillow. 2012. *Digest of Education Statistics*. NCES 2012–001. Washington: U.S. Department of Education. Accessed December 14, 2015. http://nces.ed.gov/pubs2012/2012001.pdf.

Terenzini, Patrick, Alberto Cabrera, and Elena Bernal. 2001. "Swimming Against the Tide: The Poor in American Higher Education." Research report no. 2001-1. New York: College Board.

Timpane, Michael, and Arthur Hauptman. 2004. "Improving the Academic Preparation and Performance of Low-Income Students in American Higher Education." In *America's Untapped Resource: Low-Income Students in Higher Education*, edited by Richard Kahlenburg. Ann Arbor, Mich.: Century Foundation Press.

Trusheim, Dale. 1994. "How Valid Is Self-Reported Financial Aid Information?" *Research in Higher Education* 35(3): 335–48. doi:10.1007/BF02496827.

U.S. Census Bureau. 2010. "2010 Geographic Terms and Concepts." *Geography*. Accessed December 14, 2015. http://census.gov/geo/reference/terms.html.

Zhang, Liang. 2005. "Do Measures of College Quality Matter? The Effect of College Quality on Graduates' Earnings." *Review of Higher Education* 28(4): 571–96.

Zwick, Rebecca. 2007. "College Admissions in Twenty-First-Century America: The Role of Grades, Tests, and Games of Chance." *Harvard Educational Review* 77(4): 419–28.

Beyond Earnings and Social Reproduction: Can College Lead to Good Jobs Without Reproducing Social Inequalities?

JAMES E. ROSENBAUM, CAITLIN E. AHEARN, JANET E. ROSENBAUM, AND KELLY I. BECKER

College-for-all has become the educational policy in the United States, and it has led to many changes. Postsecondary subbaccalaureate (sub-BA) credentials (certificates and associate's degrees) are an increasing portion of college credentials, and we examine the implications for the reproduction of social inequalities. We find that despite the growth of sub-BA credentials, many students who enroll in college continue to get no credentials. After replicating prior findings of sub-BA employment and earnings payoffs, using the 2004–2012 Educational Longitudinal Study (ELS) survey, we analyze the AddHealth survey to see whether sub-BA credentials are associated with jobs with nonmonetary job rewards similar to those BAs get (autonomy, career relevance, and so on). Moreover, although BA degrees often reproduce social and academic inequalities, we examine whether sub-BA credentials pose socioeconomic status (SES) and test score obstacles to credential completion, and to employment and earnings within credentials. Beyond the usual earnings payoffs in prior research, we conclude that sub-BA credentials provide ways college students can attain desirable job rewards while avoiding SES and test score obstacles. We speculate on possible reasons and policy implications.

Keywords: status-attainment model, social reproduction, nonmonetary job rewards, sub-BA degrees

U.S. society strives to give all students the opportunity to attend college, and it has largely succeeded (Grubb 1996). Prior research found that more than 80 percent of on-time high school graduates enroll in college, and the rates are similar for whites, blacks, and Hispanics (83 percent, 80 percent, 80 percent, Adelman 2003). This increase comes thanks to an implicit educational policy, referred to as college-for-all (CFA), which encourages all students to attend postsecondary institutions. Given a labor market that increasingly demands college credentials, the college-for-all ideal may be appropriate, but its implications extend beyond increased college enrollment.

Thanks to widely seen payoffs, CFA tends to encourage students to seek bachelor's degrees (BAs) but mostly ignores sub-BA credentials, such as associate's degrees (AAs) and certificates. Public service ads proclaim $1 million

---

James E. Rosenbaum is professor of sociology, education, and social policy at Northwestern University. **Caitlin E. Ahearn** is research director of the Pathways Project at Northwestern University. **Janet E. Rosenbaum** is assistant professor in the Department of Epidemiology and Biostatistics at SUNY Downstate Medical Center, Brooklyn, New York. **Kelly I. Becker** is associate director of student affairs assessment at Northwestern University.

Direct correspondence to: James E. Rosenbaum at j-rosenbaum@northwestern.edu, Institute for Policy Research, Northwestern University, 2040 Sheridan Rd., Evanston, IL 60208; Caitlin E. Ahearn at caitlinahearn2013@u.northwestern.edu; Janet E. Rosenbaum at janet.rosenbaum@downstate.edu; Kelly I. Becker at kib@u.northwestern.edu.

payoffs to BA degrees, and students have gotten this message. By 2002, 84 percent of high school sophomores expected to attain a BA degree or higher (Goyette 2008), and unlike earlier generations, students' BA plans differ minimally by grades or academic track (Reynolds et al. 2006). As students set BA goals with little regard to their academic achievement, CFA is quickly becoming synonymous with BA-for-all.

An Internet search on the question, "what percentage of Americans have college degrees?" returns information only on bachelor's degrees and four-year degrees. The Salary.com article "8 College Degrees with the Worst Return on Investment" considers only majors of BA graduates (2013). Educators, reformers, and the college-choice industry stress K-16 reforms and BA goals, but say little about sub-BA credentials (National College Advising Corps n.d.; Princeton Review n.d.; Brown 2007; Zasloff and Steckel 2014), and "College Results Online" lists only four-year colleges (Education Trust 2014). Even researchers studying upward mobility sometimes consider the BA as the only college degree, ignoring alternative degrees when classifying parental education (Massey et al. 2003, 245). In their highly praised work on high school youth, Barbara Schneider and David Stevenson (2000) warn about students' unrealistic ambitions, and advise parents to provide better information for college planning, but their warnings do not include providing information about sub-BA credentials. More than ever, students are now planning BAs with less consideration to their social backgrounds or occupational ambitions (Goyette 2008).

Of course, BA degrees are often appropriate, but should they be the only goal? Despite the desirability of BA degrees, BA expectations may have serious disadvantages for some students, which they may not realize until they are in the middle of their attempt to obtain the degree. For example, although educators advocate four-year BA degrees, BAs now take an average of six years for most students who begin in community colleges (Bound, Hershbein, and Long 2009; Stephan, Rosenbaum, and Person 2009). Yet educators rarely mention these drawbacks, so students rarely receive warning about predictable risks and costs (Rosenbaum et al. 2015).

Despite society's focus on BA completion, community colleges offer sub-BA credentials, including associate's degrees (expected two years), and certificates (expected twelve months). Certificates and AA degrees have increased fourfold since 1969, whereas BA degrees have only doubled, meaning that more students complete sub-BA credentials than BAs. About two million students in 2011 completed a certificate or AA degree, compared with the 1.7 million who completed a BA degree (Snyder and Dillow 2012, table 301.10). Much of this increase has occurred in recent years, with certificate completion growing by 79 percent between 2000 and 2012 (Kena et al. 2014, 198).

This paper seeks to broaden the usual analyses of higher education credentials by examining both BA and sub-BA outcomes. In addition, we expand prior analyses of early labor market outcomes by examining whether sub-BA credentials lead to desirable job characteristics other than earnings, and whether certificates and associate's degrees pose fewer SES or test score obstacles to completion and postgraduation outcomes than BA degrees.

COMMUNITY COLLEGE CREDENTIALS AND OUTCOMES

Although colleges aspire to provide opportunity for all students, they are often rightly accused of reproducing initial disadvantages. As we will discuss in more detail later, research finds that low-SES backgrounds and low academic achievement lead to lower BA completion rates and worse employment prospects for BA graduates (Bills 2004, chapter 3). These findings have led to a policy debate. BA-for-all advocates want to avoid placing disadvantaged students in lower credentials and therefore seek BA-for-all policies (Ayers 2011; Kahlenberg 2011). Critics argue that because many youth are unlikely to complete BA degrees, society should encourage alternative dependable pathways to good jobs, including job training programs and high school occupational programs (Samuelson 2012; Glass 2014; Gardner 2013; Steinberg 2010). Both sides recognize that low-achieving and low-SES students face added college and labor market obstacles. However, BA-for-all advocates believe that policymakers must redouble their efforts against those obstacles, and the critics suggest that society can provide other, more dependable pathways to success (Schwartz 2014). Yet the debate pits the issue as BA degrees versus vocational programs (no college), and ignores sub-BA credentials, perhaps because their value is neither understood nor recognized. Our analyses focus on providing insight into sub-BA credentials that may expand the options that educators, students, and reformers consider.

Sub-BAs may also pose different social or academic requirements than BAs. Like any academic goal, sub-BA credentials require effort and persistence, but may not require high test scores or class-related cultural capital. This study examines whether sub-BA credentials offer high-quality employment outcomes with fewer obstacles than BA degrees. As U.S. reformers attempt to improve employment opportunities for youth, they have seen the appeal of German apprenticeships, which provide students a streamlined pathway into a high-quality technical career (Hamilton 1990; Schwartz 2014). We ask whether sub-BA credentials, beside opening opportunities to BA degrees (Carnevale, Rose, and Hanson 2012), can operate like German apprenticeships in creating paths to desirable jobs (and career futures) that pose fewer SES or test score obstacles to credentials or employment outcomes than BA degrees.

In the 1980s, Steven Brint wrote that community colleges did great harm by diverting students to sub-BA credentials, which had little value at the time (Brint and Karabel 1989). More recently, however, Brint (2003) has observed that some occupational sub-BA credentials result in higher earnings than in earlier decades, a finding reinforced by recent research (Carnevale, Rose, and Hanson 2012; Holzer et al. 2011; Jacobson and Mohker 2008).

Indeed, despite advertisements announcing $1 million BA payoffs, 27 percent of those with one-year certificates earn more than the median BA graduate (Carnevale, Rose, and Hanson 2012). Reviewing many studies of earnings outcomes, Clive Belfield and Thomas Bailey find a research consensus that sub-BA credentials have significant earnings benefits. They also conclude that the "earnings premiums to education have grown over recent decades" (2011, 54–55). Sub-BA earnings premiums may be on the rise because of labor market demand for those credentials, which often prepare students for high-growth job markets such as health and information technology (Belfield and Bailey 2011). These fields maintained strong demand even in the recent recession (Holzer et al. 2011; Vuolo, Mortimer, and Staff 2014). In fact, employers often report shortages of qualified applicants for mid-skill jobs. Joshua Wyner (2014) estimates that two million mid-skill jobs, which often require sub-BA credentials, go unfilled because individuals lack qualifications.

Good jobs encompass more than just high earnings, however (Oreopoulos and Salvanes 2001). Indeed, high-paid jobs can be undesirable. Employers may offer higher earnings to compensate for undesirable job attributes: disagreeable, demanding, dangerous, dead-end, or deceptive (Rosenbaum, Stephan, and Rosenbaum 2010). Studies have examined whether sub-BA credentials are associated with improved health, less time on welfare, and lower criminal involvement (Belfield and Bailey 2011). Little research has examined the characteristics of jobs, however. In a study on job desirability, Janet Rosenbaum (2012) finds that associate's degrees are associated with health payoffs such as lower risks of smoking and obesity when compared with statistically matched high school graduates with similar high school backgrounds but no postsecondary degree. Other research suggests that job conditions may mediate health payoffs (Presser 2005; Grandner et al. 2010). Evidence indicates that job quality increases with skills requirements, suggesting that mid-skill jobs requiring sub-BA credentials may confer nonmonetary payoffs (Kalleberg 2011; Mortimer et al. 2008). Extending this interest, we study whether sub-BA credentials are related to a wide range of nonmonetary job rewards.

SOCIOLOGICAL STATUS-ATTAINMENT MODEL

According to the status-attainment model, individual attributes (such as SES or academic achievement) increase years of education, which in turn increase job outcomes (Sewell and Hauser 1980). This model hypothesizes that students with low SES, test scores, or educational plans will attain less education and therefore lower earnings than more advantaged, higher achieving, or ambitious students. Moreover, the SES differences in cultural values taught in homes (Kohn and Schooler 1983; Lareau 2011) may also confer advantages in school and work. Other research supports these predictions (DiPrete and Buchmann 2013; Jacob and Wilder 2010).

This model offers little hope for low-income or academically low-achieving students who, because of CFA, have found themselves enrolled in today's colleges. If the status-attainment prediction holds, they may receive little benefit from their time in college. Although disadvantaged students are currently entering college at unprecedented rates, this model predicts that they will receive fewer college credentials and worse labor market outcomes than more advantaged students (Dougherty 1994). Research finds reduced success for disadvantaged students pursuing BA degrees and associate's degrees with intent to transfer to a BA (Stephan, Rosenbaum, and Person 2009), but we do not know whether this is true for students pursuing a sub-BA credential as their main goal. In addition, those results are based on data from the 1990s, and recent labor market changes and sub-BA expansion may change what influences credential completion.

Although most status-attainment research focuses on BAs, students pursuing sub-BA credentials may have higher odds of attainment than if they were pursuing BAs (Grubb 1996; Carnevale, Rose, and Hanson 2012; Choy 2001). Despite policy rhetoric that students need "college-level academic skills" to benefit from college, sub-BA credentials may require lower academic skills. Indeed, some community college faculty report that some sub-BA credentials and their associated occupations require only eighth-grade academic skills (Rosenbaum, Cepa, and Rosenbaum 2013). For example, computer technicians and medical assistants must calculate proportions quickly and accurately, but these sub-BA programs do not need Algebra II, as high school requirements might suggest (Stone and Lewis 2012; Tucker 2013). Although high-status occupations sometimes require high-SES cultural capital (Rivera and Ward 2010), mid-skilled jobs demand technical skills and work ethic, but perhaps not class-related cultural capital (Lareau 2011).

We examine how student attributes are related to various credentials and labor market outcomes. Although we expect BA completion and earnings to follow the status-attainment model, we predict that sub-BA success and sub-BA labor markets may not reward economic or academic advantage to the same extent, adding a new dimension to the status-attainment model.

RESEARCH QUESTIONS

Analyzing a cohort of high school graduates in the class of 2004, from tenth grade through eight years after graduation, this study updates and extends prior findings on sub-BA attainment and outcomes for young adults. We examine the following questions:

1. What is the frequency of college enrollment and credential attainment, by college type, and test score or SES, and how do these patterns differ from a cohort twelve years earlier?

2. How are credentials related to various labor market outcomes, including employment, earnings, and a variety of nonmonetary job rewards?

3. Are SES or achievement related to credential attainment or employment outcomes within each credential?

4. Do students combine a sub-BA with a BA or choose one or the other?

Because the sub-BA earnings payoff (over high school diplomas) is already well documented in many studies (Belfield and Bailey 2011), that is not our focus. Although we run those analyses to confirm that they occur for this recent cohort, we focus mostly on other employment outcomes. We extend prior studies of nonmonetary outcomes, but instead of studying nonemployment outcomes such as health, welfare, and crime, we focus on employment and nonmonetary job rewards. Of course, policy must consider earnings, and a living wage is important, but nonmonetary job rewards are also important. This is especially true for young adults at the early stages of their careers, when they are often advised to choose jobs for their experience, training, or career preparation.

We also examine whether SES background and academic achievement predict degree completion and employment outcomes for both BAs and sub-BAs. If we find that test scores predict BA attainment, but not sub-BA attainment, that will raise questions about popular rhetoric about a single form of college readiness based on academic skills. If we find that SES or test scores are related to later labor market success for BA graduates, but not for sub-BA graduates, that may suggest that these credentials lead to career paths that pose different requirements, and do not reproduce the prior inequalities.

This is an exploratory analysis. Research to date has not examined whether sub-BA credentials are associated with better nonmonetary job rewards than a high school diploma, nor whether disadvantaged sub-BA graduates (with low SES or low test scores) have worse employment outcomes than more advantaged sub-BA graduates. These analyses may identify previously unnoticed aspects of alternative college pathways.

DATA AND METHODS

Most of our analyses use data from the nationally representative ELS, which follows the sophomore class of 2002 over ten years, through 2012. We rely mainly on data collected during the base year interview (tenth grade) and the third follow up ten years later (2012). Our sample therefore includes only individuals present in both survey years, and we use the corresponding survey weight created by ELS.

We limit all analyses to on-time high school graduates, students who graduated by the summer of 2004. On-time high school graduates are better students and have more time for credential completion, which poses a more uniform standard for judging the payoff of college credentials. In examining credential completion by age twenty-six, most analyses also exclude individuals still enrolled in college at the time of the third interview (June 2012), so individuals without credentials in our sample are no longer pursuing higher education as of 2012 (though we do not know if they return later to complete a credential). The only exception is our first table, which examines the percentage of respondents who ever enroll in college within eight years of graduating from high school. For all earnings regressions, we use the natural log of earnings in 2011 and restrict the sample to individuals who report having last attended college by December of 2010 and reported earnings for 2011. Similarly, the employment analyses, which examine employment in 2012, are limited to individuals who report having last attended college by December of 2011, which gives them some time to find employment.

Analyses begin with weighted tabulations that examine college enrollment and credential attainment, comparing students at high, middle, and low third of SES and tenth grade test score. This provides a preliminary look at today's college opportunity structure for on-time high school graduates. We compare these ELS results with a similar cohort twelve years prior, which follows the graduating class of 1992 through eight years after high school (NELS).

Using logistic and linear regression, respectively, we examine how educational attainment is related to employment status in 2012 and earnings in 2011. We then broaden our analysis by examining how various educational credentials are related to nonmonetary job outcomes in analyses based on National Longitudinal Study of Adolescent Health (AddHealth). AddHealth is also a nationally representative dataset following a sample of students in grades seven through twelve in 1995 through 2008. AddHealth was chosen because of its more thorough coverage of young adults' job characteristics.

Returning to ELS, a multinomial regression examines how student characteristics relate to attainment of various credentials. Logistic and linear regressions examine how student characteristics relate to employment and earnings within each credential category.

Question 1: What is the frequency of college enrollment and credential attainment, by college type, and test score or SES, and what changes are evident from twelve years earlier?

Current Opportunity Structure

First, descriptive statistics provide an overview of college enrollment and attainment of on-time high school graduates (table 1). This table, which includes even students still in college in 2012, finds that college-for-all largely succeeds in sending most (90 percent) on-time high school graduates to college in the eight years after high school. Even 81 percent of low-SES students attend college. Ironically, although researchers used to think college plans were necessary precursors to college attendance, now 50 percent of seniors who do not plan to attend college actually report attending in the next eight years (not shown). This highlights the new college reality that high school students who do not anticipate enrolling in college feel compelled to do so, perhaps because of labor market constraints. We should be encouraged, but not lulled into complacency, by this tremendous success. Efforts must continue to increase the high school graduation rate and to help students who did not complete high school on time to find postsecondary training.

Table 2 also shows completion rates for various credentials at two- and four-year colleges.

Here (and in later tables) we exclude students still enrolled in 2012, who may complete a degree soon. Even though most students beginning in community colleges report BA plans, only 20 percent of all students initially enrolled in a community college get a BA in the next eight years. Such dismal findings are often reported by education reformers (Ayers 2011; Kahlenberg 2011). However, broadening our notions of postsecondary success, we find many more students who first enroll in two-year colleges complete either a certificate or associate's degree (33 percent). Although more students have BA plans, individuals more frequently attain sub-BA credentials.

Reinforcing prior research (Stephan, Rosenbaum, and Person 2009), our analyses indicate that students who begin at four-year colleges have higher odds (67 percent) of completing BA degrees (table 2), and are less likely to attain sub-BA degrees than students who began at two-year colleges, at each level of SES and test score. CFA encourages even students with low academic achievement to enter college. Of students who begin in two-year colleges in the low third of test scores, we find that 11 percent of individuals complete BA degrees, but 37 percent complete sub-BA degrees. In four-year colleges, 34 percent of those with low test scores get BA degrees, and 21 percent complete sub-BA degrees (presumably by transferring, since four-year colleges rarely offer sub-BA credentials). Note that the positive relationships be-

Table 1. College Attendance, ELS (2002–2012)

	All	Test Score[a]			SES[b]		
		Low Test	Middle Test	High Test	Low SES	Middle SES	High SES
HS diploma (on time, no GED)	11,573	2,164	2,909	3,402	2,233	2,585	3,354
Percent ever attend college: 2004–2012	90.0	79.0	90.0	97.0	81.0	90.0	97.0

Source: Authors' calculations based on ELS 2002–2012.
Sample: On-time high school graduates, completed postsecondary education by June of 2012.
[a]Test score is the composite math and language arts standardized test score from 2002.
[b]Our SES variable was created by NCES through ELS, comprised of information on parents' occupations and parents' education.

Table 2. College Type and Highest Credential Attainment, ELS (2004–2012)

	All	Test Score[a]			SES[b]		
		Low Test	Middle Test	High Test	Low SES	Middle SES	High SES
First college level							
Two-year	37.0	61.0	42.0	19.0	51.0	41.0	23.0
Four-year	59.0	30.0	56.0	80.0	42.0	55.0	75.0
Started at two-year college							
Some college	46.0	51.0	42.0	44.0	49.0	47.0	41.0
Certificate	17.0	22.0	17.0	9.0	21.0	17.0	11.0
Associate's degree	16.0	15.0	18.0	16.0	16.0	16.0	15.0
Bachelor's degree plus	20.0	11.0	24.0	31.0	14.0	19.0	33.0
Started at four-year college							
Some college	22.0	45.0	26.0	15.0	36.0	26.0	15.0
Certificate	5.0	12.0	5.0	4.0	7.0	6.0	4.0
Associate's degree	5.0	9.0	7.0	3.0	8.0	6.0	4.0
Bachelor's degree plus	67.0	34.0	61.0	78.0	49.0	61.0	76.0

Source: Authors' calculations based on ELS 2002–2012.
Sample: On-time high school graduates, completed postsecondary education by June of 2012.
Note: All numbers are percentages.
[a]Test score is the composite math and language arts standardized test score from 2002.
[b]Our SES variable was created by NCES through ELS, comprised of information on parents' occupations and parents' education.

tween BA completion and test scores and SES are absent for AA completion and may move in the opposite direction for certificates. These relationships are further examined in later analyses.

Many college students fail to complete any credential. Of students who begin in two-year colleges, almost half (46 percent) have no credentials eight years after high school, whom we refer to as *some college* (table 2). Although only 23 percent of students who began in four-year colleges have no credentials, among the students with low test scores, nearly half have no credential after eight years (45 percent).

In sum, although college access is close to universal for these students, college completion is a major obstacle, especially for two-year college students and for four-year college students with low test scores. Moreover, although two-year colleges are rightly criticized for lower BA completion than four-year colleges, their rates of overall credential completion are closer to parity, if we consider the sub-BAs they confer, particularly for students with low test scores (49 percent versus 56 percent). Whether sub-BA credentials count as true success depends on employment outcomes, which we examine later, after first examining attainment patterns from twelve years earlier.

Change Since 1992

We can better understand today's college reality by comparison with the corresponding cohort from twelve years ago. Just as ELS surveyed the high school class of 2004 and followed them eight years later to 2012, a prior survey (NELS, the National Educational Longitudinal Survey) studied the high school class of 1992 and followed them eight years later (until 2000). We find changes in college enrollment and credential attainment, particularly at the sub-BA level.

Table 3. College Attendance, College Type, and Highest Credential Attainment, NELS (1992–2000)

		Test Score[a]			SES[b]		
	All	Low Test	Middle Test	High Test	Low SES	Middle SES	High SES
HS diploma (on time, no GED)	8,668	2,217	2,808	3,133	2,492	2,912	3,264
Ever attend college: 2004–2012	80.0	65.0	82.0	94.0	62.0	79.0	93.0
First college level							
Two-year	40.0	65.0	44.0	22.0	57.0	47.0	28.0
Four-year	54.0	26.0	50.0	75.0	34.0	47.0	68.0
Started at two-year college							
Some college	57.0	67.0	56.0	45.0	60.0	60.0	51.0
Certificate	6.0	7.0	5.0	8.0	8.0	6.0	5.0
Associate's degree	14.0	12.0	16.0	14.0	15.0	15.0	12.0
Bachelor's degree plus	19.0	8.0	20.0	31.0	10.0	16.0	31.0
Started at four-year college							
Some college	24.0	47.0	30.0	17.0	39.0	32.0	17.0
Certificate	1.0	4.0	1.0	1.0	3.0	1.0	1.0
Associate's degree	3.0	2.0	4.0	3.0	4.0	4.0	2.0
Bachelor's degree plus	7.0	41.0	61.0	78.0	50.0	61.0	79.0

Source: Authors' calculations based on NELS 1990–2000.
Sample: On-time high school graduates, not enrolled in a postsecondary institution in 2000.
Note: All numbers after row one are percentages.
[a]Test score is the composite math and language arts standardized test score from 1992.
[b]Our SES variable was created by NCES through ELS, comprised of information on parents' occupations and parents' education.

Table 3 indicates that fewer high school graduates enrolled in college in the earlier cohort (80 percent to 86 percent). Much of the gain occurred outside the top third of SES and test scores. For students who initially enrolled in two-year colleges, certificate completion increased from 6 percent to 17 percent (for all ages, see Kena et al. 2014). Certificate completion also increased for students who began in four-year colleges, especially for students with low test scores (from 4 percent to 12 percent). In both two- and four-year colleges, this certificate gain is larger for students in the bottom third of the distribution of test scores and SES than for more advantaged and higher-performing students. Overall, the percentage of students with no credential declined (57 percent to 46 percent), especially for those with low test scores (67 percent to 51 percent). Associate's and bachelor's degree completion changed minimally.

Research has noted the increase in certificate completion at all ages (Kena et al. 2014). Our results indicate that for young adults, this increase occurred particularly for students with low SES and low test scores. The increase in sub-BA, particularly certificate, completion seems to explain the overall increase in credential attainment, because BA attainment remains unchanged.

Question 2: How are credentials related to various labor market outcomes, including employment, earnings, and a variety of nonmonetary job rewards?

Employment Outcomes by Educational Attainment

We now examine whether credential attainment is associated with employment and earnings outcomes. For individuals who report having last attended college by the end of 2011 (n = 7596), we ran logistic regression on whether they were employed part time or full time (table 4). We find that individuals with certificates, AAs, and BAs all had significantly and increasingly higher odds of being employed (1.53, 2.07, 3.32) than high school graduates with no postsecondary enrollment. However, individuals with some college but no credential were not significantly more likely to be employed than high school graduates who did not enroll in any college (1.17, n.s.).

Seventeen studies show that sub-BA credentials increase earnings over a high school diploma (Belfield and Bailey 2011). We thus confirm a well-established finding. Consistent with prior studies, we find that BA degrees increased earnings by 34 percent, AA degrees by 22 percent, and certificates by 13 percent, all significantly higher than high school graduates' earnings. In contrast, students who get some college with no credential have no better employment or earnings than on-time high school graduates with no college. This finding

Table 4. Employment and Earnings Outcomes Regressions

	Logistic Regression of Employment Status 2012[d]	Linear Regression on Log Earnings 2011
SES 2002[a]	1.14 (1.80)	0.05 (2.77)**
Tenth grade test score[b]	1.02 (4.07)***	0.01 (4.83)***
Graduate degree[c]	4.96 (6.04)***	0.46 (8.58)***
Bachelor's degree	3.32 (8.19)***	0.34 (8.83)***
Associate's degree	2.07 (3.89)***	0.22 (4.37)***
Certificate	1.53 (2.84)**	0.13 (2.74)**
Some college	1.17 (1.36)	−0.03 (−0.73)
Hours worked per week in 2011	−	0.02 (23.92)***
Weeks Employed in 2011	−	0.03 (29.97)***
Female	0.37 (−10.91)***	−0.16 (−7.52)***
Black	1.11 (0.71)	−0.12 (−3.23)***
Hispanic	0.82 (−1.63)	0.02 (0.50)
Other Race	0.76 (−2.01)*	0.06 (1.84)
Constant	−	7.49 (86.94)***
N	7596	5,109

Source: Authors' calculations based on ELS 2002–2012.
Sample: On-time high school graduates; completed postsecondary education by the end of 2011 (employment) or the end of 2010 (earnings).
Note: T-statistics in parentheses.
[a]Our SES variable was created by NCES through ELS, comprised of information on parents' occupations and parents' education.
[b]Test score is the composite math and language arts standardized test score from 2002.
[c]On-time high school graduates are the comparison for credential coefficients.
[d]Employed (full time or part time) versus unemployed.
*$p < .05$; **$p < .01$; ***$p < .001$

Table 5. Characteristics of Individuals with Different Levels of Highest Educational Attainment

	Some College	Certificate[c]	Associate's	Bachelor's	Graduate
Low high school GPA third, honors weighted	36.0	34.0	21.0***	6.0***	2.0***
Usually had homework done tenth grade	71.0	72.0	78.0**	84.0***	88.0***
Get in trouble three or more times tenth grade	13.0	12.0	9.0	6.0***	4.0***
Skip three or more times in tenth grade	12.0	11.0	11.0	5.0***	5.0***
Low sophomore test third[a]	34.0	45.0***	29.0	9.0***	5.0***
Low SES third 2002[b]	36.0	40.0*	33.0	17.0***	11.0***
BA plans in twelfth grade	62.0	50.0***	61.0	93.0***	98.0***
Enroll in college in first term after high school	66.0	61.0**	73.0***	92.0***	94.0***
Start at a four-year college	42.0	26.0***	33.0***	84.0***	93.0***

Source: Authors' calculations based on ELS 2002–2012.
Sample: On-time high school graduates, completed postsecondary education by June of 2012.
Note: All numbers are percentages.
[a]Test score is the composite math and language arts standardized test score from 2002.
[b]Our SES variable was created by NCES through ELS, comprised of information on parents' occupations and parents' education.
[c]Significance for all credentials is compared to some college.
*$p < .05$; **$p < .01$; ***$p < .001$

has been reported in many but not all prior studies (Belfield and Bailey 2011; Grubb 2002, but see Marcotte et al. 2005), especially when examining the earnings of workers under age thirty (Day and Newburger 2002, figure 4; Carnevale, Rose, and Hanson 2012). Even in the most statistically sophisticated studies, findings conflict as to the benefits of some college (Belfield and Bailey 2011). Perhaps conflicts might be reduced if studies added key variables to the model. Some college may increase employment or earnings for students who are in certain majors, who get credits in certain skill areas, who already have certain jobs or job contacts, or who get jobs that use their skills. These variables are rarely studied, so although we can reasonably suspect that averages do not tell the whole story, we are unclear as to how, when, and for whom some college is beneficial.

However, virtually all studies agree that some college has no benefit if students get few or no credits (Grubb 2002), which is usually the case for students who do not get credentials (Rosenbaum 2001, 77). Indeed, nearly all research shows that credential attainment has significant earnings benefits over some college (Belfield and Bailey 2011, 55; Grubb 2002). At the very least, credentials increase employment in jobs that explicitly require credentials. The practical conclusion is that students at high risk of getting no credential cannot count on some college to yield better employment or earnings than a high school diploma, but completing a credential is likely to confer a significant benefit.

Are Students with Some College Less Qualified?

These findings raise the concern that individuals with some college have inferior qualifications or resources than students who get sub-BA degrees. We find that this does not appear to be the case. Students with some college have similar or better qualifications than certificate completers on a wide range of attributes likely to predict college success (table 5). Compared with those who complete certificates, some-college students have similar rates of low grade point average (GPA), homework completion, getting in trouble, and skipping school, and they are significantly more likely to be higher on SES, test scores, immediate college enrollment, starting at four-year colleges, and having BA plans. However, some-college students are significantly lower than BA completers on every positive indicator, and significantly higher on every negative indicator. Overall, some-college students fall somewhere in the middle of the sample— not as high achieving, advantaged, or motivated as BA completers, but often higher achieving and more socioeconomically advantaged than certificate completers. Of course, these variables do not measure all possible student attributes, but they cover a range of behaviors and background that are likely associated with credential completion. Based on these findings, we see no reason why individuals with some college could not have completed at least a certificate had they followed an alternative postsecondary route.

Their two largest differences from certificate graduates (BA plans and starting at four-year colleges) provide a clue as to why they did not complete certificates. We speculate that students' BA plans and four-year college beginnings may prevent students from seeing certificates' desirable features. Because educators are reluctant to promote sub-BA credentials over BA goals, we suspect that students who began college with BA plans or began at four-year colleges may not realize the value of sub-BA credentials. Many students who lack qualifications and motivation to complete BAs may be capable of completing sub-BA credentials. Unfortunately, students cannot consider sub-BA credentials if they do not know about them or their labor market potential.

Nonmonetary Job Rewards
Certain issues are rarely considered in community college literature, one of which is nonmonetary job rewards. Most national surveys follow youth only until ages twenty-five through thirty-two, a young age when earnings may not be a good indication of a promising career.

Despite claims that BAs have $1 million payoffs, a credential's average earnings may be misleading. Like studies of the U.S. Census (Baum and Ma 2013), we also find large earnings overlaps across education levels. In ELS, more than 25 percent of certificate graduates earn more than the median BA, and 25 percent of BAs earn less than the median certificate graduate (not shown). Indeed, economic theory predicts that ambitious young employees might sacrifice early earnings to get career preparation (or might enhance their earning with strenuous dead-end jobs).

To consider other reasons individuals choose jobs, we examine whether various credentials predict nonmonetary job rewards, including career-related job attributes. The AddHealth survey has an unusually rich array of such measures. Extending a prior analysis of the AddHealth survey which examined health outcomes associated with educational credentials (Janet Rosenbaum 2012), here we examine whether other nonmonetary outcomes are associated with educational credentials. Despite the usual emphasis on earnings as indicating good jobs, we find that among young working adults (ages twenty-five to thirty-two), job satisfaction is less strongly related to earnings than to certain nonmonetary job rewards, such as autonomy, career relevance, and career preparation (table 6). This suggests the possibility that these nonmonetary job rewards are valued and actively sought by young adults. We are particularly interested in the job rewards related to career preparation, which may indicate training opportunities, valuable work experiences, or inferences about future career advancement.

Further analyses examine whether college credentials are related to increased nonmonetary job rewards compared to high school graduates, after extensive controls. Table 7 shows that both AA and BA graduates report similar nonmonetary job reward payoffs (compared to high school graduates). Indeed, despite their earnings disadvantage (compared with BAs), AA degrees confer nearly all of the same nonmonetary job rewards as BAs, sometimes at similar magnitude (autonomy, satisfaction, health benefits), and sometimes less

Table 6: Correlation Between Job Satisfaction and Job Rewards Within Education Levels

	Highest Degree by 2008						
Job Rewards	HS Graduate	Some College[a]	Certificate	Associate's	Bachelor's	Graduate	All
Personal earnings	0.12	0.12	0.17	0.07	0.10	0.02	0.10
Perceived SES	0.21	0.20	0.20	0.22	0.22	0.11	0.21
Job autonomy	0.28	0.29	0.37	0.32	0.33	0.33	0.32
Job not repetitive[b]	0.13	0.17	0.14	0.14	0.19	0.11	0.17
Job related to career goals[b]	0.29	0.31	0.32	0.36	0.35	0.28	0.33
Job part of career	0.35	0.35	0.36	0.35	0.38	0.37	0.37
Achieved desired educational level	0.11	0.12	0.11	0.11	0.12	0.01	0.12
N	4470	3028	938	1058	2838	1155	10459

Source: Authors' calculations based on Adolescent Health 1995–2008.
Sample: Restricted to high school graduates who are employed full time in one job in 2008.
[a]Some college is defined as (1) reporting at wave 3 and 4 having no degree beyond high school, and (2) at least one of the following (a) having completed a year of schooling beyond twelfth grade, reported at wave 3 (n=124); (b) being currently enrolled in school at wave 3 (n=933); (c) "received any vocational education or job training in a program that lasted at least 3 months" at a community college, reported at wave 3 (n=20); (d) enrolled for at least 3 months at a "regular school", reported at wave 3 (n=1781); (e) reported at wave 4 having completed "some college" at wave 4 (n=452) in response to question " What is the highest level of education that you have achieved to date?"; (f) affirmative answer at wave 4 to "Are you currently attending a college, university, or vocational/technical school where you take courses for academic credit?" (n=56). Individuals who "received any vocational education or job training in a program that lasted at least 3 months" at Bible college or religious institution was not counted as some college (n=9). Individuals who reported at wave 4 that their highest degree was "some vocational/technical training (after high school)," (n=162) or "completed vocational/technical training (after high school)" were not counted as some college.
[b]Scale was reversed to yield positive results.

(part of a career, strenuous, day shift, irregular hours). In contrast, certificate completers report fewer job rewards than BA or AA graduates, but certificate graduates report higher satisfaction, autonomy, and job status than high school graduates. Certificate graduates are also more likely to report that their jobs are related to their career goals, are a part of their career pathways, and are providing career preparation than high school graduates.

Finally, unlike certificates, some college is not associated with greater job satisfaction, more job autonomy, or less repetitive jobs compared to high school graduates, although they get more benefits than high school graduates. Moreover, while some-college students report a weak gain in career preparation (much smaller than certificates offer), they do not report that these jobs are part of a career. Indeed, they are significantly more likely to say their jobs are unrelated to their intended careers than high school graduates, possibly because they had higher degree aspirations in the first place, and they experienced a failure that high school graduates did not experience. Some college seems to offer some material improvements (especially benefits), but not satisfaction, autonomy, variety, or jobs related to careers.

We must be cautious in accepting these ratings. Some are relatively objective, but many are subjective. However, studying earnings also has limitations, and nonpecuniary job payoffs broaden our view of attainments and perceived

Table 7. Multivariate Nonmonetary Regression Results (n=10582)

	Some College	Certificate	Associate's	Bachelor's	Graduate
Poisson regression					
Job relates to career					
Unrelated	1.11 (1.00, 1.22)*	0.64 (0.54, 0.77)****	0.93 (0.81, 1.08)	0.59 (0.51, 0.67)****	0.33 (0.27, 0.42)****
Preparation	1.15 (1.02, 1.29)*	1.45 (1.27, 1.65)****	1.17 (1.00, 1.37)*	1.27 (1.10, 1.45)***	1.23 (1.00, 1.50)*
Part of career	1.07 (0.97, 1.18)	1.49 (1.30, 1.70)****	1.40 (1.26, 1.57)****	1.64 (1.46, 1.84)****	1.96 (1.74, 2.21)****
Benefits offered					
Health benefits	1.24 (1.17, 1.31)****	1.22 (1.14, 1.30)****	1.36 (1.27, 1.46)****	1.42 (1.34, 1.51)****	1.45 (1.36, 1.56)****
Retirement benefits	1.24 (1.16, 1.32)****	1.24 (1.15, 1.35)****	1.44 (1.33, 1.56)****	1.49 (1.39, 1.59)****	1.52 (1.41, 1.64)****
Vacation benefits	1.20 (1.12, 1.29)****	1.18 (1.09, 1.26)***	1.35 (1.25, 1.45)****	1.36 (1.26, 1.46)****	1.39 (1.29, 1.50)****
Job conditions					
Day shift	1.01 (0.96, 1.08)	0.97 (0.89, 1.05)	1.10 (1.03, 1.18)**	1.26 (1.18, 1.34)****	1.25 (1.17, 1.34)****
Irregular hours	1.03 (0.90, 1.18)	1.16 (0.99, 1.36)	0.90 (0.76, 1.07)	0.82 (0.70, 0.95)**	0.90 (0.76, 1.06)
Work hard physically	0.86 (0.75, 0.98)*	0.71 (0.56, 0.90)**	0.44 (0.33, 0.57)***	0.26 (0.21, 0.34)****	0.11 (0.05, 0.22)****
Work desk job	1.70 (1.50, 1.93)***	1.50 (1.26, 1.79)***	1.90 (1.62, 2.22)***	2.51 (2.21, 2.85)****	2.08 (1.78, 2.45)****
Supervise managers	0.92 (0.75, 1.14)	0.97 (0.75, 1.26)	1.20 (0.91, 1.59)	1.07 (0.87, 1.32)	0.96 (0.75, 1.24)
Supervise others	1.15 (1.04, 1.26)**	0.99 (0.86, 1.14)	1.09 (0.94, 1.25)	1.03 (0.93, 1.15)	1.07 (0.92, 1.25)
Number Times Fired	0.77 (0.67, 0.88)***	0.76 (0.62, 0.93)***	0.61 (0.47, 0.78)***	0.47 (0.39, 0.58)****	0.30 (0.24, 0.38)****
OLS regression					
Perceived status (0–10)	0.27 (0.16, 0.39)***	0.43 (0.28, 0.58)***	0.52 (0.38, 0.66)***	1.08 (0.97, 1.20)****	1.76 (1.58, 1.94)****
Job satisfaction	0.01 (−0.00, 0.03)	0.05 (0.03, 0.06)***	0.03 (0.01, 0.04)**	0.02 (0.01, 0.04)**	0.06 (0.04, 0.08)****
Job autonomy	0.01 (−0.01, 0.04)	0.07 (0.04, 0.09)***	0.04 (0.01, 0.08)**	0.06 (0.04, 0.08)****	0.08 (0.05, 0.11)****
Job repetitive	−0.01 (−0.03, 0.01)	−0.03 (−0.06, −0.01)**	−0.06 (−0.08, −0.04)***	−0.14 (−0.16, −0.12)****	−0.20 (−0.23, −0.17)****

Source: Authors' calculations based on Adolescent Health 1995–2008.

Sample: Restricted to high school graduates who are employed full time in one job in 2008.

Control variables: demographics (race-ethnicity (black, Latino, Asian), gender); educational factors (grade average, test score, grades not reported by respondent); acculturation (nativity, parent nativity, speak English versus another language at home); and parent's socioeconomic status (parent's self-reported educational level, household income, and whether they have enough money to pay bills).

Note: Confidence interval in parentheses. Columns correspond to educational levels, and rows correspond to employment outcomes. Entries correspond to the multivariate regression coefficient predicting the outcome from the educational level.

*$p < .05$; **$p < .01$; ***$p < .001$

Table 8. Multinomial Logistic Regression of Attainment, Odds Ratios (N=6938)

	Certificate[c]	Associate's	Bachelor's	Graduate
SES 2002[a]	1.00 (0.03)	1.06 (0.68)	1.67 (8.48)***	2.29 (9.50)***
Tenth grade test score[b]	0.98 (−3.60)***	1.00 (0.12)	1.06 (11.03)***	1.11 (12.36)***
BA plans in twelfth grade	0.67 (−3.84)***	0.83 (−1.51)	4.42 (12.89)***	11.26 (6.91)***
Enroll in first term after high school	0.99 (−0.07)	1.39 (2.35)*	3.20 (9.52)***	3.48 (5.89)***
Female	1.54 (4.14)***	1.43 (3.17)**	1.48 (4.88)***	2.49 (7.83)***
Black	1.07 (0.44)	0.55 (−2.89)**	0.81 (−1.55)	1.17 (0.76)
Hispanic	1.04 (0.25)	0.83 (−1.07)	0.97 (−0.48)	1.04 (0.18)
Other race	1.04 (0.23)	0.97 (−0.16)	1.35* (2.42)	1.80 (3.56)***

Source: Authors' calculations based on ELS 2002-2012.
Sample: On-time high school graduates, not enrolled in a postsecondary institution in 2012.
Note: T-statistics in parentheses.
[a]Our SES variable was created by NCES through ELS of information on parents' occupations and parents' education.
[b]Test score is the composite math and language arts standardized test score from 2002.
[c]Some college is the reference category.
*$p < .05$; **$p < .01$; ***$p < .001$

career implications for these young adults (Oreopoulos and Salvanes 2001).

Given the highly negative views of sub-BA credentials encouraged by older research (Karabel 1979), these findings indicate that individuals themselves see some previously ignored positive attributes of jobs from certificates and AAs. Critics dismiss sub-BA credentials as leading to routine, repetitive jobs, with little autonomy, low status, and minimal training and few career opportunities. Our findings contradict those preconceptions. These reports indicate that young working adults are aware of a variety of nonmonetary job rewards, which are related to their satisfaction and may be career-related indicators. They encourage us to broaden our perspectives, and consider the possibility of alternative dimensions for judging labor market payoffs.

Question 3: Are SES or achievement related to credential attainment or employment outcomes within each credential?

Multinomial Prediction of Degree Attainment
We next examine the status attainment prediction—do low-SES or low-achieving individuals have reduced success in pursuing all credentials or is it differentiated based on credential type? To study this, we ran a multinomial logistic regression, using some-college students (with no degree or certificate) as the comparison (table 8). Gender is the only uniform effect: females have higher odds for all credentials. Additionally, immediate enrollment increases the odds of completing all credentials except certificates. Otherwise, the BAs, AAs, and certificates have different predictors. BA completion resembles the traditional findings (Sewell and Hauser 1975; Dougherty 1994): SES, test scores, and BA plans all significantly increase the likelihood of BA attainment compared with some college. In contrast, these factors do not increase the odds of an AA or certificate. Indeed, higher test scores and BA plans actually decrease the odds of certificate attainment (they increase the odds of some college).

These findings indicate that, unlike BA completion, certificates and AAs present a more level playing field for individuals with low SES and low test scores. The lack of a test score effect is consistent with faculty reports that students need only eighth-grade academic skills to get certificates or applied associates degrees in some fields (Rosenbaum, Cepa, and Rosenbaum 2013), and the doubts about the need for Algebra II for sub-BA success (Stone and Lewis 2012; Tucker 2013), noted earlier. Contrary to the usual rhetoric about college academic readiness, these findings suggest that sub-BA credential success does not require college-level academic achievement, nor high SES. Students with low test scores or low-SES backgrounds are no less successful at completing certificates or even associate's degrees than more advantaged students, all else equal.

Who Gets Higher Employment and Earnings in Each Credentials' Labor Market?

Next we examine whether SES or test scores are related to employment outcomes within each credential category. Each credential leads to different occupations, which may reward different personal attributes. If students with low test scores succeed in completing sub-BA credentials, do these graduates suffer lower employment rates or lower earnings than higher achieving graduates? It is conceivable that employers may prefer graduates with high test scores, high SES, or BA plans (perhaps a proxy for motivation), so these qualities may predict higher employment or earnings for graduates with each educational credential.

Logistic regressions analyze employment in 2012 for each credential separately (table 9, columns 1 through 4). SES does not predict employment for any credential (except those with no credential, some college). Similarly, higher test scores do not predict increased employment for any credential, except certificate graduates, which is just barely significant at t=1.98 (table 9). In addition, BA plans increase employment for students who complete BAs, but are not associated with higher employment rates for graduates of any other credential. In sum, SES, test scores, and BA plans pose few obstacles to employment for most credentials.

Looking at early earnings, we find that SES, test scores, and BA plans predict greater earnings among BA graduates, but not for individuals in the two sub-BA groups (table 8, columns 5 through 8). Thus, unlike the BA, sub-BA credentials lead to labor markets that do not hurt graduates with low SES, low test scores, or lower postsecondary plans.

Question 4: Do students combine a sub-BA with a BA or choose one or the other?

Like other researchers, we have treated students' highest credential eight years after high school as their ultimate attainment. This is consistent with the status-attainment model and the way counselors encourage students to choose a single, typically high, degree goal. Although advocates of BA expectations discourage sub-BA credentials because they lead to lower average earnings, that advice assumes that educational attainment ends after the first credential. However, those who complete certificates and AAs often combine credentials in a process referred to by reformers as *stacking*, in which they build on prior credentials (Ganzglass 2014). In the AddHealth sample of young adults, about 47 percent of BA graduates also have an AA (Rosenbaum 2012). Moreover, 19 percent of adult certificate holders also have AAs and an additional 12 percent have BAs (Carnevale, Rose, and Hanson 2012). These percentages may not seem large, but they are impressive given that, historically, community colleges have not designed explicit mechanisms by which to combine degrees.

However, it is likely that students who discovered degree ladder options in the past did so with little help from colleges. For example, in a study of twenty community college websites in Illinois and California, we saw no mention of this possibility. We also interviewed twelve counselors from various community colleges, none of whom mentioned combining degrees (Rosenbaum et al. 2015). Indeed, the only respondents who discussed degree ladders were a few community college faculty in occupational programs.

That study also included interviews with sixty-five community college students, and we found a few with plans to combine certificates with higher degrees. Doubting how long he would persist, one student was pursuing a certificate with a plan to pursue an associate degree if he succeeded. Another student was enrolled in a BA program in a four-year college, but was pursuing a certificate at a nearby community college on the side, just in case his liberal arts BA did not lead to a job. Interestingly, both students discovered this strategy from

Table 9. Predictors of Employment and Earnings by Highest Credential Attainment

	Logistic Regression of Employment Status 2012[c]				Linear Regression on Log Earnings 2011			
	Some College	Certificate	Associate's	Bachelor's	Some College	Certificate	Associate's	Bachelor's
SES 2002[a]	1.47**	1.22	0.72	0.97	0.08	-0.06	-0.11	0.08***
	(3.00)	(0.93)	(-1.06)	(-0.19)	(1.64)	(-0.81)	(-1.80)	(3.47)
Tenth grade test score[b]	1.01	1.03*	1.00	1.02	0.00	0.01	-0.00	0.00*
	(0.65)	(1.98)	(0.20)	(1.24)	(0.92)	(1.55)	(-0.04)	(2.02)
BA plans in twelfth grade	1.26	1.12	0.90	1.90*	-0.01	-0.01	-0.09	0.20*
	(1.43)	(0.42)	(-0.27)	(1.99)	(-0.14)	(-0.14)	(-1.15)	(2.36)
Enroll in first term after high school	1.87***	1.17	1.11	1.55	0.15*	0.13	0.08	-0.07
	(3.99)	(0.62)	(0.27)	(1.23)	(2.04)	(1.28)	(0.87)	(-0.65)
Hours worked per week in 2011	–	–	–	–	0.03***	0.02***	0.03***	0.02***
					(6.88)	(4.61)	(5.35)	(8.75)
Weeks employed in 2011	–	–	–	–	0.03***	0.02**	0.02***	0.02***
					(8.44)	(3.31)	(3.59)	(7.18)
Female	0.36***	0.40**	0.33**	0.39***	-0.22***	-0.38***	-0.21*	-0.09**
	(-6.54)	(-3.26)	(-2.86)	(-4.51)	(-3.59)	(-4.21)	(-2.48)	(-2.66)
Black	1.13	1.23	0.89	0.88	-0.22*	-0.13	-0.04	-0.07
	(0.53)	(0.54)	(-0.19)	(-0.33)	(-2.04)	(-0.70)	(-0.22)	(-0.81)
Hispanic	0.90	0.88	0.44	0.74	0.09	0.06	-0.03	-0.01
	(-0.51)	(-0.35)	(-1.47)	(-0.99)	(1.13)	(0.52)	(-0.23)	(-0.16)
Other race	1.22	0.59	0.35	0.89	-0.12	-0.17	-0.23	0.02
	(0.75)	(-1.36)	(-1.85)	(-0.49)	(-1.02)	(-0.89)	(-1.27)	(0.50)
Constant	–	–	–	–	7.34***	7.96***	8.23***	8.04***
					(27.94)	(16.22)	(18.59)	(34.29)
N	1845	671	536	2652	1142	417	346	2087

Source: Authors' calculations based on ELS 2002-2012.
Sample: On-time high school graduates, not enrolled in a postsecondary institution in 2012.
Note: T-statistics in parentheses.
[a]Our SES variable was created by NCES through ELS of information on parents' occupations and parents' education.
[b]Test score is the composite math and language arts standardized test score from 2002.
[c]Employed (full time or part time) versus unemployed.
* $p < .05$; ** $p < .01$; *** $p < .001$

their middle-class relatives, while none of the low-income students in our sample knew about certificates. Few students seem to know about degree ladders or their possible desirability, although many could likely benefit from this strategy.

However, some colleges do announce degree ladders, and a few go one step further by building them into their programs. These colleges structure the curriculum so that students get an automatic certificate after passing the first year's courses, an associate's degree after two years, and a BA after four years (Rosenbaum, Deil-Amen, and Person 2006). These colleges consider degree ladders an insurance policy to guarantee interim payoffs. The debate about which degree to choose disappears in these programs because everyone pursues multiple credentials simultaneously.

Although certificate and associate degree credits do not always count toward later degrees, the overlap is typically higher in new bachelors of applied science degrees (BAS), which are often in the same occupations as applied associate's degrees such as computer networking, health, and business (see also Bragg and Ruud 2012). Even if all credits do not transfer, degree ladders can provide valuable fallback options. For example, we interviewed a student who dropped out after two years because of a family crisis (Rosenbaum, Deil-Amen, and Person 2006). Although she could not complete her planned BA, she had attained a certificate and associate degree in the meantime, both of which had already improved her labor market prospects. For students who face high risks of family crises, degree ladders seem ideally suited to unpredictable interruptions.

Colleges can create procedures that take advantage of colleges' current credential options and reduce students' financial and academic risks (Rosenbaum, Deil-Amen, and Person 2006). Degree ladders, which can be developed from existing two-year college programs, allow students new options for combining credentials and create potential for increased labor market benefits. We reported a few examples, but more comprehensive research can help educators understand how these options alter student success outcomes.

CONCLUSION

Our aim is to provide a starting point for new questions about rarely considered college options and outcomes. Our central contention is that many desirable options are available that would increase youths' odds of success, but are not usually a part of their plans. We show that students with low test scores and from low-SES families complete sub-BA credentials more frequently than BAs, and that sub-BA credentials are associated with improved employment, earnings, and many nonmonetary job rewards. Moreover, while being low SES and having low test scores are significant obstacles to BA degree completion, and to earnings payoffs from BA degrees, they may not be obstacles to sub-BA credential completion or their payoffs.

Research often finds hidden obstacles to helping disadvantaged youth, and even the most well-intentioned and carefully considered reforms may have adverse effects. One famous example is Sesame Street, which aimed to reduce inequality in reading skills, but actually had greater benefits for advantaged children, which ultimately increased inequality (Cook 1975). Although reformers call for new career pathways that do not encourage traditional inequalities (Schwartz 2014), our analyses indicate that colleges already provide valuable alternative pathways in sub-BA credentials, but they are not visible and are not considered in the college-planning process in most high schools. Certificates and associate's degrees are better options than many expect, and are even associated with nonmonetary job rewards that are rarely considered by research. At a time of increasing inequality, when education often reproduces background disadvantages, these sub-BA credentials may not reproduce inequality in completion odds or in labor market outcomes, and they deserve further consideration.

Some observers criticize processes that do not reward high test scores for being unmeritocratic. However, that may be a mistaken inference in this case. Sub-BA credentials and sub-BA labor markets require many kinds of merit—effort, persistence, and technical skills, but perhaps not high-level academic or testing skills. Surgical technicians, computer network technicians, and mechanics must possess job skills, communications skills, problem-solving skills, and meticulous attention to quality, but basic math and English skills may be sufficient. Requiring high test scores for these jobs may have nothing to do with merit or performance. Moreover, with potentially reduced academic requirements for certain college credentials, a single college readiness standard is likely not enough.

The lack of SES correlation with postgraduation sub-BA outcomes is perhaps our most surprising finding. SES usually increases education and occupational attainments, often because of better schooling, social connections, or cultural capital associated with SES. However, mid-skilled jobs that require sub-BA credentials may not need the skills and cultural values emphasized in middle-class homes, meaning more students who follow that pathway can succeed (Lareau 2012). One potential explanation for the lack of disadvantages for low-income or low-achieving students may be that more advantaged students do not recognize the value of sub-BA credentials, so they do not seek them in large numbers and use their advantages to crowd out other students. A different explanation is that these credentials and their related career pathways simply may not require the cultural capital that comes from higher SES backgrounds (Laureau 2012), or these programs teach the necessary soft skills and cultural values.

One serious limitation in most research, including ours, is that credentials likely have different payoffs in different occupations (Jacobson and Mohker 2008). Even large national samples such as ELS may be too small to analyze specific occupations, and miss important nuances of sub-BA credential outcomes. The best data sets to study these issues are the universe of students in an entire state. Jacobson and Mohker took advantage of Florida's rich data to study nearly four million students to find large discrepancies by major, and future research on these issues can do the same.

Another limitation in the presented data is the age of the ELS and AddHealth samples (twenty-six to thirty-two) because credential payoff disparities may increase at older ages. Yet the employment outcomes of young adults are important. Young adults have great difficulty earning enough to support a family (Settersten and Ray 2011), and as discussed earlier, these are the foundational years for career development. Further work can examine whether our findings that certificates and AAs lead to valuable careers holds as individuals get older.

Despite those caveats, the presented analyses give hope that nontraditional students with poor odds of BA completion may be able to attain a credential with real labor market value. We have discussed at length the possibility of degree ladders, contending that the usual either-or arguments of sub-BAs versus BAs present a false dichotomy. Students do not have to pick a single degree goal, and some may benefit from planning a sequence of credentials. Some colleges even make degree ladders almost automatic. Advising procedures can make sub-BA credentials fallback options for students about to drop out of a BA program, so that students can benefit more quickly, instead of wasting several years before returning to college (Horn 1999). Future studies should examine college procedures designed to help students see how to combine credentials and their benefits.

Americans can be proud of dramatically improving college access for high school graduates, but we cannot stop there. Our society gives youth a too narrow vision of college options, careers, and the academic requirements for attaining them. In particular, while most students pursue BA degrees that may have low odds of success for the most disadvantaged among them, they often ignore valuable sub-BA credentials. We do youth a disservice by avoiding mention of sub-BAs and their desirable features. Advocates of the universal BA pursuits should reconsider blindly advising all students into a singular goal that prevents them from seeing sub-BA credentials that offer fewer academic and financial obstacles, better odds, desirable outcomes, and the potential to pursue BA plans later. Students would benefit from receiving full information on all their postsecondary options.

REFERENCES

Adelman, Clifford. 2003. "Principal Indicators of Student Academic Histories in Post-Secondary Education, 1970–2000." Washington: U.S. Department of Education, Institute of Education Sciences.

Ayers, Jeremy. 2011. "College for All or College for Some?" Washington, D.C.: Center for American Progress.

Baum, Sandy, and Jennifer Ma. 2013. *Education Pays*. Princeton, N.J.: College Board.

Belfield, Clive R., and Thomas Bailey. 2011. "The Benefits of Attending Community College: A Review of the Evidence." *Community College Review* 39(1): 46–68.

Bills, David B. 2004. *The Sociology of Education and Work*. Oxford: Blackwell Publishing.

Bound, John, Brad Hershbein, and Bridget T. Long. 2009. "Playing the Admissions Game: Reactions to Increasing College Competition." *Journal of Economic Perspectives* 23(4): 119–46.

Bragg, Debra, and Collin Ruud. 2012. "Why Applied Baccalaureates Appeal to Working Adults: From National Results to Promising Practices." *New Directions for Community Colleges* 2012(158): 73–85.

Brint, Steven. 2003. "Few Remaining Dreams: Community Colleges Since 1985." *Annals of the American Academy of Political and Social Science* 586 (March): 16–37.

Brint, Steven, and Jerome Karabel. 1989. *The Diverted Dream: Community Colleges and the Promise of Educational Opportunity in America, 1900–1985*. New York: Oxford University Press.

Brown, Duane. 2007. *Career Information, Career Counseling, and Career Development*, 9th ed. Boston, Mass.: Pearson.

Carnevale, Anthony P., Stephen J. Rose, and Andrew Hanson. 2012. "Certificates: Gateway to Gainful Employment and College Degrees." Washington, D.C.: Georgetown University Center on Education and the Workforce.

Choy, Susan. 2001. "Students Whose Parents Did Not Go to College: Postsecondary Access, Persistence, and Attainment. Findings from the Condition of Education." *NCES* report 126. Washington, D.C.: National Center for Education Statistics.

Cook, Thomas. 1975. *Sesame Street Revisited*. New York: Russell Sage Foundation.

Day, Jennifer C., and Eric C. Newburger. 2002. "The Big Payoff: Educational Attainment and Synthetic Estimates of Work-Life Earnings." *Current Population Report* P23-210. Washington: U.S. Census Bureau. https://www.census.gov/prod/2002pubs/p23-210.pdf.

DiPrete, Thomas, and Claudia Buchmann. 2013. *The Rise of Women: The Female Advantage in Education and What it Means for American Schooling*. New York: Russell Sage Foundation Press.

Dougherty, Kevin J. 1994. *The Contradictory College: The Conflicting Origins, Impacts, and Futures of the Community College*. Albany: State University of New York Press.

Education Trust. 2014. "College Results Online." Accessed Accessed February 23, 2015. http://www.edtrust.org/issues/higher-education/college-results-online.

Ganzglass, Evelyn. 2014. "Scaling 'Stackable Credentials': Implications for Implementation and Policy." Washington, D.C.: Center for Postsecondary and Economic Success at CLASP.

Gardner, Walt. 2013. "'College-for-All' Policy Bad for Students, Bad for Jobs," *Washington Times*, February 10, 2013. Accessed February 23, 2015. http://www.washingtontimes.com/news/2013/feb/10/gardnercollege-all-policy-bad-students-bad-jobs/ Reality Check blog for Education Week.

Glass, Kevin. 2014. "How 'College-For-All' Harms America's Students." *Townhall Magazine*, September 14, 2014. Accessed February 23, 2015. http://townhall.com/tipsheet/kevinglass/2014/09/14/how-collegeforall-harms-americas-students-n1891482.

Goyette, Kimberly. 2008. "College for Some to College for All: Social Background, Occupational Expectations, and Educational Expectations Over Time." *Social Science Research* 37(2): 461–84.

Grandner, Michael A., Lauren Hale, Melisa Moore, and Nirav P. Patel. 2010. "Mortality Associated with Short Sleep Duration: The Evidence, the Possible Mechanisms, and the Future." *Sleep Medicine Review* 14(3): 191–203.

Grubb, Norton W. 1996. *Working in the Middle*. San Francisco, Calif.: Jossey-Bass.

———. 2002. "Learning and Earning in the Middle, Part I: National Studies of Pre-Baccalaureate Education." *Economics of Education Review* 21(4): 299–321.

Hamilton, Stephen F. 1990. *Apprenticeship for Adult-*

hood: Preparing Youth for the Future. New York: The Free Press.

Holzer, Harry, Julia Lane, David Rosenblum, and Frederik Andersson. 2011. *Where Are All the Good Jobs Going?* New York: Russell Sage Foundation.

Horn, Laura J. 1999. "Stopouts or Stayouts? Undergraduates Who Leave College in Their First Year." Washington, D.C.: National Center for Education Statistics.

Jacobson, Lou, and Christine G. Mohker. 2008. "Pathways to Boosting the Earnings of Low-Income Students by Increasing Their Educational Attainment." Washington, D.C. / Alexandria, Va.: Hudson Institute / Center for Naval Analyses.

Jacob, Brian A., and Tamara Wilder. 2010. "Educational Expectations and Attainment." *NBER* working paper no. 15683. Cambridge, Mass.: National Bureau of Economic Research.

Kahlenberg, Richard D. 2011. "Insights and Commentary on Higher Education." *The Chronicle of Higher Education: Insights Blog.* June 9, 2011. Accessed February 24, 2015. http://chronicle.com/blogs/innovations/the-college-for-all-debate/29623.

Kalleberg, Arne. 2011. *Good Jobs, Bad Jobs.* New York: Russell Sage Foundation.

Karabel, Jerome. 1979. "The Failure of American Socialism Reconsidered." *Socialist Register* 16: 204–227.

Kena, Grace, Susan Aud, Frank Johnson, Xiaolei, Wang, Jijun Zhang, Amy Rathbun, Sidney Wilkinson-Flicker, and Paul Kristapovich. 2014. *The Condition of Education 2014.* NCES-083. Washington, D.C.: National Center for Education Statistics. Accessed February 23, 2016. http://nces.ed.gov/pubs2014/2014083.pdf.

Kohn, Melvin, and Carmi Schooler. 1983. *Work and Personality.* New York: Ablex.

Lareau, Annette. 2011. *Unequal Childhoods.* Berkeley: University of California Press.

———. 2012. "Invisible Inequality." In *Sociology of Education*, 2nd ed., edited by Alan Sadovnik. New York: Routledge.

Marcotte, Dave E., Thomas Bailey, Carey Borkoski, and Greg S. Kienzl. 2005. "The Returns of a Community College Education: Evidence from the National Education Longitudinal Survey." *Educational Evaluation and Policy Analysis* 27(2): 157–75.

Massey, Douglas, Camille Charles, Garvey Lundy, and Mary Fischer. 2003. *Source of the River: Social Origins of Freshmen at America's Selective Colleges and Universities.* Princeton, N.J.: Princeton University Press.

Mortimer, Jeylan, Mike Vuolo, Jeremy Staff, Sara Wakefield, and Wanling Xie. 2008. "Tracing the Time of 'Career' Acquisition in a Contemporary Youth Cohort." *Work and Occupations* 35(1): 44–84.

National College Advising Corps. n.d. "Our Results." Accessed February 23, 2015. http://advisingcorps.org/our-impact/our-results/.

Oreopoulos, Philip, and Kjell G. Salvanes. 2001. "Priceless: The Nonpecuniary Benefits of Schooling." *Journal of Economic Perspectives* 25(1): 159–84.

Presser, Harriet B. 2005. *Working in a 24/7 Economy: Challenges for American Families.* New York: Russell Sage Foundation.

Princeton Review. n.d. "Find the School of Your Dreams." Accessed February 23, 2015. http://www.princetonreview.com/college-education.aspx.

Reynolds, John, Michael Stewart, Ryan Macdonald, and Lacey Sischo. 2006. "Have Adolescents Become Too Ambitious? High School Seniors' Educational and Occupational Plans, 1976 to 2000." *Social Problems* 53(2): 186–206.

Rivera, Mario A., and James D. Ward. 2010. "Institutional Racism, Diversity and Public Administration." In *Diversity and Public Administration: Theory, Issues, and Perspectives*, 2nd ed., edited by Mitchell F. Rice. London: M. E. Sharpe.

Rosenbaum, James, E. 2001. *Beyond College for All.* New York: Russell Sage Foundation.

Rosenbaum, James E., Kennan Cepa, and Janet Rosenbaum. 2013. "Beyond the One-Size-Fits-All College Degree." *Context* 12(1): 49–52.

Rosenbaum, James E., Regina Deil-Amen, and Ann E. Person. 2006. *After Admission: From College Access to College Success.* New York: Russell Sage Foundation.

Rosenbaum, James E., Janet Rosenbaum, Jennifer Stephan, Amy E. Foran, and Pam Schuetz. 2015. "Beyond BA Blinders: Cultural Impediments to College Success. My 4-Year Degree Was the Longest 8 Years of My Life." In *The Cultural Matrix: Understanding Black Youth*, edited by Orlando Patterson. Cambridge, Mass.: Harvard University Press.

Rosenbaum, James E., Jennifer Stephan, and Janet

Rosenbaum. 2010. "Beyond One-Size-Fits-All College Dreams." *American Educator* 34(3): 2–13.

Rosenbaum, Janet. 2012. "Degrees of Health Disparities: Health Status Disparities Between Young Adults with High School Diplomas, Sub-Baccalaureate Degrees, and Baccalaureate Degrees." *Health Services and Outcomes Research Methodology* 12(2-3): 156–68.

Salary.com. 2013. "8 College Degrees with the Worst Return on Investment." October 23, 2013. Accessed February 23, 2015. http://www.salary.com/8-college-degrees-with-the-worst-return-on-investment/.

Samuelson, Robert J. 2012. "It's Time to Drop the College-For-All Crusade," *Washington Post*, May 27, 2012. Accessed February 24, 2015. http://www.washingtonpost.com/opinions/its-time-to-drop-the-college-for-all-crusade/2012/05/27/gJQAzcUGvU_story.html.

Schneider, Barbara L., and David Stevenson. 2000. *The Ambitious Generation: America's Teenagers, Motivated but Directionless*. New Haven, Conn.: Yale University Press.

Schwartz, Robert. 2014. "The Pursuit of Pathways." *American Educator* 38(3): 24–41.

Settersten, Richard, and Barbara Ray. 2011. *Not Quite Adults*. New York: Bantam.

Sewell, William H., and Robert M. Hauser. 1980. "The Wisconsin Longitudinal Study of Social and Psychological Factors in Aspirations and Achievements." *Research in Sociology of Education and Socialization* 1(1): 59–99.

Snyder, Thomas D., and Sally A. Dillow. 2012. *Digest of Educational Statistics*. NCES 2012–001. Washington: U.S. Department of Education. Accessed February 23, 2016. http://nces.ed.gov/pubs2012/2012001.pdf.

Steinberg, Jacques. 2010. "Plan B: Skip College." *New York Times*, May 16, 2010. Accessed February 23, 2015. http://www.nytimes.com/2010/05/16/weekinreview/16steinberg.html?pagewanted=all.

Stephan, Jennifer L., James E. Rosenbaum, and Ann E. Person. 2009. "Stratification in College Entry and Completion." *Social Science Research* 38(3): 572–93.

Stone, James, and Morgan Lewis. 2012. *College and Career Ready in the Twenty-First Century*. New York: Teachers College Press, Columbia University.

Tucker, Marc. 2013. "What Does It Really Mean to Be College and Work Ready?" Washington, D.C.: National Center on Education and the Economy.

Vuolo, Mike, Jeylan T. Mortimer, and Jeremey Staff. 2014. "Adolescent Precursors of Pathways from School to Work." *Journal of Research on Adolescence* 24(1): 145–62.

Wyner, Joshua. 2014. *What Excellent Community Colleges Do*. Cambridge, Mass.: Harvard Education Press.

Zasloff, Beth, and Joshua Steckel. 2014. *Hold Fast to Dreams*. New York: The New Press.

PART III
Policy Interventions: Incentives, Controls, and Metrics

Pricing and University Autonomy: Tuition Deregulation in Texas

JEONGEUN KIM AND KEVIN STANGE

This paper investigates changes in tuition policies in the wake of tuition deregulation in Texas, which in 2003 transferred tuition-setting authority from the state legislature to institutions. We find that price increases accelerated, particularly at the most selective institutions. Institutions also began differentiating price by undergraduate program, raising relative prices for the most costly and lucrative majors, including engineering, business, nursing, and architecture. Price increases were particularly large for institutions with the highest initial costs and for programs with a high earnings premium within institutions, though lower for institutions with more low-income students. These distinctions suggest that public postsecondary institutions respond to microeconomic incentives when given greater autonomy to set price, and take some measures to alleviate impacts on low-income students. The Texas experience suggests that decentralized price-setting generates greater price differentiation within the public higher education system, both across and within institutions.

Keywords: tuition, deregulation, differential tuition, college pricing

Colleges are increasingly being judged by the value they provide to their students as critics point to skyrocketing tuition, low graduation rates, and poor job prospects of recent graduates. Lawmakers and policymakers at many levels have joined this chorus of criticism and have been introducing ways to hold colleges more accountable for their value. The Obama administration has explored the possibility of tying federal financial aid to different measures of value, and many states have introduced performance-based funding. However, diminished direct state support for higher education has made it difficult for colleges to maintain, much less improve, the quality of their programs. In fact, John Bound, Michael Lovenheim, and Sarah Turner (2010) find that much of the decline in graduation rates since the 1970s can be traced to reductions in educational resources and enrollment shifts to less-resourced sectors.

Declines in state support have also raised affordability concerns because many institutions have responded by raising tuition. Although shifting costs to students via tuition increases would be one way to compensate for lost state revenue, this option is limited for many public colleges and universities that have limited flexibility to set prices. The responsibility for setting tuition is left to individual institutions in only ten states; state legislatures or other broad government boards have primary authority in the others (Carlson 2011). This pattern is changing, however, as a

Jeongeun Kim is assistant professor at Mary Lou Fulton Teachers College, Arizona State University. **Kevin Stange** is assistant professor at Ford School of Public Policy, University of Michigan.

Direct correspondence to: Jeongeun Kim, Mary Lou Fulton Teachers College, Arizona State University, 1050 S Forest Mall, Tempe, AZ 85281, Jeongeun.Kim@asu.edu; and Kevin Stange, Ford School of Public Policy, University of Michigan, 735 S. State Street, Ann Arbor, MI, 48109, kstange@umich.edu.

handful of states (Florida, Virginia, Texas) decentralized tuition-setting authority in some way recently, and lawmakers in New York, Washington, Ohio, and Wisconsin have considered doing so (Camou and Patton 2012; Deaton 2006; Marley and Herzog 2015; McBain 2010).

Despite the policy relevance and potential impacts on access and affordability, evidence is scant on how public institutions alter their tuition levels or policies when given more autonomy over tuition-setting. Much research on university pricing has focused on private, particularly elite, institutions (Clotfelter 1996; Ehrenberg 2001; Epple, Romano, and Sieg 2006) and generally not on tuition-setting structures. Findings are mixed in the limited analysis of the public sector that has examined tuition-setting and governance structures. Robert Lowry (2001) finds that tuition at public universities is higher when a state has multiple governing boards, Michael Rizzo and Ronald Ehrenberg (2004) find no relationship, and Michael McLendon, James Hearn, and Robert Hammond (2013) find that tuition is lower in states with more governing boards. Because the number of governing boards in each state varies little over time, each of these studies essentially relies on the cross-sectional relationship between state governance structures and tuition levels, which may be subject to various forms of bias.[1] Stella Flores and Justin Shepard (2014) examine the effect of tuition deregulation at seven Texas institutions and find that institution-level price has accelerated but effects on enrollment of underrepresented minority students is mixed. The behavior of private universities is unlikely to provide a clear model of how public institutions will respond to greater pricing authority, as public institutions have a formal responsibility for educating their in-state residents that private institutions do not (Weisbrod, Ballou, and Asch 2008). Furthermore, if state lawmakers internalized institutional objectives before deregulation, shifts in the nominal responsibility for setting prices could have minimal impact. For all these reasons, an empirical examination of whether and how public institutions alter prices when given more authority to do so is essential.

To answer these questions, this study describes the experience of public universities in the state of Texas, which underwent an enormous change in pricing control in 2003 when tuition-setting authority was transferred from the state legislature to the governing board of each public university. Texas is a particularly good setting to examine the topic of deregulation in light of its institutional diversity and the scope of the policy changes. We make three contributions to prior work. First, we focus on a sharp change in the financial independence of public universities specifically as it relates to tuition-setting authority, rather than on cross-sectional relationships between general measures of governance structure and tuition levels. Examining tuition changes around a known policy change and for a fixed set of institutions eliminates many sources of bias inherent in previous cross-sectional work. Second, in addition to studying institution-level price variation, we also examine program-specific prices within institutions. Prior research on price-setting has focused on overall institution-level price with no systematic analysis of price differences across programs within institutions. The program-specific analysis in this study is enabled by novel data about pricing practices at a program level within institutions, which we assembled from numerous historical and archival sources. Within-institution analysis is important because many institutions have turned to or are considering differential tuition to maintain program quality in the face of diminished state appropriations. Third, we focus broadly on public four-year colleges and universities in the state, rather than on private institutions or selective public flagships. This is important as the ma-

---

1. Rizzo and Ehrenberg (2004) do use panel data, but omit governing board measures from their longitudinal analysis presumably because they do not change much over time. McLendon and his colleagues (2013) incorporate several measures of governance structure (including number of governing boards) in longitudinal analysis that includes institution fixed effects, but do not explicitly assess the extent to which governing board measures actually change over time, which is necessary for identification.

jority of college students attend public four-year colleges outside the flagships.

In our analysis, we first compare the experience of Texas to other states using institution-level data and a difference-in-differences approach. We find that price increases accelerated across the state in the wake of deregulation. In fact, the raw price gap between public universities in Texas and elsewhere closed in the years following deregulation. Event study estimates suggest that college prices in Texas were trending similarly to those in other states in the years leading up to deregulation, but diverged immediately afterwards. Relative price growth was particularly large at the most selective institutions and was not fully offset by additional grant aid, thus Texas college students' net price increased considerably. We next look within Texas, comparing price growth across institutions and programs. We find that price increases were particularly large for those institutions with the greatest initial costs, for high-cost fields, and for the most lucrative and selective programs within institutions. Institutions with many low-income students experienced lower price growth and additional grant aid also offset some of the price growth for low-income students. One implication is that deregulation resulted in much greater differentiation within the public higher education system in Texas.

These results suggest that public institutions respond to microeconomic incentives when setting prices but take measures to mitigate impacts on low-income students. Although it may not be surprising that institutions altered prices following deregulation, the specific patterns of these changes were unknown beforehand and are potentially informative about the differing objectives of institutions and state lawmakers. State lawmakers appear to place relatively more value on broad-based affordability, having maintained low and uniform sticker prices prior to deregulation. Institutions, on the other hand, appear to place relatively more weight on program quality and desire greater differentiation, both across programs and institutions. Whether these patterns reflect different objectives (such as a different conception of social welfare on the part of institutions) or differences in information (institutions may have better information about the appropriate level of differentiation), we cannot tell. Regardless, the balance struck between affordability and quality objectives clearly depends on the nominal price-setter, which numerous states have recently altered (or considered altering). The equity and efficiency consequences of these price changes ultimately hinges on how they affected the sorting of students into programs, changed institutional capacity, and impacted program quality. A necessary first step to addressing these normative issues is to document and understand how public institutions change their pricing practices when given full autonomy to do so.

BACKGROUND

Texas has a large and diverse public higher education system that includes thirty-nine four-year colleges, which range from very selective top research universities to relatively unselective regional campuses. As in many other states, these institutions have historically relied heavily on state appropriations as the main source of funding. In 2000, state appropriations accounted for 38 percent of the revenue at four-year institutions, and tuition for 18 percent (South Regional Education Board 2013), though appropriations have been declining in Texas for last five years (Palmer 2013).[2]

State appropriations in Texas are determined by a funding formula that reimburses institutions a fixed rate for the number of weighted semester credit hours its students earn. Weights, which vary across five academic levels and twenty discipline areas, are determined by cost differences.[3] Importantly,

---

2. In 2005, state appropriations accounted for 24.6 percent of the revenue at four-year institutions, and tuition accounted for 19.2 percent.

3. The five levels include lower division undergraduates, upper division undergraduates, graduate students, doctoral students, and professional students. The twenty discipline areas are liberal arts, science, fine arts, teacher education, agriculture, engineering, home economics, law, social sciences, library sciences, development

weights within these level-discipline cells are the same across all institutions; a flagship institution receives the same appropriation for a lower-division liberal arts course as a less selective institution, despite potentially investing more resources in this course. Thus institutions whose students would demand (or benefit from) a greater level of investment in a given discipline-level will find it difficult to do so because this spending would not be reimbursed by the state.

Higher tuition and fees is one way that institutions could potentially fund greater levels of investment than is supported by the state. Historically, however, tuition and fees in Texas were controlled quite closely by the state legislature. Tuition at public universities consists of statutory and designated tuition (THECB 2010b). Statutory tuition is a tuition charge authorized under Texas Education Code (TEC) 54.051, which is a fixed rate per credit hour that differs only by residency status, but is otherwise constant across institutions. Designated tuition is a charge authorized by TEC 54.0513 that permits institutions to impose an additional tuition charge that the governing board of the institution deems appropriate and necessary. Designated tuition, previously known as a building use fee, was intended to permit institutions with greater costs to capture some of that cost through fees. Though designated tuition charges were determined by institutions, the legislature historically capped designated tuition at the level of statutory tuition.

In addition to the statutory and designated tuition, universities were allowed to charge mandatory and course fees. Under TEC 55.16, amended in 2001, all public institutions were allowed to charge extra fees for costs associated with services or activities. Mandatory fees are charged to a student on enrollment to provide services available to every student. On the other hand, course fees include fees charged for students enrolled in a particular course, or discretionary fees for students participating in a special activity.

Tuition Deregulation

In response to the economic downturn, the state decreased revenue appropriations in 2002 (Hernandez 2009). With leadership from the state's research-intensive universities, particularly the University of Texas (UT) and Texas A&M systems, many institutions advocated for more flexibility in setting tuitions in this time of reduced state support. The UT system leadership argued that the traditional tuition model did not provide enough pricing options for the array of services offered and did not adequately consider variation across institutions in terms of market demand, types of programs offered or the national prominence of these programs (University of Texas 2008), claiming that a "deregulated environment is a more efficient environment" (Hall 2003). The argument was that tuition flexibility would not only permit maintenance of existing levels of service, but also increase institutional agility to anticipate and meet statewide educational and economic development needs. Institutions would be able to actively engage in enrollment management using the market forces of supply and demand. Furthermore, the advocates insisted that tuition deregulation would improve institutional performance as the market-driven pricing models encourage students to take higher course loads and minimize exposure to tuition escalation.

In September 2003, the legislature passed HB 3015, which modified TEC 54.0513 to allow governing boards of public universities to set different designated tuition rates, with no upper limit. The amount can also vary by program, course level, academic period, term, and credit load and any other dimension institutions deem appropriate.

The major concern about tuition deregulation was that large tuition increases may create financial burdens for low-income students. Thus the deregulation came with a requirement that 20 percent of the proceeds from Texas resident undergraduate rates greater than $46 per school credit hour be set aside to

---

education, vocational training, physical training, health services, pharmacy, business administration, optometry, teacher education practice, technology, nursing, and veterinary medicine. Weights are normalized to 1.00 for lower division liberal arts courses, and are updated every few years (THECB 2010a).

provide financial assistance to students.[4] In addition, the legislature mandated that every institution participating in tuition deregulation had to meet performance criteria and show progress toward the goals outlined in the Texas master plan for higher education (McBain 2010).

Review of Literature
Most research on college price-setting has examined the determinants of institution-level price, focusing on state appropriations, federal and state aid programs, market pressure, and governance structures.[5]

State Appropriations
Given the significant dependence of public institutions on public subsidizes, several researchers have investigated how state context matters for public institutions' pricing (Hearn, Griswold, and Marine 1996; Kane 1999; Paulsen 2000; Toutkoushian and Hollis 1998). Declines in state support are followed by increases in in-state tuition in subsequent years (Koshal and Koshal 2000) and higher net tuition revenue (Lowry 2001). Rizzo and Ehrenberg (2004) also find that higher state appropriations per students are associated with lower tuition, though the elasticity is far from unity.

The impact of state finance on tuition might also be mediated by institutional characteristics. Michael McLendon, James Hearn, and Robert Hammond (2013) find that as state appropriation increases, tuition at public flagships grows more slowly. Factors such as proportion of out-of-state students also influence tuition levels. Rizzo and Ehrenberg (2004) also show that schools with higher Barron's selectivity rankings, higher endowment per student, higher ratio of graduate to undergraduate students, and higher seating capacity charge more in-state undergraduate tuition.

Federal and State Aid
Several studies have investigated whether institutions capture the benefits of federal and state aid programs by increasing tuition, the so-called Bennett Hypothesis. Private selective institutions do capture some of the benefits of Pell Grants via higher net tuition, though public institutions do not appear to do so (Singell and Stone 2007; Turner 2012). Bridget Long (2004) finds that the Georgia HOPE scholarship decreased tuition at public institutions by 3 percent but increased it at private institutions by about 5 percent. The author explains these different patterns by the limited flexibility of public schools to raise tuition and the nature of the scholarship. Rizzo and Ehrenberg (2004) find somewhat mixed results on state merit-aid programs, depending on the states. Yet this study showed that more generous Pell Grant and federal subsidized loans significantly increased in-state tuition.

Market Structure
Caroline Hoxby (1997) presents the most comprehensive study on the changing market structure of higher education and its implication for institution quality and price. Using changes in several exogenous factors as instruments (telecommunications, travel costs, use of standardized admissions tests, tuition reciprocity agreements), she found that market expansion resulted in greater vertical differentiation, higher average quality, and increased average price as students increasingly sorted based on ability. Colleges also increased subsidies to high ability students, whose input quality is high.

This study and several others find significant differences between public and private institutions in response to market changes: the increase in tuition and subsidizes were most significant at elite private institutions (Clotfel-

---

4. Of the 20 percent, 5 percent funds the Texas B-On-Time Loan Program, which is a no-interest loan where the entire loan amount can be forgiven upon graduation if students graduate with a minimum of B grade GPA. The remaining 15 percent is allocated for each institution's need-based financial aid.

5. A long literature on the effects of tuition increases on student enrollment and success is indirectly relevant here in that students' enrollment responses should influence institutions' pricing decisions (for a recent overview of this literature, see Kane 1999; for program-specific enrollment responses to price, see Shin and Milton 2008; Stange 2015).

ter 1996). One explanation is that public institutions' ability to change tuition in response to market forces is often constrained by state policies and political pressures. Although institutions aggressively seek resources, various pressures from local governments, interest groups, alumni, governing boards, and appointment and evaluation of leaderships can also impact pricing decisions (Ehrenberg 2001).

Governance Structure

In light of these observed differences between public and private institutions and the vast differences in public institutions across states, several researchers have also examined governance structures as a mediating factor. Lowry (2001) finds that in the states where public universities have more financial autonomy, tuition and fee revenues tend to be higher. On the contrary, Rizzo and Ehrenberg (2004) find no evidence for the relationship between autonomous governance structures and higher tuition. This finding is echoed by McLendon, Hearn, and Hammond (2013), who find that having a weak governing board (a measure of institutional autonomy) has no significant association with tuition prices. A limitation of prior work on governance structures is that such structures rarely change over time. Previous work may thus conflate the effects of governance structure per se with other state-level factors that are correlated with it.

Program-Specific Pricing

Almost all previous research on price-setting focuses on factors that determine overall institution-level price and offers no analysis of price differences across programs within institutions. This is surprising, because many institutions have turned to differential tuition to maintain program quality in the face of diminished state appropriations. Differential pricing is particularly compelling for costly majors and for those that lead to jobs with higher economic returns (Ehrenberg 2007; Heller 2006; Mortenson 2004; Ward and Douglass 2005).

Only recently have these practices been documented on a national scale. In a broad survey of 165 public research universities, Glen Nelson (2008) finds that 45 percent of schools have at least one undergraduate program with differential tuition or fees in 2008, with most implementing them in the past decade. Many others, such as the University of California System, have recently considered such a scheme. Differential pricing by level, independent of major program, is more rare, but still present at some institutions (Ehrenberg 2012; Simone 2010). A recent survey found a continuation of this trend: Ehrenberg (2012) reports that 42 percent of all public doctoral institutions had some form of tuition differential in 2010–2011, as did many public master's-level (18 percent) and bachelor's-level (30 percent) public institutions, and that growth has been steady since the mid-1990s (Cornell Higher Education Research Institute 2012). In survey responses, campus administrators perceived that differential tuition increased tuition revenue, but did not perceive any effects on total enrollment or enrollment by major (Nelson 2008), particularly that of minority students (Ravenscroft and Enyeart 2009). Incremental tuition revenue is allocated to colleges or departments in most cases, and the central administration keeps part of differential tuition revenue at some institutions. The tuition revenue is spent on teaching expenditure (reduction of faculty-student ratio, increases in faculty salaries), equipment and technology support, and financial aid (Ravenscroft and Enyeart 2009).

THEORETICAL FRAMEWORK

To structure our empirical work, we briefly sketch several prominent economic factors potentially influencing public institutions' pricing behavior in the wake of tuition deregulation.[6] We pay particular attention to factors that explain why institutions may increase prices for particular programs rather than at the same rate across the board. Our starting point is a model of price-setting where univer-

---

6. This discussion glosses over the fact that the changes we document empirically result from a shift in price-setting autonomy from state lawmakers to institutions themselves. If lawmakers were completely internalizing the objectives of the institutions prior to deregulation, we would see little change in price following deregulation and would thus be unable to quantify the importance of the factors described.

sities have some market power (demand is not perfectly price elastic) and offer multiple products, such as training in different academic disciplines. Market power can arise either from students' geographic immobility or vertical differentiation with a small number of options at each quality level. Universities are assumed to choose prices and spending levels to maximize an objective (such as prestige, surplus, diversity, or student success) subject to a budget constraint that educational spending must be covered by tuition and state revenue.[7]

A first prediction is that institutions or programs with greater costs at baseline should charge higher prices after deregulation. Disciplines require different teaching technologies, creating variation in costs of facilities or faculty salary (Johnson and Turner 2009; Thornton 2007). For instance, engineering instruction is much more costly than instruction in liberal arts (Middaugh et al. 2003). In some academic fields, faculty can command greater compensation because of private-sector competition, and this may force institutions to generate more revenue to retain them (Deaton 2006). Before deregulation, institutions did not have the flexibility to align price very closely with inherent costs, thus some programs were underpriced relative to cost. This resulted in cross-subsidization across academic disciplines, from low-cost—such as the humanities and social sciences—to high-cost—such as fine arts, agriculture, business, and engineering (James 1978; Zemsky, Wegner, and Massy 2005). From this perspective, differential pricing alleviates undue expense on students in less expensive majors (Harwell 2013). Given pricing flexibility, universities will likely increase prices for costly majors and moderate increases for lower-cost ones (Berg and Hoenack 1987; Hoenack and Weiler 1975; Yanikoski and Wilson 1984). Although differential tuition could benefit low-income students who enter low-cost fields (Little, O'Toole, and Wetzel 1997), it may also hamper access to high-cost ones. Institutions concerned about access may thus allocate part of the incremental revenue to financial aid.

An observably similar, though conceptually distinct, prediction is that price increases should be greatest for those programs already making the largest educational investments before deregulation. Vertical differentiation across institutions arises from heterogeneous demand for college quality and complementarity between student ability and college quality (Hoxby 2009; Rothschild and White 1995). Price regulation constrains the extent of quality differentiation because students with high demand for educational inputs are not able to obtain (and pay for) them. Deregulation thus should increase price and educational inputs most dramatically at institutions and for programs that already had high levels of inputs, similar to the effects of increased market competition (Hoxby 1997, 2009). When proposing higher tuition, institutions emphasize the need to enhance quality through additional resources, which can be used for faculty hiring and salary increase, smaller classes, better facilities, and more student supports.[8] Departments' quest for quality and reputation are further driven by schools' desire to obtain resource parity with peer institutions (for example, Texas A&M University 2010), which may be most salient for the most well-resourced institutions at baseline.

A second prediction is that institutions and programs facing more elastic demand should be more reluctant to raise price. This is a basic tenet of monopolistic pricing and has been examined in the context of university pricing (Ehrenberg and Sherman 1987; Epple, Romano, and Seig 2006). At the program level, demand for majors may be less elastic if students expect the degree to pay off in the job market much more than their next alternative (such as business) or if the degree is required for entry to

---

[7]. We do not take a stand on institutional objective, though the predictions we make likely hold for several plausible institutional objective functions. Furthermore, institutions have other sources of revenue too, including alumni donations and federal and state grants. We ignore these in this study.

[8]. Texas A&M and the University of Houston report that additional revenue, beyond the 20 percent set aside for financial aid, is largely retained by the colleges and spent at the discretion of the dean of the colleges (Ravenscroft and Enyeart 2009).

the related occupation (such as nursing). Although it is difficult to infer demand elasticity directly without putting more structure on the nature of the higher education market, we propose several markers for demand elasticity at the institution and program level.

Third, it is likely that institutions whose students are lower income or otherwise underrepresented in college would, all else equal, have more restrained price increases following deregulation. Public universities have multiple objectives, including providing access to postsecondary education for socioeconomically disadvantaged students. In fact, increasing access and success for disadvantaged students was one of the main objectives of Texas' master plan for higher education in 2000 (THECB 2000). Price increases at institutions that serve many low-income students may thus be particularly detrimental to states' access goals. Finally, institutions' pricing decisions following deregulation could reflect other objectives, such as responding to market needs for certain types of work forces (Deaton 2006). For example, institutions may not want to increase price for certain majors deemed critical to the local workforce. We do not investigate this factor directly.

CROSS-STATE COMPARISONS

We begin our analysis by contrasting the experience of public universities in Texas to similar universities in other states, which were not subject to the regulatory change. From the Integrated Postsecondary Education Data System (IPEDS), we assemble data on in-state tuition and fees, revenues by category, and total enrollment for each public four-year university in the country from 2000 to 2010.[9] To this data we merge on information about Barron's selectivity in 2004 and the state unemployment rate in each year. The full sample includes a total of 6,599 observations, corresponding to thirty-two Texas institutions and approximately 570 non-Texas institutions per year for eleven years. Figure 1 situates Texas institutions in the national landscape, depicting the average in-state tuition and fees at Texas and all non-Texas public universities over time. Although both groups of institutions have been raising prices over this period, the price jump at Texas universities in 2004 is notable. In fact, Texas universities proceed to increase prices at a higher rate and ultimately close the price gap by 2008. Figure 2 examines revenue sources. Though all universities have become more dependent on tuition revenue over time, Texas universities depend more on tuition in the postderegulation period (figure 2). The share of revenue coming from state appropriations also dropped in Texas relative to other institutions following deregulation, though it recovered eventually (figure 3).

To examine the robustness of these patterns to various control groups and to perform statistical inference, we estimate a generalized difference-in-differences (or event study) model. Specifically we regress an outcome (such as in-state tuition and fees) on an indicator for the institution being a Texas public institution, a full set of year fixed effects, and interactions between these year fixed effects and whether the institution is a Texas public university.

$$Y_{jt} = \beta_0 \cdot \text{Texas Public}_j + \sum_{s=2000}^{2010} \gamma_t 1(\text{year}_t = s) + \beta_t 1(\text{year}_t = s) \cdot \text{Texas Public}_j + e_{jt}$$

We omit the interaction term for 2003, setting this year as our base year against which we measure changes in relative price. The model produces a set of coefficients β_t indicating the difference in prices between Texas and non-Texas public universities in each year over and above what prevailed in 2003. Coefficients for the years prior to deregulation offer a test of whether Texas and non-Texas institutions were trending similarly before deregulation. In most of our analysis, we restrict our sample to institutions in sixteen southeastern and southwestern states,[10] though we also examine other sets of institutions as potential control groups.

---

9. We do not adjust nominal variables (prices and revenues) for inflation as aggregate price trends will be absorbed by trends in control institutions.

10. These states include Alabama, Arkansas, Florida, Georgia, Kentucky, Louisiana, Mississippi, North Carolina, South Carolina, Tennessee, Virginia, and West Virginia in the Southeast and Arizona, New Mexico, Oklahoma, and Texas in the Southwest.

Figure 1. Average Tuition and Fees

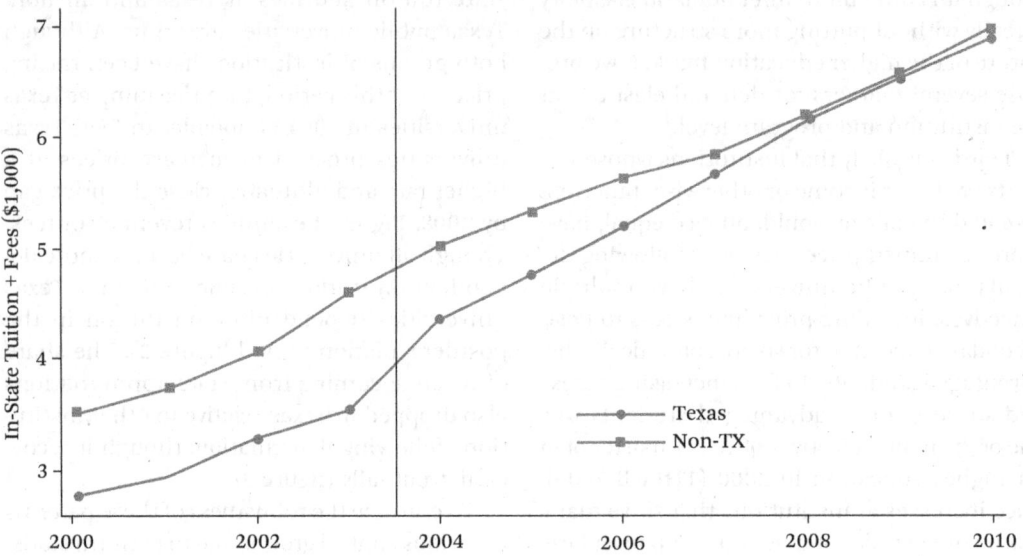

Sources: Authors' calculations based on IPEDS.
Note: The vertical line refers to 2003 when the bill targeting tuition deregulation was passed. Averages are weighted by total undergraduate enrollment. Nonweighted graphs look similar. Sample includes all public four-year institutions in the United States (public universities in Texas versus public universities in all other states).

Figure 2. Share of Revenue from Tuition

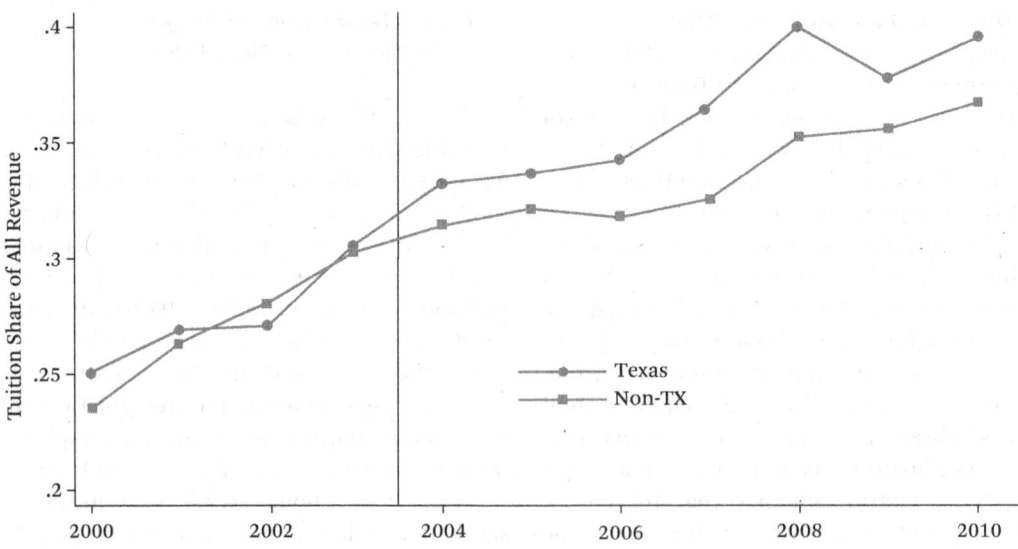

Sources: Authors' calculations.
Notes: The vertical line refers to 2003 when the bill targeting tuition deregulation was passed. Averages are weighted by total undergraduate enrollment. Nonweighted graphs look similar. Sample includes all public four-year institutions in the United States (public universities in Texas versus public universities in all other states).

Figure 3. Share of Revenue from State Appropriations

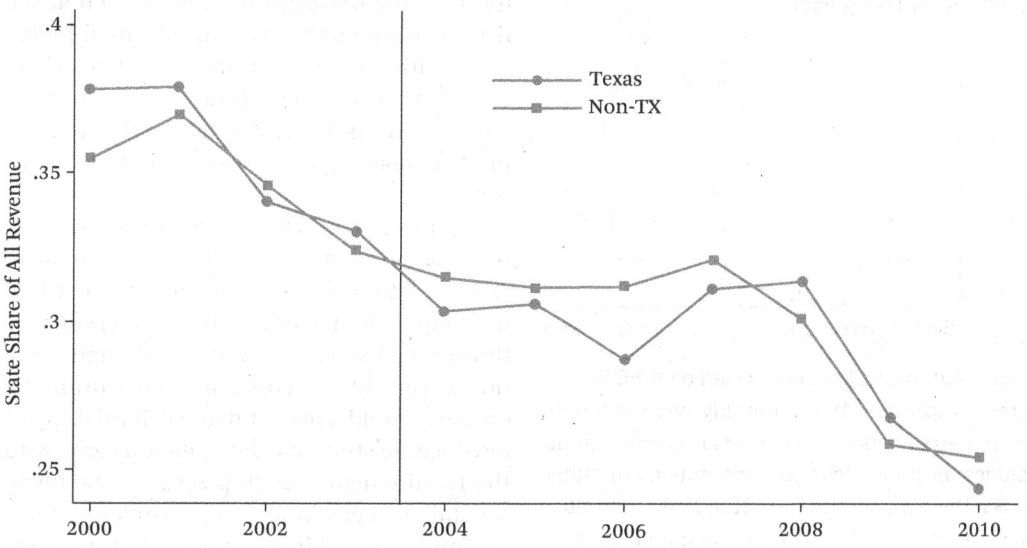

Sources: Authors' calculations based on IPEDS.
Notes: The vertical line refers to 2003 when the bill targeting tuition deregulation was passed. Averages are weighted by total undergraduate enrollment. Nonweighted graphs look similar. Sample includes all public four-year institutions in the United States (public universities in Texas versus public universities in all other states).

This restricted sample includes approximately 184 non-Texas institutions per year and a total of 2,096 non-Texas observations (for summary statistics, see table A1). Our analysis weights each observation according to its total undergraduate enrollment, though unweighted results are quite similar for all the outcomes we examine. As a robustness check, we also control for the state unemployment rate in some specifications, because Texas may have experienced a different economic shock during the recession, which could lead us to falsely attribute outcome differences to deregulation. To account for the possibility that state-specific factors may make the pricing decisions of institutions correlated within states, we cluster standard errors by state.

Figure 4 plots the point estimates and 95 percent confidence interval of the β_ts for in-state tuition and required fees, estimated using all public institutions in the Southeast or Southwest as controls. Although no trend difference is discernable between Texas and other states before deregulation, the relative price in Texas rises sharply in 2004 and continues to grow through 2009. Ultimately in-state sticker price increases by almost $1,500 within five years of deregulation, netting out the time trend for non-Texas institutions.[11] A lack of trend prior to deregulation suggests that Texas and non-Texas institutions had similar price trajectories prior to deregulation and might have been expected to continue this pattern in the absence of deregulation.[12]

---

11. Though not reported here, these patterns are mostly unchanged if we use different control groups, namely, all public institutions, only the Southeast, only the Southwest, or the Southeast excluding Florida. Texas private institutions do not provide a good control group as their tuition rates have been rising relative to Texas public institutions even before deregulation.

12. Tables A2 and A3 report estimates using various other control groups, not weighted by enrollment, and controlling for state unemployment rate. Estimates from these other specifications are usually similar qualitatively and quantitatively as our base model.

Figure 4. Estimates of Tuition and Fee Changes ($1,000) After Deregulation

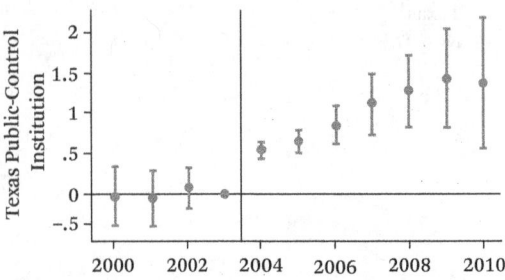

Source: Authors' calculation based on IPEDS.
Notes: Graph reports event-study point estimate and 95 percent confidence interval. Control group includes all public four-year institutions in either the Southwest or Southeast. Standard errors clustered by state. Estimates are weighted by total undergraduate enrollment.

Figure 5 separates institutions by selectivity. The steepest price increase is seen at the five institutions that Barron's deemed highly competitive or very competitive (UT-Austin, UT-Dallas, Texas A&M, Texas State—San Marcos, and Texas Tech), though sizable relative price increases are seen in all other sectors as well.[13]

Figures 6, 7, and 8 examine two alternative, revenue-based, measures of price. In figure 6, estimates for tuition and fee revenue per full-time-equivalent student are very similar to those for in-state sticker price, though more noisy. To address concerns that tuition increases would create financial hardship for low-income students, deregulation came with the requirement that 20 percent of the incremental proceeds from resident undergraduate tuition be set aside to fund need-based institutional aid and loan programs. Figure 7 pre-

Figure 5. Estimates of Tuition and Fee Changes ($1,000) After Deregulation, by Selectivity

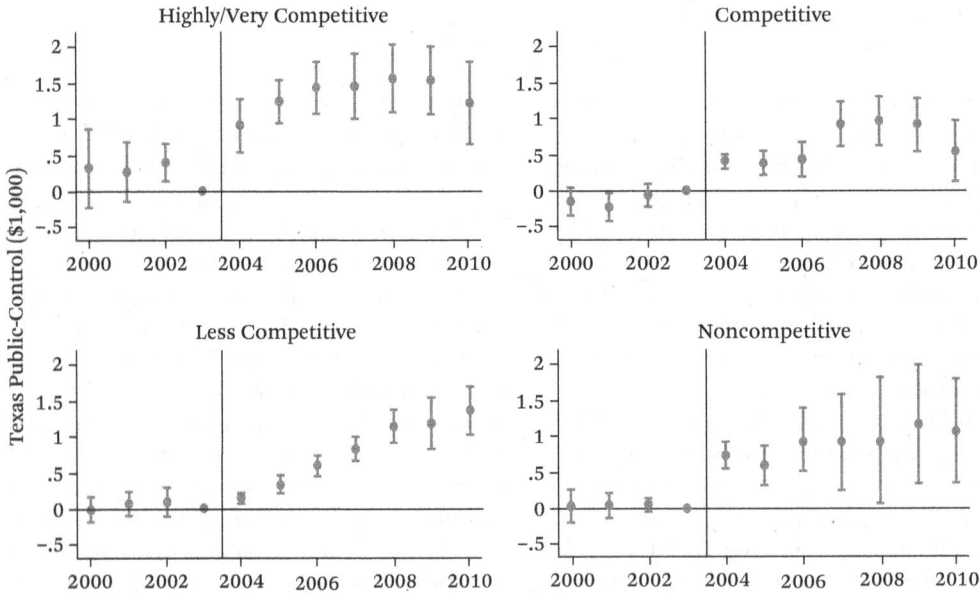

Source: Authors' calculations based on IPEDS.
Notes: Graph reports event-study point estimate and 95 percent confidence interval, separately by selectivity group. Control group includes all public four-year institutions in either the Southwest or Southeast. Standard errors clustered by state. Estimates are weighted by total undergraduate enrollment.

13. We do see large price increases in the noncompetitive sector as well, but given the few institutions in this sector in Texas (six), these results are quite imprecise, especially for later years.

Figure 6. Estimates of Changes in Tuition and Fee Revenue (per FTE, $1,000) After Deregulation

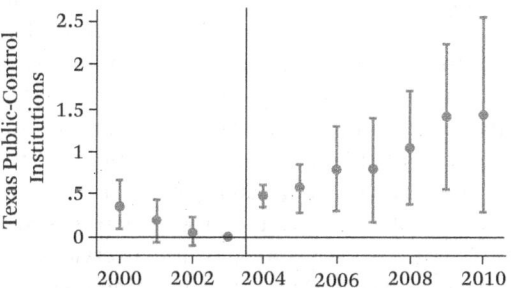

Source: Authors' calculations based on IPEDS.
Notes: Graph reports event-study point estimate and 95 percent confidence interval. Tuition and fee revenue per FTE includes students from all levels, not exclusively undergraduate. Control group includes all public four-year institutions in Southwest or Southeast. Standard errors clustered by state. Estimates are weighted by total undergraduate enrollment.

Figure 7. Estimates of Changes in Net Tuition Revenue (per FTE, $1,000) After Deregulation

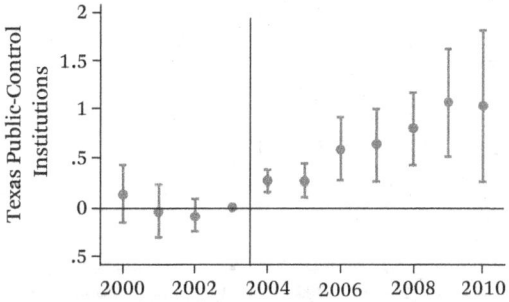

Source: Authors' calculations based on IPEDS.
Notes: Graph reports event-study point estimate and 95 percent confidence interval. Tuition and fee revenue per FTE includes students from all levels, not exclusively undergraduate. Net tuition revenue equals tuition revenue minus institutional grant expenditure. Control group includes all public four-year institutions in Southwest or Southeast. Standard errors clustered by state. Estimates are weighted by total undergraduate enrollment.

sents estimates of changes in net tuition revenue (tuition revenue minus institutional grants) following deregulation. Although the magnitude is somewhat smaller than for sticker price, the general pattern is quite similar. This trend suggests that some of the additional tuition revenue was devoted to financial aid. Figure 8 indicates that Texas public institutions have increased institutional grant aid after deregulation, compared with their counterparts in the Southeast and Southwest.

Figure 9 examines changes in state appropriations per student following deregulation using the same difference-in-differences model. Texas institutions had a similar path of state support in the years leading up to deregulation, though a sizable drop in state support in the four years following. The decline, which was partially enabled by deregulation through political compromise, is thus an alternative explanation for the steep tuition increases immediately after deregulation. Interestingly, Texas institutions continued to expand their prices relative to peer institution through 2008 and 2009, despite state appropriations having returned to parity.

Figure 8. Estimates of Changes in Institutional Grant Aid (per FTE, $1,000) After Deregulation

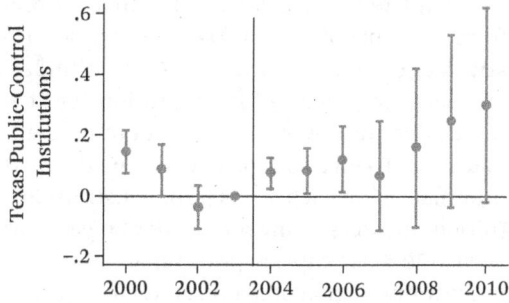

Source: Authors' calculations based on IPEDS.
Notes: Graph reports event-study point estimate and 95 percent confidence interval. Institutional grant aid per FTE includes students from all levels, not exclusively undergraduate. Control group includes all public four-year institutions in Southwest or Southeast. Standard errors clustered by state. Estimates are weighted by total undergraduate enrollment.

Figure 9. Estimates of Changes in State Appropriations per FTE ($1,000) After Deregulation

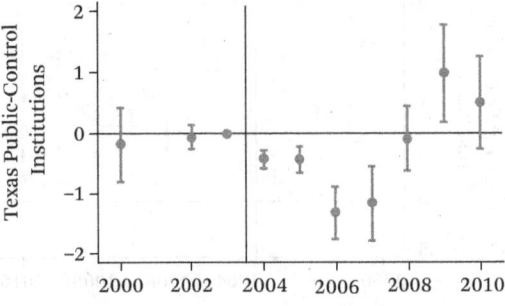

Source: Authors' calculations based on IPEDS.
Notes: Graph reports event-study point estimate and 95 percent confidence interval. State appropriations revenue per FTE includes students from all levels, not exclusively undergraduate. Control group includes all public four-year institutions in either the Southwest or Southeast. Standard errors clustered by state. Estimates are weighted by total undergraduate enrollment.

WITHIN TEXAS COMPARISONS

Data and Measures

Although information on average or typical tuition and fees are available for institutions from a number of standard sources, no systematic data exist about prices of specific undergraduate programs within institutions or how these prices vary with credit load or undergraduate level. To fill this gap, we collected detailed information on each Texas public institution's tuition and fees from the academic years of 2000 to 2011. We capture price separately by the five-way interaction of major, credit load, entering cohort, residency, and undergraduate level. This level of granularity is critical because many Texas institutions adopted price schedules that vary according to all of these characteristics. Our data come from historical universities' tuition and fee schedule documents, university catalogs, and campus and system documents on tuition policy, obtained from a number of sources. We include only tuition and fees (sticker price) for on-campus, undergraduate students. Tuition is the sum of statutory tuition and designated tuition, and fees include only mandatory fees, excluding voluntary or incremental fees. We also include program fees, which are charged to all students who enrolled in specific programs or schools with regard to advising and career services, instructional technology, and learning resource centers.

To examine the correlates of price changes, we also collected information about programs and institutions in 2002, the year before deregulation legislation passed and two years before it became effective, from several other sources. Information about expenditure by discipline and level was obtained from the Public General Academic Institution Expenditure Study, conducted by the Texas Higher Education Coordinating Board (THECB). The study provides information about the relative expenditure per student credit hour for twenty disciplines and five levels of instruction, using lower-division liberal arts courses as the reference. Instruction expenditure is calculated based on teaching salary, academic support expenses, institutional support, student services, and departmental operating expenses. We are able to estimate total grant aid (and thus net price) for needy students using micro data contained in the financial aid database compiled by THECB (2003–2011). These micro data contain grant aid information for all students who are eligible for need-based aid and enrolled in a Texas public institution. From this data we estimate the total, Pell, and non–Pell Grant aid for need-eligible in-state juniors enrolled full time, averaged separately for each program, institution, and year whenever there are at least five students.[14]

We constructed two proxies for demand

---

14. The financial aid data has a few caveats. First, it only consistently includes students that receive need-based aid, so net price can only be constructed for this group. Second, the target sample for the database changes over time. From 2001 to 2006 the database includes only students who received any type of need-based aid, or any type of aid that requires a need analysis. From 2007 to 2009, the database included students who are enrolled and completed either a FAFSA or TASFA (Texas Application for State Financial Aid), some of which may not have received any aid. Since 2010, the database was expanded to include students who did not apply for

elasticity at the program level. First, we created indicators of whether each program used an admissions process that was separate from that for overall freshman admissions to the university in 2002, collected from the same sources as the price information. This typically means that admissions to these programs were more selective than for other majors. Second, we estimate the average ten-year log earnings difference between enrollees of each program and Texas high school graduates who do not enroll in a Texas public postsecondary institution from the high school cohort of 2000 from student earnings micro data.[15] These data were obtained from merged student records obtained from the Texas Education Agency, Texas Higher Education Coordinating Board, and the Texas Workforce Commission, housed at the UT-Dallas Education Research Center as part of the Texas Schools Project. As a robustness check, we also use log earnings estimates adjusted to control for sex, race-ethnicity, free-lunch status, and high school exit exam scores. We interpret higher selectivity and higher earnings potential as markers for programs facing less elastic demand. Finally, we calculated the freshman acceptance rate from THECB data to characterize overall institutional selectively. The proportion of students receiving federal grant aid (a proxy for low-income) for the institution overall was drawn from IPEDS.

Although we collected price data on all academic programs, in the analysis we restrict our sample to liberal arts, engineering, business, nursing, and architecture programs. Liberal arts is the base program against which we compare the price and cost of others and the four others are the ones for which differential pricing is implemented most frequently (Nelson 2008).

Method

We aim to document and characterize how institutions' program-specific pricing changed following tuition deregulation. We begin with descriptive analysis, depicting price trends over time, across institution, and across programs. We also describe the various nonstandard pricing policies that institutions adopted following deregulation. These trends and practices have not previously been documented for the state of Texas and, as far as we can find, for any set of institutions following a pricing policy shift as dramatic as tuition deregulation.

To investigate the specific role of different factors in explaining these price trends, we look at the dollar change in total price (tuition + fees) for each program as a function of fixed characteristics of each program and institution prior to deregulation. We estimate equation (1) using OLS.

$$\Delta Price_{j,k} = \beta_0 + \beta_1 \left(\tfrac{Exp}{SCH}\right)_{jk,2002} + \beta_2(Selective_{jk}) + \beta_3(LnEarnings_{jk}) + \delta_k + \beta_z Z_j + \varepsilon_{jk} \quad (1)$$

Our main outcome, $\Delta Price_{j,k}$, is the change in price for program k at institution j between Fall 2003 (the last term before deregulation took effect) and Fall 2011.[16] We investigate sev-

---

need-based aid, but received merit or performance-based aid. In order to keep our sample of students consistent, we restrict to students that received a positive amount of grant aid from at least one need-based aid program (Pell, SEOG, Texas Grant, TPEG, or HB 3015). Finally, data confidentiality requirements prevent us from disclosing grant aid for observations with fewer than five students. Thus analysis of program-specific net price will be performed on fewer observations than that for sticker price.

15. Specifically, for all Texas high school graduates from the class of 2000 we regress log quarterly earnings measured ten or more years after graduation on indicators for first enrollment in one of about three hundred institution-major programs (plus community college). The estimated coefficients on these indicators provide the log earnings difference between enrollees in these programs and high school graduates who did not enroll in a Texas public postsecondary institution within two years of high school. These measures come from ongoing work in which one of the authors is examining the impact of price deregulation in Texas on the sorting of students to different programs.

16. Results are substantively very similar if 2002 is used as the base year. Pooling multiple years of price data and including many interactions between time, postderegulation, and our covariates does not improve precision since our main variables of interest are time-invariant.

Figure 10. Tuition and Fees by Institution

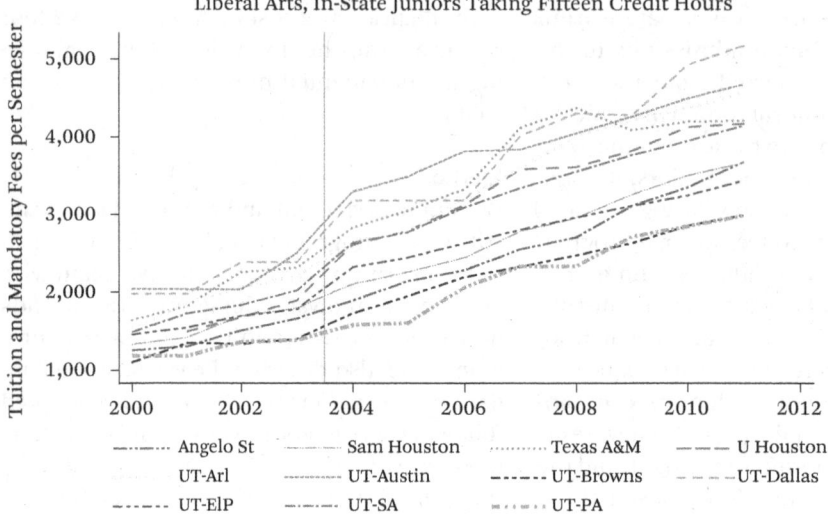

Source: Authors' calculations.

eral categories of explanatory variables. Our theoretical framework suggests that programs that have greater costs in the baseline period should have larger increases in price when they are permitted greater price-setting flexibility. Because institutions that spend more within narrow disciplines and levels are not provided greater funding per student, these institutions have an incentive to charge more when they are permitted to do so. The coefficient on $\left(\frac{Exp}{SCH}\right)_{jk,2002}$ captures whether programs that are more costly to provide experienced larger increases in price following deregulation. This cost variation is both across and within institutions, across programs. Second, $Selective_{jk}$ is an indicator for whether program k at institution j had a separate or selective admissions policy in 2002 that was distinct from that for other majors. For instance, students at UT-Arlington have to apply separately to enter the engineering program, where applicants are required to present higher minimum SAT or ACT scores than other majors. We use this variable as a proxy for a program having excess demand. Third, $LnEarnings_{jk}$ measures the earnings premium that students enrolled in program k at institution j have relative to high school graduates that do not enroll in a Texas postsecondary institution. Programs (within institutions) having excess demand or higher earnings premiums should face a less elastic demand and thus could raise prices without curtailing enrollment. Fourth, we examine a small set of institutional characteristics, Z_j, such as overall selectivity and demographic composition (percentage eligible for Pell). Finally, in some specifications we include program or institution fixed effects (replacing institutional characteristics) to examine cross-program price changes after netting out overall price increases at institutions.

Descriptive Evidence

Figure 10 depicts the trend in the total price (tuition plus mandatory fees) for several institutions from 2000 to 2011 for in-state juniors majoring in liberal arts and taking fifteen credit hours. The tuition and fees for each institution increased considerably following deregulation, a notable jump occurring in the first year institutions had tuition-setting authority. On average, tuition is increased by $1,782 (95 percent) from 2003 to 2011.[17] However, variation around this average is fairly sig-

---

17. THECB (2010b) reported that between the fall of 2003 and the fall of 2009 the statewide average of total academic charges for a student taking fifteen semester credit hours increased by 72 percent, some $1,389.

nificant, UT-Dallas raising prices by $2,783 (117 percent) and the University of Houston-Victoria by $1,084 (59 percent).

In addition, three forms of new pricing structures emerged: differential, flat-rate, and guaranteed. Institutions' use of these practices following deregulation is summarized in table 1. More than one-third (thirteen) of the universities began differentiating tuition by major or program or assigned program-specific fees that had the same effect, referred to as *differential tuition*. The programs typically affected are engineering (ten), business (twelve), nursing (six), and architecture (four). Many of these were ad-

Table 1. Summary of Pricing Policies Adopted by Texas Public Universities Since 2003

	Differential Pricing by Level?	Differential Pricing by Field? (Which Fields?)	Flat Pricing?	Guaranteed Tuition?
University of Texas at Arlington	yes (upper)	engineering, nursing, business, architecture, liberal arts, visual and performing arts, sciences, education	yes	no
University of Texas at Austin	no	architecture, business, communication, education, engineering, fine arts, liberal arts, natural sciences, nursing, pharmacy, social work, geosciences	yes	no
University of Texas at Brownsville	no	no	yes	no
University of Texas at Dallas	yes (lower)	engineering and computer sciences, business, natural sciences and math	yes	yes
University of Texas at El Paso	no	engineering, nursing, business		no
University of Texas at San Antonio	no	no	no	no
University of Texas at Tyler	no	no	no	no
University of Texas-Pan American	no	no	no	no
University of Texas of the Permian Basin	no	no	no	no
Texas A&M University	yes (upper)	business; architecture, engineering, bio & agricultural engineering	yes	no
Texas A&M International University	no	no	no	no
Texas A&M University-Commerce	no	no	no	no
Texas A&M University-Corpus Christi	no	no	no	no
Texas A&M University-San Antonio	no data	no data	no data	no data
Texas A&M University-Kingsville	no	no	no	no
Prairie View A&M University	no	business, nursing, engineering	no	no

Table 1. (cont.)

	Differential Pricing by Level?	Differential Pricing by Field? (Which Fields?)	Flat Pricing?	Guaranteed Tuition?
Tarleton State University	no	business, nursing & health professions, engineering and technology (*2013)	no	no
Texas A&M University-Texakana	no data	no data	no data	no data
West Texas A&M University	no	no	no	no
Texas A&M University-Central Texas	no data	no data	no data	no data
University of Houston	no	architecture, business, education, engineering, hotel & restaurant business, liberal arts & social sciences, social work, technology	no	no
University of Houston-Clear Lake	no	business	no	no
University of Houston-Downtown	no	business	no	no
University of Houston-Victoria	no	no	no	no
University of North Texas	no	no	yes	no
University of North Texas at Dallas	no	no	no	no
Lamar University	no	no	no	no
Sam Houston State University	no	no	no	no
Sul Ross State University	no	no	no	no
Texas State University	no	no	no	no
Angelo State University	no	no	no	no
Texas Tech University	no	agriculture, business, engineering	no	no
Midwestern State University	no	no	no	no
Stephen F. Austin State University	no	no	no	no
Texas Southern University	no	business, education, science & tech, humanities, fine arts, & social sciences	no	no
Texas Woman's University	no	nursing	no	no

Sources: Authors' compilation.

opted in 2004. Cost varied across institutions and programs even before deregulation, given variation in fees and that some institutions were not hitting the cap on designated tuition. However, the increase in the dispersion of prices across institutions and programs from 2004 onward is quite clear (figure 11).

In adopting differential pricing by program, Texas's colleges and universities joined a national trend of universities implementing more complex pricing policies over the past few decades. Ronald Ehrenberg (2012), Glen Nelson (2008), and Kevin Stange (2015) each find that many public universities have ad-

Figure 11. Price Spread Across Institution and Program

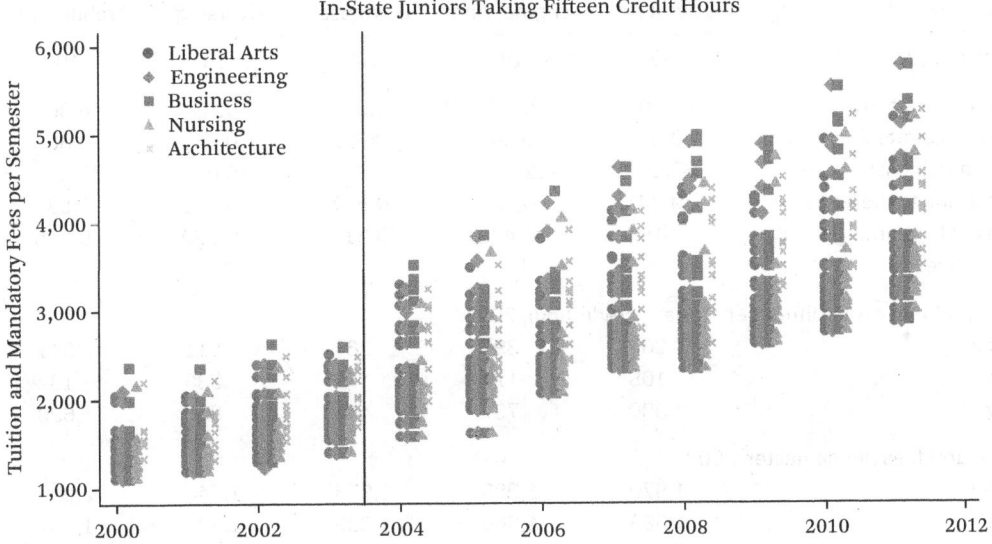

Source: Authors' calculations.

opted differential pricing by program over the past two decades. Furthermore, the programs targeted by Texas are quite similar to those for which differential pricing is used nationally. Only three institutions differentiated price by level, which is surprising given the huge cost differences between upper and lower division coursework. Finally, six schools combined all tuition, mandatory fess, program fees, and course fees into a single price that applies to all students taking a full credit load or higher, referred to as *flat-rate pricing*. Steven Hemelt and Kevin Stange (2014) find modest to no effect of flat (versus per credit) pricing on the average number of credits taken and earned, suggesting that flat pricing may not increase student graduation despite reducing tuition revenue. Finally, one school fixed a tuition rate for each entering cohort (referred to as *guaranteed tuition*), though this is now mandated of all institutions as of 2012 (Texas Guaranteed Tuition Plan 2012).

Difference Regressions
To characterize the role of economic factors in institutions' pricing decisions, we now turn to simple regression analysis. The top of table 2 summarizes our measures of program cost and excess demand, separately by program. Across all institutions, colleges spend $208 per undergraduate student credit hour in liberal arts, ranging from $108 to $390 across institutions. The other four programs we examine are all significantly more expensive, including $397 for engineering, $267 for business, $511 for nursing, and $341 for architecture. Because these programs are much more expensive than liberal arts, it is not surprising that these are targeted for differential pricing. Interestingly, variation is considerable across institutions in the expenditure devoted to these programs. Furthermore, about one-third of these programs have a separate (and likely more selective) application process. We interpret this as a measure of excess demand for enrollment in the program. Finally, enrollees in engineering, business, and architecture experience higher earnings premiums than students in liberal arts, even after adjusting for student achievement and demographic characteristics.

As our primary outcome, we calculate the per-semester price change from 2003 to 2011 for each program at each institution. Table 2 also summarizes the variation in price of these five programs across institutions. Because price data is available for only some years and

Table 2. Characteristics of Five Programs, 2003

	Liberal Arts	Engineering	Business	Nursing	Architecture
Number of programs	27	14	27	13	10
Program is selective	0.00	0.57	0.30	0.23	0.30
Acceptance rate (institution)	0.82	0.84	0.82	0.84	0.80
Fraction Pell (institution)	37.3	32.4	37.3	40.0	22.9
Log earnings difference	0.241	0.839	0.517	0.169	0.532
Adjusted log earnings difference	0.151	0.478	0.313	0.120	0.345
Undergraduate expenditure per student credit hour, 2002					
Mean	208	397	267	511	341
Min	108	174	177	333	132
Max	390	737	456	869	690
Tuition and fees per semester, 2003					
Mean	1,870	1,985	1,873	1,740	2,099
Min	1,389	1,389	1,389	1,389	1,687
Max	2,508	2,387	2,590	2,308	2,474
Change in tuition and fees per semester, 2003 to 2011					
Mean	1,782	2,129	1,887	1,854	2,214
Min	1,084	1,330	1,084	1,423	1,812
Max	2,783	3,383	3,383	2,873	3,360
Grant aid (need-eligible students), 2003					
Total grant aid	4,243	4,997	4,380	4,663	4,454
Pell Grant aid	2,390	2,404	2,366	2,374	2,083
Non-Pell Grant aid	1,852	2,592	2,014	2,289	2,371
Net tuition and fees per semester (need-eligible students), 2003					
Mean	−251	−479	−317	−563	−94
Min	−1,355	−1,780	−1,369	−1,463	−1,453
Max	505	240	696	12	470
Change in net tuition and fees per semester (need-eligible students), 2003 to 2011					
Mean	408	264	460	397	577
Min	−967	−966	−467	−342	−67
Max	1,796	2,613	2,199	1,158	1,739
Change in grant aid (need-eligible students), 2003 to 2011					
Total grant aid	1,371	2,003	1,427	1,478	1,731
Pell Grant aid	1,009	902	976	912	859
Non-Pell Grant aid	362	1,102	452	565	871

Sources: Authors' compilation. Undergraduate expenditure per student credit hour and acceptance rate from THECB. Whether a program is selective and sticker price information from various archival sources. Log earnings difference is for 2000 enrollees in each program measured ten years after enrollment, relative to earnings for high school graduates who did not enroll in a Texas public institution. Adjusted log earnings estimates control for student race, sex, free-lunch status, and high school exit exam scores. Average grant aid and net tuition estimated from student-level data contained in the Financial Aid Database compiled by THECB. See text for details.

not all institutions have nursing and architecture programs, this table and our subsequent analysis relies on ninety-one observations: twenty-seven liberal arts programs, fourteen engineering programs, twenty-seven business programs, thirteen nursing programs, and ten architecture programs. As in the earlier figures, average price and range of prices was similar across all five programs prior to deregulation in 2003. The third panel depicts changes in price from 2003 to 2011. Average price nearly doubled, increasing by $1,782 for liberal arts programs, about $70 more for nursing programs, $100 more for business programs, $350 more for engineering, and $430 more for architecture programs. However, these averages mask quite a bit of heterogeneity in price response. The standard deviation and range (maximum-minimum) of price changes was quite a bit higher for engineering, business, and architecture. Meanwhile, the actual amount students pay (net tuition and fees) might not show the same variation across programs in part because grant aid partially offsets sticker price increases. Between 2003 and 2011, the average change in the net tuition for need-eligible students was actually lowest in engineering, whose students experienced the largest increase in non–Pell Grant aid. The change in the Pell Grant aid was similar across the programs.

Table 3 examines the correlates of price changes for liberal arts programs. Expenditure per student (combining lower and upper division courses) has no relationship with the price change following deregulation, though the estimate is imprecise.[18] Specifications (2) through (4) examine the correlation with three other economic factors: the institutional acceptance rate, the proportion of students receiving federal grant aid (a marker for the proportion who are low income), and log earnings premium. Institutions with a low acceptance rate and greater earnings premiums see larger price increases, consistent with the prediction that excess demand enables institutions to raise prices. However, institutions with many low-income students (as proxied by the proportion of students receiving federal grant aid) have more restrained increases. When these variables are examined together (specification 5), we find that institutions with the greatest price increases following tuition deregulation have higher expenditure per student credit hour and fewer low-income students than before deregulation. Selectivity and earnings premiums do not have a consistent relationship with price increases of liberal arts programs. Finally, specifications (6) through (9) examine the correlates of changes in grant aid and net price. Schools with greater expenditure per student at baseline increase grant aid for needy students the most following deregulation, particularly with non-Pell aid. Increases in net price was also significantly lower for schools with more low-income students.

Table 4 examines price changes for four particular programs which experienced greater price increases than liberal arts. Here we find much weaker support for the importance of baseline program-specific cost to predicting price increases. Earnings premiums, program selectivity, and overall institution characteristics (such as liberal arts expenditure, institution selectivity, and student income) are fairly strong predictive of price changes, but program-specific expenditure is not. Price increased more for programs that had higher earnings premiums or separate admissions processes (a marker for excess demand), yet did not for more expensive programs regardless of which other characteristics are controlled for. Although selective programs see larger price increases than nonselective ones, they also provide more grant aid, particularly grants other than Pell. This suggests that the net tuition for selective programs did not rise as fast for needy students as sticker price did. Programs with high earnings premiums see an increase in net price, as additional grant aid

---

18. Figures A1 and A2 plot the price changes against baseline expenditure in 2002 (figure A1) and earnings premiums (figure A2), separately by program. It is clear that the price increase is greatest in engineering and architecture programs with the greatest expenditure at baseline, but not so for business, liberal arts, or nursing. Price increases are strongly positively correlated with earnings premiums for all majors other than architecture.

Table 3. Predictors of Price Changes, Liberal Arts

	Price Change from 2003 to 2011 (mean = $1,782)					Change from 2003 to 2011 (Students with Need Aid)			
						Net Price ($442)	Total Grants ($1,387)	Pell Grant ($985)	Other Grant ($402)
	(1)	(2)	(3)	(4)	(5)	(6)	(7)	(8)	(9)
Expenditure per SCH in liberal arts (lower and upper division ugrad)	0.0642 (1.554)				2.231* (1.241)	-1.515 (2.380)	3.408* (1.903)	0.165 (0.683)	3.243 (2.009)
Acceptance rate (institution)		-379.1 (523.0)			86.19 (585.9)	-341.5 (765.6)	442.8 (1.189)	900.1 (625.4)	-457.2 (1.797)
% Students with federal grant aid (institution)			-10.96*** (2.957)		-13.29** (4.799)	-20.53*** (7.155)	7.441 (8.477)	11.39** (4.823)	-3.947 (10.95)
Log earnings difference (relative to non-enrollees)				900.7** (374.7)	-106.1 (312.8)	-653.1 (1,021)	821.8 (920.4)	700.3** (312.6)	121.5 (966.0)
Constant	1,769*** (291.9)	2,120*** (467.4)	2,218*** (135.2)	1,585*** (106.1)	1,817*** (458.0)	1,930*** (661.5)	-153.4 (990.0)	-382.4 (518.4)	229.0 (1,467)
Observations	27	26	26	26	25	24	24	24	24
R^2	0.000	0.030	0.296	0.254	0.376	0.316	0.314	0.574	0.172

Source: Authors' calculations.

Notes: SCH refers to school credit hours. Sample includes all liberal arts programs at Texas public universities for which sticker price (tuition plus mandatory fees) was available in both 2003 and 2011. Price includes tuition plus mandatory fees for in-state juniors taking 15 credits in the Fall. Average grant aid and net price is calculated for all full-time in-state juniors with a declared major in liberal arts or English who received one of the main need-based aid programs (Pell, SEOG, Texas Grant, TPEG, HB3015). Grant aid amounts are annual, but are divided in half when calculating net price. Log earnings difference is for 2000 enrollees in humanities measured ten years after enrollment, relative to earnings for high school graduates who did not enroll in a Texas public institution. Robust standard errors in parentheses.

*$p < .1$, **$p < .05$, ***$p < .01$

Table 4. Predictors of Price Changes by Program, Four Programs Pooled

	Price Change from 2003 to 2011 (mean = $1,984)						Change from 2003 to 2011 (Students with Need Aid)			
							Net Price ($432)	Total Grants ($1,595)	Pell Grant ($932)	Other Grant ($664)
	(1)	(2)	(3)	(4)	(5)	(6)	(7)	(8)	(9)	(10)
Expenditure per SCH in program (lower and upper division ugrad)	0.510 (0.406)			0.700 (0.471)	0.802 (0.658)	0.482 (0.566)	0.0467 (0.711)	0.206 (0.474)	0.0606 (0.214)	0.145 (0.449)
Selective program		350.4** (140.9)		111.5 (183.9)	115.6 (198.9)	-11.29 (178.5)	-242.2 (225.7)	268.5* (157.2)	-75.35 (70.99)	343.8** (144.2)
Log earnings difference (relative to non-enrollees)			506.1*** (178.6)	552.1*** (203.7)	559.2** (232.8)	337.1* (200.2)	457.7 (368.9)	521.4** (252.5)	-392.1*** (78.50)	913.5*** (251.9)
Expenditure per SCH in liberal arts (lower and upper division ugrad)						2.906** (1.236)				
Acceptance rate (institution)						-231.9 (469.6)				
% Students with federal grant aid (institution)						-10.86** (4.771)				
Engineering					-3.450 (241.8)	58.13 (220.1)	-240.5 (302.2)	147.7 (242.5)	218.8** (101.5)	-71.13 (191.5)

Table 4. *(cont.)*

	Price Change from 2003 to 2011 (mean = $1,984)					Change from 2003 to 2011 (Students with Need Aid)			
						Net Price ($432)	Total Grants ($1595)	Pell Grant ($932)	Other Grant ($664)
	(1)	(2)	(3)	(4)	(5)	(6)	(7)	(8)	(9)	(10)
Business					46.23	44.61	1.055	-129.4	166.2	-295.5*
					(211.6)	(183.9)	(242.2)	(218.1)	(105.6)	(174.2)
Architecture						284.8	142.2	130.6	143.1	33.36	109.7
					(223.4)	(246.5)	(285.2)	(222.4)	(110.5)	(189.3)
Nursing (reference)										
Constant	1,802***	1,864***	1,746***	1,429***	1,323***	1,604***	298.9	1,157***	1,019***	138.0
	(143.5)	(82.42)	(95.33)	(182.5)	(337.3)	(453.5)	(363.6)	(292.6)	(129.5)	(244.3)
Observations	64	64	62	62	62	61	57	57	57	57
R^2	0.023	0.091	0.127	0.191	0.223	0.403	0.060	0.299	0.232	0.484

Source: Authors' calculations.

Notes: SCH refers to school credit hours. Sample includes all engineering, business, architecture, and nursing programs at Texas public universities for which sticker price (tuition plus mandatory fees) was available in both 2003 and 2011. Price includes tuition plus mandatory fees for in-state juniors taking fifteen credits in the fall semester. Average grant aid and net price is calculated for all full-time in-state juniors with a declared major in one of these four programs that received one of the main need-based aid programs (Pell, SEOG, Texas Grant, TPEG, HB3015). Grant aid amounts are annual, but are divided in half when calculating net price. Log earnings difference is for 2000 enrollees in each program measured ten years after enrollment, relative to earnings for high school graduates who did not enroll in a Texas public institution. Robust standard errors in parentheses.

* $p < .1$, ** $p < .05$, *** $p < .01$

was not sufficient to offset tuition increases.[19] Results are qualitatively similar regardless of whether earnings premiums are adjusted for student covariates or whether lower or upper division undergraduate courses are used to construct the expenditure measure.[20]

DISCUSSION AND CONCLUSION

This research investigates changes in tuition policies in the wake of tuition deregulation in Texas. Texas offers a unique case study of a massive policy change that provided public higher education institutions with greater autonomy and flexibility to determine prices. Many institutions took advantage of this flexibility, accelerating price increases and adopting alternative pricing structures, particularly differential pricing by undergraduate program, after the deregulation. Engineering, business, nursing, and architecture programs were the most common targets for differential pricing, mirroring national trends. The UT and Texas A&M systems actively supported tuition deregulation because they believed the change would make them flexible to market demands and faculty hiring, which in turn would enhance their prestige and quality of education (University of Texas 2008). The assumption is that the quality of their educational offerings was held artificially low when prices were set by the legislature. Meanwhile, other institutions in the state that still had physical capacity to accommodate additional enrollment were hesitant of the changes (Hernandez 2009) and have been reluctant to enact differential prices.

Our findings are broadly consistent with these economic rationales. We find that overall price increases (for students in the liberal arts) were greatest at institutions that were already spending more per student and that had fewer low-income students. Program-specific price is largely influenced by earnings premiums, selectivity, and overall spending at the institution. Because the state funding formula does not consider cross-institution differences in spending within fields, this behavior can be explained by the desire of more resource-intensive institutions to pay for their additional spending via price increases. The importance of alumni earnings and student income suggests that institutions also consider the demand and access consequences of the price changes, as institutions with less elastic demand and higher-income students are more able to increase price without harming enrollment. Finally, lucrative programs also increased grant aid for low-income students, somewhat offsetting the increase in sticker price faced by these students. Thus demand and cost may function as important contingencies for public universities in setting prices (Morphew and Eckel 2009; Yanikoski and Wilson 1984).

These results may shed light on the objectives of public universities, particularly in comparison with state lawmakers. State lawmakers set low and uniform sticker prices prior to deregulation, suggesting value placed on broad-based affordability. Institutions, on the other hand, appear to desire a greater level of differentiation (between and within institutions) and a higher level of program quality. The balance struck between the dual objectives of affordability and quality clearly depends on the nominal price-setter, though whether this reflects differences in objectives or information between institutions and lawmakers remains unclear. In a time when public institutions face scrutiny but diminished public support, many are exploring various financial models to maintain and improve scale, breadth of activities, and the ability to pursue public good (Duderstadt and Womack 2003). Figure 12 suggests that the increase in tuition and fees in the post-

---

19. Table A4 estimates models for each program separately. The pattern for engineering, business, and nursing programs are qualitatively similar: those programs that were initially devoting more resources to their students prior to deregulation did not increase their price appreciably following deregulation but programs with greater earnings premiums did. This general pattern mostly holds after controlling for expenditure in liberal arts and the selectivity and income of students at the institution overall. Architecture has a different pattern than the other three, with baseline expenditure predictive of postderegulation price changes but earnings premiums unpredictive.

20. These robustness results are reported in appendix tables A5 and A6.

Figure 12. Estimates of Changes in Educational and General Expenses per FTE ($1,000) After Deregulation

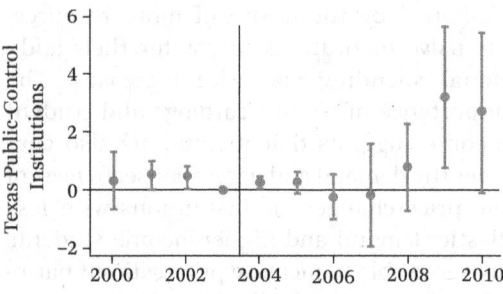

Source: Authors' calculations based on IPEDS.
Notes: Graph reports event-study point estimate and 95 percent confidence interval. Total educational and general expenses per FTE includes students from all levels, not exclusively undergraduate. Control group includes all public four-year institutions in either the Southwest or Southeast. Standard errors clustered by state. Estimates are weighted by total undergraduate enrollment. Nonweighted graphs look very similar.

deregulation period ultimately enabled higher levels of education and related activities at an institutional level. Yet how differential tuition shifted the revenues and expenses for different activities across academic programs within institutions is not well understood, in part because revenue allocation is at the discretion of the dean of the college at some universities in the state (Ravenscroft and Enyeart 2009).

Although our analysis is intended to be entirely positive, the normative implications of greater differentiation can be framed around a potential trade-off between efficiency and equity that depends on institution and student responses to deregulation-enabled price changes. Differential pricing could increase efficiency by aligning price more closely with marginal costs or by facilitating more quality differentiation across programs if there is strong complementarity between student ability and resources (Hoxby 2009; Rothschild and White 1995). In fact, efficiency concerns were the primary justification for tuition deregulation (University of Texas 2008).

On the other hand, differential pricing and greater price dispersion could also widen socioeconomic gaps, as price increased overall and most dramatically at the most selective and best-resourced programs. These changes could price lower-income students out of desirable programs or make completion more difficult. However, we do find that institutional grant aid increased more in Texas following deregulation and that more selective programs awarded more non-Pell Grant aid for students in financial need, offsetting some of the increases in sticker price. This increase in institutional grant aid for students who are eligible for need-based might reflect the requirement that came with the deregulation to allocate 20 percent of the incremental to institution's need-based financial aid. Whether this additional aid fully mitigated impacts on access or would have occurred had institutions not been required to set aside part of the raised revenue for need-based aid remains an open question.

The increase in educational spending documented in figure 12 does suggest that institutions use the increased revenue for improving academic quality. At a department level, some schools report making significant investments in new computer labs and reduced class sizes with differential tuition dollars (for example, Totzke, 2011). Again, whether these improvements in quality were particularly important to the success of low-income students or simply widened existing resource gaps between programs serving poor and nonpoor students remains unclear. Across many universities nationally, Stange (2015) finds that differential pricing for engineering is associated with fewer engineering degrees granted particularly for female and black students, but his analysis is unable to separate price (demand) and program quality (supply) channels. A full accounting of the equity and efficiency consequences of deregulation requires an assessment of how it altered the sorting of students into programs, changed institutional capacity, and impacted program quality.[21] A necessary first step to answering these questions is to simply document and understand how institutions alter pricing practices when given full autonomy to do so.

---

21. One of the authors (Stange) is currently investigating these issues in collaboration with Rodney Andrews from University of Texas at Dallas.

APPENDIX

Figure A1. Price Change and Initial Instructional Expenditure

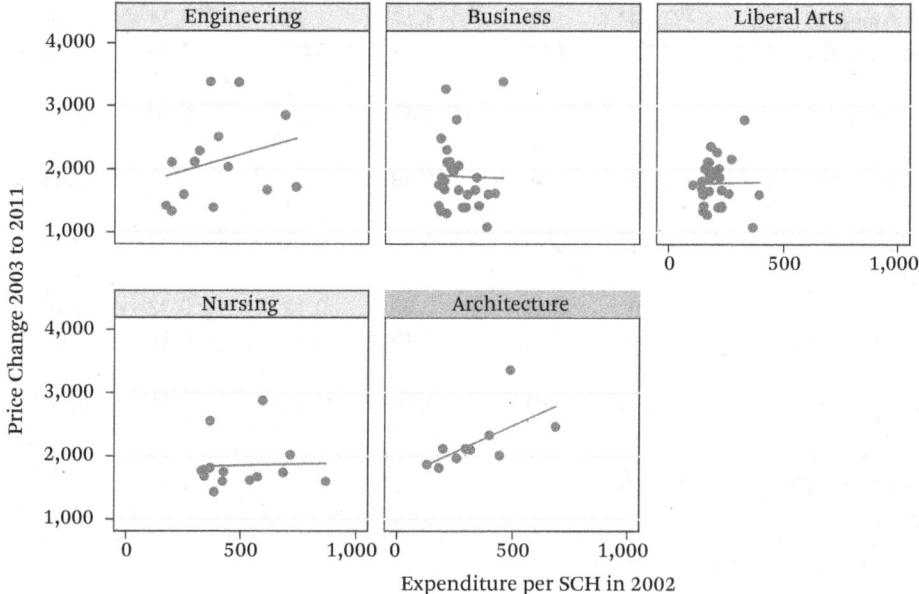

Source: Authors' calculations.

Figure A2. Price Change and Log Earnings Premium

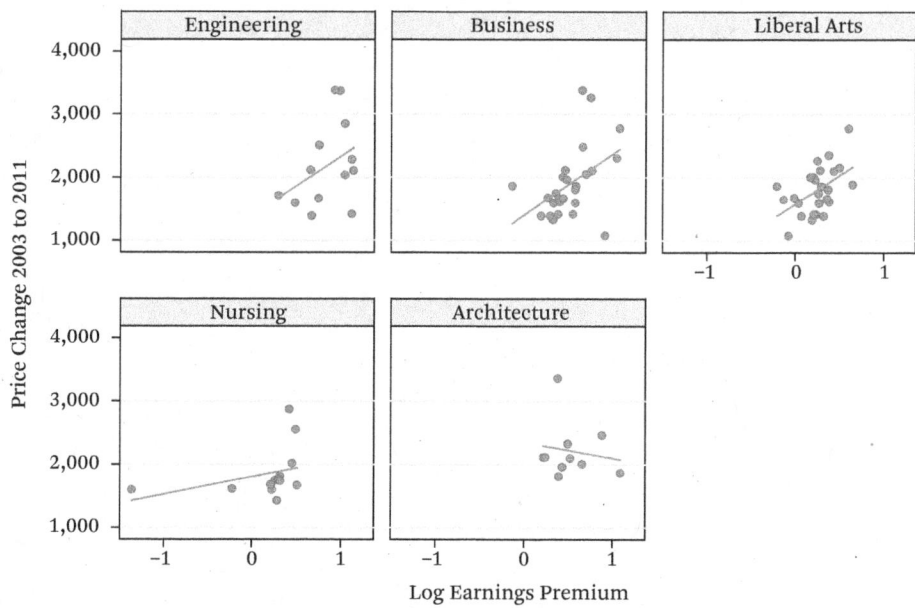

Source: Authors' calculations.

Table A1. IPEDS Sample Characteristics

	Full Sample		Non-Texas Public in SE/SW		Texas Public	
	Mean	SD	Mean	SD	Mean	SD
In-state tuition + fees ($1,000)	4.18	1.78	4.17	1.81	4.24	1.60
Tuition and fee revenue per FTE ($1,000)	6.73	2.97	6.62	3.00	7.39	2.64
Net tuition revenue per FTE ($1,000)	5.57	2.56	5.47	2.58	6.20	2.31
State appropriations per FTE ($1,000)	9.38	8.40	9.58	8.95	8.26	3.65
Share of revenue state appropriations	0.35	0.11	0.35	0.11	0.37	0.10
Share of revenue from tuition	0.29	0.12	0.28	0.12	0.33	0.10
Institutional grant or tuition revenue	0.16	0.12	0.16	0.12	0.15	0.09
Undergraduate enrollment	9,583	8,807	9,143	8,558	12,203	9,777
Number of observations	2,448		2,096		352	
Number of institutions in 2003	216		184		32	
Number of states	16		15		1	

Source: Authors' calculations based on IPEDS.

Table A2. Texas Versus Non-Texas Sticker Price Estimates, Robustness

	Dependent Variable: In-State Tuition and Fee Changes ($1,000)						
	Control Group: SE/SW Public			Control Group			
	Base Model	Un-weighted	Control for Unemployment Rate	All Public	SE Public	SE without FL	SW Public
	(1)	(2)	(3)	(4)	(5)	(6)	(7)
2000	−0.013	0.083	−0.051	0.293***	−0.053	0.157	0.206
	(0.187)	(0.139)	(0.309)	(0.109)	(0.211)	(0.162)	(0.159)
2001	−0.051	0.062	−0.103	0.248**	−0.100	0.108	0.244
	(0.178)	(0.133)	(0.341)	(0.101)	(0.199)	(0.139)	(0.167)
2002	0.074	0.084	0.059	0.264***	0.017	0.166	0.416
	(0.132)	(0.096)	(0.165)	(0.086)	(0.140)	(0.099)	(0.197)
2004	0.535***	0.365***	0.520***	0.403***	0.545***	0.529***	0.461***
	(0.053)	(0.038)	(0.108)	(0.076)	(0.060)	(0.074)	(0.069)
2005	0.654***	0.442***	0.611**	0.490***	0.670***	0.624***	0.545***
	(0.069)	(0.048)	(0.239)	(0.094)	(0.078)	(0.089)	(0.092)
2006	0.848***	0.628***	0.814***	0.638***	0.871***	0.752***	0.694***
	(0.120)	(0.093)	(0.221)	(0.129)	(0.137)	(0.131)	(0.077)
2007	1.114***	0.888***	1.048**	0.874***	1.147***	0.914***	0.899***
	(0.192)	(0.134)	(0.382)	(0.146)	(0.219)	(0.168)	(0.092)
2008	1.268***	1.010***	1.144	1.025***	1.326***	1.066***	0.885**
	(0.226)	(0.175)	(0.655)	(0.175)	(0.248)	(0.208)	(0.174)
2009	1.424***	1.169***	1.231	1.017***	1.518***	1.104***	0.779
	(0.309)	(0.209)	(0.984)	(0.228)	(0.323)	(0.205)	(0.531)
2010	1.364***	1.145***	1.185	0.968***	1.480***	0.894***	0.549
	(0.411)	(0.281)	(0.945)	(0.286)	(0.428)	(0.219)	(0.765)
Observations	2,411	2,412	2,411	6,293	2,110	1,921	652
R^2	0.327	0.269	0.328	0.220	0.305	0.413	0.638

Source: Authors' calculations.

Notes: Model includes indicator for Texas public institution, year fixed effects, and interactions between year fixed effects and indicator for Texas public institution. Table reports coefficients on these interactions. Interaction term for 2003 is omitted group so point estimates represent price differences over and above the difference that prevailed in 2003. All models (except 2) are weighted by undergraduate enrollment. Control group for base model includes all public four-year institutions in either the Southwest or Southeast. Standard errors clustered by state.

*$p < .1$, **$p < .05$, ***$p < .01$

Table A3. Texas Versus Non-Texas Net Price Estimates, Robustness

	Dependent Variable: Net Tuition Revenue per FTE ($1,000)						
	Control Group: SE/SW Public			Control Group			
	Base model	Un-weighted	Control for unemployment rate	All public	SE Public	SE without FL	SW public
	(1)	(2)	(3)	(4)	(5)	(6)	(7)
2000	0.140	0.227	0.135	0.322***	0.141	0.225	0.132
	(0.150)	(0.212)	(0.291)	(0.115)	(0.174)	(0.215)	(0.146)
2001	−0.032	0.040	−0.038	0.129	−0.074	0.050	0.213
	(0.140)	(0.146)	(0.315)	(0.080)	(0.156)	(0.157)	(0.179)
2002	−0.079	−0.006	−0.081	0.051	−0.128	−0.051	0.216
	(0.085)	(0.111)	(0.124)	(0.072)	(0.084)	(0.086)	(0.159)
2004	0.283***	0.169**	0.281***	0.203***	0.275***	0.220***	0.328***
	(0.057)	(0.076)	(0.076)	(0.048)	(0.068)	(0.068)	(0.051)
2005	0.279***	0.321***	0.274	0.185**	0.284**	0.214*	0.239
	(0.086)	(0.106)	(0.216)	(0.083)	(0.098)	(0.104)	(0.152)
2006	0.606***	0.541***	0.602**	0.496***	0.676***	0.540***	0.152
	(0.161)	(0.118)	(0.209)	(0.125)	(0.159)	(0.156)	(0.443)
2007	0.642***	0.910***	0.634	0.517***	0.727***	0.568**	0.066
	(0.193)	(0.108)	(0.362)	(0.157)	(0.188)	(0.203)	(0.549)
2008	0.806***	0.982***	0.792	0.608***	0.870***	0.738**	0.381
	(0.186)	(0.124)	(0.633)	(0.161)	(0.197)	(0.244)	(0.288)
2009	1.069***	1.142***	1.046	0.820***	1.158***	0.845**	0.444
	(0.282)	(0.142)	(0.978)	(0.210)	(0.295)	(0.301)	(0.439)
2010	1.037**	0.955***	1.016	0.710**	1.147**	0.621*	0.261
	(0.394)	(0.171)	(0.934)	(0.285)	(0.410)	(0.294)	(0.768)
Observations	2,386	2,400	2,386	6,227	2,104	1,915	631
R^2	0.319	0.230	0.319	0.218	0.313	0.342	0.518

Source: Authors' calculations.

Notes: Model includes indicator for Texas public institution, year fixed effects, and interactions between year fixed effects and indicator for Texas public institution. Table reports coefficients on these interactions. Interaction term for 2003 is omitted group so point estimates represent price differences over and above the difference that prevailed in 2003. All models (except 2) are weighted by undergraduate enrollment. Control group for base model includes all public four-year institutions in either the Southwest or Southeast. Standard errors clustered by state.

*$p < .1$, **$p < .05$, ***$p < .01$

Table A4. Predictors of Price Changes by Program, Separately by Program

	Engineering		Business		Nursing		Architecture	
	(1)	(2)	(3)	(4)	(5)	(6)	(7)	(8)
Expenditure per SCH in program (lower and upper division ugrad)	2.313 (1.294)	0.145 (1.699)	-0.0633 (2.210)	1.708 (2.757)	0.398 (0.688)	0.297 (0.598)	2.575* (1.092)	4.097** (0.900)
Selective program	-433.1 (564.0)	-67.36 (502.6)	280.1 (261.3)	239.0 (242.1)	375.7 (334.2)	1,013 (691.7)	-516.1 (375.0)	-463.0* (162.0)
Log earnings difference (relative to non-enrollees)	1,411** (547.6)	-458.1 (1,985)	797.8 (492.6)	630.9 (530.6)	271.4 (199.7)	184.5 (473.2)	-198.4 (292.6)	-263.1 (252.2)
Expenditure per SCH in liberal arts (lower and upper division ugrad)		3.631 (3.355)		0.528 (2.478)		1.319 (3.188)		-11.86* (4.925)
Acceptance rate (institution)		-3,035 (2,158)		-79.56 (567.1)		2,146 (1,121)		-4,842*** (311.8)
% Students w Federal grant aid (institution)		-3.081 (27.47)		-12.70 (9.978)		-12.61** (4.567)		47.37** (8.735)
Constant	319.4 (550.2)	4,456 (3,774)	1,428** (676.4)	1,520** (569.2)	1,518*** (392.3)	-125.0 (935.4)	1,595*** (278.6)	6,146*** (647.3)
Observations	13	13	26	25	13	13	10	10
R^2	0.298	0.526	0.257	0.475	0.319	0.646	0.641	0.968

Source: Authors' calculations.

Notes: SCH refers to school credit hours. Sample includes all engineering, business, architecture, and nursing programs at Texas public universities for which sticker price (tuition plus mandatory fees) was available in both 2003 and 2011. Price includes tuition plus mandatory fees for in-state juniors taking fifteen credits in the fall semester. Robust standard errors in parentheses.

* $p < .1$, ** $p < .05$, *** $p < .01$

Table A5. Robustness of Price Change Results, Liberal Arts Programs

	Price Change from 2003 to 2011 (mean = $1,782)			
	(1)	(2)	(3)	(4)
Expenditure per SCH in liberal arts	2.231*	2.446*		
(lower and upper division ugrad)	(1.241)	(1.245)		
Acceptance rate	86.19	57.96	18.96	210.8
(institution)	(585.9)	(541.9)	(548.5)	(688.2)
% Students with federal grant aid	−13.29**	−13.54**	−12.31**	−10.57**
(institution)	(4.799)	(4.866)	(4.378)	(3.726)
Log earnings difference	−106.1		48.12	127.9
(relative to non-enrollees)	(312.8)		(321.3)	(263.9)
Adjusted log earnings difference		−370.6		
(relative to non-enrollees)		(319.1)		
Expenditure per SCH			1.215	
(lower division ugrad)			(0.817)	
Expenditure per SCH				2.538***
(upper division ugrad)				(0.800)
Constant	1,817***	1,835***	2,029***	1,292*
	(458.0)	(415.1)	(397.5)	(627.0)
Observations	25	25	25	25
R^2	0.376	0.392	0.330	0.509

Source: Authors' calculations.

Notes: SCH refers to school credit hours. Sample includes all liberal arts programs at Texas public universities for which sticker price (tuition plus mandatory fees) was available in both 2003 and 2011. Price includes tuition plus mandatory fees for in-state juniors taking fifteen credits in the fall semester. Log earnings difference is for 2000 enrollees in each program measured ten years after enrollment, relative to earnings for high school graduates who did not enroll in a Texas public institution. Adjusted log earnings estimates control for student race, sex, free-lunch status, and high school exit exam scores. Robust standard errors in parentheses.

*$p < .1$, **$p < .05$, ***$p < .01$

Table A6. Robustness of Price Change Results, Four Programs Pooled

	Price change from 2003 to 2011 (mean = $1,782)			
	(1)	(2)	(3)	(4)
Expenditure per SCH in program	0.802	0.783		
(lower and upper division ugrad)	(0.658)	(0.678)		
Selective program	115.6	136.8	202.8	95.71
	(198.9)	(203.5)	(191.5)	(201.2)
Log earnings difference	559.2**		459.2*	566.2**
(relative to non-enrollees)	(232.8)		(245.7)	(230.7)
Adjusted log earnings difference		496.5*		
(relative to non-enrollees)		(248.8)		
Expenditure per SCH			0.140	
(lower division ugrad)			(0.625)	
Expenditure per SCH				0.851
(upper division ugrad)				(0.644)
Major fixed effects	Yes	Yes	Yes	Yes
Constant	1,323***	1,363***	1,670***	1,289***
	(337.3)	(346.6)	(290.6)	(336.3)
Observations	62	62	62	62
R^2	0.223	0.192	0.194	0.228

Source: Authors' calculations.

Notes: SCH refers to school credit hours. Sample includes all engineering, business, architecture, and nursing programs at Texas public universities for which sticker price (tuition plus mandatory fees) was available in both 2003 and 2011. Price includes tuition plus mandatory fees for in-state juniors taking fifteen credits in the fall semester. Log earnings difference is for 2000 enrollees in each program measured ten years after enrollment, relative to earnings for high school graduates who did not enroll in a Texas public institution. Adjusted log earnings estimates control for student race, sex, free-lunch status, and high school exit exam scores. Robust standard errors in parentheses.

*$p < .1$, **$p < .05$, ***$p < .01$

REFERENCES

Berg, David J., and Stephen A. Hoenack. 1987. "The Concept of Cost-Related Tuition and its Implementation at the University of Minnesota." *Journal of Higher Education* 58(3): 276–305.

Bound, John, Michael Lovenheim, and Sarah Turner. 2010 "Why Have College Completion Rates Declined: Marginal Students or Marginal College?" *American Economic Journal: Applied Economics* 2(3): 129–57.

Camou, Michelle, and Wendy Patton. 2012. "Deregulation and Higher Education: Potential Impact on Access, Affordability, and Achievement in Ohio." *Policy Matters Ohio*, September. Accessed December 14, 2015. http://www.policymattersohio.org/wp-content/uploads/2012/10/HigherEd_Oct2012.pdf.

Carlson, Andrew. 2011. "State Tuition, Fees, and Financial Assistance Policies for Public Colleges and Universities, 2010–2011." Boulder, Colo.: State Higher Education Executive Officers.

Clotfelter, Charles T. 1996. *Buying the Best: Cost Escalation in Elite Higher Education*. Princeton, N.J.: Princeton University Press.

Cornell Higher Education Research Institute. 2012. "2011 Survey of Differential Tuition at Public Higher Education Institutions." Ithaca, N.Y.: Cornell University. Accessed February 23, 2016. https://www.ilr.cornell.edu/cheri/surveys.

Deaton, Steven B. 2006. "Policy Shifts in Tuition Setting Authority in the American States: An Event History Analysis of State Policy Adoption." Ph.D. diss., Vanderbilt University, Nashville, TN.

Duderstadt, James J., and Farris W. Womack. 2003. *The Future of the Public University in America: Beyond the Crossroad*. Baltimore, Md.: The Johns Hopkins University Press.

Ehrenberg, Ronald G. 2001. "The Supply of American Higher Education Institutions." *ILR School* working paper. Ithaca, N.Y.: Cornell University. Accessed December 14, 2015. https://net.edu cause.edu/ir/library/pdf/ffpfp0102.pdf.

———. 2007. "The Economics of Tuition and Fees in American Higher Education." *ILR School* working paper. Ithaca, N.Y.: Cornell University.

———. 2012. "American Higher Education in Transition." *Journal of Economic Perspectives* 26(1): 193–216.

Ehrenberg, Ronald G., and Daniel R. Sherman. 1987. "Optimal Financial Aid Policies for a Selective University." *NBER* working paper no. 1014. Cambridge, Mass.: National Bureau of Economic Research. Accessed December 14, 2015. http://www.nber.org/papers/w1014.

Epple, Dennis, Richard Romano, and Holger Seig. 2006. "Admission, Tuition, and Financial Aid Policies in the Market for Higher Education." *Econometrica* 74(4): 885–928.

Flores, Stella M., and Justin C. Shepard. 2014. "Pricing Out the Disadvantaged? The Effect of Tuition Deregulation in Texas Public Four-Year Institutions." *Annals of the American Academy of Political and Social Science* 655 (September): 99–122.

Hall, Delaney. 2003. "Lawmakers Deregulate UT Tuition." *Daily Texan*, June 2. Accessed December 14, 2015. http://www.utwatch.org/oldnews/texan_tuitionderegualted_6_02_03.html.

Harwell, Erica J. 2013. "Students' Perceptions of Differential Tuition Based on Academic Program and the Impact on Major Choice." Ph.D. diss., University of Illinois at Urbana-Champaign.

Hearn, James C., Carolyn P. Griswold, and Ginger. M. Marine. 1996. "Region, Resources, and Reason: A Contextual Analysis of State Tuition and State Aid Policies." *Research in Higher Education* 37(3): 241–78.

Heller, Donald E. 2006. "State Support of Higher Education: Past, Present, and Future." In *Privatization and Public Universities*, edited by Douglas M. Priest and Edward P. St. John. Bloomington: Indiana University Press.

Hemelt, Steven W., and Kevin Stange. 2014. "The Effect of Marginal Price on Student Progress at Public Universities." *NBER* working paper no. 20779. Cambridge, Mass.: National Bureau of Economic Research.

Hernandez, José Carlos. 2009. "Student Price Response: The Effect of Tuition Deregulation in Texas on Student Enrollment Trends in Texas Public Institutions of Higher Education." Ph.D. diss., University of Texas at El Paso.

Hoenack, Stephen A., and William C. Weiler. 1975. "Cost-Related Tuition Policies and University Enrollments." *Journal of Human Resources* 10(3): 332–60.

Hoxby, Caroline M. 1997. "How the Changing Market Structure of U.S. Higher Education Explains College Tuition." *NBER* working paper no. 6323. Cambridge, Mass.: National Bureau of Economic Research. Accessed February 23, 2016. http://www.nber.org/papers/w6323.pdf.

———. 2009. "The Changing Selectivity of American

Colleges." *Journal of Economic Perspectives* 23(4): 95–118.

James, Estelle. 1978. "Product Mix and Cost Disaggregation: A Reinterpretation of the Economics of Higher Education." *Journal of Human Resources* 13(2): 157–86.

Johnson, William R., and Sarah Turner. 2009. "Faculty Without Students: Resource Allocation in Higher Education." *Journal of Economic Perspectives* 23(2): 169–90.

Kane, Thomas J. 1999. *The Price of Admission: Rethinking How Americans Pay for College*. Washington, D.C. / New York: Brookings Institution / Russell Sage Foundation.

Koshal, Rajindar K., and Monjulika Koshal. 2000. "State Appropriation and Higher Education Tuition: What Is the Relationship?" *Education Economics* 8(1): 81–89.

Little, Michael W., Dennis O'Toole, and James Wetzel. 1997. "The Price Differential's Impact on Retention, Recruitment, and Quality in a Public University." *Journal of Marketing for Higher Education* 8(2): 37–51.

Long, Bridget Terry. 2004. "How Do Financial Aid Policies Affect College? The Institutional Impact of the Georgia HOPE Scholarship." *Journal of Human Resources* 39(4): 1045–66.

Lowry, Robert C. 2001. "Governmental Structure, Trustee Selection, and Public University Prices and Spending: Multiple Means to Similar Ends." *American Journal of Political Science* 45(4): 845–61.

Marley, Patrick, and Karen Herzog. 2015. "Walker Opens Door to UW System Tuition Limits After 2017." *Milwaukee-Wisconsin Journal Sentinel*, February 12. Accessed December 14, 2015. http://www.jsonline.com/news/statepolitics/walker-opens-door-to-uw-system-tuition-cap-after-2017-b99443872z1-291673721.html.

McBain, Lesley. 2010. "Tuition-Setting Authority and Deregulation at State Colleges and Universities." A Higher Education Policy Brief. Washington, D.C.: American Association of State Colleges and Universities. Accessed December 14, 2015. http://www.aascu.org/policy/publications/policy-matters/2010/tuitionsettingauthority.pdf.

McLendon, Michael K., James C. Hearn, and Robert G. Hammond. 2013. "Pricing the Flagships: The Politics of Tuition Setting at Public Research Universities." Raleigh: North Carolina State University. Accessed December 14, 2015. http://www4.ncsu.edu/~rghammon/Pricing_the_Flagships.pdf.

Middaugh, Michael F., Rosalina Graham, and Abdus Shahid. 2003. *A National Study of Higher Education Instructional Expenditures: The Delaware Study of Instructional Costs and Productivity*. NCES 2003-161. Washington: U.S. Department of Education. Accessed December 14, 2015. http://nces.ed.gov/pubs2003/2003161.pdf.

Morphew, Christopher C., and Peter D. Eckel. 2009. *Privatizing the Public University: Perspectives from Across the Academy*. Baltimore, Md.: Johns Hopkins University Press.

Mortenson, Thomas G. 2004. *Postsecondary Education Opportunity*. Report no. 139. Oskaloosa, IA: Mortenson Research Seminar on Public Policy Analysis of Opportunity for Postsecondary Education.

Nelson, Glen R. 2008. "Differential Tuition by Undergraduate Major: Its Use, Amount, and Impact at Public Research Universities." Ph.D. diss., University of Nebraska–Lincoln.

Palmer, Jim. 2013. "Grapevine: An Annual Compilation of Data on State Fiscal Support for Higher Education." Normal, Ill.: Grapevine. Last updated January 2015. Accessed January 2, 2016. http://education.illinoisstate.edu/grapevine.

Paulsen, Michael B. 2000. "Economic Perspectives on Rising College Tuition: A Theoretical and Empirical Exploration." In *Higher Education: Handbook of Theory and Research*, vol. 15, edited by J. C. Smart. New York: Agathon Press.

Ravensoft, Michael, and Christine Enyeart. 2009. "Differential Tuition at Public Universities: Models and Implementation Strategies." Custom Research Brief, March 19. Washington, D.C.: Education Advisory Board.

Rizzo Michael J., and Ronald G. Ehrenberg. 2004. "Resident and Non-Resident Tuition and Enrollment at State Flagship Universities." In *College Choices: The Economics of Where to Go, When to Go, and How to Pay for It*, edited by Caroline M. Hoxby. Chicago: University of Chicago Press.

Rothschild, Michael, and Lawrence J. White. 1995. "The Analysis of the Pricing of Higher Education and Other Services in Which the Customers Are Inputs." *Journal of Political Economy* 103(3): 573–86.

Shin, Jung Cheol, and Sande Milton. 2008. "Student Response to Tuition Increase by Academic Majors: Empirical Grounds for a Cost-Related Tuition Policy." *Higher Education* 55: 719–34.

Simone, Sean. 2010. "Tuition and Fee Differentiation at Degree Granting Postsecondary Education Institutions." An AIR/NCES Data Policy Fellowship Report. May 2010. Washington: U.S. Department of Education.

Singell, Larry D., and Joe A. Stone. 2007. "For Whom the Pell Tolls: The Response of University Tuition to Federal Grants-in-Aid." *Economics of Education Review* 26(3): 285–95.

South Regional Education Board 2013. "Higher Education Finance & Budgets (By-College Funding): Funding for Higher Education Related Operations." Last updated June 2013. Accessed December 14, 2015. http://www.sreb.org/page/1359/data_library_higher_ed_finance_budgets.html#By_College_Public_Funding.

Stange, Kevin M. 2015. "Differential Pricing in Undergraduate Education: Effects on Degree Production by Field." *Journal of Policy Analysis and Management* 34(1): 107–35.

Texas A&M University. 2010. "Proposal for Differential Tuition: Dwight Look College of Engineering." College Station, Tex.: Texas A&M University. Accessed January 2, 2016. http://sec.tamu.edu/upload/documents/LCOE%20Differential%20Tuition-11_08_10.pdf.

Texas Guaranteed Tuition Plan. 2012. "Plan Overview." Accessed January 2, 2016. http://www.tgtp.org/details/overview.html.

Texas Higher Education Coordinating Board (THECB). 2000. "Closing the Gaps: The Texas Higher Education Plan." Austin: THECB. Accessed December 14, 2015. http://www.thecb.state.tx.us/.

———. 2010a. "General Academic Institutions Expenditure Study (formerly Cost Study)." Austin: THECB. Accessed January 2, 2016. http://www.thecb.state.tx.us/index.cfm?objectid=50067F8C-D180-18DE-B88C060BCE74E409.

———. 2010b. "Overview: Tuition Deregulation." Austin: THECB. Accessed January 2, 2016. http://www.thecb.state.tx.us/reports/pdf/2010.pdf.

Thornton, Saranna. 2007. "Financial Inequality In Higher Education: The Annual Report on the Economic Status of the Profession, 2006–2007." Washington, D.C.: American Association of University Professors.

Totzke, Deana. 2011. "Electrical Engineering Opens New Student Computer Lab with Differential Tuition Dollars." College Station, Tex.: Dwight Look College of Engineering, Texas A&M University. Accessed Jan 2, 2016. https://engineering.tamu.edu/news/2011/11/11/electrical-engineering-opens-new-student-computer-lab-with-differential-tuition-dollars.

Toutkoushian, Robert K., and Paula Hollis. 1998. "Using Panel Data to Examine Legislative Demand for Higher Education." *Education Economics* 6(2): 141–57.

Turner, Nicholas. 2012. "Who Benefits from Student Aid? The Economic Incidence of Tax-Based Federal Student Aid." *Economics of Education Review* 31(4): 463–81.

University of Texas. 2008. "Access and Affordability: Frequently Asked Questions." Austin: The University of Texas System. Accessed Jan 2, 2016. http://web.archive.org/web/20080517022159/http://www.utsystem.edu/Affordability/faq.htm.

Ward, David, and John Aubrey Douglass. 2005. "The Dynamics of Variable Fees: Exploring Institutional and Public Policy Responses." *CSHE* occasional paper no. 5.05. Berkeley: University of California.

Weisbrod, Burton A., Jeffrey P. Ballou, and Evelyn D. Asch. 2008. *Mission and Money: Understanding the University*. New York: Cambridge University Press.

Yanikoski, Richard A., and Richard F. Wilson. 1984. "Differential Pricing of Undergraduate Education." *Journal of Higher Education* 55(6): 735–50.

Zemsky, Robert, Gregory R. Wegner, and William F. Massy. 2005. "Today's Colleges Must Be Market Smart and Mission Centered." *Chronicle of Higher Education*, July 15.

Looking Inside the Black Box of Performance Funding for Higher Education: Policy Instruments, Organizational Obstacles, and Intended and Unintended Impacts

KEVIN J. DOUGHERTY, SOSANYA M. JONES, HANA LAHR, REBECCA S. NATOW, LARA PHEATT, AND VIKASH REDDY

For several decades, policymakers have been concerned about increasing the efficiency and effectiveness of postsecondary institutions. In recent years, performance funding—which directly connects state funding to an institution's performance on indicators such as student persistence, credit accrual, and college completion—has become a particularly attractive way of pursuing better college outcomes. But even as states have made an enormous investment in performance funding, troubling questions have been raised about whether performance funding has the effects intended and whether it also produces substantial negative side effects in the form of restrictions in access for underrepresented students and weakening of academic standards. This paper addresses these troubling questions by drawing on data richer than heretofore available. In addition to drawing on the existing body of research on performance funding, it reports data from a study of the implementation of performance funding in three leading states (Indiana, Ohio, and Tennessee) and its impacts on three universities and three community colleges in each state.

Keywords: performance funding, performance-based funding, outcomes-based funding, higher education accountability, educational accountability, public accountability, performance management, performance-based management, quality assurance, higher education policy, college quality

Kevin J. Dougherty is associate professor of education policy and senior research associate at the Community College Research Center at Teachers College, Columbia University. **Sosanya M. Jones** is assistant professor of qualitative research methods and higher education at Southern Illinois University at Carbondale. **Hana Lahr** is a doctoral student in education policy and research associate at the Community College Research Center at Teachers College, Columbia University. **Rebecca S. Natow** is senior research associate at the Community College Research Center at Teachers College, Columbia University. **Lara Pheatt** is a doctoral student in politics and education and research associate at the Community College Research Center at Teachers College, Columbia University. **Vikash Reddy** is a doctoral student in politics and education and research associate at the Community College Research Center at Teachers College, Columbia University.

We wish to thank Lumina Foundation for its support for this research. The views expressed in this report are those of its authors and do not necessarily represent the views of Lumina Foundation, its officers or employees. We also wish to thank Ronald Abrams, Steven Brint, Charles Clotfelter, Kevin Corcoran, Russ Deaton, Alicia Dowd, William Doyle, Nicholas Hillman, Davis Jenkins, Alison Kadlec, Marcus Kolb, Vanessa Morest, John Muffo, Richard Petrick, Jeffrey Stanley, Susan Shelton, David Tandberg, Sean Tierney, and William Zumeta for their comments on earlier papers and reports that have fed into this paper. Any remaining errors are our own. Direct correspondence to: Kevin Dougherty at dougherty@tc.edu, Teachers College, Columbia University, Box 11, 525 W. 120th St., New York, NY 10027; Sosanya M. Jones at smjones@siu.edu; Hana Lahr at hel2112@tc.columbia.edu; Rebecca S. Natow at rebeccanatow@yahoo.com; Lara Pheatt at lep2148@tc.columbia.edu; Vikash Reddy at vtr2107@tc.columbia.edu.

For several decades, policymakers have been concerned about increasing the efficiency and effectiveness of postsecondary institutions. In recent years, performance funding—which directly connects state funding to an institution's performance on indicators such as student persistence, credit accrual, and college completion—has become a particularly attractive way of pursuing better college outcomes (Burke 2002; Burke and Associates 2005; Complete College America 2013; Dougherty and Natow 2015; Harnisch 2011; Lumina Foundation 2009; Jones 2013; Reindl and Jones 2012; Reindl and Reyna 2011; Zumeta and Kinne 2011). As of November 2015, thirty-three states have implemented performance funding programs, with several more states planning to start one within the next few years (Dougherty and Natow 2015; National Conference of State Legislatures 2015). But even as states have made an enormous investment in performance funding, troubling questions have been raised about whether performance funding has the effects intended and whether it also produces substantial negative side effects in the form of restrictions in access for underrepresented students and weakening of academic standards (Dougherty and Reddy 2013).

This paper addresses these troubling questions by drawing on data richer than heretofore available. In addition to drawing on the existing body of research on performance funding, it reports data from a study of the implementation of performance funding in three leading states (Indiana, Ohio, and Tennessee) and its impacts on three universities and three community colleges in each state (Dougherty et al. 2014b; Dougherty et al., forthcoming).

Conceptualizing the Nature and Process of Performance Funding

The goal of perform funding is to improve college and university performance, especially with regard to student outcomes such as persistence, completion of developmental (remedial) education and key college-level courses, accrual of course credits, degree completion, transfer, and job placement. These outcomes often constitute the indicators that performance funding programs use to allocate higher education appropriations.

Two kinds of performance funding programs can be usefully distinguished (Dougherty and Natow 2015; Dougherty and Reddy 2013; Snyder 2011, 2015). Performance funding 1.0 (PF 1.0) takes the form of a bonus, over and above regular state funding for higher education. The typical size of this bonus is between 1 and 5 percent of state funding (Burke 2002; Dougherty and Reddy 2013). Tennessee established its PF 1.0 program in 1979 (the first in the nation), and it exists to this day. Ohio did so in 1995 and 1997 (with the introduction of the Performance and Success Challenges), and Indiana in 2007 (Dougherty and Natow 2015; Dougherty and Reddy 2013). Performance funding 2.0 (PF 2.0) programs differ from PF 1.0 in that performance funding no longer takes the form of a bonus but rather is part and parcel of the regular state base funding for higher education. Often as well, the proportion of state appropriations funding for higher education tied to performance metrics can be much higher, as high as 80 to 90 percent in Ohio and Tennessee. Indiana and Ohio established PF 2.0 programs in 2009, followed by Tennessee in 2010 (Dougherty and Natow 2015; Dougherty and Reddy 2013).[1]

To understand how performance funding has operated, we draw on various research literatures. These include research on performance funding (see Burke 2002; Burke and Associates 2005; Dougherty and Reddy 2013), performance management in government (see Heinrich and Marschke 2010; Moynihan 2008), organizational learning (see Argyris and Schön 1996; Dowd and Tong 2007; Witham and Bensimon 2012), implementation theory and principal-agent theory (see Honig 2006; Lane and Kivisto 2008), and organizational change theory in higher education (see Kezar 2012).

Performance funding policies embody "theories of action" (Argyris and Schön 1996) involving causal sequences by which desired outcomes will be produced. These sequences typically involve specific "policy instruments"

---

[1]. Unlike the other two states, Tennessee did not discontinue its earlier PF 1.0 program. It now operates both types of programs.

or "mechanisms that translate substantive policy goals into concrete actions" (McDonnell and Elmore 1987, 134). The theory of action typically laid out by advocates of performance funding is that performance funding will stimulate institutional changes in academic and student-service policies, programs, and practices that in turn will result in improved student outcomes. Typically, policymakers do not specify particular institutional changes (Dougherty et al. 2014a). The main policy instrument considered by performance funding advocates is providing financial incentives that mimic the profits for businesses (Dougherty et al. 2014a; also see Burke and Associates 2005, 304; Dougherty and Reddy 2013; Massy 2011). Applied to higher education institutions, this financial incentives theory of action—which is akin to resource-dependence theory (Pfeffer and Salancik 1978)—holds that the institutions are revenue maximizers and will make a strong effort to improve their performance if the amount of funding involved is significant enough (Burke 2002, 266–72; Dougherty et al. 2014a). This policy instrument also flows from principal-agent theory, which stresses that there is often a misalignment between the interests of principals and their agents (Lane and Kivisto 2008). Monetary incentives flowing from the principals (the state) therefore become a device to bring the interests of the agents (college officials) into better alignment with those of the principals.

Despite the emphasis on financial incentives, advocates of performance funding programs have also considered other policy instruments. One is providing information to college officials and faculty about the goals and intended methods of performance funding as a means to to catalyze institutional change; the aim is to persuade colleges of the importance of improved student outcomes (Dougherty et al. 2014a; Dougherty and Reddy 2013; Massy 2011; Reddy et al. 2014; see also Anderson 2014; Ewell 1999; Rutschow et al. 2011). The idea is that once college and university personnel are convinced that a goal is socially valued and legitimate, they will modify their behavior. This instrument parallels the soft side of *coercive isomorphism*, which may manifest itself as pressure from governmental mandates and societal expectations (DiMaggio and Powell 1991).

Another instrument takes the form of making colleges aware of their student outcomes, particularly in comparison with other colleges. The aim is to mobilize feelings of pride and status striving (Burke and Associates 2005; Dougherty et al. 2014a; Dougherty and Reddy 2013; see also Baldwin et al. 2011; Dowd and Tong 2007; Witham and Bensimon 2012).

Advocates of performance funding have given little attention to another important policy instrument: building up the capacity of colleges to respond to the demands of performance funding, particularly through effective organizational learning in which they examine areas of substandard performance, devise new ways to improve that performance, and evaluate the effectiveness of those methods (Reddy et al. 2014; see also Jenkins 2011; Kerrigan 2010; Kezar 2005; McDonnell and Elmore 1987; Witham and Bensimon 2012). However, we examine the degree to which states have actually used this instrument as part of their performance funding programs, because capacity building has been a major feature of several recent high profile, foundation-sponsored initiatives to improve community college performance, including Achieving the Dream and Completion by Design (Nodine, Venezia, and Bracco 2011; Rutschow et al. 2011). Both programs have featured offering colleges "coaches" who work with senior administrators and institutional researchers to improve their analysis of student outcomes and decide on institutional changes to improve outcomes.

Changes in colleges' revenues from the state, in their awareness of the state's priorities and of their performance in relation to those priorities, and in their organizational capacities can be termed the immediate impacts of performance funding. To be effective, these impacts must in turn stimulate intermediate institutional changes involving changes to institutional policies, programs, and practices that will presumably lead to the ultimate impacts policymakers seek, such as more graduates or increased rates of job placement (Dougherty and Reddy 2013).

We also need to consider the unintended impacts of and frequent obstacles to performance funding (Dougherty and Reddy 2013; Lahr et al. 2014; Pheatt et al. 2014; see also Heinrich and Marschke 2010; Moynihan 2008). Unintended impacts are results that are not intended by the policy creators but that arise as side effects of policy initiatives (Merton 1976). In the case of performance funding, they may include lowering academic standards for enrolled students or narrowing institutional missions to focus on areas rewarded by performance funding (Dougherty and Reddy 2013). Such impacts may arise when public agencies—whether in education, workforce training, health care, or social services—encounter difficulties in easily realizing the intended impacts of performance accountability by using legitimate means and instead resort to less legitimate means, such as lowering service delivery standards or restricting the intake of harder-to-serve clients (Forsythe 2001; Grizzle 2002; Heinrich and Marschke 2010; Moynihan 2008; Radin 2006; Rothstein 2008a, 2008b; also see Merton 1968, 1976; Mica, Peisert, and Winczorek 2012). The obstacles are characteristics of the performance funding program or of the target higher education institutions that impede the ability of institutions to effectively respond to the demands of the performance funding program using legitimate methods. They can take such forms as colleges' lack of organizational capacity to adequately understand their performance problems and develop feasible and effective solutions (Dougherty and Reddy 2013).

Research Questions

The analysis in this paper is organized around six main research questions: First, what policy instruments have states used as a part of their performance funding (PF) programs to influence the behavior of institutions? What have been the immediate impacts of those instruments? Second, what deliberative processes have colleges used to determine how to respond to performance funding? Third, how have colleges altered their academic and student services policies, programs, and practices in ways that relate to performance funding goals? Fourth, what have the impacts of performance funding programs been on student outcomes? Fifth, have there been obstacles to securing the impacts intended by PF advocates? Finally, have there been unintended outcomes of PF?

Research Methods

To answer these questions, we analyzed the performance funding experiences of three states (Indiana, Ohio, and Tennessee) and within each state, three community colleges and three public universities. For data triangulation, we conducted numerous interviews in each of the three states with a diverse range of individuals involved with performance funding. We also analyzed available documentary data, including public agency reports, newspaper articles, institutional websites, and academic research studies (books, journal articles, and doctoral dissertations).

Why Indiana, Ohio, and Tennessee? These three states are leaders in performance funding—particularly PF 2.0—but otherwise differ substantially in the histories of their performance funding programs and in their political and socioeconomic structures, as table 1 shows.

In terms of policy history, Tennessee established a performance funding 1.0 program in 1979, the first state to do so. Ohio first adopted it much later, in 1995, Indiana later still, in 2007. In 2009, Indiana and Ohio adopted new PF 2.0 programs, and Tennessee followed in 2010 (Dougherty and Natow 2015; Dougherty and Reddy 2013). The Ohio and Tennessee PF 2.0 programs tie a much larger proportion of state appropriations for higher education to performance indicators than Indiana does: 80 to 90 percent as compared with 6 percent in Indiana.

The states also differ in the degree of centralization of their public governance systems for higher education. All but one of Indiana's community college campuses operate under a single governing board (Ivy Tech), and its university campuses operate under five governing boards.[2] At the other extreme, in Ohio, all twenty-three of the community colleges and all

---

2. The Ivy Tech system in Indiana operates as a single community college, with the separate campuses reporting to a Central Office. Only one public two-year college—Vincennes University—is not part of the Ivy Tech system.

Table 1. Programmatic, Political, Social, and Economic Characteristics of the Case Study States

State Characteristic	Indiana	Ohio	Tennessee
1. Year performance funding was established[a]			
1.0 program	2007	1995	1979
2.0 program	2009	2009	2010
2. Sectors of public higher education covered by the state's performance funding 2.0 program	Universities and community colleges	Universities and community colleges	Universities and community colleges
3. Proportion of state appropriations based on performance funding 2.0 indicators	6% of higher education funding (fiscal year 2013–2014)	80% of funding for universities and 50% of funding for community colleges (fiscal year 2013–2014)	Approximately 85 to 90% of state higher education appropriations; the remainder is accounted for by utilities, major equipment, and similar expenses
4. State's higher education governance structure at the time performance funding 2.0 was adopted			
Coordinating board for all public higher education in the state	X	X	X
Governing boards for *each* public university or university system in state	X	X	X (for the five University of Tennessee campuses)
Governing board for *all* community colleges	X		X (all public community colleges and universities other than the University of Tennessee)
Governing board for each community college		X	
5. State political culture: Proportion in state identifying as conservative (1996–2003)	37.9%	34.4%	39.3%
6. Governor's institutional powers on a scale of 1 to 5 (2010)	3.25	3.75	2.75
7. Professionalism of the legislature (2009)	22nd	5th	37th
8. Index of party competition (2007–2011)	0.871	0.926	0.913
9. State's population as of 2010	6,484,000	11,537,000	6,346,000
10. State's per capita personal income as of 2010	$34,943	$36,395	$35,307
11. Residents over age twenty-four holding at least a bachelor's degree (2009)	22.5%	24.1%	23.0%

Sources: Authors' compilation based on Dougherty and Reddy 2013 (rows 1, 2); author interviews (3); McGuinness 2003 and author interviews (4); Erikson, Wright, and McIver 2006 (5); Ferguson 2013 (6); Hamm and Moncrief 2013 (7); Holbrook and La Raja 2013 (8); U.S. Census Bureau 2012 (9–11).

Notes: Ferguson applies a five-point scale based on the following six features: the number of executive branch officials separately elected, the tenure potential of the governor, the governor's powers of appointment, the governor's budgetary power, the governor's veto power, and whether the governor's party controls the legislature. The average rating for all fifty states across all of these features is 3.3. Hamm and Moncrief use rankings on Squire's index (based on legislative salary, the amount of permanent staff, and the length of the legislative session). Holbrook and La Raja report the Ranney interparty competition index, with larger numbers meaning more competition, on a 0.5 to 1.0 scale.

[a] We chose to focus on the date that performance funding was adopted rather than on a later date of implementation or full phase-in (if applicable), because as of the adoption date, institutions were likely to have been aware that performance funding had been adopted and were probably considering institutional responses by at least that point.

thirteen of the university main campuses have their own governing boards (McGuiness 2003).

The states also vary significantly in political culture and structures (Gray, Hanson, and Kousser 2012). Tennessee and Indiana are above average in the conservatism of their electorates, whereas Ohio is very near the national average (Erikson, Wright, and McIver 2006). The three states also differ in the characteristics of their political institutions, with Ohio's governor having more institutional power and its legislature a higher degree of legislative professionalism than Indiana's or Tennessee's (Ferguson 2013; Hamm and Moncrief 2013). Moreover, Ohio and Tennessee tend to have greater political party competition than Indiana (Holbrook and La Raja 2013).

Finally, the states differ considerably in their social characteristics: population, income, and education. Ohio's population is substantially larger, wealthier, and better educated than those of Indiana and Tennessee, as shown in table 1.

Which Colleges and Universities?
This study examines the experiences of eighteen public higher education institutions with performance funding: nine community colleges and nine universities. The community colleges and universities differ in their expected capacity to respond effectively to performance funding. Using data from the Integrated Postsecondary Education Data System (IPEDS) survey of 2011 and other data, expected organizational capacity was measured based on college resources (IPED data on revenues per full-time equivalent student), data-analytic capacity (ratings by two experts in each state), and number of at-risk students (IPEDS data on percentage of students receiving Pell Grants and percentage of minority students). We rated all the community colleges in each state as being in the top, middle, and bottom third on each of these three dimensions, summed the ratings, and picked one college in each state from each third. We have labeled these colleges as having high, medium, or low capacity. We also rated all the public universities in each state along the same dimensions and selected two universities that were high and low in their expected capacity to respond to performance funding, using the same capacity measure as for the community colleges. We labeled these universities either high 1 or low. For comparison, we also selected a third university in each state that was also high capacity but not a research-intensive institution. We labeled it high 2.

Data Collection and Analysis
We interviewed 261 state officials, state-level political actors, and institutional administrators and faculty at the eighteen institutions (see table 2). We also drew on documentary sources such as public agency reports, newspaper articles, and academic research studies (books, journal articles, and doctoral dissertations) to supplement our findings. At the state level, we interviewed higher education commission officials, gubernatorial advisors, legislators and members of their staff, business leaders, and researchers and consultants. The institutional respondents included senior administrators (the president and the vice presidents reporting to the president), deans and other middle-level academic administrators, nonacademic middle-level administrators such as the director of institutional research, chairs of different departments representing a range of disciplines and degrees of exposure to outside accountability demands, and the chair of the faculty senate. We relied on the department chairs and the chair of the faculty senate to illuminate the range of faculty opinion.

The interviews were semistructured and lasted approximately one to two hours. Although we used a standard protocol, we adapted it to each interviewee and to material that emerged during an interview. Moreover, after conducting a cross-case analysis of our initial community college interviews, we added several questions to the interview protocol we used for our remaining community college and university interviews to better pinpoint certain processes and impacts. All institutions and interviewees were promised confidentiality, and we have masked their identities.

The interviews were transcribed and coded using the Atlas.ti qualitative data analysis software system. We also coded documentary materials if they were in a format that allowed im-

Table 2. Categories of Interviewees

Category	IN	OH	TN
State-level officials			
State higher education officials	3	5	9
Legislators and staff	4	2	5
Gubernatorial advisors	1	2	3
Business leaders	1	1	0
Other (consultants, researchers, other)	1	1	1
Subtotal	10	11	18
Institutional-level—community colleges			
Senior administrators	10	16	12
Mid-level administrators—nonacademic	5	4	10
Mid-level administrators—academic	11	5	10
Faculty	8	13	6
Subtotal	34	38	38
Institutional-level—universities			
Senior administrators	15	16	11
Mid-level administrators—nonacademic	4	3	9
Mid-level administrators—academic	6	9	6
Faculty	12	13	8
Subtotal	37	41	34
Total	81	90	90

Source: Authors' compilation.

porting it into Atlas. Our coding scheme began with an initial list of "start" or thematic codes drawn from our conceptual framework, but we added and altered codes as necessary as we proceeded with data collection and analysis. New codes were added and existing codes modified as we discovered unexpected patterns in our data during our periodic cross-case analyses of the interviews. To analyze the data, we ran queries in Atlas based on our key coding categories. Using this output, we created analytic tables comparing how different interviewees at different kinds of institutions perceived the implementation and operation of performance funding.

POLICY INSTRUMENTS AND THEIR IMMEDIATE IMPACTS

We begin by describing the four policy instruments that could be used for performance funding: financial incentives; disseminating information about the goals and methods of performance funding; communicating to colleges how they are doing on the state performance funding metrics; and building up institutional capacity to respond to performance funding. We analyze how these instruments were used in our three states and what immediate impacts they had on institutions. Our documentary analysis and interviews with campus personnel yield substantial evidence that the first three instruments are all operating and having substantial impact in our three states. Although the financial incentives seemed to have the most impact, it is also clear that the two informational instruments also had important impacts of their own. Little evidence indicates, however, that building up institutional capacity was a significant policy instrument used by those states and that it had much of any impact (for a full analysis, see Dougherty et al., forthcoming; Reddy et al. 2014).

Financial Incentives

We find evidence that college leaders are following the money and that college personnel further down the institutional hierarchy (such as faculty and mid-level administrators) are aware that student outcomes now impact their institution's bottom line. To be sure, of our 141 institutional respondents who felt comfortable assessing the size of annual budget variations, two-thirds indicated that their state's performance funding program had little to no impact on their college's budget.[3] However, most of our institutional respondents also reported that the financial incentives attached to performance funding were having a substantial impact on campus efforts to improve student outcomes. Of the 124 institutional respondents answering this question,[4] half (61) rated the impact as high. A mid-level administrator at a university in Tennessee put it this way:

> I think it does have a big impact. And I think it establishes sort of officially that this is the business that we're in, and we always should have been in this business. But now we're going to be funded, and anybody who wants to do anything creative, new, expanding whatever, they are going to have to sort of justify it by the funding that comes with these numbers. So yeah, I mean, I think it's a sea change, at least for us on this campus.

Disseminating Information on PF Goals and Methods

Disseminating information as to what the state priorities are and just how performance funding is intended to function can further help to align the motivations of policymakers and campus personnel (see Anderson 2014). State actors and institutional personnel in all three states testified to extensive efforts on the part of state higher education officials to communicate the goals and methods of their performance funding programs to local college personnel, either directly from the state or indirectly through senior college administrators. However, we also received many responses indicating that awareness of the programs was quite uneven within institutions. Nearly one-fifth (38 of 222) of our respondents stated that they had not received any communication—direct or indirect—from the state on the goals and methods of performance funding. Those reports tended to be concentrated among faculty and middle-level administrators (for similar findings on Washington State, see Jenkins et al. 2012). The main explanations for this lack of awareness involved competing demands on faculty time and attention, lack of faculty involvement in decision-making situations where performance funding was relevant, administrative decisions to hold back information when they felt it was not relevant to faculty, and communications breakdowns. In the end, however, of the 123 institutional respondents who rated the impact of the dissemination of information about program goals and methods on college efforts to improve student outcomes, 46 percent did so as high and 27 percent as medium. For example, a dean at an Indiana community college said this:

> They're really letting people know, "This is a serious issue." And again, like I said, it's not all being driven by the fact that its money involved, but there's an awful lot of "It's the right thing to do. This is a serious problem for the country; we need to see what we can do to solve that problem."

Disseminating Information on Institutional Performance

Our data indicate that state efforts to mold institutional action through provision of information about how the institutions were doing on the state metrics were spottier and had less impact than their efforts to disseminate information about state goals. More than a third (79 of 221) of our institutional respondents said

---

3. Several factors mitigated against a big financial impact: the use of three-year rolling averages rather than annual statistics; hold-harmless provisions in the first few years of the programs that limited their impact; the declining state share of total institutional revenues and concomitant rise in the tuition share of revenues; and—in Indiana and in Ohio for community colleges until recently—the small proportion of state funding driven by performance indicators (for more detail, see Reddy et al. 2014).

4. This represented 56 percent of our institutional respondents. This number was kept down in good part by the fact that we did not begin asking this question until after our first round of interviews in Ohio and Tennessee.

there was no communication, direct or indirect, from the state. Moreover, a large proportion did not respond when we asked them what impact state communication may have had on institutional efforts to improve student outcomes. Still, the impact of information about institutional performance could be considerable. Of the 101 who responded, 51 percent rated the impact as high and 27 percent as medium. A senior administrator of an Ohio university described the ability of performance funding programs to induce status-competition between institutions:

> I'd say the financial impact was completely overshadowed by these other features about this university's reputation and where it really wanted to focus and maintain its status, relative to the other public institutions in the state as well as some of the private schools with whom we know we compete for similar students.

Building Up Organizational Capacity

We find little evidence that building organizational capacity—to collect and analyze data on student outcomes, devise and fund interventions to improve them, and evaluate those interventions—was an important policy instrument in implementing performance funding. To be sure, the state officials we interviewed did mention some efforts to build up the capacity of colleges, such as Ohio's building of a state data infrastructure that would make it easier for colleges to analyze data and Tennessee hosting two-day College Completion Academies at which participating institutions could learn about institutional practices to improve student outcomes (Dougherty et al. 2014a). Still, among the 173 institutional respondents who rated the extent of state effort to build up institutional capacity, 95 percent rated it as low or nonexistent. A mid-level Tennessee university administrator observed:

> I just think the state is saying, "It's up to you to find efficiencies, and it's up to you to do what you need to do to increase outcomes. And if you do a good job, we're going to give you more money." But they didn't [give] any kind of seed money to start any of these new things.

This weak state effort to build up the capacity of colleges to collect and analyze data on student outcomes, determine effective ways to improve them, pay the cost of those interventions, and evaluate their effectiveness is important. It contributes to one of the obstacles colleges encounter in trying to respond to performance funding: inadequate organizational capacity. We return to this point later.

We have no reason to believe that Indiana, Ohio, and Tennessee are unusual in their lack of sustained attention to capacity building. Little evidence indicates that others states with performance funding programs are devoting much attention to it either. We regard this lack of attention as a central problem with performance funding programs as they now exist.

ORGANIZATIONAL LEARNING IN RESPONSE TO PERFORMANCE FUNDING

In our interviews, we asked respondents about what kind of deliberative process their colleges used to consider how to respond to the pressure from the state performance funding program for improved student outcomes (Dougherty et al., forthcoming; Jones et al. 2015). We discovered that the colleges relied both on their established bureaucratic processes and on special purpose deliberative structures to investigate and make decisions about policies and practices that would improve performance funding outcomes. The established bureaucratic "general administrative structures" have a long-standing place in the administrative hierarchy, typically existed before performance funding was implemented, and most likely will continue if performance funding were to end. They take such forms as a designated position, such as vice president for student effectiveness, or regularly constituted groups, such as a president's or dean's council. A dean at a Tennessee community college listed a variety of general purpose deliberative structures used to respond to performance funding:

> There's a vice president's council which makes some decisions and then we have a

learning council which is more the academic deans and the directors of financial aid and admissions ... all those folks who are the support for the academic side of the house. And so, yes, we come together and we talk about what performance funding indicators ... what we want those to be, what we think we can reach, how much we want to put into this particular indicator and how much we want to put into that one. And then we, as deans, take it back to our departments for conversations and get inputs from our departments.

However, we also found that colleges frequently used more informal and temporary organizational structures to monitor and improve their performance on state funding metrics. These "special purpose deliberative structures" have been set up for a specific goal, are often newer, are not part of the main bureaucratic administrative structure, and are not intended to be permanent. They take such forms as strategic planning committees, accreditation self-study task forces, or college committees to coordinate an institution's response to external initiatives such as the Achieving the Dream and Completion by Design initiative of the Lumina and Gates Foundations, which work with colleges to improve student outcomes. For example, in Indiana, special purpose structures arose in response to community colleges' involvement with the Achieving the Dream (ATD) initiative and then became devices for responding to performance funding. A senior administrator at an Indiana community college noted how its ATD committee became the college's vehicle for deliberation on how to respond to performance funding:

> Once we joined Achieving the Dream ... we convened panels of faculty and staff from the various regions to address individual issues like student orientation, individual academic plans, and these groups of faculty and staff came up with several proposals.... We have not to my knowledge had any meetings specifically for performance funding. We do have meetings on a regular basis though on, again, the Achieving the Dream goals. But this kind of similar, like I say, the performance funding has just kind of fallen [into a] one-to-one relationship with our Achieving the Dream efforts.

INSTITUTIONAL CHANGES IN KEEPING WITH THE AIMS OF PERFORMANCE FUNDING

In this section we examine how universities and community colleges in all three states altered their academic and student services policies, programs, and practices following the advent of performance funding in ways that relate to achieving the goals of performance funding. A major theme is the difficulty in disentangling the impact of performance funding from other factors that operated concurrently (for the full analysis, see Dougherty et al., forthcoming; Natow et al. 2014).

Determining the Impact of Performance Funding

In our interviews, we asked our institutional respondents what changes their institutions made in response to performance funding. However, many of our respondents found it difficult to answer this question in any simple way. They noted that performance funding has been but one of several concurrent external influences that seek to improve higher education institutional outcomes. States have recommended or even legislatively mandated such institutional changes as lowering the number of credits required for degrees, enhancing course articulation and transfer, and reforming developmental (remedial) education. Institutions are also influenced by accreditors, foundations, and other nonprofit associations—such as the Gates and Lumina foundations and Complete College America—that fund or otherwise advocate for particular reforms. In light of all of these concurrent influences, it is difficult to differentiate the impact of performance funding from that of other external influences (for a similar finding on Washington State, see Jenkins et al. 2012). For example, when asked about programmatic changes in response to performance funding, a senior administrator at a Tennessee university said this:

I think part of the challenge with your question is that the things that I'm walking through [with you] are not just simply because of the new [performance funding] formula or the old formula. They are the result of policy directives from the board. They are the results of questions from regional and professional accrediting entities. They are the result of public pressures. So it's not just simply the formula, it's a national mood and a national conversation around the importance of completion.

On the whole, there is reason to believe that the coincidence of performance funding with other policy initiatives to improve student outcomes has produced synergy rather than interference. Institutional responses to a given external initiative were often quite useful to responding as well to performance funding demands. Colleges frequently used special purpose deliberative structures developed to respond to accreditation demands or initiatives such as Achieving the Dream to also craft their responses to performance funding.

Changes in Academic Policies, Programs, and Practices

The two most common campus-level academic changes following performance funding adoption have been to alter developmental (remedial) education and change course articulation and transfer. Other commonly adopted academic practices include changes to tuition and financial aid policies, registration and graduation procedures, and student services departments (Natow et al. 2014).

Developmental Education

Respondents at ten of our eighteen institutions—particularly at community colleges but also at some universities—reported making changes in developmental education (also known as remedial education). Changes to developmental education involved both curricular and instructional changes. A way one community college in our sample restructured its developmental education was through preterm remediation, in which students could enroll in remedial classes during the summer before their first fall term. In other instances, developmental education students were enrolled in developmental courses at the same time as college-level courses. In Indiana, this corequisite model is a statewide mandate for community colleges separate from the performance funding program (Ivy Tech Community College 2014).

Performance funding provided an incentive for this insofar as developmental education success was a performance indicator for community colleges in Ohio and Tennessee. At the same time, in all three states, developmental education reform was mandated or incentivized by state legislation or other state or private initiatives separate from performance funding (Boatman 2012; Ivy Tech Community College 2014; Quint et al. 2013). Thus, although the developmental education reforms in these states are certainly consistent with the goals of performance funding, other forces were influential as well. It is difficult to know the extent that performance funding influenced these changes.

Course Articulation and Transfer

Another common academic change, which was reported at eight of our eighteen institutions, was to improve course articulation and transfer, particularly between community colleges and universities. Performance funding certainly played a role because transfer numbers are a performance funding metric in Ohio and Tennessee. The performance-based funding formulas in those two states reward colleges for students transferring out to another institution with twelve or more credits (Ohio Board of Regents 2013; Tennessee Higher Education Commission 2011a, 2011b). But other influences are also at work. The Complete College Tennessee Act that revamped the higher education funding formula also mandated other efforts to improve transfer between community colleges and universities (State of Tennessee 2010).

Changes in Student-Services Policies, Programs, and Practices

The two most commonly made campus-level student services changes after performance funding was adopted have been to change advising and counseling services as well as tutoring and supplemental instruction (for other changes, see Natow et al. 2014).

Advising and Counseling

All eighteen of our institutions made changes in advising and counseling. Such changes included adding more academic advisors or counselors, creating online advising systems, asking faculty members to play a greater role in student advising, and using early alert or early warning systems that notify advisors when students are in danger of dropping out. Institutions saw these changes as helping improve institutional performance on performance funding metrics for credit accrual and degree completion. However, it was also clear that some of these institutional responses were also seen as driven by state-mandated changes that were independent of performance funding.

Tutoring and Supplemental Instruction

Next to advising, the student services changes made with the most frequency involved tutoring and supplemental instruction. Respondents at thirteen of our eighteen institutions reported such changes. Tutoring changes included creating new tutoring centers, providing online tutoring, and requiring faculty to meet personally with students.

STUDENT OUTCOMES

Given the rather extensive changes institutions have made in response to performance funding, the question is whether this has resulted in a significant improvement in student outcomes. As it happens, we have no research definitively establishing that.

To be sure, we do have evidence that graduation numbers in Indiana, Ohio, and Tennessee have risen faster than enrollment in the years since the introduction of the performance funding 2.0 programs in those states (see Dougherty et al., forthcoming; Postsecondary Analytics 2013). However, this by no means settles the issue. Even if student outcomes improve after the introduction of performance funding, the improvements could be influenced by many other factors, such as growing enrollments (which alone could produce rising graduation numbers), modifications to state tuition and financial aid policies, and other efforts to improve student outcomes (such as recent state initiatives to improve counseling and advising, developmental education, and transfer between institutions). Hence, it is important to conduct multivariate statistical analyses that strive to control for the many other factors that might account for improvements in student outcomes.

Most of these multivariate analyses focus on graduation from public four-year colleges, though some also consider graduation from community colleges and retention in both two-year and four-year colleges. The studies compare states with and without performance funding using a variety of multivariate statistical techniques (such as difference-in-differences or hierarchical linear modeling) and controlling for a variety of institutional characteristics (such as median test scores, student income and racial composition, and institutional spending on instruction), state policies (such as average tuition for two-year and four-year colleges, state financial aid per student, and state appropriations per student), and state socioeconomic characteristics and conditions (such as population size and state unemployment rate) (Dougherty and Reddy 2013, table A2; Dougherty et al., forthcoming).

Four-Year College Graduation

Most of these studies focus on baccalaureate completions at public four-year colleges, analyzing either graduation rates or number of degrees awarded. The predominant finding is that performance funding does not have a significant impact on four-year graduation for institutions and states (Hillman, Tandberg, and Gross 2014; Larocca and Carr 2012; Rutherford and Rabovsky 2014; Sanford and Hunter 2011; Shin 2010; Shin and Milton 2004; Tandberg and Hillman 2014; Umbricht, Fernandez, and Ortagus 2015). For example, using a difference-in-differences design with state and year fixed effects to compare states with and without performance funding, David Tandberg and Nicholas Hillman (2014) examine the impact of performance funding on number of baccalaureate degrees awarded by public four-year colleges. They control for various higher education system characteristics (including percentage of students enrolled in the public four-year sector, in-state tuition at public two-year and four-year colleges, state aid per public FTE, and state appropriations per public FTE) and various state-level socioeconomic characteristics (including population size, poverty rate, unemployment rate, and gross state product per capita). Comparing states with and without performance funding for four-year colleges, the authors find no average impact of performance funding on changes between 1990 and 2010 in the number of baccalaureate degrees awarded by states with performance funding. As a robustness check, they do comparisons involving lagged and nonlagged effects and three different comparison groups of states without performance funding: all states, states contiguous to performance funding states, and states with coordinating-planning boards (the type most common among performance funding states).

Although the multivariate analyses of four-year graduation do not find that performance funding on average has an impact, there is an interesting finding. Tandberg and Hillman (2014) find that performance funding had a positive impact on bachelor's degree production beginning seven years after the performance funding programs were established in the few states that had programs lasting that long. They note that this suggests that performance funding programs may need some time before they produce effects. Programs are sometimes phased in over time. Institutions need time to react to performance funding demands and make necessary changes. And enough time needs to pass to see students through to graduation, which often comes five or six years after college entrance (Tandberg and Hillman 2014; see also Dougherty et al., forthcoming).

Two-Year College Graduation

Two multivariate studies have been conducted on the impact of performance funding on student completions at community colleges (Hillman, Tandberg, and Fryar 2015; Tandberg, Hillman, and Barakat 2014). The authors find a significant impact on completion of short-term certificates but no impact, on average, on completion of long-term certificates or associate degrees. The latter finding has some interesting wrinkles, however.

Using a difference-in-differences fixed effects analysis comparing institutions in states with performance funding and those in various combinations of states without performance funding for community colleges (all states and neighboring states),[5] two recent studies find that performance funding has no impact, on average, on associate degree completion (Hillman, Tandberg, and Fryar 2015; Tandberg, Hillman, and Barakat 2014). The control variables included higher education characteristics and state or local socioeconomic characteristics.[6] However, despite finding no average effect, both studies did find more localized impacts of interest. Tandberg and his colleagues (2014) find that—across six separate equations—four states evidence a significant positive impact of performance funding on associate's degree completion, although they also find evidence of a negative impact in six states, mixed impacts in three states, and no impact in six states. Moreover, Hillman and his colleagues (2015) find that performance funding for community colleges in Washington had a delayed impact on associate's degree completion beginning four years after the program was established in 2007. They also find a positive impact of Washington's Student Achievement Initiative on short-term certificate awards (less than one-year) in comparisons of Washington

---

5. Tandberg, Hillman, and Barakat (2014) also include states with state coordinating or planning boards as a comparison group.

6. For the Tandberg and colleagues (2014) study, the higher education system control variables include include percentage of students enrolled in the community college sector, in-state tuition at public two-year and four-year colleges, state aid per public FTE, and state appropriations per public FTE and the socioeconomic controls included state population size, poverty rate, and unemployment rate. For the Hillman and colleagues (2015) study, the higher education institution controls included percentage enrolled part-time, percentage white, percentage of revenues from state appropriations, tuition and fees, and federal and state grant aid per FTE, whereas the socioeconomic control variables were size of county labor force and county unemployment rate.

with three combinations of states. However, performance funding had a negative impact on the awarding of long-term certificates.

Retention at Four-Year and Two-Year Colleges

A few multivariate studies have also been conducted of retention rates and almost without exception they find no impact of performance funding. Roger Larocca and Douglas Carr (2012) find that two-year colleges in states with performance funding had higher one-year retention rates than their counterparts in states without performance funding. However, Hillman, Tandberg, and Fryar (2015) find no impact of performance funding on community college retention in Washington. Four other studies also found no effect of performance funding on retention in public four-year colleges (Huang 2010; Larocca and Carr 2012; Rutherford and Rabovsky 2014; Sanford and Hunter 2011).

In sum, the multivariate studies conducted to date largely fail to find evidence that performance funding improves retention and graduation. However, several interesting findings of more localized effects involve delayed effects on four-year college graduation, impacts on short-term community college certificates, and, in some states, impacts on community college associate's degrees.

These multivariate studies primarily examined PF 1.0 programs, which do not tie much state funding to performance indicators. Although PF2.0 programs have become much more common, only a few existed before 2007 (see Dougherty and Natow 2015). Hence, only a few PF 2.0 programs are captured by the existing studies of performance funding impacts through 2010, and they are captured very early in their development. We have only three studies that examine performance funding 2.0 programs in any depth (Hillman, Tandberg, and Gross 2014; Hillman, Tandberg, and Fryar 2015; Umbricht, Fernandez, and Ortagus 2015). Nonetheless, it is instructive that all three find that performance funding 2.0 programs do not have a significant impact on student outcomes. For example, Hillman and his colleagues (2015) examine the impacts of performance funding in Indiana, Ohio, and Tennessee using a difference-in-differences analysis, controlling for the local unemployment rate and the following institutional characteristics: enrollment, proportion of students who are white, proportion part-time, tuition level, operating revenues, and revenues from the state. In eleven of twelve models (four for each state), they find that performance funding had no multiyear average positive impact on graduation numbers.[7]

Performance Funding Outcomes Outside Higher Education

Studies of the impact of performance accountability programs in other policy areas besides higher education have arrived at mixed results. Studies of the federal No Child Left Behind program and of similar state accountability programs in Florida and Texas have found evidence of significant impacts on student achievement, though these impacts are not uniform across subjects and grades (Dee and Jacob 2011; Deming et al. 2013; Rouse et al. 2007). On the other hand, a study of the impact of the Schoolwide Performance Bonus Program in New York City found no impact on student achievement (Marsh et al. 2011). Similarly, studies of the performance standards attached to the Job Training Partnership Act (JTPA) programs have also yielded mixed findings. They find that JTPA did lead training centers to produce the intended results in terms of immediate employment and short-term earnings improvement. However, those immediate results are very weakly correlated with earnings and employment eighteen and thirty months after completing training (Cragg 1997; Heckman, Heinrich, and Smith 2011).

If performance funding for higher education so far has had less impact than performance accountability in other policy areas, it could be simply because, until recently, it has not been tied to that much state funding. More

---

[7]. When the authors examine performance on outcomes year by year, significant impacts begin appearing two to three years after the state PF 2.0 programs were established, particularly in Indiana. This raises the possibility that performance funding may have lagged effects.

pronounced impacts could emerge if states follow the lead of Tennessee and Ohio in tying much larger portions of state funding for higher education to performance metrics, though we do not yet have definitive data on what impact those programs have had (Dougherty et al., forthcoming). However, the lack of impact of performance funding for higher education so far could also be testimony to the substantial obstacles it encounters to its effective operation. Could the lack of impact stem from obstacles institutions and campus personnel encounter in responding effectively to performance funding (Dougherty and Reddy 2013; Hillman, Tandberg, and Gross 2014; Tandberg, Hillman, and Barakat 2014)? If so, what forms do such obstacles take? We now turn to analyzing the obstacles that higher education institutions encounter in responding to the demands of performance funding programs.

OBSTACLES TO EFFECTIVELY RESPONDING TO PERFORMANCE FUNDING

Consistent with previous research (Dougherty and Reddy 2013), we find that institutions in our three states encounter several persistent obstacles that hinder their efforts to perform well on the state metrics. Our respondents perceived improvement in student outcomes as primarily inhibited by the demographic and academic composition of their student bodies (in the case of community colleges and broad-access public universities), inappropriate performance funding metrics, and insufficient institutional capacity. Other obstacles mentioned less often included institutional resistance, inadequate state funding of higher education, insufficient institutional knowledge of performance funding, instability in performance funding, indicators, and measures, and insufficient state funding of performance funding (for our full analysis, see Dougherty et al., forthcoming; Pheatt et al. 2014).

Student Composition

With regard to student composition, sixty-three of our respondents at sixteen of the eighteen institutions stated that the most difficult obstacle they perceived to responding to the funding formula is that open-access institutions enroll many at-risk students who face social and economic challenges that make it difficult for them to persist and graduate and therefore contribute to good institutional results on state performance metrics. When asked about specific ways student composition hinders institutional performance, twenty respondents at ten institutions (mostly community colleges) pointed to student academic preparation. Their institutions, they reported, take in many students who are not well prepared academically and therefore less likely to do well on the state metrics, particularly graduation. An Ohio community college dean noted this:

> I think our student population comes in incredibly unprepared and without the foundations skills, without what would be considered college level reading, writing and comprehension. So quite honestly . . . they just don't have the skills—whether it be that they never learned how to study in high school, whether it be they got passed through high school—but they just don't know how to attack college and the level of work that's required in a college class.

Similarly, seventeen respondents at nine institutions (again mostly community colleges) pointed to the fact that a good number of their students come in without a desire for a degree, which also makes it less likely they will graduate. In fact, among college entrants surveyed in their first year as part of the 2003–2004 Beginning Postsecondary Students survey, 16 percent of two-year entrants but only 6 percent of four-year entrants stated that they did not intend to receive a certificate or degree (Berkner and Choy 2008, 7–8). From a high-level community college administrator in Tennessee, we heard this:

> I think all of our sister institutions that are community colleges will be experiencing something very similar. . . . The students that come to community college may not all be intending to earn an associate's degree. They may be coming to upgrade some of their skills as incumbent workers. There may be

some students that are coming back to retool in certain areas. So a completion agenda may not always be first and foremost for a community college student the same way it would be for a four-year university student.

Although it is clear that these sentiments are heartfelt on the part of our community college respondents, they could have a self-serving element. The great stress on student composition as an obstacle could verge on "blaming the victim" and allow institutions to escape from having to examine how their policies and programs might be contributing to poor student outcomes (Kezar et al. 2008; Witham and Bensimon 2012). On the other hand, it would be unfair to the broad-access two-year and four-year colleges to argue that they do not face obstacles greater than those that selective resource-rich four-year institutions face.

Inappropriate Metrics

In good part because of the differences between institutions in student composition and organizational mission, many of our respondents (sixty-one respondents at seventeen institutions) also stated that institutional responsiveness to performance funding was often hindered by a poor match between performance funding metrics and institutional missions and capacities. Respondents at community colleges often perceived the state performance funding programs as being unfair insofar as they held them to the same graduation expectations as four-year institutions. These respondents argued that many students at community colleges do not intend to get a degree, unlike students at four-year institutions, or will have difficulty doing so in a timely fashion given their poorer academic preparation and more difficult life circumstances. As a senior community college administrator in Indiana noted,

> The state [is] not understanding the mission of the community college, as compared to four-year universities. And they evaluate us on the same plane, or they try to. For example, people in a community college have a different mission. They may be married, they may be working, and they may be laid off.... It could be all of those things in life that can screw you up.... We should not be judged the same.

Meanwhile, respondents at high-capacity universities, particularly in Indiana, were frustrated because they felt their institutions had little room to improve. They felt there was a ceiling effect in that institutions already doing well had little room to make big jumps in student outcomes.

Inadequate Organizational Capacity

Finally, many of our respondents (forty-two respondents at fourteen institutions) pointed to their institutions' lack of organizational capacity. The most frequently reported deficiency involved too little institutional research (IR) capacity. A Tennessee community college dean noted, "Any time you talk about implementing any programs or additional assessment ... anything of that nature ... [it] requires resources. And our IR department is woefully understaffed." This underscores the importance of state support for the development of IR capacity. But as we note in our discussion of policy instruments, capacity building of this sort is something that the states have not paid much attention to (Dougherty et al., forthcoming; Reddy et al. 2014).

Tennessee had considerably fewer respondents mentioning obstacles than Indiana and Ohio did. This may in part be because Tennessee has had the longest history of performance funding, so more of the kinks may have been worked out, and college respondents may have become more comfortable with performance funding. Also, our data suggest that—in good part because of a long history of extensive consultation between the state higher education coordinating board and institutional officials (Dougherty and Natow 2015)—Tennessee college administrators and faculty were more aware of and better understood the performance funding policy in their state than did their counterparts in Indiana and Ohio. This would lessen reports of insufficient knowledge as an obstacle (see Reddy et al. 2014).

The presence of reported obstacles to institutions being able to respond effectively to performance funding pressures raises the specter that they may resort to illegitimate methods to succeed (Dougherty and Reddy 2013; Moynihan 2008). The sociologist Robert Merton identified this conjunction of high societal pressure to succeed but structural constraints on being able to do so legitimately—a condition he termed "anomie," following the lead of Emile Durkheim—as a major source of deviance (Merton 1968, 1976). Do we see the organizational equivalent in the case of higher education institutions exposed to strong pressure to perform well by performance funding programs but also facing significant obstacles to doing so? That is the subject of our next section.

UNINTENDED IMPACTS OF PERFORMANCE FUNDING

Besides its intended impacts, performance funding can also generate unintended impacts not desired by policy framers.[8] Our respondents reported numerous undesired impacts, actual and potential, particularly weakening of academic standards and restrictions in college admissions of less-prepared students who might not do as well on performance measures. These negative unintended impacts have been reported as well in Dougherty and Reddy's review of the literature on performance funding in higher education (2013). Moreover, similar impacts—involving deterioration in service delivery quality and adverse risk selection (or "cream skimming") appear in analyses of the use of performance accountability in K-12 education (Rothstein 2008a, 2008b), social welfare programs (Wells and Johnson 2001), workforce training programs (Heckman et al. 2011; Rothstein 2008b), health care (Lake, Kvam, and Gold 2005; Rothstein 2008b; Stecher and Kirby 2004), and public services generally (Grizzle 2002; Heinrich and Marschke 2010; Moynihan 2008).

We classified instances as actual or observed when the interviewee discussed that an impact has occurred or concrete steps have been taken toward producing it (for example, specific steps have been already taken by the college to change admission practices in ways that restrict access for certain kinds of students). Unintended impacts are classified as potential if the respondent noted the possibility of a certain impact occurring, but it has not yet occurred or no clear steps have yet been taken toward producing it.

The unintended impacts most commonly mentioned were restrictions in admissions to college and weakening of academic standards. Others included compliance costs, less institutional cooperation, decrease in staff morale, reduced emphasis on missions not rewarded by performance funding, and weaker faculty voice in academic governance (see Dougherty et al., forthcoming; Lahr et al. 2014).

These unintended impacts may bear an important connection to the obstacles we analyze earlier. When institutions are not successful using legitimate methods because they encounter major obstacles, they may resort to illegitimate ones to realize socially expected goals (see Merton 1968, 1976; Mica, Peisert, and Winczorek 2012).

Admission Restriction

Sixty-seven interviewees at five of nine community colleges and five of nine universities reported that restriction of admissions was an actual or potential unintended impact of performance funding. Forty-one mentioned a potential impact that might occur, twenty-six reported an impact that had occurred. All but one report of an actual impact came from university respondents.

Restriction of admission could improve institutional performance on performance funding metrics by lessening the proportion of students who are less prepared academically and otherwise less likely to graduate. For example, a senior administrator from an Indiana four-year institution said that because of the pres-

---

8. However, we should add that those outcomes—though unintended by policy designers—may actually be intended by institutional actors. They may be quite happy to make their institutions more selective, even if this is not the intent of the state performance funding program. We wish to thank Dr. Tiffany Jones of the Southern Education Foundation for her recommendation that we clarify what is unintended and intended in the impacts of performance funding.

sure from performance funding, the institution is less likely to offer admission to "weaker" students "because if they are weaker . . . there is a chance they will bring down your performance numbers." This might make organizational sense, but it is a troubling development at the societal level. Community colleges and broad-access four-year colleges have historically been committed to increasing opportunity for higher education for less advantaged students. It is very troubling if they begin to back away from this mission at a time when concern is great about increasing inequality in access to higher education (Karen and Dougherty 2005; Mettler 2014).

According to our respondents, restriction of admission of students who are less likely to graduate could occur through a variety of means, such as higher admission requirements, selective recruitment, and shifting institutional financial aid toward better-prepared students (see also Lambert 2015; Umbricht, Fernandez, and Ortagus 2015).

Higher Admissions Requirements
Clearly, colleges can restrict admission of less-prepared students by requiring higher standardized test scores and grade point averages or by decreasing the number of conditionally admitted students who are accepted. A mid-level nonacademic administrator at an Ohio university noted,

> Instead of a graduation rate of 80 percent, we really need to bump that up so that we have a higher graduation rate. And some of that is being achieved by [changing] the type of student that we bring in. . . . So by raising our average ACT score of our incoming class by one point, the question is, "Can we anticipate then higher course completions, higher number of degrees awarded?" . . . So yes, there's a deliberate approach being made by our enrollment management office.

Selective Recruitment
To maximize the likelihood that they enroll students more likely to graduate, institutions are increasing or might increase their efforts to attract better-prepared students, including suburban, out-of-state, and international students. At the same time, respondents discussed how their institutions might deemphasize or are deemphasizing recruitment of students from high schools with many less well-prepared students. A senior administrator at a four-year institution in Ohio observed,

> There's a recognition [as has been brought up in some discussions] of the fact . . . that the more we focus on suburban kids with high GPAs and high ACT scores, the less we're able to serve . . . an urban population that tends to be from poorer school districts. . . . I mean there's a tension between continuing to recruit a very diverse student population and being an urban-serving institution and being an institution that has high performing students who are successful in getting a degree. (quoted in Lahr et al. 2014)

As it happens, a news article in the *Dayton Daily News* (Lambert 2015) reported that a number of Ohio universities are increasing their efforts to recruit students from suburban high schools. A senior administrator at an Ohio public university is quoted as stating, "We are telling our recruiters to expand the variety of schools they go to. If you're in Dayton, maybe not go to just Dayton Public, but also to Beavercreek and Centerville" (quoted in Lambert 2015).

Shifting the Focus of Financial Aid
Admissions can also be affected by shifting the focus of a college's financial aid funds from assisting needy students to attracting better-prepared ones through so-called merit aid. A senior administrator at an Ohio community college explained how performance funding could encourage the college to offer scholarships to higher performing students who are more likely to complete:

> My theory is that we're going to be raising the bar for who we give some of our scholarships to. As I told the president, if it was my business I would be looking for ways to attract people that I thought were very likely to complete. And along with that, I would be looking for what are the tendencies or what are the attributes for those that tend to be non-

completers. Now I think that raises some ethical questions because we are an open-access institution, and so we still need to offer that access, but I think we also need to tweak and, again, encourage more completions as opposed to just numbers of enrollment.

Weakening Academic Standards

Fifty-five respondents at eight of nine community colleges and five of nine universities noted that performance funding could or did result in colleges lowering their academic standards in order to keep up their retention and graduation rates. Two-thirds of these reports involved potential impacts but one-third involved impacts that respondents stated had occurred. Our respondents observed that academic standards are or could be weakened principally by lessening academic demands in class or reducing degree requirements.

Lessening Class Demands

A senior campus administrator at an Indiana community college worried that the push for completions, the most heavily weighted metric within the Indiana performance-based funding formula, will force faculty and institutions to move students through to graduation without care for whether academic standards are maintained: "It's putting faculty in a position of the easiest way out is to lower the standards and get people through. And so it's something that's of great concern I think." Similarly, a faculty member at an Ohio university discussed a feeling of "pressure" not to fail students by inflating grades:

> Well, in an effort to promote student success, there is a substantial pressure to minimize the failure rates of the students in some of these undergraduate courses. And of course that would translate into inflation of grades in order to make sure that the students are passing all of these courses and so forth. So I as a faculty member have a concern as to the watering down of our course materials as well as the quality of our majors, the programs.

Calling attention to courses with low completion rates can lead faculty to decrease their academic demands (and therefore to grade more easily) to achieve higher rates of course completion.

Reducing Degree Requirements

Several respondents noted that their respective institutions recently have changed degree requirements to ensure that students receive their degrees as soon as possible. Although removing unnecessary barriers to graduation may often be a good change, the focus on rapid credential attainment can also affect learning negatively. Degree requirements can be weakened by reducing the number of credits required to complete a degree and by having students take easier courses. In Tennessee, a college dean cited watering down of academic demands to achieve higher completion numbers as a potential unintended impact of performance funding:

> The push is to get students to graduate, or at least the message that we get is [that] students have to graduate. There's concern among faculty [that] that's going to become the overriding goal and they're going to be forced to water down the curriculum, which does not sit well with faculty on any level. . . . A number of the programs have [a] very set curriculum, and there seems to be a push to change that just so that you can get students to be able to graduate. In other words, to substitute courses that aren't necessarily in the curriculum and that doesn't always sit well [with faculty].

Many of our reports of unintended impacts involved *potential* impacts, that is, forecasts of what might happen, particularly if performance funding demands get more intense. These reports could simply be testimony more to our respondents' fears than to their understanding of processes actually unfolding. Still, half of the impacts mentioned were ones we classified as *observed*, reports not of possible impacts but of ones that occurred. Furthermore, we have to keep in mind that our interviews occurred before Indiana, Tennessee, and especially Ohio had fully phased in their performance funding programs. Hence, we have to wonder how many of the potential unintended impacts mentioned might in time become actual. Finally, even if we conclude that the potential unintended impacts will mostly remain only potential, they still testify to a widespread disquiet among higher education administrators and faculty that needs to be addressed by the advocates of performance funding.

The total number of reported unintended impacts varies across our three states, with Tennessee reporting the fewest and Ohio the most, and Indiana somewhere between. Again, a possible explanation for why Tennessee has the lowest number of reports is that of all three states it has had the longest history with performance funding. This may have allowed institutions more time to become used to performance funding and for the state to come up with solutions to unintended impacts that emerged. In addition, the high number of mentions in Ohio may in part be due to the fact that its program was extensively revised during our interviews there. The program may thus have weighed heavily on the minds of faculty and administrators, contributing to the higher number of unintended impacts reported.

SUMMARY AND CONCLUSIONS

We have analyzed the implementation and impacts of performance funding through the lens of three states regarded by many as leaders in that movement: Indiana, Ohio, and Tennessee. Based on extensive interviews with state officials and with staff of eighteen colleges and universities in those three states, we describe the policy instruments those states use to implement performance funding, the deliberative processes colleges use to devise their responses to performance funding, the impact of performance funding on institutional policies and programs and eventually on student outcomes, the obstacles institutions encountered in responding to performance funding demands, and the unintended impacts that ensued.

With regard to policy instruments, we find that states clearly deployed three: financial incentives, dissemination of information on the goals and intended methods of performance funding, and communication to institutions about their performance on the state metrics. Our respondents reported that these three instruments had a significant impact on institutional efforts to improve student outcomes. Although it is clear that the financial incentives were the most important policy instrument, it is also clear that the two informational policy instruments exerted an impact that supplemented and amplified the financial incentive. However, we saw little evidence of another possible instrument playing a significant role: building up the capacity of institutions to respond effectively to performance funding. For example, little evidence indicated any state efforts to enhance the capacity of institutions to collect and analyze data on student outcomes, to determine what might be the most effective solutions to improving those outcomes, to finance the implementation of those solutions, or to evaluate the effectiveness of those interventions. This absence contributes to an important obstacle encountered by colleges in responding to performance funding demands: insufficient organizational capacity.

In responding to performance funding, institutions drew on both general purpose deliberative structures rooted in their bureaucracy and more evanescent special purpose deliberative structures. The latter often arose to address other initiatives—such as accreditation association demands—the colleges were responding to, but they also played a major role in institutional response to performance funding.

Performance funding clearly spurred institutions to change their institutional policies and programs in order to improve student outcomes. However, many of our respondents found it difficult to gauge the relative importance of performance funding, given that it has been only one of several concurrent initiatives that states, accrediting associations, and policy groups have undertaken to improve student outcomes. Still, it appears that this joint influence produced synergy rather than interference, with responses to other external initiatives also facilitating college responses to performance funding. The two most commonly made campus-level academic changes following performance funding adoption have been to alter developmental (remedial) education and improve course articulation and transfer between community colleges and universities.

Meanwhile, the two most common student services changes have been to revamp advising and counseling services and to change tutoring and supplemental instruction.

Even if student outcomes improve after performance funding is introduced, these improvements could be tied to many other factors, such as rising enrollments, changes in state tuition and financial aid policies, initiatives by state governments, national policy groups, and accrediting associations to improve student outcomes, and institutional decisions to admit fewer at-risk students who are less likely to graduate. In Indiana, Ohio, and Tennessee, graduation numbers have increased at a greater rate than enrollments since the advent of their PF 2.0 programs. However, we cannot in any way conclude that performance funding in these three states is producing these better student outcomes because these figures do not control for a host of other possible causes. This caution is strongly reinforced by the fact that multivariate analyses of performance funding programs largely fail to find evidence that performance funding improves graduation or retention, although there is evidence of some interesting localized impacts. However, these multivariate studies primarily examined PF 1.0 programs. We need more multivariate analyses of the more intensive PF 2.0 programs in states such as Ohio and Tennessee before we can reach definitive conclusions about PF 2.0.

If the impact of performance funding on student outcomes is limited, it may be attributable in part to obstacles that institutions encounter in responding to PF demands. We find that institutions in our three states encounter several persistent obstacles. Our respondents most often pointed to the presence of many at-risk students (particularly in the case of community colleges and broad-access public universities), inappropriate performance funding metrics that did not align well with institutional missions and characteristics, and inadequate institutional capacity.

Our interviewees also frequently reported performance funding impacts not publicly intended by those who designed the policies. These negative unintended impacts are similar to those reported by studies of performance accountability in other public services (Grizzle 2002; Heckman et al. 2011; Heinrich and Marschke 2010; Moynihan 2008; Rothstein 2008a, 2008b). The most commonly mentioned unintended impacts were restrictions in admissions to college and weakening of academic standards. These impacts may be rooted in the obstacles colleges encounter in responding to performance funding. They may resort to actions that are socially harmful because they allow them to meet external demands placed on their organizations when socially legitimate means are proving inadequate (see Merton 1968, 1976).

Our findings have a number of implications for research. Clearly, we need more multivariate studies of the impact of performance funding. We do not have enough studies of PF 2.0 programs, particularly ones that have been operating for a number of years, are fully phased in, and involve a large share of state funding for higher education, as in Tennessee and Ohio. We also need more studies that examine PF impacts on two-year college outcomes. This multivariate research should examine not just whether a state has performance funding but also the features of that program: for example, how long it has been in place, what proportion of total institutional funding it affects, which particular performance metrics drive funding allocations, and what other state programs affecting student outcomes (such as initiatives to revamp developmental education or improve transfer pathways) are operating alongside PF. In doing this, researchers should keep in mind that features of a state's performance funding program can vary significantly over time (see Dougherty and Natow 2015). Finally, new studies should examine PF impacts not just on student outcomes but also on intermediate institutional processes that may produce improvements in student outcomes, such as institutional changes in developmental education, student advising, or institutional research.

Our findings also have important implications for policymaking. To reduce unintended impacts of performance funding, policymakers need to protect academic standards and reduce the temptation to restrict admission of at-risk students. To protect academic standards, states and institutions can assess student learning, collect data on changes in degree requirements and course grade distributions, and survey faculty members to find out whether they are feeling pressure to weaken academic standards. To reduce restriction of student admissions, states should provide incentives for admitting and graduating at-risk students and compare only institutions with similar missions and student composition (Dougherty and Reddy 2013; Dougherty et al., forthcoming; Jenkins and Shulock 2013; and Shulock and Jenkins 2011). These efforts would be enhanced by those to overcome the obstacles institutions encounter in responding effectively to performance funding and lead them to be tempted to use illegitimate methods to be successful. States should aid colleges with many at-risk students to better meet the needs of their students, create performance indicators and measures that better align with institutional missions, and act strongly to improve the capacity of colleges to engage in organizational learning (for more, see Dougherty et al., forthcoming).

This is a particularly important time to reflect on performance funding for higher education. It is now operating in over thirty states, with more in prospect, and it comes with great expectations that it will significantly improve student outcomes. It has seized the attention of college administrators and faculty and spurred—along with other policy initiatives—sizable changes in college academic and student-support policies, programs, and practices. At the same time, we do not have as yet conclusive evidence that performance funding does indeed improve student outcomes in any significant way. Moreover, we have evidence that it may produce troubling unintended impacts such as a weakening of academic standards and restrictions in the admission of less prepared and less advantaged students at a time of rising inequality in higher education. Clearly, performance funding deserves close attention both from policymakers and from researchers.

REFERENCES

Anderson, James E. 2014. *Public Policymaking*, 8th ed. Boston, Mass.: Wadsworth.

Argyris, Chris, and Donald A. Schön. 1996. *Organizational Learning II: Theory, Methods, and Practice*. Reading, Mass.: Addison-Wesley.

Baldwin, Christopher, Estela M. Bensimon, Alicia C. Dowd, and Lisa Kleiman. 2011. "Measuring Student Success." *New Directions for Community Colleges* 153(Spring): 75–88.

Berkner, Lutz, and Susan Choy. 2008. *Descriptive Summary of 2003-04 Beginning Postsecondary Students: Three Years Later*. NCES 2008-174. Washington, D.C.: National Center for Education Statistics.

Boatman, Angela. 2012. "Evaluating Institutional Efforts to Streamline Postsecondary Remediation: The Causal Effects of the Tennessee Developmental Course Redesign Initiative on Early Student Academic Success." NCPR working paper. New York: National Center for Postsecondary Research. Accessed February 23, 2016. http://www.postsecondaryresearch.org/i/a/document/22651_BoatmanTNFINAL.pdf.

Burke, Joseph C., ed. 2002. *Funding Public Colleges and Universities: Popularity, Problems, and Prospects*. Albany: State University of New York Press.

Burke, Joseph C., and Associates, eds. 2005. *Achieving Accountability in Higher Education: Balancing Public, Academic, and Market Demands*. San Francisco, Calif.: Jossey-Bass.

Complete College America. 2013. "The Game Changers: Are States Implementing the Best Reforms to Get More College Graduates?" Washington, D.C.: Complete College America.

Cragg, Michael. 1997. "Performance Incentives in the Public Sector: Evidence from the Job Training Partnership Act." *Journal of Law, Economics, and Organization* 13(1): 147–68.

Dee, Thomas, and Brian Jacob. 2011. "The Impact of No Child Left Behind on Student Achievement." *Journal of Policy Analysis and Management* 30(3): 418–46.

Deming, David J., Sarah Cohodes, Jennifer Jennings, and Christopher Jencks. 2013. "School Accountability, Postsecondary Attainment, and Earnings." *NBER* working paper no. 19444. Cambridge, Mass.: National Bureau of Economic Research.

DiMaggio, Paul J., and Walter W. Powell. 1991. "The Iron Cage Revisited: Institutional Isomorphism and Collective Rationality in Organizational Fields." In *The New Institutionalism in Organizational Analysis*, edited by W. W. Powell and

P. J. DiMaggio. Chicago: University of Chicago Press.

Dougherty, Kevin J., Sosanya M. Jones, Hana Lahr, Rebecca S. Natow, Lara Pheatt, and Vikash Reddy. 2014a. "Envisioning Performance Funding Impacts: The Espoused Theories of Action for State Higher Education Performance Funding in Three States." CCRC working paper no. 63. New York: Columbia University. Accessed February 23, 2016. http://ccrc.tc.columbia.edu/publications/envisioning-performance-funding-impacts.html.

———. 2014b. "Performance Funding for Higher Education: Forms, Origins, Impacts, and Futures." Annals of the American Academy of Political and Social Science 655(1): 163–84.

———. Forthcoming. Performance Funding for Higher Education. Baltimore, Md.: Johns Hopkins University Press.

Dougherty, Kevin J., and Rebecca S. Natow. 2015. The Politics of Performance Funding for Higher Education: Origins, Discontinuations, and Transformations. Baltimore, Md.: Johns Hopkins University Press.

Dougherty, Kevin J., and Vikash Reddy. 2013. Performance Funding for Higher Education: What Are the Mechanisms? What Are the Impacts? ASHE Higher Education Report. San Francisco, Calif.: Jossey-Bass.

Dowd, Alicia C., and Vincent P. Tong. 2007. "Accountability, Assessment, and the Scholarship of 'Best Practice.'" In Higher Education: Handbook of Theory and Research, vol. 22, edited by J. C. Smart. Dordrecht: Springer.

Erikson, Robert S., Gerald C. Wright, and John P. McIver. 2006. "Public Opinion in the States: A Quarter Century of Change and Stability." In Public Opinion in State Politics, edited by Jeffrey E. Cohen. Stanford, Calif.: Stanford University Press.

Ewell, Peter T. 1999. "Linking Performance Measures to Resource Allocation: Exploring Unmapped Terrain." Quality in Higher Education 5(3): 191–209.

Ferguson, Margaret. 2013. "Governors and the Executive Branch." In Politics in the American States, 10th ed., edited by Virginia Gray, Russell L. Hanson, and Thad Kousser. Washington, D.C.: CQ Press.

Forsythe, Dall W., ed. 2001. Quicker, Better, Cheaper? Managing Performance in American Government. Albany, N.Y.: Rockefeller Institute Press.

Gray, Virginia, Russell Hanson, and Thad Kousser, eds. 2012. Politics in the American States: A Comparative Analysis, 10th ed. Washington, D.C.: CQ Press.

Grizzle, Gloria A. 2002. "Performance Measurement and Dysfunction: The Dark Side of Quantifying Work." Public Performance and Management Review 25(4): 363–69.

Hamm, Keith E., and Gary F. Moncrief. 2013. "Legislative Politics in the States." In Politics in the American States, 10th ed., edited by Virginia Gray, Russell Hanson, and Thad Kousser. Washington, D.C.: CQ Press.

Harnisch, Thomas L. 2011. "Performance-Based Funding: A Re-Emerging Strategy in Public Higher Education Financing." A Higher Education Policy Brief. Washington, D.C.: American Association of State Colleges and Universities.

Heckman, James J., Carolyn J. Heinrich, Pascal Courty, Gerald Marschke, and Jeffrey Smith. 2011. The Performance of Performance Standards. Kalamazoo, Mich.: W. E. Upjohn Institute.

Heckman, James J., Carolyn J. Heinrich, and Jeffrey Smith. 2011. "Do Short-Run Performance Measures Predict Long-Run Impacts?" In The Performance of Performance Standards, edited by James J. Heckman et al. Kalamazoo, Mich.: W. E. Upjohn Institute.

Heinrich, Carolyn J., and Gerald Marschke. 2010. "Incentives and Their Dynamics in Public Sector Performance Management Systems." Journal of Policy Analysis and Management 29(1): 183–208.

Hillman, Nicholas W., Alisa F. Fryar, David A. Tandberg, and Valerie Crespin-Trujillo. 2015. "Evaluating the Efficacy of Performance Funding in Three States: Tennessee, Ohio, and Indiana." Unpublished paper. University of Wisconsin, Madison.

Hillman, Nicholas W., David A. Tandberg, and Alisa H. Fryar. 2015. "Evaluating the Impacts of 'New' Performance Funding in Higher Education." Educational Evaluation and Policy Analysis. doi: 10.3102/0162373714560224.

Hillman, Nicholas W, David A. Tandberg, and Jacob P. K. Gross. 2014. "Performance Funding in Higher Education: Do Financial Incentives Impact College Completions?" Journal of Higher Education 85(6): 826–57.

Holbrook, Thomas M., and Raymond J. La Raja. 2013. "Parties and Elections." In Politics in the American States, 10th ed., edited by Virginia Gray, Russell L. Hanson, and Thad Kousser. Washington, D.C.: CQ Press.

Honig, Meredith I. 2006. "Complexity and Policy Implementation: Challenges and Opportunities for the Field." In *New Directions in Education Policy Implementation: Confronting Complexity*, edited by Meredith I. Honig. Albany: State University of New York Press.

Huang, Y. 2010. "Performance Funding and Retention Rates." Unpublished paper. Michigan State University.

Ivy Tech Community College. 2014. "The Co-Requisite Initiative: An Initial Assessment of Its Impact at Ivy Tech Community College—Central Indiana Region." Presentation, March 25. Indianapolis, Ind.: Ivy Tech Community College. Accessed February 23, 2016. https://s3.amazonaws.com/jngi_pub/gce14/Co-Requisite+Initiative.pdf.

Jenkins, Davis. 2011. "Redesigning Community Colleges for Completion: Lessons from Research on High-Performance Organizations." *CCRC* working paper no. 24. New York: Columbia University.

Jenkins, Davis, and Nancy Shulock. 2013. "Metrics, Dollars, and Systems Change: Learning from Washington's Student Achievement Initiative to Design Effective Postsecondary Performance Funding Policies." State Policy Brief. New York: Columbia University, Teachers College, Community College Research Center.

Jenkins, Davis, John Wachen, Colleen Moore, and Nancy Shulock. 2012. "Washington State Student Achievement Initiative Policy Study: Final Report." New York: Columbia University, Teachers College, Community College Research Center.

Jones, Dennis P. 2013. "Outcomes-Based Funding: The Wave of Implementation." Indianapolis, Ind.: Complete College America. Accessed February 23, 2016. http://www.completecollege.org/pdfs/Outcomes-Based-Funding-Report-Final.pdf.

Jones, Sosanya M., Kevin J. Dougherty, Jana Lahr, Rebecca S. Natow, Lara Pheatt, and Vikash Reddy. 2015. "Organizational Learning by Colleges Responding to Performance Funding: Deliberative Structures and Their Challenges." *CCRC* working paper no. 79. New York: Columbia University.

Karen, David, and Kevin J. Dougherty. 2005. "Necessary But Not Sufficient: Higher Education as a Strategy of Social Mobility." In *Higher Education and the Color Line*, edited by Gary Orfield, Patricia Marin, and Catherine Horn. Cambridge, Mass.: Harvard Education Press.

Kerrigan, Monica R. 2010. "Data-Driven Decision Making in Community Colleges: New Technical Requirements for Institutional Organizations." EdD diss., Columbia University, Teachers College, New York.

Kezar, Adrianna. 2005. "What Campuses Need to Know About Organizational Learning and the Learning Organization." *New Directions for Higher Education* 131(Autumn): 7–22.

———. 2012. "Organizational Change in a Global, Postmodern World." In *The Organization of Higher Education: Managing Colleges for a New Era*, edited by M. Bastedo. Baltimore, Md.: Johns Hopkins University Press.

Kezar, Adrianna, William J. Glenn, Jaime Lester, and Jonathan Nakamoto. 2008. "Examining Organizational Contextual Features That Affect Implementation of Equity Initiatives." *Journal of Higher Education* 79(2): 125–59.

Lahr, Hana, Lara Pheatt, Kevin J. Dougherty, Sosonya M. Jones, Rebecca S. Natow, and Vikash Reddy. 2014. "Unintended Impacts of Performance Funding on Community Colleges and Universities in Three States." *CCRC* working paper no. 78. New York: Columbia University.

Lake, Tim, Chris Kvam, and Marsha Gold. 2005. "Literature Review: Using Quality Information for Health Care Decisions and Quality Improvement." Cambridge, Mass.: Mathematica Policy Research.

Lambert, Lance. 2015. "State Funding Pushes Up College Standards: Ohio's New Funding Formula Puts a Premium on 'College-Ready' High School Graduates." *Dayton Daily News*, August 22.

Lane, Jason E., and Jussi A. Kivisto. 2008. "Interests, Information, and Incentives in Higher Education: Principal-Agent Theory and Its Potential Applications to the Study of Higher Education Governance." In *Higher Education: Handbook of Theory and Research*, edited by J. C. Smart. New York: Springer.

Larocca, Roger, and Douglas Carr. 2012. "Higher Education Performance Funding: Identifying Impacts of Formula Characteristics on Graduation and Retention Rates." Paper presented to the Western Social Science Association Annual Conference. Oakland, Mich.: Oakland University.

Lumina Foundation. 2009. "Four Steps to Finishing First: An Agenda for Increasing College Productivity to Create a Better-Educated Society." Indianapolis, Ind.: Lumina Foundation. Accessed February 23, 2016. http://www.luminafoundation.org/publications/Four_Steps_to_Finishing_First_in_Higher_Education.pdf.

Marsh, Julie A., Matthew G. Springer, Daniel F. McCaffrey, Kun Yuan, Scott Epstein, Julia Koppich, Nidhi Kalra, Catherine DiMartino, and Art Peng. 2011. *A Big Apple for Educators: New York City's Experiment with Schoolwide Performance Bonuses*. Santa Monica, Calif.: RAND Corp.

Massy, William F. 2011. "Managerial and Political Strategies for Handling Accountability." In *Accountability in Higher Education*, edited by B. Stensaker and L. Harvey. New York: Routledge.

McDonnell, Lorraine M., and Richard F. Elmore. 1987. "Getting the Job Done: Alternative Policy Instruments." *Educational Evaluation and Policy Analysis* 9(2): 133–52.

McGuinness, Aims C., Jr. 2003. "Models of Postsecondary Education Coordination and Governance in the States." StateNote Report. Denver, Colo.: Education Commission of the States.

Merton, Roberty K. 1968. *Social Theory and Social Structure*, revised and enlarged ed. New York: Free Press.

———. 1976. *Sociological Ambivalence and Other Essays*. New York: Free Press.

Mettler, Suzanne. 2014. *Degrees of Inequality: How the Politics of Higher Education Sabotaged the American Dream*. New York: Basic Books.

Mica, Adrianna, Arkadiusz Peisert, and Jan Winczorek, eds. 2012. *Sociology and the Unintended*. New York: Peter Lang.

Moynihan, Daniel P. 2008. The *Dynamics of Performance Management: Constructing Information and Reform*. Washington, D.C.: Georgetown University Press.

National Conference of State Legislatures. 2015. "Performance-Based Funding for Higher Education." Accessed December 16, 2015. http://www.ncsl.org/research/education/performance-funding.aspx.

Natow, Rebecca S., Lara Pheatt, Kevin J. Dougherty, Sosanya M. Jones, Hana Lahr, and Vikash Reddy. 2014. "Institutional Changes to Organizational Policies, Practices, and Programs Following the Adoption of State-Level Performance Funding Policies." *CCRC* working paper no. 76. New York: Columbia University.

Nodine, Thad, Andrea Venezia, and Kathy Bracco. 2011. "Changing Course: A Guide to Increasing Student Completion in Community Colleges." San Francisco: WestEd. Accessed February 23, 2016. http://knowledgecenter.completionbydesign.org/sites/default/files/changing_course_V1_fb_10032011.pdf.

Ohio Board of Regents. 2013. "Draft State Share of Instruction FY2014 with FY2013 Actuals." Columbus.: Ohio Board of Regents.

Pfeffer, Jeffrey, and Gerald Salancik. 1978. *The External Control of Organizations*. New York: Harper & Row.

Pheatt, Lara, Hana Lahr, Kevin J. Dougherty, Sosanya M. Jones, Rebecca S. Natow, and Vikash Reddy. 2014. "Obstacles to the Effective Implementation of Performance Funding: A Multi-State Cross-Case Analysis." *CCRC* working paper no. 77. New York: Columbia University.

Postsecondary Analytics. 2013. *What's Working? Outcomes-Based Funding in Tennessee*. Washington, D.C.: HCM Associates.

Quint, Janet C., Shanna S. Jaggars, D. Crystal Byndloss, and Asya Magazinnik. 2013. *Bringing Developmental Education to Scale: Lessons from the Developmental Education Initiative*. New York: MDRC. Accessed February 23, 2016. http://www.mdrc.org/sites/default/files/Bringing percent 20Developmental percent20Education per cent20to percent20Scale percent20FR.pdf.

Radin, Beryl A. 2006. *Challenging the Performance Movement: Accountability, Complexity, and Democratic Values*. Washington, D.C.: Georgetown University Press.

Reddy, Vikash, Hana Lahr, Kevin J. Dougherty, Sosanya M. Jones, Rebecca S. Natow, and Lara Pheatt. 2014. "Policy Instruments in Service of Performance Funding: A Study of Performance Funding in Three States." *CCRC* working paper no. 75. New York: Columbia University.

Reindl, Travis, and Dennis P. Jones. 2012. "Raising the Bar: Strategies for Increasing Postsecondary Educational Attainment with Limited Resources." Presentation to the NGA National Summit on State Government Redesign. Washington, D.C. (December 5, 2012).

Reindl, Travis, and Ryan Reyna. 2011. "From Information to Action: Revamping Higher Education Accountability Systems." Washington, D.C.: National Governor's Association. Accessed February 23, 2016. http://www.nga.org/files/live/sites/NGA/files/pdf/1107C2Calif.CTIONGUIDE.PDF.

Rothstein, Richard. 2008a. *Grading Education: Getting Accountability Right*. New York: Teachers College Press.

———. 2008b. "Holding Accountability to Account: How Scholarship and Experience in Other Fields Inform Exploration of Performance Incentives in Education." Working paper no. 2008-04. Washington, D.C.: Economic Policy Institute. Accessed February 23, 2016. http://www.epi.org/publication/wp_accountability/.

Rouse, Cecilia E., Jane Hannaway, Dan Goldhaber, and David Figlio. 2007. "Feeling the Florida Heat? How Low-Performing Schools Respond to Voucher and Accountability Pressure." Washington, D.C.: Urban Institute.

Rutherford, Amanda, and Thomas Rabovsky. 2014. "Evaluating Impacts of Performance Funding Policies on Student Outcomes in Higher Education." *The Annals of the American Academy of Political and Social Science* 655(1): 185–206.

Rutschow, Elizabeth Z., Lashawn Richburg-Hayes, Thomas Brock. Genevieve Orr, Oscar Cerna, Dan Cullinan, Monica R. Kerrigan, Davis Jenkins, Susan Gooden, and Kasey Martin. 2011. *Turning the Tide: Five Years of Achieving the Dream in Community Colleges*. New York: MDRC.

Sanford, Thomas, and James M. Hunter. 2011. "Impact of Performance Funding on Retention and Graduation Rates." *Educational Policy Analysis Archives* 19(33): 1–30.

Shin, Jung-Cheol. 2010. "Impacts of Performance-Based Accountability on Institutional Performance in the U.S." *Higher Education* 60(1): 47–68.

Shin, Jung-Cheol, and Sande Milton. 2004. "The Effects of Performance Budgeting and Funding Programs on Graduation Rate in Public Four-Year Colleges and Universities." *Education Policy Analysis Archives* 12(22): 1–26.

Shulock, Nancy, and Davis Jenkins. 2011. "Performance Incentives to Improve Community College Completion: Learning From Washington State's Student Achievement Initiative." A State Policy Brief. New York: Columbia University, Teachers College, Community College Research Center. Accessed February 23, 2016. http://ccrc.tc.columbia.edu/publications/performance-incentives-college-completion.html.

Snyder, Martha J. 2011. "Role of Performance Funding in Higher Education's Reform Agenda: A Glance at Some State Trends." Presentation given at the Annual Legislative Institute on Higher Education, National Conference of State Legislatures. Denver, Colo. (October 2011).

———. 2015. "Driving Better Outcomes: Typology and Principles to Inform Outcomes-Based Funding Models." Washington, D.C.: HCM Strategists.

State of Tennessee. 2010. "Complete College Tennessee Act of 2010." Tenn. Stat. 2010. Nashville: Tennessee Higher Education Commission. Accessed December 16, 2015. http://www.tn.gov/thec/topic/complete-college-tn-act.

Stecher, Brian, and Sheila N. Kirby, eds. 2004. *Organizational Improvement and Accountability: Lessons for Education from Other Sectors*. Santa Monica, Calif.: RAND Corp.

Tandberg, David A, and Nicholas W. Hillman. 2014. "State Higher Education Performance Funding: Data, Outcomes, and Causal Relationships." *Journal of Education Finance* 39(3): 222–43.

Tandberg, David A., Nicholas W. Hillman, and Mohamed Barakat. 2014. "State Higher Education Performance Funding for Community Colleges: Diverse Effects and Policy Implications." *Teachers College Record* 116(12): 1–31.

Tennessee Higher Education Commission. 2011a. "Outcomes Formula Technical Details." Presentation. Nashville (May 17, 2011). Accessed December 16, 2015. http://slideplayer.com/slide/4021430/.

———. 2011b. "Outcomes Based Funding Formula." Accessed December 16, 2015. http://tn.gov/thec/article/2010-2015-funding-formula.

Umbricht, Mark R., Frank Fernandez, and Justin C. Ortagus. 2015. "An Examination of the (Un)Intended Consequences of Performance Funding in Higher Education." *Educational Policy*: 1—31. doi: 10.1177/0895904815614398.

U.S. Census Bureau. 2012. *Statistical Abstract of the United States, 2012*. Washington, D.C.: Government Printing Office. Accessed February 23, 2016. https://www.census.gov/library/publications/2011/compendia/statab/131ed.html.

Wells, Susan J., and Michelle Johnson-Motoyama. 2001. "Selecting Outcome Measures for Child Welfare Settings: Lessons for Use in Performance Management." *Children and Youth Services Review* 23(2): 169–99.

Witham, Keith A., and Estela M. Bensimon. 2012. "Creating a Culture of Inquiry Around Equity and

Student Success." In *Creating Campus Cultures: Fostering Success Among Racially Diverse Student Populations*, edited by Samuel D. Museus and Uma M. Jayakumar. New York: Routledge.

Zumeta, William, and Alicia Kinne. 2011. "Accountability Policies: Directions Old and New." In *The States and Public Higher Education Policy: Affordability, Access, and Accountability*, 2nd ed., edited by Donald E. Heller. Baltimore, Md.: Johns Hopkins University Press.

The Promises and Pitfalls of Measuring Community College Quality

MICHAL KURLAENDER, SCOTT CARRELL, AND
JACOB JACKSON

In this paper we explore the community college (institutional) effect on student outcomes in the nation's largest public two-year higher education system—the California Community College system. We investigate whether there are significant differences in student outcomes across community college campuses after adjusting for observed student differences and potential unobserved determinates that drive selection. To do so, we leverage a unique administrative dataset that links community college students to their K–12 records in order to control for key student inputs. We find meaningful differences in student outcomes across California's Community Colleges, after adjusting for differences in student inputs. We also compare college rankings based on unadjusted mean differences with college rankings adjusted for student inputs. Our results suggest that policymakers wishing to rank schools based on quality should adjust such rankings for differences in student-level inputs across campuses.

Keywords: community colleges, college quality, transfer

Identifying college quality has been a key element of the Obama administration's efforts to increase accountability in higher education. In 2013, the White House launched the College Scorecard with the goal of providing students and their families information about the "cost, value, and quality" of specific colleges in order to make more informed decisions (U.S. Department of Education 2015). Beyond transparency, the administration is also pushing for performance-based funding in higher education (White House 2013). Specifically, President Obama's proposal aims, by 2018, to tie federal aid to a rating system of colleges based on affordability, student completion rates, and graduate earnings.

Much discussion has been had on these ratings, and has included skepticism about the quality of the data used for the ratings and whether, as the president of the University of California system Janet Napolitano states, "criteria can be developed that are in the end meaningful" (Anderson 2013). Admittedly, policymakers have recognized the host of issues in developing the accountability metrics, and have solicited feedback on the college ratings methodology.

Among the many critiques of the rating systems is whether it is reasonable to compare institutions that are quite different from one another in terms of the institutional goals and the student populations served. Some have noted that even if scorecard rankings are adjusted for institutional or individual differences across campuses, biases will still favor elite institutions and institutions that serve

Michal Kurlaender is associate professor of education at the University of California, Davis. **Scott Carrell** is associate professor of economics at the University of California, Davis. **Jacob Jackson** is research fellow at the Public Policy Institute of California.

We thank the California Community College Chancellor's Office and the California Department of Education for their assistance with data access. Opinions reflect those of the authors and do not necessarily reflect those of the state agencies providing data. Direct correspondence to: Michal Kurlaender at mkurlaender@ucdavis.edu, University of California Davis, One Shields Ave., Davis, CA 95616; Scott Carrell at secarrell@ucdavis.edu, University of California Davis, One Shields Ave., Davis, CA 95616; Jacob Jackson at jackson@ppic.org, Senator Office Building, 1121 L Street, Suite 801, Sacramento, California 95814.

more traditional college students (Gross 2013). Relatedly, others worry that a rating system, particularly one tied to performance is "antithetical" to the open access mission of community colleges (Fain 2013).

The idea of performance-based accountability may be novel in higher education, but in K–12 it has been at the heart of both federal and state accountability systems, which developed—albeit to varying success—structures to grade K–12 schools on a variety of performance measures. Long before state and federal accountability systems took hold, school leaders and the research community were preoccupied with understanding the unique effects of schools on individual outcomes. Nearly fifty years after the Coleman Report, many scholarly efforts have been made to isolate the specific contribution of schools on student outcomes, controlling for individual and family characteristics.

Several studies since this canonical report, which concluded that the differences between K–12 schools account for only a small fraction of differences in pupil achievement, find that school characteristics explain less than 20 percent of the variation in student outcomes, though one study concludes that as much as 40 percent is attributable to schools, even after taking into account students' family background (Startz 2012; Borman and Dowling 2010; Rumberger and Palardy 2005; Rivkin, Hanushek, and Kain 2005; Goldhaber et al. 2010). In higher education, however, school effects have primarily focused on college selectivity, or have been constrained by existing aggregate data and small samples.

In this paper, we explore the community college (institutional) effect on student outcomes in the nation's largest public two-year higher education system—the California Community College system. We seek to know whether differences in student outcomes across community college campuses are significant after adjusting for observed student differences and potential unobserved determinates that drive selection. Additionally, we ask whether college rankings based on unadjusted mean differences across campuses provide meaningful information. To do so, we leverage a unique administrative dataset that links community college students to their K–12 records to control for key student inputs.

Results show that differences in student outcomes across the 108 California Community Colleges in our sample, after adjusting for differences in student inputs, are meaningful. For example, our lower-bound estimates show that going from the 10th to 90th percentile of campus quality is associated with a 3.68 (37.3 percent) increase in student transfer units earned, an 0.14 (20.8 percent) increase in the probability of persisting, an 0.09 (42.2 percent) increase in the probability of transferring to a four-year college, and an 0.08 (26.6 percent) increase in the probability of completion. We also show that college rankings based on unadjusted mean differences can be quite misleading. After adjusting for differences across campus, the average school rank changed by over thirty ranks. Our results suggest that policymakers wishing to rank schools based on quality should adjust such rankings for differences in student-level inputs across campuses.

BACKGROUND

Research on college quality has focused largely on more selective four-year colleges and universities, and on the relationship between college quality and graduates' earnings. Reasons for students wanting to attend elite private and public universities are sound. More selective institutions appear to have a higher payoff in terms of persistence to degree completion (Alon and Tienda 2005; Bowen, Chingos, and McPherson 2009; Small and Winship 2007; Long 2008), graduate or professional school attendance (Mullen, Goyette, and Soares 2003), and earnings later in life (Black and Smith 2006; Hoekstra 2009; Long 2008; Monks 2000). However, empirical work on the effect of college quality on earnings is a bit more mixed (Brand and Halaby 2006; Dale and Krueger 2002; Hoekstra 2009; Hoxby 2009).

The difficulty in establishing a college effect results from the nonrandom selection of students into colleges of varying qualities (Black and Smith 2004). Namely, the characteristics that lead students to apply to particular colleges may be the same ones that lead to better postenrollment outcomes. Prior work has addressed this challenge largely through conditioning on key observable characteristics of students, namely, academic qualifications. To more fully address self-selection, Stacy Dale and Alan Krueger (2002, 2012) adjust for the observed set of institutions to which students submitted an application. They argue that the application set reflects students' perceptions, or "self-revelation," about their academic potential (2002); students who apply to more selective colleges and universities do so because they believe they can succeed in such environments. They find relatively small differences in outcomes between students who attended elite universities and those who were admitted but chose to attend a less selective university. Jesse Cunha and Trey Miller (2014) examine institutional differences in student outcomes across Texas's thirty traditional four-year public colleges. Their results show that controlling for student background characteristics (race, gender, free lunch, SAT score, and so on), the quality of high school attended, and application behavior significantly reduces the mean differences in average earned income, persistence and graduation across four-year college campuses. However, recent papers that exploit a regression discontinuity approach in the probability of admissions find larger positive returns to attending a more selective university (Hoekstra 2009; Anelli 2014).

Community colleges are the primary point of access to higher education for many Americans, yet research on quality differences between community colleges has been scant. The multiple missions and goals of community colleges have been well documented in the academic literature (Rosenbaum 2001; Dougherty 1994; Grubb 1991; Brint and Karabel 1989). Community colleges have also captured the attention of policymakers concerned with improving workforce shortages and the overall economic health of the nation (see The White House 2010). The Obama administration identified community colleges as key drivers in the push to increase the stock of college graduates in the United States and to raise the skills of the American workforce. "It's time to reform our community college so that they provide Americans of all ages a chance to learn the skills and knowledge necessary to compete for the jobs of the future," President Obama remarked at a White House Summit on Community Colleges.

The distinct mission and open access nature of community colleges and the diverse goals of the students they serve make it difficult to assess differences in quality across campuses. First, it is often unclear which outcomes should actually be measured (Bailey et al. 2006). Moreover, selection issues into community colleges may differ from those between four-year institutions. Nevertheless, community college quality has been a key component of the national conversation about higher education accountability. This paper is not the first to explore institutional quality differences among community colleges. A recent study explored variation in success measures across North Carolina's fifty-eight community colleges, and finds that conditional on student differences, colleges were largely indistinguishable from one another in degree receipt or transfer coursework, save for the differences between the very top and very bottom performing colleges (Clotfelter et al. 2013). Other efforts have looked at the role of different institutional inputs as proxies for institutional quality. In particular, Kevin Stange (2012) exploits differences in instructional expenditures per student across community colleges and finds no impact on student attainment, degree receipt, or transfer. This finding corroborates with Juan Calcagno and his colleagues (2008), though they identify several other institutional characteristics that do influence student outcomes. Specifically, larger enrollment, more minority students, and more part-time faculty are associated with lower degree attainment and lower four-year transfer rates (Calcagno et al. 2008).

In this paper, we explore institutional effects of community colleges in the state with the largest public two-year community college system, using a unique administrative dataset that links students' K-12 data to postsecondary schooling at community college.

Setting

California is home to the largest public higher education system, including its 112-campus community college system. Two-thirds of all California college students attend a community college. The role of community colleges as a vehicle in human capital production was the cornerstone of California's 1960 *Master Plan for Higher Education*, which stipulated that the California community college system will admit "any student capable of benefiting from instruction" (State of California 1960).[1] Over the years, the system has grown and its schools have been applauded for remaining affordable, open access institutions. However, the colleges are also continually criticized for producing weak outcomes, in particular low degree receipt and transfer rates to four-year institutions (Shulock and Moore 2007; Sengupta and Jepsen 2006).

Several years before Obama's proposed college scorecard, California leaders initiated greater transparency and accountability in performance through the Student Success Act, signed into law by Governor Brown in 2012. Among the components of this act is an accountability scorecard, the Student Success Scorecard, that tracks several key dimensions in student success: remedial course progression rate; persistence rates; completion of a minimum of thirty units (roughly equivalent to one year of full-time enrollment status); sub-baccalaureate degree receipt and transfer status, and certificate, degree or transfer among career and technical educationn (CTE) students. This scorecard is not focused on comparing institutions, rather on performance improvement over time within institutions. Nevertheless, policymakers desire critical information about the effectiveness of the postsecondary system to improve human capital production in the state and to increase postsecondary degree receipt.

In 2013, the community college system in California (CCC) served more than 2.5 million students from a tremendous range of demographic and academic backgrounds. California's community colleges are situated in urban, suburban, and rural areas of the state, and their students come from public high schools that are both among the best and among the worst in the nation. California is an ideal state to explore institutional differences at community colleges because of the large number of institutions present, and because of the larger governance structure of the CCC system and its articulation to the state's public four-year colleges. Moreover, the diversity of California's community college population reflects the student populations of other states in the United States and the mainstream public two-year colleges that educate them. Given the diversity of California's students and public schools, and the increasing diversity of students entering the nation's colleges and universities,[2] we believe that other states can learn important lessons from California's public postsecondary institutions.

RESEARCH DESIGN

To explore institutional differences between community colleges, we use an administrative dataset that links four cohorts of California high school juniors to the community college system. These data were provided by the California Community College Chancellor's Office and the California Department of Education. Because California does not have an individual identifier that follows students from K–12 to postsecondary schooling, we linked all transcript and completion data for four first-time

---

1. The master plan articulated the distinct functions of each of the state's three public postsecondary segments. The University of California (UC) is designated as the state's primary academic research institution and is reserved for the top one eighth of the State's graduating high school class. The California State University (CSU) is primarily to serve the top one-third of California's high school graduating class in undergraduate training, and graduate training through the master's degree, focusing primarily on professional training such as teacher education. Finally, the California Community Colleges are to provide academic instruction for students through the first two years of undergraduate education (lower division), as well as provide vocational instruction, remedial instruction, English as a second language courses, adult noncredit instruction, community service courses, and workforce training services.

2. Between 2007 and 2018, the number of students enrolled in a college or university is expected to increase by 4 percent for whites but by 38 percent for Hispanics, 29 percent for Asian–Pacific Islanders, and 26 percent for African Americans (Hussar and Bailey 2009).

freshmen fall-semester cohorts (2004–2008) age seventeen to nineteen enrolled at a California community college with the census of California eleventh-grade students with standardized test score data. The match, performed on name and birth date, high school attended, and cohort, initially captured 69 percent of first-time freshmen ages seventeen through nineteen enrolled at a California community college (consistent with similar studies conducted by the California Community College Chancellor's Office matched to K–12 data).[3]

The California Community Colleges is an open access system, one in which any student can take any number of courses at any time, including, for example, while enrolled in high school, or the summer before college for those who intend to start as first-time freshman at a four-year institution. In addition, community colleges serve multiple goals, including facilitating transfer to four-year universities, subbaccalaureate degree and certificate, career and technical education, basic skills instruction, and supporting lifelong learning. We restrict the sample for our study to first-time freshman at the community college, of traditional age. We built cohorts of students who started in the summer or fall within one year of graduating high school, who attempted more than two courses (six units) in their first year, and had complete high school test and demographic information. This sample contains 254,865 students across 108 California community college campuses.[4]

Measures

We measure four outcomes intended to capture community college success in the short term through credit accumulation and persistence into year two, as well as through degree-certificate receipt and four-year transfer. First, we measure how many transferrable units a student completes during the first year. This includes units that are transferrable to California's public four-year universities (the University of California system and the California State University system) that were taken at any community college. Second, we measure whether a student persists to the second year of community college. This outcome indicates whether a student attempts any units in the fall semester after the first year at any community college in California. Third, we measure whether a student ever transfers to a four-year college. Using National Student Clearinghouse data that the CCC Chancellor's office linked with their own data, we are able to tell whether a student transferred to a four-year college at any point after attending a California community college. Last, we measure degree-certificate completion at a community college. This measure indicates whether a student earned an AA degree, or a sixty-unit certificate, or transferred to a four-year university. These outcomes represent only a few of the community college system's many goals, and as such are not meant to be an exhaustive list of how we might examine community college quality or effectiveness.

Our data are unique in that we have the ability to connect a student's performance and outcomes at community college with his or her high school data. As community colleges are open access, students do not submit transcripts from their high school, and have not necessarily taken college entrance exams such as the SAT or ACT to enter. As a result, community colleges often know very little about their students' educational backgrounds. Researchers interested in understanding the community college population often face the same constraints. Examining the outcomes of

---

3. Our match rates may be the result of several considerations. First, the name match occurred on the first three letters of a student's first name and last name, leading to many duplicates. Students may have entered different names or birthdays at the community college. Students may have omitted information at either system. Second, the denominator may also be too high; not all community college students attended California high schools. Finally, students who did attend a California high school, but did not take the eleventh grade standardized tests were not included in the high school data.

4. We excluded the three campuses that use the quarter system, as well as three adult education campuses. Summer students were allowed in the sample only if they took enough units in their first year to guarantee they also took units in the fall.

community colleges without considering the educational backgrounds of the students enrolling in that college may confound college effects with students' self-selection.

To address ubiquitous selection issues, we adjust our estimates of quality for important background information about a student's high school academic performance. We measure a student's performance on the eleventh grade English and mathematics California Standardized Tests (CSTs).[5] We also determine which math course a student took in eleventh grade. In addition, we measure race-ethnicity, gender, and parent education levels from the high school file as sets of binary variables.

To account for high school quality, we include the Academic Performance Index (API) of high school attended. Importantly, as students are enrolling in community college, they are asked about their goals for attending community college. Students can pick from a list of fifteen choices, including transfer with an associate's degree, transfer without an associate's degree, vocation certification, discover interests, improve basic skills, undecided, and others. We include students' self-reported goals as an additional covariate for their postsecondary degree intentions. Last, we add additional controls for college-level by cohort means of our individual characteristics (eleventh grade CST math and English scores, race-ethnicity, gender, parental education, API, and student goal). Table 1 includes descriptive statistics on all of our measures at the individual level; table 2 includes descriptive statistics at the college level.[6]

Empirical Methods

We begin by examining our outcomes across the community colleges in our sample. Figure 1 presents the distribution of total transfer units, proportion persisting to year 2, proportion transfer, and proportion completing across our 108 community colleges. To motivate the importance of accounting for student inputs, we plot each outcome against students' eleventh grade math test scores at the college level (figure 2).

From these simple scatterplots it is clear that average higher student test scores are associated with better average college outcomes. However, we also note considerable variation in average outcomes for students with similar high school test scores.

To examine whether there are significant differences in quality across community college campuses, we estimate the following linear random effects model:

$$Y_{iscty} = \beta_0 + \beta_1 x_i + \beta_2 \bar{x}_{cy} + \beta_3 w_s + \lambda_t + \phi_y + \zeta_c + \varepsilon_{iscty}$$

where Y_{iscty} is our outcome variable of interest (transfer units earned, persistence into year two, transfer to a four-year institutions, or degree-certificate completion) for individual i, from high school s, who is a first-time freshman enrolled at community college c, in term t in year y; x_i is a vector of individual-level characteristics (race-ethnicity, gender, parental education, and eleventh grade math and English language arts test scores), $\bar{x}_{cy}$ are community college by cohort means of x_i, and w_s is a measure of the quality of the high school (California's API score)[7] attended for each in-

---

5. We include CST scaled scores, which are approximately normally distributed across the state.

6. Unlike the four-year college quality literature, we do not account for students' college choice set since most community college students enroll in the school closest to where they attended high school. Using nationally representative data, Stange (2012) finds that in contrast to four-year college students, community college students do not appear to travel farther in search of higher quality campuses, and, importantly, "conditional on attending a school other than the closest one, there does not appear to be a relationship between student characteristics, school characteristics, and distance traveled among community college students" (2012, 81).

7. The Academic Performance Index (API) is a measure of California schools' academic performance and growth. It is the chief component of California's Public Schools Accountability Act, passed in 1999. API is composed of schools' state standardized test scores and results on the California High School Exit Exam; scores range from a low of 200 to a high of 1,000.

Table 1. Sample Descriptive Statistics (n=254,865)

Variable	Mean	SD	Min	Max
Outcomes				
Transfer units in year one	11.88	9.61	0	60
Ever transfer	0.27	0.44	0	1
Persist to year two	0.80	0.40	0	1
Complete ever	0.34	0.47	0	1
Covariates				
English test score	333.65	55.70	150	600
Math test score	291.64	48.98	150	600
Asian	0.08	0.27	0	1
Pacific Islander	0.01	0.08	0	1
Filipino	0.05	0.21	0	1
Hispanic	0.39	0.49	0	1
Black	0.07	0.25	0	1
White	0.40	0.49	0	1
Did not state	0.01	0.08	0	1
Multiple race	0.00	0.00	0	1
Female	0.50	0.50	0	1
Parents less than high school	0.15	0.36	0	1
Parents high school diploma	0.22	0.41	0	1
Parents some college	0.28	0.45	0	1
Parents college graduate	0.25	0.43	0	1
Parents did not state	0.10	0.30	0	1
Cohort 2005	0.14	0.35	0	1
Cohort 2006	0.20	0.40	0	1
Cohort 2007	0.22	0.41	0	1
Cohort 2008	0.23	0.42	0	1
Cohort 2009	0.21	0.41	0	1
Fall	0.82	0.38	0	1
Summer	0.18	0.38	0	1
High school API	707.91	79.00	272	987
Goal: transfer with AA	0.46	0.50	0	1
Goal: transfer without AA	0.12	0.32	0	1
Goal: two-year AA degree	0.04	0.19	0	1
Goal: two-year vocational degree	0.01	0.10	0	1
Goal: vocational certification	0.01	0.08	0	1
Goal: undecided	0.14	0.34	0	1
Goal: unreported	0.13	0.33	0	1

Source: Authors' calculations based on data from the California Community College Chancellor's Office.

Table 2. Sample Descriptive Statistics by College (n=108)

Variable	Mean	SD	Min	Max
Outcomes				
Transfer units in year one	11.44	2.44	4.96	17.39
Ever transfer	0.25	0.08	0.06	0.43
Persist to year 2	0.77	0.07	0.53	0.90
Complete ever	0.33	0.08	0.09	0.52
Covariates				
English test score (std)	−0.05	0.27	−0.79	0.56
Math test score (std)	−0.04	0.25	−0.72	0.44
Transfer units in year one	11.44	2.44	4.96	17.39
Ever transfer	0.25	0.08	0.06	0.43
Persist to year two	0.77	0.07	0.53	0.90
Complete ever	0.33	0.08	0.09	0.52
English test score (std)	−0.05	0.27	−0.79	0.56
Math test score (std)	−0.04	0.25	−0.72	0.44
Asian	0.07	0.07	0.00	0.37
Pacific Islander	0.01	0.01	0.00	0.05
Filipino	0.04	0.05	0.00	0.27
Hispanic	0.37	0.20	0.06	0.91
Black	0.08	0.11	0.01	0.69
White	0.41	0.22	0.01	0.85
Did not state	0.01	0.01	0.00	0.05
Multiple race	0.00	0.00	0.00	0.00
Female	0.50	0.04	0.39	0.65
Parents less than high school	0.16	0.10	0.01	0.48
Parents high school diploma	0.22	0.05	0.10	0.37
Parents some college	0.28	0.07	0.15	0.54
Parents college graduate	0.24	0.07	0.05	0.41
Parent did not state	0.10	0.05	0.02	0.22
Cohort 2005	0.12	0.09	0.00	0.48
Cohort 2006	0.18	0.10	0.00	0.52
Cohort 2007	0.21	0.10	0.00	0.75
Cohort 2008	0.23	0.11	0.00	0.63
Cohort 2009	0.26	0.19	0.04	1.00
High school API	703.26	45.03	588.34	799.11
Goal: transfer with AA	0.43	0.12	0.06	0.67
Goal: transfer without AA	0.10	0.05	0.00	0.25
Goal: two-year AA degree	0.04	0.03	0.00	0.25
Goal: two-year vocational degree	0.01	0.01	0.00	0.07
Goal: vocational certification	0.01	0.01	0.00	0.07
Goal: undecided	0.15	0.07	0.00	0.33
Goal: unreported	0.12	0.16	0.00	0.84

Source: Authors' calculations based on data from the California Community College Chancellor's Office.

Figure 1. Distribution of Outcomes by College

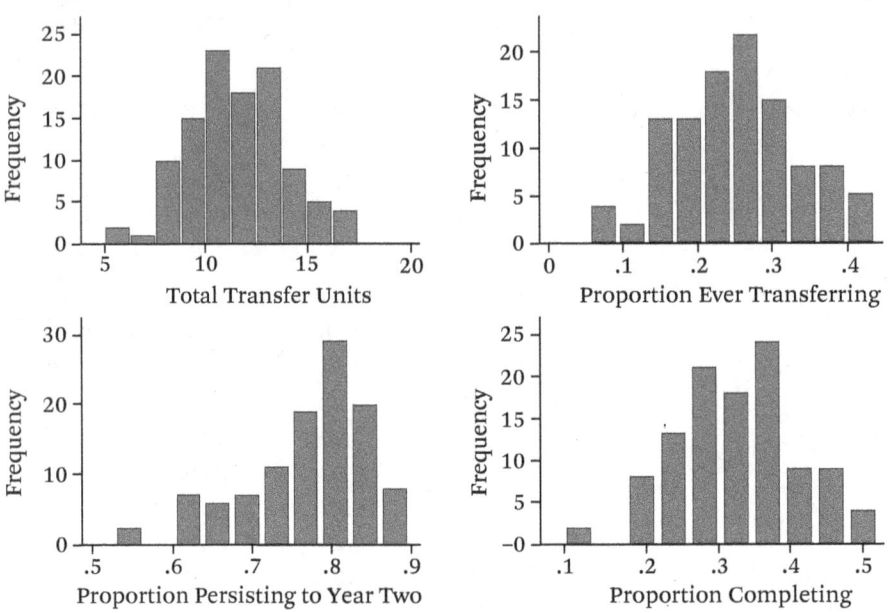

Source: Authors' calculations based on data from the California Community College Chancellor's Office.

Figure 2. Average College Outcomes Against Students' Eleventh Grade Math Test Scores

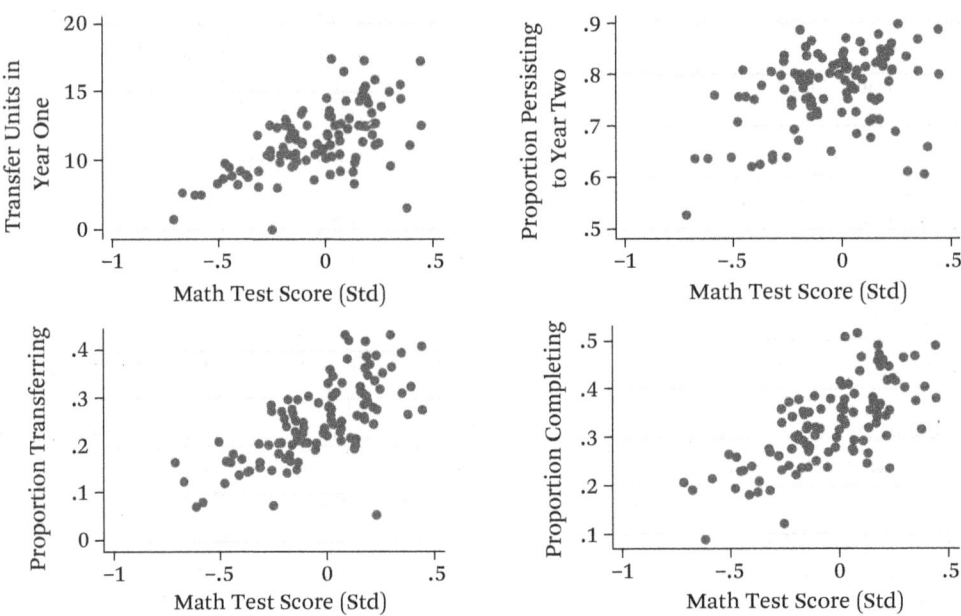

Source: Authors' calculations based on data from the California Community College Chancellor's Office.

dividual. And ε_{iscty} is the individual-level error term.

The main parameter of interest is the community college random effect, ζ_c.[8] We estimate $\hat{\zeta}_c$ using an empirical Bayes shrinkage estimator to adjust for reliability. The empirical Bayes estimates are best linear unbiased predictors (BLUPs) of each community college's random effect (quality), which takes into account the variance (signal to noise) and the number of observations (students) at each college campus. Estimates of ζ_c with a higher variance and a fewer number of observations are shrunk toward zero (Rabe-Hesketh and Skrondal 2008).

The empirical Bayes technique is commonly used in measuring the quality of hospitals (Dimick, Staiger, and Birkmeyer 2010), schools or neighborhoods (Altonji and Mansfield 2014), and teachers (Kane, Rockoff, and Staiger 2008; Carrell and West 2010). In particular, we use methodologies similar to those recently used in the literature to rank hospital quality, which shows the importance of adjusting mortality rates for patient risk (Parker et al. 2006) and statistical reliability (caseload size) (Dimick, Staiger, and Burkmeir 2010). In our context, we similarly adjust our college rankings for "student risk" (such as student preparation, quality, and unobserved determinants of selection) as well as potential noise in our estimates driven by differences in campus size and student population.

RESULTS

Are there measured differences in college outcomes?

Because we are interested in knowing whether student outcomes differ across community college campuses, we start by examining whether variation in our estimates of $\hat{\zeta}_c$'s for our various outcomes of interest is significant. Table 3 presents results of the estimated variance, σ_ζ^2, in our college effects for various specifications of equation (1). High values of σ_ζ^2 indicate there is significant variation in student outcomes across community college campuses, while low values of σ_ζ^2 would indicate that there is little difference in student outcomes across campuses (that is, no difference in college "quality").

In row 1, we start with the most naïve estimates, which include only a year-by-semester indicator variable. We use these estimates as our baseline model for comparative purposes and consider this to be the upper bound of the campus effects. These unadjusted estimates are analogous to comparing means (adjusted for reliability) in student outcomes across campuses. Estimates of σ_ζ^2 in row 1 show considerable variation in mean outcomes across California's community college campuses.

For ease of interpretation, we discuss these effects in standard deviation units. For our transfer units completed outcome in column 1, the estimated variance in the college effect of 4.86 suggests that a one standard deviation difference in campus quality is associated with an average difference of 2.18 transfer units completed in the first year for each student at that campus. Likewise, variation across campuses in our other three outcome measures is signficant. A one standard deviation increase in campus quality is associated with a 6.3 percentage point increase in the probability of persisting to year two ($\sigma_\zeta^2 = 0.0042$), a 7.3 percentage point increase in the probability of transferring to a four-year college ($\sigma_\zeta^2 = 0.0056$), and a 7.3 percentage point increase in the probability of completion ($\sigma_\zeta^2 = 0.0056$).[9]

One potential concern is that our estimates of σ_ζ^2 may be biased due to differences in student quality (aptitude, motivation, and so on) across campuses. That is, the mean differences in student outcomes across campuses that we measure in row 1 may not be due to real differences in college quality, but rather to differences (observable or unobservable) in student-

---

8. We use a random effects model instead of fixed effects model due to the efficiency (minimum variance) of the random effects model. However, our findings are qualitatively similar when using a fixed effects framework.

9. Completion appears to be driven almost entirely by transfer; that is, few students who do not transfer appear to complete AA degrees, as such, these two outcomes are likely measuring close to the same thing.

Table 3. Regression Results from Random Effects Models

Model		Variance of Random Effects Estimates			
		Transfer Units	Persist to Y2	Ever Transfer	Ever Complete
M1	Year/term	4.86	0.0042	0.0056	0.0056
M2	Test scores	3.69	0.0040	0.0034	0.0035
M3	Demographics	3.46	0.0038	0.0025	0.0029
M4	Goal	3.09	0.0032	0.0021	0.0025
M5	School API	3.07	0.0031	0.0017	0.0022
M6	College Means	2.96	0.0027	0.0016	0.0020
	% Variance reduced M1 to M5	37%	26%	70%	60%
	% Variance reduced M1 to M6	39%	36%	71%	64%

Source: Authors' calculations based on data from the California Community College Chancellor's Office.

level inputs (such as ability). To highlight this potential bias, figure 2 shows considerable variation across campuses in our measures of student ability. The across campus standard deviation in eleventh grade CST math and English scores is 0.25 and 0.27 standard deviation, respectively.

Therefore, in results shown in rows 2 through 5 of table 3, we sequentially adjust our estimates of ζ_c for a host of student-level covariates. This procedure is analogous to the hospital quality literature that calculates "risk adjusted" mortality rates by controlling for patient observable characteristics (Dimick, Staiger, and Birkmeyer 2010). Results in row 2 control for eleventh grade math and English standardized test scores. Row 3 additionally controls for our vector of individual-level demographic characteristics (race-ethnicity, gender, and parental education level). Results in row 4 add a measure of student motivation, which is an indicator for student's reported goal to transfer to a four-year college. Finally, in row 5 we add a measure of the quality of the high school that each student attended, as measured by California's API score.

The pattern of results in rows 2 through 5 suggests that controlling for differences in student-level observable characteristics accounts for some, but not all of the differences in student outcomes across community colleges. Results for our transfer units earned outcome in column 1 show that the estimated variance in the college effects shrinks by 37 percent when going from our basic model to the fully saturated model. Despite this decrease, there still remains considerable variation in our estimated college effects, with a one standard deviation increase in campus quality associated with a 1.73 increase in the average number of transfer units completed by each student ($\sigma_\zeta^2 = 3.07$).

Examining results for our other three outcomes of interest, we find that controlling for student-level covariates shrinks the estimated variance in college quality by 26 percent for our persistence outcome, 70 percent for our transfer outcome, and 60 percent for completion. Again, despite these rather large decreases in the variance of the estimated college effects, considerable variation remains in student outcomes across campuses. A one standard deviation increase in college quality is associated with a 0.053 increase in the probability of persisting ($\sigma_\zeta^2 = 0.0031$), a 0.039 increase in the probability of transferring ($\sigma_\zeta^2 = 0.0017$), and a 0.045 increase in the probability of completion ($\sigma_\zeta^2 = 0.0022$). Graphical representations of the BLUPs from model 5 are presented in figure 3.

Although the estimates shown in row 5 control for a rich set of individual-level *observable* characteristics, there remains potential concern that our campus quality estimates may still be biased due to selection on *unobservables* that are correlated with college choice (Altonji, Elder, and Tabor 2005). To directly address this concern, recent work by Joseph Altonji and Richard Mansfield (2014) shows that

Figure 3. Ranked College Effects by Outcome

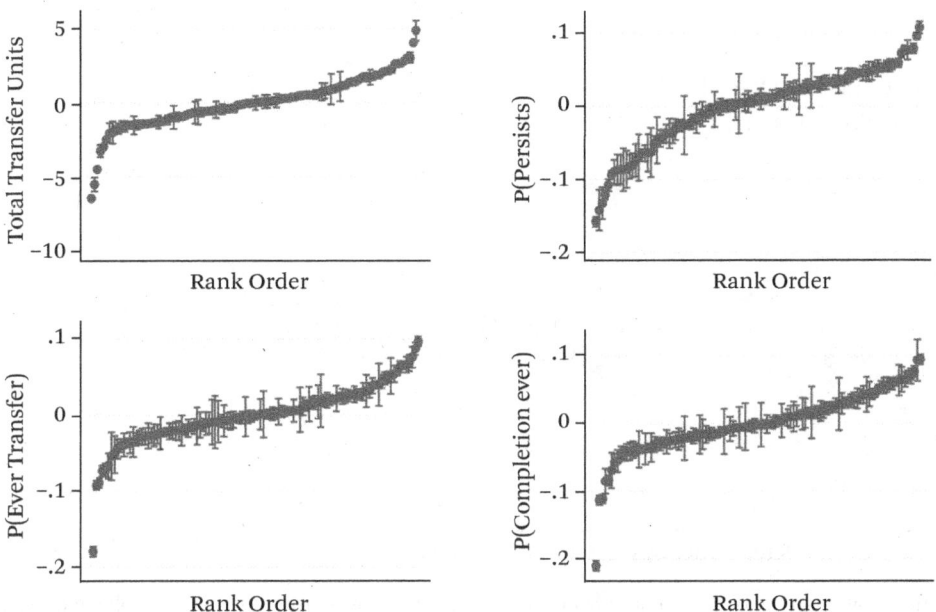

Source: Authors' calculations based on data from the California Community College Chancellor's Office.

controlling for group averages of observed individual-level characteristics adequately controls for selection on unobservables and provides a *lower bound* of the estimated variance in school quality effects.[10]

Therefore, in results shown in row 6 we additionally control for college by cohort-level means of our individual characteristics (eleventh grade CST math and English scores, race-ethnicity, gender, parental education and API score). We find that controlling for college-level covariates shrinks the estimated variance in college quality over the naïve model (model 1) by 39 percent for transfer units, 36 percent for our persistence outcome, 71 percent for our transfer outcome, and 64 percent for completion. Model 5 remains our preferred specification, however, even in this highly specified model, we still find considerable variation in student outcomes across community college campuses.

Exploring Campus Ranking

Given recent proposals by the Obama administration to create a college scorecard, it is particularly critical to determine how stable (or unstable) our college quality estimates, $\hat{\zeta}_c$, are across specifications with various control variables. On the one hand, if our naïve estimates in row 1 result in a similar rank ordering of colleges as the fully saturated estimates in rows 5 and 6, then scorecards based on unadjusted mean outcomes will provide meaningful information to prospective students. On the other hand, if the rank ordering of the estimated $\hat{\zeta}_c$'s are unstable across specifications, it is critical that college scorecards be adjusted for various student-level inputs.[11]

---

10. Altonji and Mansfield (2014) show that, under reasonable assumptions, controlling for group means of individual-level characteristics "also controls for all of the across-group variation in the unobservable individual characteristics." This procedure provides a lower bound of the school quality effects because school quality is likely an unobservable that drives individual selection.

11. Both hospital rankings and teacher quality rankings have been shown to be sensitive to controlling for individual characteristics (see, for example, Kane and Staiger 2008; Dimick, Staiger, and Birkmeyer 2010).

Figure 4. Unadjusted College Effects Compared to Adjusted Effects for Transfer Units in First Year

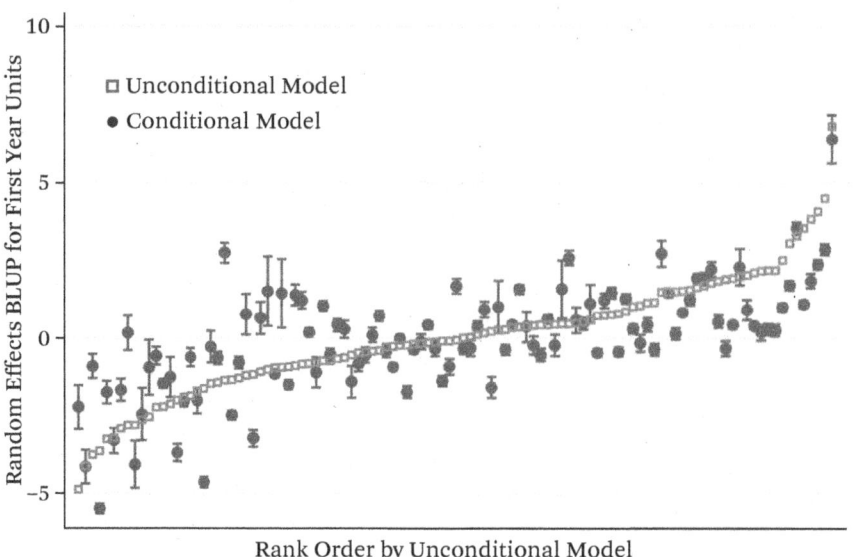

Source: Authors' calculations based on data from the California Community College Chancellor's Office.

To help answer this question, we examine how the rank ordering of our college quality estimates change after controlling for our set of observable student characteristics. Figure 4 graphically presents the unadjusted and adjusted estimated college quality effects for our transfer unit outcome (our preferred specification model 5 from table 3).

The squares represent the unadjusted effects, and the dots the effects and 95 percent confidence intervals after adjusting for student-level covariates. This graph highlights two important findings: schools at the very bottom and very top end of the quality distribution tend to stay at the bottom and top of the rankings, and movement up and down in the middle of the distribution is considerable. This result indicates that unadjusted mean outcomes may be valuable in predicting the very best and very worst colleges, but they likely do a poor job in predicting the variation in college quality in the middle of the distribution. The same pattern can be noted in the other outcomes not pictured.

In a more detailed look at how the rankings of college quality change when adjusting for student-level covariates, figure 5 plots rank changes in transfer units in the first year by campus. This graph show that the rank ordering of campuses change considerably after controlling for covariates. The average campus changed plus or minus thirty ranks, the largest positive change being seventy-five and the largest drop, negative forty-nine.

These results highlight the importance of controlling for student-level inputs when estimating college quality. They also throw caution to policymakers who may be tempted to rank colleges based on unadjusted mean outcome measures such as graduation rates or post-graduation wages.

CONCLUSION

Understanding quality differences among educational institutions has been a preoccupation of both policymakers and social scientists for more than half a century (Coleman 1966). It is well established that individual ability and socioeconomic factors bear a stronger relation to academic achievement than the school attended. In fact, when these factors are statistically controlled for, it appears that differences between schools account for only a small fraction of differences in pupil achievement. Yet the influence of institutional quality differences in the postsecondary setting, particularly

Figure 5. Change in Rank from Unadjusted to Fully Specified Model

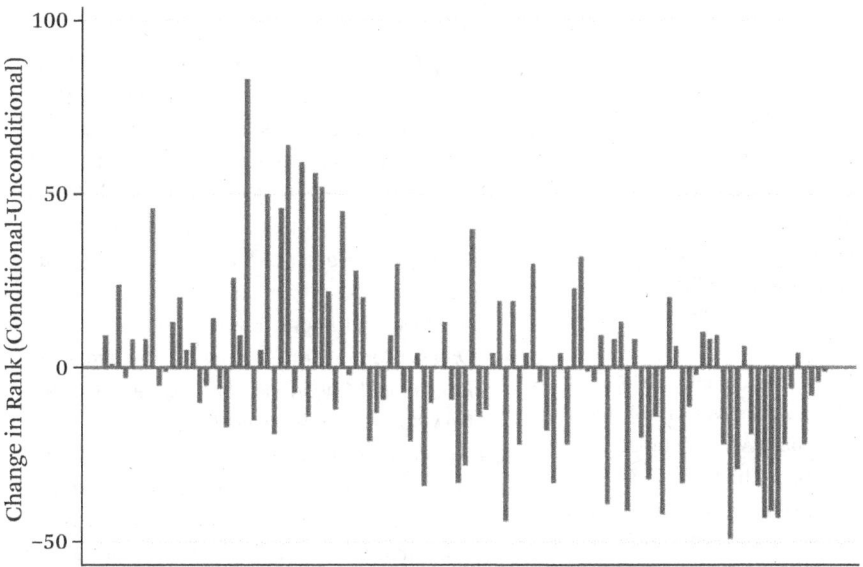

Source: Authors' calculations based on data from the California Community College Chancellor's Office.
Note: Colleges ordered by unconditional rank.

at the less selective two-year sector, where the majority of Americans begin their postsecondary schooling, has rarely been explored.

To help fill this gap, we use data from California's Community College System to examine whether differences in student outcomes across college campuses are significant. Our results show considerable differences across campuses in both short-term and longer-term student outcomes. However, much of these differences are accounted for by student inputs, namely measured ability, demographic characteristics, college goals, and unobservables that drive college selection. Nevertheless, after controlling for these inputs, our results show that important differences between colleges remain. What is the marginal impact of being at a better quality college? Our lower-bound estimates indicate that going from the 10th to 90th percentile of campus quality is associated with a 3.68 (37.3 percent) increase in student transfer units earned, a 0.14 (20.8 percent) increase in the probability of persisting, an 0.09 (42.2 percent) increase in the probability of transferring to a four-year college, and an 0.08 (26.6 percent) increase in the probability of completion.

A natural follow-up question is what observable institutional differences, if any, might be driving these effects? A close treatment of what might account for these institutional differences in our setting is beyond the scope of this paper. However, prior work has identified several characteristics that may be associated with student success, including peer quality, faculty quality, class size or faculty-student ratio, and a variety of measures for college costs (Long 2008; Calcagno et al. 2008; Bailey et al. 2006; Jacoby 2006).

Finally, identifying institutional effects is not purely an academic exercise. In today's policy environment, practitioners and higher education leaders are looking to identify the conditions and characteristics of postsecondary institutions that lead to student success. Given the recent push by policymakers to provide college scorecards, our analysis furthers that goal for a critical segment of higher education, public open access community colleges, and the diverse students they serve. Our results show that college rankings based on unadjusted mean differences can be quite misleading. After adjusting for student-level differences across campus, the average school rank in our sample changed by plus or minus thirty ranks. Our results suggest that policymakers wishing to rank schools based on quality should adjust such rankings for differences across campuses in student-level inputs.

REFERENCES

Alon, Sigal, and Marta Tienda. 2005. "Assessing the 'Mismatch' Hypothesis: Differentials in College Graduation Rates by Institutional Selectivity." *Sociology of Education* 78(4): 294–315.

Altonji, Joseph G., Todd E. Elder, and Christopher R. Taber. 2005. "Selection on Observed and Unobserved Variables: Assessing the Effectiveness of Catholic Schools," *Journal of Political Economy* 113(1): 151–84.

Altonji, Joseph, and Richard Mansfield. 2014. "Group-Average Observables as Controls for Sorting on Unobservables When Estimating Group Treatment Effects: The Case of School and Neighborhood Effects." *NBER* working paper no. 20781. Cambridge, Mass.: National Bureau of Economic Research.

Anderson, Nick. 2013. "Napolitano, University of California President, 'Deeply Skeptical' of Obama College Rating Plan." *Washington Post*, December 6, 2013, Nick Anderson, *The Washington Post*. Accessed December 17, 2015. http://www.washingtonpost.com/local/education/napolitano-uc-president-deeply-skeptical-of-keyassumption-in-obama-college-rating-plan/2013/12/06/f4f505fa-5eb8-11e3-bc56-c6ca94801fac_story.html.

Anelli, Massimo. 2014. "Returns to Elite College Education: A Quasi-Experimental Analysis." Job Market paper. Davis: University of California. Accessed December 16, 2015. http://www.econ.ku.dk/Kalender/seminarer/28012015/paper/MassimoAnelli_JobMarketPaper.pdf.

Bailey, Thomas, Juan Carlos Calcagno, Davis Jenkins, Timothy Leinbach, and Gregory Kienzl. 2006. "Is Student-Right-to-Know All You Should Know? An Analysis of Community College Graduation Rates." *Research in Higher Education* 47(5): 491–519.

Black, Dan, and Jeffrey Smith. 2004. "How Robust Is the Evidence on the Effects of College Quality? Evidence from Matching." *Journal of Econometrics* 121(1–2): 99–124.

———. 2006. "Estimating the Returns to College Quality with Multiple Proxies for Quality." *Journal of Labor Economics* 24(3): 701–28.

Borman, Geoffrey, and Maritza Dowling. 2010. "Schools and Inequality: A Multilevel Analysis of Coleman's Equality of Educational Opportunity Data." *Teachers College Record* 112(5): 1201–46.

Bowen, William G., Matthew M. Chingos, and Michael McPherson. 2009. *Crossing the Finish Line*. Princeton, N.J.: Princeton University Press.

Brand, Jennie E., and Charles N. Halaby. 2006. "Regression and Matching Estimates of the Effects of Elite College Attendance on Educational and Career Achievement." *Social Science Research* 35(3): 749–70.

Brint, Steve, and Jerome Karabel. 1989. *The Diverted Dream: Community Colleges and the Promise of Educational Opportunity in America, 1900–1985*. New York: Oxford University Press.

Calcagno, Juan Carlos, Thomas Bailey, Davis Jenkins, Gregory Kienzl, and Timothy Leinbach. 2008. "Community College Student Success: What Institutional Characteristics Make a Difference?" *Economics of Education Review* 27(6): 632–45.

Carrell, Scott E., and James E. West. 2010. "Does Professor Quality Matter? Evidence from Random Assignment of Students to Professors," *Journal of Political Economy* 118(3): 409–32.

Clotfelter, Charles T., Helen F. Ladd, Clara G. Muschkin, and Jacob L. Vigdor. 2013. "Success in Community College: Do Institutions Differ?" *Research in Higher Education* 54(7): 805–24.

Coleman, James S. 1966. "Equality of Educational Opportunity." Office of Education Pub no. 101-228-169. Washington: U.S. Department of Health, Education, and Welfare.

Cunha, Jesse M., and Trey Miller. 2014. "Measuring Value-Added in Higher Education: Possibilities and Limitations in the Use of Administrative Data." *Economics of Education Review* 42(1): 64–77.

Dale, Stacy B., and Alan B. Krueger. 2002. "Estimating the Payoff to Attending a More Selective College: An Application of Selection on Observables and Unobservables." *Quarterly Journal of Economics* 117(4): 1491–527.

Dale, Stacy B., and Alan B. Krueger. 2012. "Estimating the Return to College Selectivity over the Career Using Administrative Earning Data." *NBER* working paper no. 17159. Cambridge, Mass.: National Bureau of Economic Research.

Dimick, Justin, Douglas Staiger, and John Birkmeyer. 2010. "Ranking Hospitals on Surgical Mortality:

The Importance of Reliability Adjustment." *Health Services Research* 45(6): 1614–29.

Dougherty, Kevin J. 1994. *The Contradictory College: The Conflicting Origins, Impacts, and Futures of the Community College*. Albany: State University of New York Press.

Fain, Paul. 2013. "Performance Funding Goes Federal." *Inside Higher Ed*, August 23. Accessed December 17, 2013. https://www.insidehighered.com/news/2013/08/23/higher-education-leaders-respond-obamas-ambitous-ratings-system-plan.

Goldhaber, Dan, Stephanie Liddle, Roddy Theobald, and Joe Walch. 2010. "Teacher Effectiveness and the Achievement of Washington's Students in Mathematics." *CEDR* working paper 2010-06. Seattle: University of Washington.

Gross, Karen. 2013. "Ratings Are Not So Easy." *Inside Higher Ed*, August 23. Accessed December 17, 2015. https://www.insidehighered.com/views/2013/08/23/obamas-ratings-system-may-be-difficult-pull-essay.

Grubb, W. Norton. 1991. "The Decline of Community College Transfer Rates: Evidence from National Longitudinal Surveys." *Journal of Higher Education* 62(2): 194–222.

Hoekstra, Mark. 2009. "The Effect of Attending the Flagship State University on Earnings: A Discontinuity-Based Approach." *Review of Economics and Statistics* 91(4): 717–24.

Hoxby, Caroline M. 2009. "The Changing Selectivity of American Colleges." *Journal of Economic Perspectives* 23(4): 95–118.

Hussar, William J., and Tabitha M. Bailey. 2009. *Projections of Education Statistics to 2018*, 37th ed. NCES 2009-062. Washington: U.S. Department of Education.

Jacoby, Daniel. 2006. "Effects of Part-Time Faculty Employment on Community College Graduation Rates." *Journal of Higher Education* 77(6): 1081–103.

Kane, Thomas J., Jonah E. Rockoff, and Douglas O. Staiger. 2008. "What Does Certification Tell Us About Teacher Effectiveness? Evidence from New York City." *Economics of Education Review* 27(6): 615–31.

Kane, Thomas J., and Douglas O. Staiger. 2008. "Estimating Teacher Impacts on Student Achievement: An Experimental Evaluation." *NBER* working paper no. 14607. Cambridge, Mass.: National Bureau of Economic Research. Accessed February 24, 2016. http://www.nber.org/papers/w14607.

Long, Mark C. 2008. "College Quality and Early Adult Outcomes." *Economics of Education Review* 27(5): 588–602.

Monks, James. 2000. "The Returns to Individual and College Characteristics: Evidence from the National Longitudinal Survey of Youth." *Economics of Education Review* 19(3): 279–89.

Mullen, Ann L., Kimberly Goyette, and Joseph A. Soares. 2003. "Who Goes to Graduate School? Social and Academic Correlates of Educational Continuation After College." *Sociology of Education* 76(2): 143–69.

Parker, Joseph P., Zhongmin Li, Cheryl L. Damberg, Beat Danielsen, and David M. Carlisle. 2006. "Administrative Versus Clinical Data for Coronary Artery Bypass Graft Surgery Report Cards: The View from California." *Medical Care* 44(7): 687–95.

Rabe-Hesketh, Sophia, and Anders Skrondal. 2008. *Multilevel and Longitudinal Modeling Using Stata*, 2nd ed. College Station, Tex.: Stata Press.

Rivkin, Steven G., Eric A. Hanushek, and John F. Kain. 2005. "Teachers, Schools and Academic Achievement." *Econometrica* 73(2): 417–58.

Rosenbaum, James. 2001. *Beyond College for All: Career Paths for the Forgotten Half*. New York: Russell Sage Foundation.

Rumberger, Russell, and Gregory Palardy. 2005. "Does Segregation Still Matter? The Impact of Student Composition on Academic Achievement in High School." *Teachers College Record* 107(9): 1999–2045.

Sengupta, Ria, and Christopher Jepsen. 2006. "California's Community College Students." *California Counts: Population Trends and Profiles* 8(2): 1–24.

Shulock, Nancy, and Colleen Moore. 2007. "Rules of the Game: How State Policy Creates Barriers to Degree Completion and Impedes Student Success in the California Community Colleges." Sacramento, Calif.: Institute for Higher Education and Leadership.

Small, Mario L., and Christopher Winship. 2007. "Black Students' Graduation from Elite Colleges: Institutional Characteristics and Between-Institution Differences." *Social Science Research* 36(2007): 1257–75.

Stange, Kevin. 2012. "Ability Sorting and the Importance of College Quality to Student Achievement: Evidence from Community Colleges." *Education Finance and Policy* 7(1): 74–105.

Startz, Richard. 2012. "Policy Evaluation Versus Explanation of Outcomes in Education: That Is, Is It the Teachers? Is It the Parents?" *Education Finance and Policy* 7(3): 1–15.

State of California. 1960. *A Master Plan for Higher Education in California: 1960–1975*. Sacramento: California State Department of Education. Accessed December 17, 2015. http://www.ucop.edu/acadinit/mastplan/MasterPlan1960.pdf.

U.S. Department of Education. 2015. "College Scorecard." Accessed December 17, 2015. https://collegescorecard.ed.gov.

The White House. 2010. "The White House Summit on Community Colleges: Summit Report." Washington, D.C. Accessed December 17, 2015. https://www.whitehouse.gov/sites/default/files/uploads/community_college_summit_report.pdf.

———. 2013. "Fact Sheet on the President's Plan to Make College More Affordable: A Better Bargain for the Middle Class." Washington, D.C.: Office of the Press Secretary. Accessed December 17, 2015. https://www.whitehouse.gov/the-press-office/2013/08/22/fact-sheet-president-s-plan-make-college-more-affordable-better-bargain-.

PART IV

Teaching and Learning: Contexts and Practices

Aligning Science Achievement and STEM Expectations for College Success: A Comparative Study of Curricular Standardization

SIQI HAN AND CLAUDIA BUCHMANN

Lack of preparation in science leads to high rates of attrition among science, technology, engineering, and mathematics (STEM) majors, even among students who are highly oriented toward STEM. Using data for twenty-seven countries from the 2006 Program for International Student Assessment, we compare the United States with other industrialized countries in terms of fifteen-year-olds' science achievement and their expectations to focus on STEM in the future. The United States trails most countries in the mean science achievement of the general student population and among students expecting to pursue STEM majors or careers. Lack of curricular standardization in the United States is related to this lower science achievement. Countries with higher curricular standardization exhibit higher average science achievement scores; science achievement and students' future orientation toward science are also better aligned in these countries. We discuss the implications of these findings for American colleges and universities as they seek to reduce student attrition in STEM fields.

Keywords: STEM attrition, curriculum; standardization, science achievement, cross-national research

In response to growing concern about the declining U.S. competitiveness in the global economy (National Academy of Sciences 2007), in 2009 the Obama administration launched the Educate to Innovate campaign to improve the participation rates and performance of U.S. students in science, technology, engineering and math (STEM). More recently, the President's Council of Advisors on Science and Technology urged institutions of higher education to increase the rates of students earning degrees in STEM fields. The council predicts that the United States needs more than a million STEM professionals over the next decade than are currently projected if the country is to remain a global leader in science (Olson and Riordan 2012).

About half of all college students in science, technology, engineering and math leave STEM fields before completing a college degree. Using data that tracked students from 2003 onward, the U.S. Department of Education reported that while 28 percent of all bachelor's degree candidates declared a STEM major, nearly half (48 percent) of this group had left STEM fields by 2009. Among these STEM leavers about half switched to a non-STEM degree and half dropped out of college. While the at-

Siqi Han is a Ph.D. candidate of sociology at the Ohio State University. **Claudia Buchmann** is professor and chair of sociology at the Ohio State University.

Direct correspondence to: Siqi Han, Department of Sociology, The Ohio State University, 238 Townshend Hall, 1885 Neil Avenue Mall, Columbus, OH 43210, Han.607@osu.edu; and Claudia Buchmann, Department of Sociology, The Ohio State University, 211 Townshend Hall, 1885 Neil Avenue Mall, Columbus, OH 43210, Buchmann.4@osu.edu.

trition rate in STEM is similar to attrition rates for other majors, increasing STEM retention in college by even a small percentage could be a cost-effective way to produce the STEM professionals that the nation needs (Chen and Soldner 2013).

Lynn Reimer and her colleagues (this volume) focus on one potential way to increase student retention in STEM—improving the learning experiences of students in undergraduate STEM courses. Although enhancing undergraduate STEM courses could help reduce the high rates of attrition from STEM majors, even the best instruction in undergraduate courses may come too late for students who arrive at college with a lack of science knowledge and preparation. Research finds that lack of preparation in science leads to high rates of departure from STEM fields, even among students who are highly oriented toward STEM (Chen and Soldner 2013). Thus the very diverse levels of science proficiency that American students bring with them to college create an additional challenge for colleges and universities as they seek to increase the rates of students earning degrees in STEM fields.

This paper examines student science achievement in the precollege years, focusing on students who indicate they plan to major in science or pursue a science career. It compares the United States with other industrialized countries in terms of science achievement and determines the degree to which cross-national variations in standardization of the curriculum are related to science achievement, net of other country-level factors such as teacher quality and economic development. Curricular standardization refers to the degree to which students within a nation are exposed to the same curriculum. In this paper, we distinguish between three degrees of curricular standardization: educational systems in which the central government determines the curriculum for all students in the nation; educational systems in which regional or local agencies have some ability to adapt the centrally mandated curriculum; and educational systems in which there is no central government intervention in designing the curriculum, such that students within the same nation may be exposed to very different curricula. We then examine cross-national variations in students' future orientations toward STEM to determine whether curricular standardization is related to the alignment of students' science achievement with their plans to pursue a STEM major or career. We use data from the Program for International Student Assessment (PISA) 2006. In addition to assessing the science achievement of fifteen-year-olds in fifty-seven countries, PISA collects extensive data on student backgrounds and their expectations about the future. Conducted by the Organization for Economic Development and Cooperation (OECD) and widely used in comparative research on education, PISA is considered to be the best source of comparative cross-national data on adolescents' science achievement, orientations toward science, and their educational experiences more generally. These data do not allow us to establish a direct causal link between curricular standardization and the propensity of students to choose STEM fields. However, if among similarly situated students, those in countries with more standardized curricula are more likely to major in STEM fields, the correlation would be consistent with the hypothesis that curricular standardization is related to differential rates of choosing STEM majors. Future research could build on this preliminary evidence to understand how structural variations in educational systems matter for student preferences and other outcomes.

Our analyses indicate that the mean science achievement scores of both the general student population and students aspiring to enter STEM fields are lower in the United States than in most other developed countries. This outcome is related, in part, to the lack of standardization of the curriculum in the United States. We find that countries in which all students are exposed to a more standardized curriculum in primary and secondary school have higher average science achievement scores, net of other factors. In these countries, students' science achievement and future orientation toward science are also better aligned, in that higher achievers are significantly more likely to consider pursuing a STEM major or career than lower achievers. In countries that lack a standardized science curriculum, such as the United States, the greater diversity of science preparation for students who arrive on campus expecting to pursue a STEM degree poses a challenge to college and universities; we discuss the implications of these findings for higher education institutions as they seek to reduce student attrition in STEM fields.

BACKGROUND

It is well established that individual educational and occupational choices are shaped during adolescence, when students start to clarify their personal identities and ambitions. Proficiency in science and expectations to pursue a science career during the adolescent years are especially important precursors to the subsequent likelihood of completing a STEM degree in college. Using nationally representative data that followed students from eighth grade to young adulthood, Robert Tai and his colleagues (2006) examine whether science-related career expectations among eighth graders predicted the field of the college degrees they earned several years later. Among students who earned a bachelor's degree, those who as eighth graders expected to have science-related careers at age thirty were 1.9 times more likely to earn a life science degree than those who did not expect a science-related career and 3.4 times more likely to earn physical science and engineering degrees than students without such expectations.

The Tai and colleagues findings underscore the importance of the alignment between achievement and expectations in predicting the likelihood of earning a college degree in science. Fifty-one percent of all high achievers (those who scored at least one standard deviation above the average in math) who also expected to pursue science-related careers completed a bachelor's degree in the physical sciences or engineering. In contrast, 34 percent of average achievers who expected a science-related career attained such a degree. Only 19 percent of high achievers who expected a non-science career and 10 percent of average achievers who expected a nonscience career attained a degree in the physical sciences/engineering (Tai et al. 2006, 1144).

Using longitudinal data that followed students over their college years, Todd Stinebricker and Ralph Stinebricker (2011) find that when students enter college they are as open to a math or science major as they are to any other, but many students move away from math and science after realizing that their grades in that field will be substantially lower than they expected. Further, changes in beliefs about grade performance tend to arise because students realize that their ability in math and science is lower than they thought rather than because they realize that they are not willing to put substantial effort into math or science majors. These findings suggest that students are more likely to be pushed out of STEM fields due to their poorer than expected performance, thus leading to high rates of attrition from STEM majors. Along with prior achievement, race and gender matter; much research has examined gender and racial differences in science achievement and expectations in an attempt to understand why women and minorities remain underrepresented in STEM fields (Maple and Stage 1991; Xie and Shauman 2006).

Beyond individual-level factors, the structure of educational systems has been found to be related to individuals' performance and preferences, as well as the variation in these factors across the student population. For example, nations vary greatly in the degree of standardization in their educational systems.[1] In highly standardized systems, all students are exposed to a standardized curriculum and learning standards are mandated by a central-

---

1. Research has considered how two other aspects of the organization of national educational systems matter for individual educational outcomes: *differentiation*—how and when students are tracked between or within schools by ability level and *vocational specificity*—the extent to which the content of education is related to the knowledge of an occupation (Allmendinger 1989; Shavit and Muller 1998). These aspects are beyond the scope of this paper.

ized body. In many standardized systems, to gain a given credential, students are also required to demonstrate their curricular knowledge by passing exit examinations centrally administered by an education authority. Students' exam performance may also determine university admission and preferred fields of study (Bishop 1997, 2006).

Research finds that nations with standardized curricula and exit exams tend to have less inequality in student performance. Some evidence suggests that standardization is related to smaller performance gaps among secondary students from different class backgrounds (Ayalon and Gamoran 2000) and smaller gender inequalities in math achievement (Ayalon and Livneh 2013). Other research finds that standardization is related to smaller negative effects of tracking (Bol et al. 2014) and reduces opportunities for school decision makers to favor their own interests over student performance (Wößmann 2005).

The potential benefits of standardization can be illustrated from the perspectives of students, parents, teachers, and schools. For students, standardized curricula and examinations serve as incentives or extrinsic rewards for them to take more rigorous courses and spend more time on homework (Bishop 2006). In standardized systems, students in different tracks and schools are exposed to the same curricula and standards, so their exposure to knowledge is much more equal (Ayalon and Livneh 2013). Moreover, when educational decisions are based on students' performance in externally administered centralized examinations, parents have ample information on the performance of their children against an established standard (Wößmann 2005). As a result, both students and their parents may be better able to monitor their educational progress and gain a clearer understanding of how their achievement, as measured by test scores, compares to that of other students in the nation. Indeed, Hyunjoon Park (2008) finds that the greater accountability and transparency of standardized education systems enables parents and students from all socioeconomic backgrounds to assess and monitor the student's performance in comparison to established standards. Finally, in countries with a highly standardized curriculum, teachers and school administrators are not allowed to modify the content of curricula or exams according to students' ability grouping (Stevenson and Baker 1991). Instead, teachers tend to invest much effort in helping all students meet nationally mandated standards, regardless of students' ability level or class background (Bol et al. 2014).

In contrast to highly standardized educational systems found in much of the world, the U.S. educational system has long been marked by a lack of standardization. Historically, curricula, teacher training, learning standards and a host of other factors have been determined at the state and district level rather than the national level. This highly decentralized education decision-making leads to substantial variation in educational curricula across the nation. For example, in Kansas, debate has raged for years about whether to teach evolution, such that some students have not learned the principles of evolution and key biological concepts essential to a comprehensive science education (Subotnik, Edmiston, and Rayhack 2007).

Since the 1990s, however, the United States has been moving toward greater curricular standardization, at least at the state level. By the early 2000s, every state had developed and adopted its own learning standards and had a definition of proficiency requirements for each grade level and high school graduation. In an attempt to create greater curricular standardization, many state leaders agreed in 2009 to develop the Common Core State Standards. By June 2014, forty-three states had adopted unified, internationally benchmarked standards in math and language arts for kindergarten through twelfth grade with the goal of providing students with the necessary knowledge and skills for college and the workforce (Grossman, Reyna, and Shipton 2011). The development of standards for science is the next step in this process (National Research Council 2012). It is an open question whether the Common Core will fulfill the goal of a unified system of national curricular standards applicable to all states and districts and whether the purported benefits of greater curricular standardization will be realized.

Curricular Standardization, Science Achievement, and Expectations

Most research to date has considered how standardization relates to students' achievement in mathematics or reading. We know of no research that has considered the relationship between curricular standardization and science achievement. It is reasonable to expect that in standardized systems, where all students are exposed to science and math curricula more equally and their course-taking patterns are more homogeneous, overall student achievement in science may be higher. Thus, we predict hypothesis 1: *Countries in which all students are exposed to the same curriculum and standards exhibit higher mean science achievement.* Additionally, a more standard exposure for all students to the science curriculum may mean that students cannot activate their preferences and thus avoid science coursework, thus we predict hypothesis 2: *In countries where all students are exposed to a standard curriculum, gender and social class gaps in science achievement are smaller.*

Finally, we predict that standardized systems may be more effective in strengthening the linkage between science performance and future orientation toward a STEM major or career such that in countries with standardized educational systems, high science achievers may be more likely to pursue science-based fields of study and careers. This is because they gain valuable information about their standing relative to the whole student population and are more likely to consider this information in their subsequent educational decisions and career choices. In contrast, in countries that lack curricular standardization, such as the United States, students receive weak and highly varied signals about their performance in specific academic domains and students' science achievement and their interest in science should be less aligned. Thus we predict hypothesis 3: *The higher the curricular standardization is, the greater the alignment of students' science achievement and their future orientation toward STEM fields.*

DATA AND METHODS

We compare the United States with several other industrialized countries on metrics related to students' performance in science and their expectations to focus on STEM in the future. We then examine whether the alignment between adolescents' science achievement and their plans to major in a STEM field in college vary with the institutional features of national educational systems, net of individual-level factors. One goal of this analysis is to examine whether the low level of standardization in the U.S. educational system is related, in part, to the high attrition rate of college students from STEM fields in the United States.

The main source of data for this study is PISA 2006, an international survey testing fifteen-year-old students' cognitive skills on math, reading, and science. It collects data from all OECD countries and several non-OECD countries on one of the three subjects every three years. The latest survey to focus on science proficiency and engagement was completed in 2006 and included fifty-seven countries. Because we are interested in comparing the United States to other industrialized countries, we exclude countries whose gross domestic product (GDP) per capita is below $12,000 in 2005, as calculated by the World Bank (2005) to produce a sample of 211,766 students in twenty-seven countries.

The analyses proceed in three stages. First, we examine the descriptive statistics for all countries to see how the United States compares in terms of student science performance. We then select the subset of students in each country who indicate that they plan to major in STEM or pursue a STEM career, and describe the average science performance of this group of students who, on the basis of their plans, are most likely to pursue a STEM major in college. Finally, we use hierarchical linear modeling to examine whether national level variations in the organization of educational systems are related to adolescents' science achievement and the alignment of science achievement with plans to major or work in a STEM field in the future, net of individual-level factors and other country-level factors.

Specifically, we determine whether the

level of standardization of the educational curriculum within a country is related to mean student science achievement as well as a greater alignment of students' science achievement with their plans to pursue a STEM major or career, such that students who score high on the science test are more likely to consider a future in STEM. For this analysis, we pool the twenty-seven countries and run a hierarchical linear model, adding two dummy variables—highly standardized curriculum and moderately standardized curriculum—as country-level independent variables, with unstandardized curriculum as the reference category. Again, these analyses do not establish causal relationships between curricular standardization and students' science performance or their future orientation toward a science major or career. Although we control for several country-level factors for which data are available and that may be related to performance or future orientation, other unobserved country-level factors through which curricular standardization operates are possible. Nonetheless, these analyses can determine whether a correlation between curricular standardization and these outcomes, net of other factors, exists for a wide range of countries.

Variables

Future Orientation Toward STEM

We use the PISA future orientation index to measure students' future plans to major in STEM or pursue a STEM career. It is based on students' level of agreement with four statements: *I would like to work in a career involving science; I would like to study science after secondary school; I would like to work on science projects as an adult; I would like to spend my life doing advanced science*. This index is especially relevant to the study of how attitudes during adolescence translate into the subsequent choice to major in a STEM field or to pursue a STEM career later in life. The index was constructed so that the average OECD student has an index value of zero and about two-thirds of the OECD student population scored between the value of –1 and 1 (OECD 2007). A positive value indicates a student responded more positively to the questions used to comprise the index than students on average across all OECD countries; a negative value indicates that a student responded less positively than the OECD average.[2]

Science Achievement

The PISA data include comparable achievement scores for each student derived using state-of-the-art assessment methodology. Five plausible values of the science test score were used as a representation of the range of students' science abilities. The plausible values transfer a point estimate of achievement to a distributional estimate of achievement. We make use of the plausible values of student science achievement in generating all descriptive statistics.

Curricular Standardization

Following Guillermo Montt (2011), we categorize national educational systems into three types: systems in which the central government determines the curriculum, systems in which regional or local agencies have some ability to adapt the centrally mandated curriculum, and countries in which there is no central government intervention in designing the curriculum. The information about curricular standardization is based on *World Data on Education Edition 6* (UNESCO 2006). We generate a dummy variable for highly standardized systems, and a dummy variable for moderately standardized systems, to contrast with the unstandardized systems in our models. In seven of the twenty-seven countries, the central government has primary responsibility for determining the curriculum. The majority (sixteen)

---

2. In other analyses (not shown) we used an alternative measurement of future STEM orientation: student responses to the PISA question asking what occupation they expect to attain by age thirty and coded students as expecting a STEM occupation versus expecting a non-STEM occupation. Because results using either indicator as the dependent variable in the analysis were markedly similar, we report only results using the future orientation index here, as this index captures a more holistic conception of future orientation, which includes students' preference for a STEM field of study in college.

fall into the second category, where regional or local agencies have some ability to adapt the centrally mandated curriculum. In four countries, including the United States, the government has no responsibility for designing the curriculum or setting curricular standards.[3] This curricular standardization measurement closely corresponds to whether a country has a central exit exam: three of the four countries where the government has no responsibility for designing curriculum also have no central exit examinations. Six of the seven countries where the government determines the curriculum also have central exit examinations.

This measure captures variation across countries in the degree to which students are exposed to the same or different content of learning. In countries where the curriculum is centrally determined, all students are exposed to the same science curriculum and in many cases, students are required to demonstrate their science knowledge on an externally based exit exam. In countries like the United States where curricular content is determined at the state and district level, variation in student exposure to science content is significant and evaluated with assessments that are also highly variable across states and districts. As the United States moves toward greater curricular standardization with the implementation of the Common Core Standards, the comparison of countries with different levels of curricular standardization may provide useful predictions of the possible impact of rising curricular standardization in the United States.

Individual-Level Controls
We control for a wide range of individual-level variables. In the analysis of science achievement, we include gender, immigrant status, family socioeconomic status (SES), science self-efficacy, science learning hours, and science activities as control variables. Prior research has established that females and immigrants tend to earn lower scores on science tests relative to males and native students (Levels and Dronkers 2008). In contrast, students from higher SES families have score advantages over other students. Students are coded as immigrants if they are either foreign born or native born to immigrant parents. Family SES is measured by an index of economic, social, and cultural status (ESCS index). PISA derived this index from student's home possessions, the highest level occupation of either parent, and the highest level of education of either parent expressed as years of schooling (OECD 2009).

Additionally, research has determined that students' self-efficacy in sciences (Areepattamannil and Kaur 2012) as well as the time they spend in science-related activities and their knowledge about science-related careers (Kjærnsli and Lie 2011) are related to science achievement and may shape students' future orientation toward STEM. Thus we include a measure of science self-efficacy, based on students' ratings of the ease with which they believe they could perform eight specific scientific tasks. Science activities are measured by students' reports of how frequently they watch television, borrow or buy books, visit websites, listen to radio, read magazines and newspapers, or attend a club related to science. Science learning hours is measured by the hours spent in science classes. In the analysis of future orientation toward STEM fields, we include these individual-level controls as well as controls for individual science achievement and career information about STEM fields in predicting future orientation. Coupled with high achievement in science, more information about science careers should boost understanding and preparation for a future in the field, and also reduce stereotypes about who goes into science (Kjærnsli and Lie 2011).

---

3. Systems in which the central government determines the curriculum include: France, Greece, Iceland, Italy, Luxembourg, the Netherlands, and Slovenia. Systems in which regional or local agencies have some ability to adapt the centrally mandated curriculum include Australia, Canada, the Czech Republic, Finland, Germany, Ireland, Israel, Japan, New Zealand, Norway, Portugal, Korea, Spain, Sweden, Switzerland, and the UK. Countries with no central government intervention in designing the curriculum include Austria, Belgium, Denmark, and the United States.

This variable is derived from students' reports of their level of information about science-related careers, the steps to take if they want a science-related career, as well as the kind of companies that hire people for science-related careers.[4]

Country-Level Controls

Although curricular standardization is the key independent variable of interest, we control for several other country-level variables to ensure that the relationships between standardization and the outcome variables are robust, net of these other factors. We include GDP per capita and Gini coefficient in 2005, which measure the level of economic development and economic inequality of a country. Research shows that more economically developed countries have higher quality educational systems and thus higher levels of achievement as measured by test scores (Baker, Goesling, and LeTendre 2002). At the same time, students (especially female students) in these countries are less likely to aspire to study in a STEM field or pursue a STEM career (Charles and Bradley 2009). In highly unequal societies, family resources may be distributed more unequally, which may contribute to the unequal performance and expectations among students from different social classes (Chiu and Khoo 2005). Also, the more unequal the gender distribution in college STEM fields within a country, the less likely fifteen-year-old girls may be to expect to enter STEM fields (McDaniel 2010). Thus we created a measure of the gender segregation in field of study for each country. This measure, based on OECD estimates (Vincent-Lancrin 2008), ranges from zero to fifty with an average of twenty-seven across all OECD countries in 2005.[5]

Teacher quality is related to students' achievement (Goldhaber and Brewer 2000) and also may be related to their future orientation toward STEM fields. Countries such as Finland that earn high achievement scores on cross-national assessments are known for their high-quality teachers (Darling-Hammond 2010). We created an average teacher quality measure for each country indicating the number of teachers with a college degree or higher in each school in the country. Finally, prior research finds that the achievement of peers is related both to students' own academic self-concept and to their actual achievement. When a student is immersed in an environment where peers generally have high achievement levels, a student's self-concept as well as her actual achievement may be depressed through the process of comparing herself to these high-achieving peers (Nagengast and Marsh 2012; Marsh and Hau 2003; Marsh et al. 2015). To account for this possibility, we aggregated the individual-level science achievement scores into a country-level science achievement score and include it in both hierarchical linear models (HLM). Moreover, some high-achieving countries (Japan and New Zealand, for example) tend to have below-average levels of self-efficacy, and some low-achieving countries (such as the United States and Portugal) tend to have above-average levels of self-efficacy. In the analysis where students' future orientation is the dependent variable, we control for the national average of science self-efficacy because it is reasonable to assume that this pattern may reflect some country-level cultural aspects that affect student motivation and learning. The descriptive statistics of all variables are included in table 1.

4. Family SES, science self-efficacy, science activities, and career information about STEM are measured by PISA indexes. As described, each index is scaled so that the average OECD student has an index value of zero and about two thirds of the OECD student population scored between the value of –1 and 1 (OECD 2007). A positive value indicates that a student responded more positively to the questions used to comprise the index than the average OECD student; a negative value indicates that a student responded less positively than the average OECD student.

5. The OECD source file does not provide estimates for Israel, Luxemburg, and Slovenia, so we assign these three countries the average value of the sample countries, which is 28.33.

Table 1. Descriptive Statistics for All Variables Used in the Analyses

	Mean	SD	Min	Max
Individual-level variables (N=211,766)				
Female (% female)	49.74	0.50	0.00	1.00
Immigrant status (% immigrant)	10.23	0.30	0.00	1.00
Family SES (ESCS index)	0.10	0.91	−5.66	3.34
Science Self-efficacy	−0.02	1.01	−3.77	3.22
Science learning hours	3.00	1.87	0.00	6.00
Science activities	−0.08	0.99	−1.69	3.38
Science career information	0.04	0.99	−2.44	2.53
Science achievement				
Plausible value 1	508.00	98.82	23.72	920.48
Plausible value 2	508.20	98.92	23.44	924.21
Plausible value 3	508.00	98.84	23.72	897.91
Plausible value 4	507.94	99.00	21.39	883.18
Plausible value 5	508.08	98.93	22.79	952.19
Country-level variables (N=27)				
Moderately standardized curriculum	59.26	0.50	0	1
Highly standardized curriculum	25.93	0.45	0	1
GDP per capita 2005	36,168.62	12,721.53	13,318	79,594
Gini coefficient 2005	32.08	4.32	24.70	40.80
Gender segregation index	26.46	5.04	20.00	43.00
Teacher quality	28.59	14.51	3.02	53.27
Average science score	506.33	22.75	453.90	563.32
Average science self-efficacy	−0.01	0.17	−0.53	0.22

Source: Authors' calculations based on PISA 2006.

Note: Mean and SD of five plausible values of science achievement are individual estimates, applying the Balanced Repeated Replication methods with Fay's adjustment. The mean and SD do not equal the OECD average (500, 100) because only twenty-seven countries are selected for analysis. Similarly, the means and indexes of the PISA indexes do not equal the OECD average (0 and 1). Science achievement, national average science achievement, and GDP per capita are grand-mean centered when entered into HLM analyses. Science learning hours is originally an interval variable; to calculate the mean value, we take the midpoint of each interval. For example, if the student's learning time is two to four hours, we give assign the student a 3.

Methods

Our HLM analyses begin with a model that includes all individual-level variables in the model and allows for country-specific random effects. Then, we add country-level variables to the model and focus mainly on whether curricular standardization is related to different intercepts of student achievement or future orientation (γ_{01j}). The final models add cross-level interactions to the previous model to assess whether the relationship between student achievement and future orientation significantly varies in countries with different levels of curricular standardization. This requires modeling the slope of science score to be predicted by curricular standardization (γ_{11j}).[6] We add interactions between curricular standardization and gender (γ_{21j}) and SES (γ_{31j}) to examine whether the gender gap and the social class gap in science achievement and science orien-

---

[6]. In the actual model, the variable consists of two dummies, highly and moderately standardized systems, as indicated in the variable section. For simplicity, in the formula below we present them as one item.

Figure 1. Mean Science Score and Standard Deviation, by Country

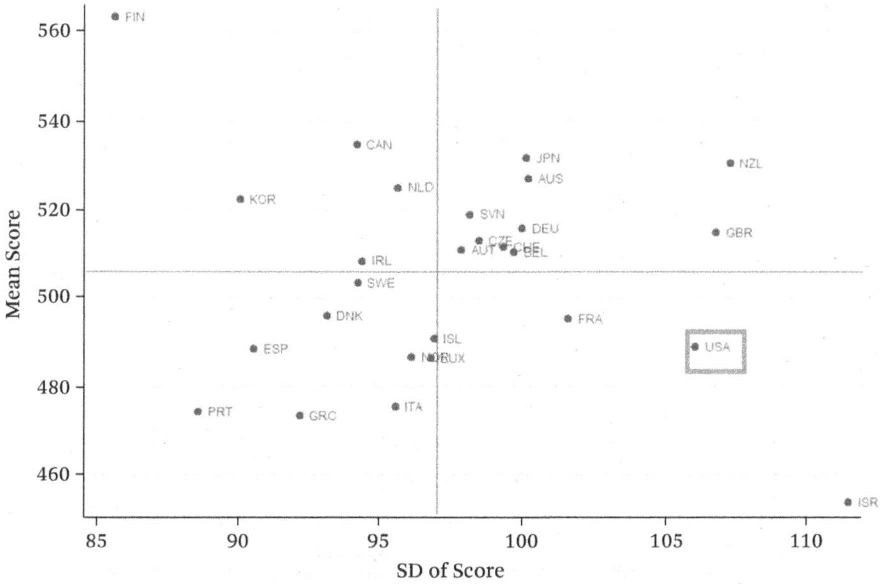

AUS	Australia	DNK	Denmark	ISL	Iceland	NOR	Norway
AUT	Austria	ESP	Spain	ISR	Israel	NZL	New Zealand
BEL	Belgium	FIN	Finland	ITA	Italy	PRT	Portugal
CAN	Canada	FRA	France	JPN	Japan	SVN	Slovenia
CHE	Switzerland	GBR	United Kingdom	KOR	Korea	SWE	Sweden
CZE	Czech Republic	GRC	Greece	LUX	Luxembourg	USA	United States
DEU	Germany	IRL	Ireland	NLD	Netherlands		

Source: Authors' calculations based on PISA 2006.

tation differ by level of curricular standardization at the country level. The final HLM equation is as follows:

Level 1: $Y_{ij} = \beta_{0j} + \beta_{1j}X_{1ij}(\text{score}) + \beta_{2j}X_{2ij}(\text{gender}) + \beta_{3j}X_{3ij}(\text{SES}) + \beta_{xj}X_{xij} \ldots + r_{ij}$

Level 2: $\beta_{0j} = \gamma_{00} + \gamma_{01j}(\text{curricular standardization}) + \gamma_{0xj} + \ldots \mu_{0j}$

$\beta_{1j} = \gamma_{10} + \gamma_{11j}(\text{curricular standardization}) + \mu_{1j}$
$\beta_{2j} = \gamma_{20} + \gamma_{21j}(\text{curricular standardization}) + \mu_{2j}$
$\beta_{3j} = \gamma_{30} + \gamma_{31j}(\text{curricular standardization}) + \mu_{3j}$[7]

RESULTS

1. How do U.S. students compare with students in other countries in terms of science achievement?

Figure 1 shows the relationship between country-level mean science scores and standard deviation in science scores for the full student population surveyed in each country. The scenario of a high average and low variability in scores is optimal because it indicates that a large proportion of students are achieving a high level of science proficiency. Finland demonstrates this pattern most clearly and far exceeds all other countries in that it exhibits a high mean science score (563) and a low variability in scores (SD=85). Canada, Japan, Korea, the Netherlands, and Australia are also high-achieving countries in this regard. The United States, Great Britain, and New Zealand have relatively high standard deviations, meaning that students' science scores vary substantially. But whereas the New Zealand shows high variability (SD= 107) coupled with high mean achievement (530), the United States has a low

---

7. This is a demonstration of the HLM analysis on future orientation. In the HLM analysis of science performance, test score is a dependent variable rather than an independent variable.

Figure 2. Mean Science Achievement for Aspiring Students, by Country

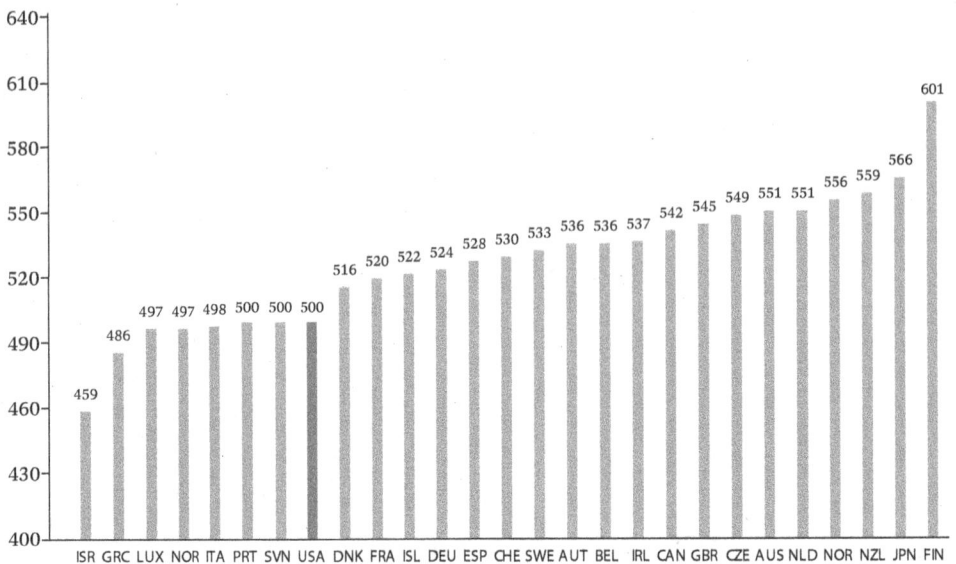

Source: Authors' calculations based on PISA 2006.
Note: Refer to figure 1 for country codes.

mean achievement score (489) relative to most other countries.

2. How do U.S. students who aspire to major in STEM and pursue STEM careers compare in terms of performance in science?

We have shown evidence for the high dropout rate of U.S. STEM students, and argued that it is in part because of a lack of mastery to science knowledge and skills at the earlier stages of education. The lack of mastery is undoubtedly reflected by the lower average science score for the United States. At the same time, many low performers may not expect to pursue a science field of study or career and thus will not enter the science pipeline. For this reason, it is useful to compare the achievement levels of students wanting to pursue a STEM major or career. For them to attain their goals, they need to have been well prepared in high school on basic science knowledge and skills to meet the academic requirements in college STEM fields. Students who aspire to major in STEM fields but have low science achievement scores are more likely to struggle in college STEM courses and are at much greater risk for switching out of STEM into other majors or dropping out of college completely. In fact, statistics from the U.S. Department of Education show that 48 percent of STEM majors leave their initial STEM field (Chen and Soldner 2013).

Figure 2 shows average science score by country for the subset of students who aspire to a science career according to whether their future orientation index is above average (index>0) (aspiring students). The average score of aspiring students in the United States is 500. Although higher than that of the full sample of U.S. students, the mean score of aspiring students in the United States is lower than those of their counterparts in most other developed countries including Australia (551), Canada (542), Finland (601), and Japan (566). Thus, even among students highly oriented toward STEM, the United States trails most other developed countries in science performance.

At the same time, if most aspiring students attain a level of proficiency in science that prepares them for college-level study in STEM, the lower average score itself may be less of a concern. For this reason, it is informative to compare aspiring students in the United States with aspiring students in other countries in terms of proficiency levels. PISA uses profi-

Figure 3. Distribution of Proficiency Levels of Aspiring Students, by Country

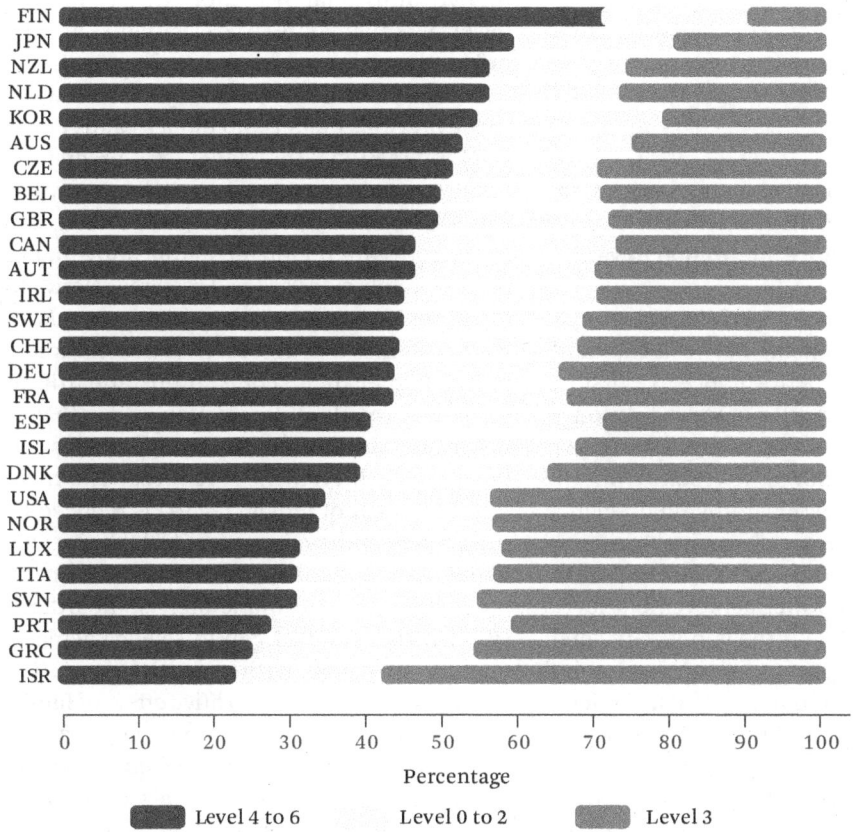

Source: Authors' calculations based on PISA 2006.
Note: Refer to figure 1 for country codes.

ciency levels to interpret science test scores. The seven levels run from below level 1 (which we coded 0) to 6. According to PISA (OECD 2007), students at level 1 have only limited scientific knowledge that can be applied to a few familiar situations. At levels 2 and 3, they can clearly describe scientific issues in a range of contexts and apply simple models or inquiry strategies. At level 4, they can work effectively with situations and issues that involve explicit phenomena, and communicate decisions using scientific knowledge and evidence. Students who achieve proficiency levels 5 and 6 can consistently identify, explain, and apply scientific knowledge and knowledge about science in a variety of complex life situations. Moreover, they clearly and consistently demonstrate both advanced scientific thinking and reasoning and a willingness to use their scientific understanding to support solutions in unfamiliar scientific technological situations. Accordingly, the percentages of students attaining level 1 to level 6 across OECD countries are 94.8 percent, 80.8 percent, 56.7 percent, 29.3 percent, 9.0 percent and 1.3 percent. Figure 3 presents the distribution of proficiency levels for aspiring students in each country. To simplify the presentation, we combine levels 0, 1, 2, 4, 5, and 6 into larger categories. The U.S. numbers on level 4 or higher proves quite low. The majority are in the 0 to 3 range, clear evidence of a lack of proficiency for college STEM coursework. In contrast, Finland, Japan, and New Zealand have the highest percentage of aspiring students who reached proficiency level 4 or higher and much smaller percentages of students at proficiency levels 3 or lower. In sum, the U.S. educational system appears to be less efficient in aligning students' future orientation toward STEM fields with their levels of science achievement. This situation could be one factor related to the high rate of attrition among college STEM majors in the United States.

3. Is the degree of curricular standardization related to the alignment of science achievement and future orientation toward STEM fields?

To speak to this question and the existing literature on the relationship between standardization and student performance, we first examine whether curricular standardization is related to higher overall student science performance. Table 2 shows the results from the HLM analysis predicting individual science performance. The first model includes only individual-level predictors. It shows that female students have lower achievement levels than male students, but the gap is very small (–1.5 points). Immigrant students lag behind native students by about 26 points. Students from higher socioeconomic families (27 points higher than lower SES families) and those who report higher science self-efficacy (27 points higher than low self-efficacy students) have significantly higher science scores. Not surprisingly, students who spend more hours learning science in class and who are engaged in more science activities also earn substantially higher science scores (13 points and 3 points respectively). These results align with previous findings that gender (Ayalon and Livneh 2013), immigrant status, socioeconomic status (Levels, Dronkers, and Jencks 2014), self-efficacy (Bishop 2006), and academic intensity (Montt 2011) matter for student performance in science.

The second model adds the dummy variables for standardization to the first model. Without controlling for other level 2 predictors, a moderately standardized curriculum is related to a 40-point gain in science performance, and a highly standardized curriculum is related to a 27-point gain in science performance. In countries where the average science achievement and teacher quality are higher, individual students' science achievement is also higher. In countries where economic inequality as measured by the Gini coefficient is higher, individual students' achievement is lower. No other country-level variables are significantly related to science achievement.

Model 3 adds other country-level controls to the previous model, and model 4 adds cross-level interactions. Individual-level predictors' effects remain largely unchanged. However, with other country level controls added, science scores are no longer significantly higher in moderately standardized systems relative to unstandardized systems. In highly standardized systems, average science scores are 12 points higher than scores in unstandardized systems. Cross-level interactions show that in highly standardized systems, the gender gap in science achievement is reduced. The main negative effect of female (–0.92) is reduced by the positive interaction effect (2.23) between a highly standardized system and gender. On the other hand, it is in moderately standardized systems that the SES gap in science achievement is attenuated. With a negative interaction effect (–4.43), the main positive effect of family SES is reduced, indicating that such systems may allow for more educational equality across social classes. In sum, our analysis supports the argument that curricular standardization is related to improved individual student science performance, but it is significantly related to a smaller gender gap in science achievement in highly standardized systems, and to a smaller class gap in science achievement in moderately standardized systems, net of other individual and country-level factors.

Table 3 shows the results from analyses that examine future orientation toward majoring in STEM or pursuing a STEM career. Recall that the dependent variable is measured as an index with a mean of 0 and a standard deviation of 1, where values above 0 indicate a higher level of future orientation than average. In addition to examining the relationship between individual- and country-level factors and students' future orientation toward STEM, these analyses address the question of whether curricular standardization is related to the alignment between students' science achievement and their future orientation toward STEM. Table 3 presents four models. The first includes the same set of individual-level independent

Table 2. HLM Estimates of the Relationship Between Individual-Level and Country-Level Factors and Science Achievement

	Model 1	Model 2	Model 3	Model 4
Individual-level variables				
Female	−1.53**	−1.53**	−1.53**	−0.92**
	(0.72)	(0.72)	(0.72)	(0.42)
Immigrant	−26.70***	−26.70***	−26.68***	−25.77***
	(4.90)	(4.91)	(4.91)	(4.93)
Family SES	27.08***	27.09***	27.08***	29.76***
	(1.84)	(1.84)	(1.84)	(1.20)
Science self-efficacy	26.82***	26.82***	26.82***	26.72***
	(1.31)	(1.31)	(1.31)	(1.29)
Science learning hours	13.42***	13.42***	13.41***	13.34***
	(0.67)	(0.67)	(0.67)	(0.67)
Science activities	2.92**	2.92**	2.93**	3.01**
	(1.21)	(1.21)	(1.21)	(1.20)
Country-level variations				
Standardization				
Unstandardized		Reference	Group	
Moderately standardized		40.23***	−1.81	2.96
		(8.54)	(5.85)	(5.74)
Highly standardized		26.77***	9.94**	12.42**
		(5.83)	(4.09)	(4.55)
GDP per capita			0.00	0.00
			(0.00)	(0.00)
Gini coefficient			−1.43**	−1.62**
			(0.49)	(0.53)
Gender segregation index			0.35	0.46
			(0.37)	(0.33)
Teacher quality			0.14	0.44**
			(0.16)	(0.13)
Average science score			0.74***	0.67***
			(0.10)	(0.07)
Cross-level variations				
Moderately standardized*female				1.62
				(1.38)
Highly standardized*female				2.23**
				(1.05)
Moderately standardized*family SES				−4.43**
				(1.35)
Highly standardized*family SES				0.00
				(1.97)
Intercept	466.57***	444.86***	490.69***	482.54***
	(11.32)	(3.61)	(20.51)	(23.68)
Country-level random effect – μ_0		300.97	48.90	63.91
Individual-level random effect – r		6780.83	6780.83	6764.76

Source: Authors' calculations based on PISA 2006.
Note: Models are weighted by PISA final student weight.
*p < .1; **p < .05; ***p < .01

Table 3. HLM Estimates of the Relationship between Individual-level and Country-level Factors and Future Orientation toward Science

	Model 1	Model 2	Model 3	Model 4
Individual-level variables				
Female	−0.08***	−0.08**	−0.08**	−0.03
	(0.03)	(0.03)	(0.03)	(0.02)
Immigrant	0.12***	0.12***	0.12***	0.12***
	(0.01)	(0.01)	(0.01)	(0.01)
Family SES	−0.02***	−0.02**	−0.02***	−0.02**
	(0.00)	(0.00)	(0.01)	(0.01)
Science achievement	0.001***	0.001***	0.001***	0.001***
	(0.000)	(0.000)	(0.000)	(0.000)
Science self-efficacy	0.08***	0.08***	0.08***	0.08***
	(0.00)	(0.00)	(0.00)	(0.00)
Science learning hours	0.02***	0.03***	0.03***	0.03***
	(0.01)	(0.01)	(0.01)	(0.01)
Science activities	0.32***	0.36***	0.36***	0.35***
	(0.01)	(0.01)	(0.01)	(0.01)
Science career information	0.21***	0.21***	0.21***	0.20***
	(0.00)	(0.00)	(0.00)	(0.00)
Country-level variations				
Standardization				
Unstandardized		Reference	Group	
Moderately standardized		−0.18**	−0.03	0.03
		(0.06)	(0.09)	(0.08)
Highly standardized		−0.14***	−0.08	−0.03
		(0.03)	(0.07)	(0.08)
GDP per capita			0.00	0.00
			(0.00)	(0.00)
Gini coefficient			0.02**	0.02**
			(0.01)	(0.01)
Gender segregation index			0.01	0.00
			(0.01)	(0.00)
Teacher quality			0.00	0.00
			(0.00)	(0.00)
Average science score			−0.003**	−0.002*
			(0.001)	(0.001)
Average science self-efficacy			−0.39**	−0.35**
			(0.14)	(0.14)
Cross-level Variations				
Moderately standardized*female				−0.10**
				(0.03)
Highly standardized*female				−0.09*
				(0.05)
Moderately standardized*family SES				0.01
				(0.01)
Highly standardized*family SES				−0.01
				(0.02)

Table 3. (Cont.)

	Model 1	Model 2	Model 3	Model 4
Moderately standardized*science score				0.0005**
				(0.0001)
Highly standardized*science score				0.0005**
				(0.0002)
Intercept	−0.04	0.06	−0.94**	−0.95**
	(0.07)	(0.04)	(0.34)	(0.36)
Country-level random effect μ_0		0.01	0.01	0.01
Individual-level random effect – r		0.68	0.68	0.67

Source: Authors' calculations based on PISA 2006.
Note: Models are weighted by PISA final student weight.
$*p < .1; **p < .05; ***p < .01$

variables from table 2; the second and third models add the same set of country-level independent variables in table 2. The last adds three cross-level interactions: curricular standardization interacted with individual-level science score, curricular standardization interacted with gender, and curricular standardization interacted with SES. Of primary interest is the interaction between curricular standardization and individual-level science score: a significant positive interaction indicates that an increase in students' science performance is related to a larger gain in their future orientation in standardized systems than in unstandardized systems.

Because the future orientation variable is an index, the values of the coefficients are not directly interpretable. The directions of the relationships are telling, however. Model 1 shows that females and higher SES students are less likely to be oriented to a STEM field of study or career. Immigrants, students with higher achievement or self-efficacy in science, students who spend more hours studying science or who received more STEM career information, and those who are more involved in science activities are all more likely to have a future orientation toward STEM.

Model 2 includes only the two main level-2 predictors: highly and moderately standardized education systems. It shows that in both education systems, future orientation toward science is lower than that in unstandardized systems, and the differences are significant. It is not surprising to see these negative effects, given that we have discussed that in unstandardized systems such as the United States, students tend to have less realistic expectations or aspirations, usually not matched with a comparable level of achievement that will facilitate the realization of such expectations or aspirations.

Model 3 shows that the individual-level independent variables' effects remain largely unchanged, and that several country-level variables are significantly related to future orientation. The more unequal a country (indicated by a higher Gini coefficient), the higher students' future orientation toward STEM, possibly because they regard STEM as a mobility channel. The higher average science achievement and science self-efficacy, the lower students' future orientation toward STEM. The negative relationship between national average achievement and personal future orientation speaks to the social comparison theory previously discussed. When compared with a group of high-achieving students, a student might underestimate her own ability for learning science, and thus be less oriented toward a STEM major or career. The negative relationship between the national average self-efficacy and future orientation might be driven by countries such as Japan and Korea that have low average self-efficacy but a high proportion of STEM college graduates and a large STEM labor force.

In the last model, curricular standardization is not related to the value of the intercept, but there is no reason to expect that it should be related to higher future orientations toward STEM for all students; rather we predict that in countries with higher levels of curricular standardization, students' science performance and their future orientations toward STEM are better aligned. To investigate this possibility, model 3 adds the cross-level interaction of curricular standardization and student science achievement, along with two other cross-level interactions. As hypothesized, students' achievement is better aligned with their future orientation in countries with higher levels of curricular standardization than similarly situated students in countries with less curricular standardization.

To put this finding in substantive terms, imagine a hypothetical comparison of four students of the same background except for their science proficiency levels and future orientations. The four students include a pair from the United States and a pair from France. Each pair has one student at proficiency level 3 and another at level 4. Because the average test score gap between level 3 and level 4 is about 75 points, and the coefficient for individual test score on future orientation is 0.001, we can expect the level 4 students to have higher future orientation than level 3 students. However, the advantage in future orientation for the level 4 student in France (which has a highly standardized curriculum) is significantly larger than for the level 4 student in the United States (with no standardized curriculum). In the United States, the level 4 student's future orientation is 0.075 higher than the level 3 student (0.001*75=0.075); while in France, the level 4 student's future orientation is 0.11 higher than the level 3 student (0.001+0.0005) *75=0.11). Considering that the real gap in future orientation between a level 3 student and a level 4 student in the United States is 0.21,[8] a gap of 0.04 (0.11–0.075) is a considerably large effect. In other words, curricular standardization appears to be related to a stronger alignment between students' future orientation toward STEM and their achievement in science.

DISCUSSION AND CONCLUSION

In terms of the science performance of the entire student population and the subset of students who expect to pursue STEM majors or careers, the United States trails many industrialized countries. We compared the United States with several other industrialized countries in terms of students' science achievement and their orientation to focus on STEM in the future. The United States exhibits both lower mean science achievement and greater variation in science performance than most other countries in the sample (figure 1). Although aspiring students in the United States achieve more in the sciences than the general U.S. student population, their mean achievement and proficiency levels are still lower than those of their counterparts in other countries.

We then considered whether curricular standardization is related to student achievement in science and the alignment of student science achievement with their future orientation toward STEM. Countries with standardized educational systems generally have higher student achievement in science, as evidenced by significantly higher mean test scores. Additionally, more standardized educational systems show a stronger linkage between science performance and future orientation toward study or a career in science, such that high achievers in science indicate a greater likelihood of pursuing science-based majors and careers in the future. This relationship may be due in part to the fact that standardized systems provide students with valuable information about their standing relative to the general student population that students use in their subsequent educational decisions and career choices. These analyses do not establish causal relationships between curricular standardization and students' science performance or their future orientation toward a science major or career. Moreover, beyond the individual- and country-level factors included in our models, other unexamined country-level factors through which curricular standardization operates may exist. At any rate, correlations are strong be-

---

8. For the entire sample of countries, the gap between level 3 and level 4 ranges between 0.10 in Slovenia and 0.41 in Spain. Two-thirds of the countries have a gap in between 0.20 to 0.35. Country-specific data on these gaps are available on request.

tween curricular standardization and student science achievement as well as between curricular standardization and the alignment of science performance and future orientation toward study or a career in science, net of other factors, for a wide range of countries. It is possible that in countries that lack curricular standardization, such as the United States, students do not receive such clear signals about their performance in specific academic domains and thus their science achievement and their interest in science are less aligned.

In addition to standardization, the primary factor of interest here, other national-level features may well distinguish the performance and future orientations of students in some countries from others. For example, if in some countries STEM majors generate higher labor market returns, students may strive for better science performance in secondary school and may be more motivated to choose a STEM major in college in those countries relative to countries where STEM majors are not highly remunerated. It is also possible that major cultural differences between countries play a role in explaining the cross-national variations in students' achievement and future plans to major in STEM and pursue STEM careers. While investigating these possibilities is beyond the scope of this paper, future research along these lines may prove fruitful.

At the individual level, students with higher levels of science self-efficacy and those who spend more time learning science and in science-related activities have higher science achievement scores, net of other factors (table 2). These findings suggest that devoting more hours of the school day to learning science and providing opportunities for students to engage in science-related activities may be promising avenues to boost student achievement in science. These recommendations align with those of research findings that students' greater exposure to math and science courses in high school is significantly related to their grades in college-level science courses (Sadler and Tai 2007). That students' information about science careers is significantly correlated with students' expectations to pursue science majors or careers in the future, net of other factors (table 3), further suggests that providing concrete information about science careers and the skills needed for them may help adolescents align their skills and career expectations.

In light of the diversity of skills and preparation of incoming students, what can higher education do to improve retention rates in STEM fields? Many colleges and universities use placement tests to determine which students need more preparation via remedial coursework before enrolling in the first year gateway science courses, as Lynn Riemer and colleagues discuss elsewhere in this volume. Colleges and universities might consider expanding placement tests and programs that help bridge the gap in student science preparation prior to their enrollment in gateway science courses. Such steps, coupled with the improvements to instruction in gateway courses, as Reimer and colleagues suggest, may prove to be cost-effective ways to produce the STEM professionals the nation needs.

REFERENCES

Allmendinger, Jutta. 1989. "Educational Systems and Labor Market Outcomes." *European Sociological Review* 5(3): 231–50.

Areepattamannil, Shaljan, and Berinderjeet Kaur. 2012. "Factors Predicting Science Achievement of Immigrant and Non-Immigrant Students: A Multilevel Analysis." *International Journal of Science and Mathematics Education* 11(5): 1183–207. doi:10.1007/s10763-012-9369-5.

Ayalon, Hanna, and Adam Gamoran. 2000. "Stratification in Academic Secondary Programs and Educational Inequality in Israel and the United States." *Comparative Education Review* 44(1): 54–80.

Ayalon, Hanna, and Idit Livneh. 2013. "Educational Standardization and Gender Differences in Mathematics Achievement: A Comparative Study." *Social Science Research* 42(2): 432–45. doi:10.1016/j.ssresearch.2012.10.001.

Baker, David P., Brian Goesling, and Gerald K. LeTendre. 2002. "Socioeconomic Status, School Quality, and National Economic Development: A Cross-National Analysis of the 'Heyneman-Loxley Effect' on Mathematics and Science Achievement." *Comparative Education Review* 46(3): 291–312. doi:10.1086/341159.

Bishop, John H. 1997. "The Effect of National Standards and Curriculum-Based Exams on Achievement." *American Economic Review* 87(2): 260–64.

———. 2006. "Drinking from the Fountain of Knowledge: Student Incentive to Study and Learn—Externalities, Information Problems and Peer Pressure." In *Handbook of the Economics of Education*, vol. 2, edited by Eric Hanushek and Finis Welch. Amsterdam: Elsevier. Accessed February 23, 2016. http://www.sciencedirect.com/science/article/pii/S1574069206020150.

Bol, Thijs, Jacqueline Witschge, Herman G. Van de Werfhorst, and Jaap Dronkers. 2014. "Curricular Tracking and Central Examinations: Counterbalancing the Impact of Social Background on Student Achievement in 36 Countries." *Social Forces* 92(4): 1545–72. doi:10.1093/sf/sou003.

Charles, Maria, and Karen Bradley. 2009. "Indulging Our Gendered Selves? Sex Segregation by Field of Study in 44 Countries." *American Journal of Sociology* 114(4): 924–76.

Chen, Xianglei, and Matthew Soldner. 2013. *STEM Attrition: College Students' Paths into and out of STEM Fields. Statistical Analysis Report*. NCES 2014–001. Washington: U.S. Department of Education. Accessed February 23, 2016. http://files.eric.ed.gov/fulltext/ED544470.pdf.

Chiu, Ming Ming, and Lawrence Khoo. 2005. "Effects of Resources, Inequality, and Privilege Bias on Achievement: Country, School, and Student Level Analyses." *American Educational Research Journal* 42(4): 575–603. doi:10.3102/00028312042004575.

Darling-Hammond, Linda. 2010. *The Flat World and Education: How America's Commitment to Equity Will Determine Our Future*. New York: Teachers College Press.

Goldhaber, Dan D., and Dominic J. Brewer. 2000. "Does Teacher Certification Matter? High School Teacher Certification Status and Student Achievement." *Educational Evaluation and Policy Analysis* 22(2): 129–45. doi:10.3102/01623737022002129.

Grossman, Tabitha, Ryan Reyna, and Stephanie Shipton. 2011. *Realizing the Potential: How Governors Can Lead Effective Implementation of the Common Core State Standards*. Washington, D.C.: National Governors Assocation, Center for Best Practices. Accessed February 23, 2016. http://eric.ed.gov/?id=ED532524.

Kjærnsli, Marit, and Svein Lie. 2011. "Students' Preference for Science Careers: International Comparisons Based on PISA 2006." *International Journal of Science Education* 33(1): 121–44. doi:10.1080/09500693.2010.518642.

Levels, Mark, and Jaap Dronkers. 2008. "Educational Performance of Native and Immigrant Children from Various Countries of Origin." *Ethnic and Racial Studies* 31(8): 1404–25. doi:10.1080/01419870701682238.

Levels, Mark, Jaap Dronkers, and Christopher Jencks. 2014. "Mind the Gap: Compositional, Cultural and Institutional Explanations for Numeracy Skills Disparities Between Adult Immigrants and Natives in Western Countries." *HKS Faculty Research* working paper RWP14-020. Cambridge, Mass.: Harvard University. Accessed February 23, 2016. https://research.hks.harvard.edu/publications/getFile.aspx?Id=1048.

Maple, Sue A., and Frances K. Stage. 1991. "Influences on the Choice of Math/Science Major by Gender and Ethnicity." *American Educational Research Journal* 28(1): 37–60. doi:10.3102/00028312028001037.

Marsh, Herbert W., Adel Salah Abduljabbar, Philip D. Parker, Alexandre J. S. Morin, Faisal Abdelfattah, Benjamin Nagengast, Jens Möller, and Maher M. Abu-Hilal. 2015. "The Internal/External Frame of Reference Model of Self-Concept and Achievement Relations Age-Cohort and Cross-Cultural Differences." *American Educational Research Journal* 52(1): 168–202. doi:10.3102/0002831214549453.

Marsh, Herbert W., and Kit-Tai Hau. 2003. "Big-Fish—Little-Pond Effect on Academic Self-Concept: A Cross-Cultural (26-Country) Test of the Negative Effects of Academically Selective Schools." *American Psychologist* 58(5): 364–76. doi:10.1037/0003-066X.58.5.364.

McDaniel, Anne. 2010. "Cross-National Gender Gaps in Educational Expectations: The Influence of National-Level Gender Ideology and Educational Systems." *Comparative Education Review* 54(1): 27–50. doi:10.1086/648060.

Montt, Guillermo. 2011. "Cross-National Differences in Educational Achievement Inequality." *Sociology of Education* 84(1): 49–68. doi:10.1177/0038040710392717.

Nagengast, Benjamin, and Herbert W. Marsh. 2012. "Big Fish in Little Ponds Aspire More: Mediation and Cross-Cultural Generalizability of School-Average Ability Effects on Self-Concept and Career Aspirations in Science." *Journal of Educational Psychology* 104(4): 1033–53. doi:10.1037/a0027697.

National Academy of Sciences. 2007. *Rising Above the Gathering Storm: Energizing and Employing America for a Brighter Economic Future*. Washington, D.C.: National Academies Press. Accessed February 23, 2016. http://www.nap.edu/catalog/11463/rising-above-the-gathering-storm-energizing-and-employing-america-for.

National Research Council. 2012. *A Framework for K-12 Science Education: Practices, Crosscutting Concepts, and Core Ideas*. Washington, D.C.: National Academies Press. Accessed February 23, 2016. http://www.nap.edu/catalog/13165/a-framework-for-k-12-science-education-practices-crosscutting-concepts.

OECD. 2007. *PISA 2006: Science Competencies for Tomorrow*, vol. 1. Paris: Organization for Economic Cooperation and Development. Accessed February 23, 2016. http://www.oecd-ilibrary.org/content/book/9789264040014-en.

———. 2009. *PISA Data Analysis Manual: SPSS*, 2nd ed. Paris: Organization for Economic Cooperation and Development. Accessed February 23, 2016. http://www.oecd-ilibrary.org/content/book/9789264056275-en.

Olson, Steve, and Donna Gerardi Riordan. 2012. *Engage to Excel: Producing One Million Additional College Graduates with Degrees in Science, Technology, Engineering, and Mathematics*. Washington, D.C.: Executive Office of the President. Accessed February 23, 2016. http://files.eric.ed.gov/fulltext/ED541511.pdf.

Park, Hyunjoon. 2008. "The Varied Educational Effects of Parent-Child Communication: A Comparative Study of Fourteen Countries." *Comparative Education Review* 52(2): 219–43. doi:10.1086/524044.

Sadler, Philip M., and Robert H. Tai. 2007. "The Two High-School Pillars Supporting College." *Science* 317(5837): 457–58. doi:10.1126/science.1144214.

Shavit, Yossi, and Walter Muller. 1998. *From School to Work. A Comparative Study of Educational Qualifications and Occupational Destinations*. New York: Oxford University Press. Accessed February 23, 2016. http://eric.ed.gov/?id=ED419142.

Stevenson, David Lee, and David P. Baker. 1991. "State Control of the Curriculum and Classroom Instruction." *Sociology of Education* 64(1): 1–10. doi:10.2307/2112887.

Stinebrickner, Todd R., and Ralph Stinebrickner. 2011. "Math or Science? Using Longitudinal Expectations Data to Examine the Process of Choosing a College Major." *NBER* working paper no. 16869. Cambridge, Mass.: National Bureau of Economic Research. Accessed February 23, 2016. http://www.nber.org/papers/w16869.

Subotnik, Rena, Ashley Edmiston, and Kristin Rayhack. 2007. "Developing National Policies in STEM Talent Development: Obstacles and Opportunities." In *Science Education: Models and Networking of Student Research Training*, 28–38. Amsterdam: IOS Press.

Tai, Robert H., Christine Qi Liu, Adam V. Maltese, and Xitao Fan. 2006. "Planning Early for Careers in." *Science* 312(5777): 1143–44. doi:10.1126/science.1128690.

UNESCO. 2006. "World Data on Education Sixth Edition, 2006/07." International Bureau of Education. Accessed December 17, 2015. http://www.ibe.unesco.org/en/services/online-materials/world-data-on-education/sixth-edition-2006-07.html.

Vincent-Lancrin, Stéphan. 2008. "The Reversal of Gender Inequalities in Higher Education." In *Higher Education to 2030*, vol. 1, *Demography*, 265–98. Paris: OECD Publishing. Accessed February 23, 2016. http://www.oecd-ilibrary.org/content/chapter/9789264040663-11-en.

World Bank. 2005. "GDP per Capita in (Constant 2005 US$)." Accessed December 17, 2015. http://data.worldbank.org/indicator/NY.GDP.PCAP.KD.

Wößmann, Ludger. 2005. "The Effect Heterogeneity of Central Examinations: Evidence from TIMSS, TIMSS-Repeat and PISA." *Education Economics* 13(2): 143–69. doi:10.1080/09645290500031165.

Xie, Yu, and Kimberlee A. Shauman. 2006. *Women in Science: Career Processes and Outcomes*. Cambridge, Mass.: Harvard University Press.

Evaluating Promising Practices in Undergraduate STEM Lecture Courses

LYNN C. REIMER, KATERINA SCHENKE, TUTRANG NGUYEN, DIANE K. O'DOWD, THURSTON DOMINA, AND MARK WARSCHAUER

Over the course of one year, we systematically observed instruction in nearly all large gateway STEM courses at the University of California, Irvine to assess the prevalence of promising instructional practices and their implications for student success. More than half of the courses included promising instructional practices. Our most conservative student fixed-effects models suggest that students earn slightly higher grades in courses where instructors use explicit epistemological instruction, frequent assessment, and interactive instruction. Although we find no evidence to suggest that these strategies have lasting effects for the average UC Irvine student, we do find they have unique positive effects on the achievement of first-generation college students.

Keywords: STEM, promising practices, undergraduate lectures, first generation

Global labor markets increasingly demand professionals with sophisticated skills in science, technology, engineering, and mathematics (STEM) (Lansiquot et al. 2011; Vergara et al. 2009). However, too few U.S. college graduates have these in-demand skills (Goldin and Katz 2009; Levy and Murnane 2012). Instruction in undergraduate STEM courses may be partly to blame, as many are organized into large lectures in which expert teachers transmit knowledge with minimal student interaction; it is argued that this course design contributes to attrition from STEM majors during the first undergraduate years (Baillie and Fitzgerald 2010; Kyle 1997; McGinn and Roth 1999; Mervis 2010; NAE 2005). In this study, we investigate the effectiveness of several instructional practices that have been proposed to reform large introductory STEM courses. Our study consists of one year of detailed observations of the instructional practices in forty sections of eight large introductory STEM courses at the University of California, Irvine (UCI). By linking these observations to administrative records of nearly five thousand undergraduates enrolled in these courses, we examine whether instructional practices identified as "promising" by leading national organizations influence students' course grades, odds of enrolling in the next STEM course, and their grades in the sub-

Lynn C. Reimer is a National Science Foundation graduate research fellow at the University of California, Irvine. **Katerina Schenke** is a postdoctoral researcher at the University of California, Los Angeles. **Tutrang Nguyen** is a doctoral student at the University of California, Irvine. **Diane K. O'Dowd** is professor and vice provost at the University of California, Irvine. **Thurston Domina** is associate professor at the University of North Carolina, Chapel Hill. **Mark Warschauer** is professor and interim dean at the University of California, Irvine.

This material is based on work supported by the National Science Foundation under Grant Number 1256500. Direct correspondence to: Lynn C. Reimer at lcreimer@uci.edu, School of Education, University of California, Irvine, CA 92697; Katerina Schenke at kschenke@ucla.edu, National Center for Research on Evaluation, Standards, and Student Testing, University of California, Los Angeles, CA 90095; Tutrang Nguyen at tutrann@uci.edu, School of Education, University of California, Irvine, CA 92697; Diane K. O'Dowd at dkodowd@uci.edu, School of Biological Sciences, University of California, Irvine, CA 92697; Thurston Domina at tdomina@email.unc.edu, School of Education, University of North Carolina, Chapel Hill, NC 27599; Mark Warschauer at markw@uci.edu, School of Education, University of California, Irvine, CA 92697.

sequent course (Nielsen 2011). Our analyses provide a preliminary look at the relationship between widely implemented promising instructional practices and student outcomes using a student-level cross-course fixed-effects design to control for time-variant observable student characteristics as well as time-invariant student characteristics. We find that students earn slightly higher grades in courses that use promising instructional practices. However, we find no evidence that promising instructional practices have longer-term achievement effects across the entire student population, with the exception of first-generation college students, who may derive some post-class benefits from exposure to promising instructional practices.

We draw on reports from the National Academy of Sciences (NAS) and the National Research Council (NRC) in which promising practices were identified from a review of the research in undergraduate STEM education (Hake 1998; NAE 2005; Nielsen 2011; Wolter et al. 2011). We focus on three of the practices that figure prominently in the NAS/NRC recommendations: explicit instruction in epistemology or "thinking like a scientist," formative and summative assessment, and group-based or interactive learning. Although these instructional practices have a strong theoretical basis and intuitive appeal, findings about the effectiveness of these practices remain unclear. In particular, much of the research supporting promising instructional practices comes from evaluations of highly motivated and trained instructors in low-enrollment course settings or larger, discipline-specific studies (NAE 2005; Nielsen 2011). To address this gap, we systematically observe instruction across a variety of STEM disciplines and link these observations to student-level administrative data. Taking advantage of the instructional variation that we observe across these courses, we estimate the relation between exposure to instructional methods and grades in observed STEM courses, enrollment in subsequent courses toward STEM degrees, and grades in subsequent STEM courses. By focusing analysis on students who are exposed to multiple instructional styles across different classes and observing the extent to which this within-student variation is associated with variation in subsequent persistence and success in STEM courses, our approach makes it possible to separate the effects of these instructional practices from potentially confounding student characteristics.

BACKGROUND

Demand for employees in STEM is projected to outpace demand for employees in other occupations (NSB 2010). However, the number of STEM graduates from U.S. higher education is not keeping pace (Felder, Felder, and Dietz 1998; NSB 2010). Furthermore, STEM employers report that too many recent graduates are poorly prepared for the problem-solving tasks required in real-world applications (NAE 2005; Vergara et al. 2009).

Efforts to reform undergraduate STEM education highlight the first two years of undergraduate education as a critical period (Tinto 2006; Upcraft, Gardner, and Barefoot 2005). During these early years, many American undergraduates are enrolled in large lecture courses. Although these courses provide an efficient mechanism for disciplinary experts to communicate information, they may fail to provide adequate scaffolding for students to engage, learn, and experience success. Given this, many argue that traditionally organized, large lecture courses are ineffective settings for facilitating the skill development required for persistence in STEM majors (Mervis 2010). Many colleges and universities have begun to promote more active and engaged learning in the interest of improving scientific understanding and retention in STEM disciplines.

Several studies estimate associations between instructional practices and student outcomes, including motivation and course satisfaction, test performance, content retention and recall, and mastery of conceptual reasoning and problem-solving skills (Colliver 2000; Newman 2005; Chaplin 2009; Knight and Wood 2005; Michael 2006; Dougherty et al. 1995; Gijbels et al. 2005; Strobel and van Barneveld 2009, 43; Antepohl and Herzig 1999; Crouch and Mazur 2001; Deslauriers, Schelew, and Wieman 2011; Dochy et al. 2003; Lansiquot et al. 2011). This literature provides broad guidelines for instruction based primarily on small-scale evaluations of promising instructional practices on specific student outcomes such as problem-solving abilities (Singer, Nielsen, and Schweingruber 2012; Deslauriers, Schelew, and Wieman 2011). For example, one experimental study, in which students were randomly assigned either to instructors trained to facilitate student interaction or to one of the control course sections, indicates that interaction improves students' attendance, engagement, and conceptual knowledge (Deslauriers, Schelew, and Wieman 2011, 862).[1] Although these results are encouraging and typical of other disciplines, the research literature is fragmented with little evidence assessing the extent to which practices effective in one discipline setting (such as physics) can successfully transfer to other disciplinary settings (Singer, Nielsen, and Schweingruber 2012).

Extant studies of promising instructional practices in introductory STEM courses commonly feature instructors with extensive pedagogical training and interest, showcased in courses with relatively small enrollments and rich instructional resources (Han and Finkelstein 2013). A meta-analysis of 225 studies found that active learning increases student performance in science, engineering, and mathematics. Student performance included examinations and concept inventories (N = 158 studies) and odds of failing the course (N = 67 studies) (Freeman et al. 2014). Although this meta-analysis provides no data on the size of the study courses or the degree of instructional training, it notes that results are stronger when class size is under fifty and that instructors in these studies volunteered to incorporate active learning pedagogies. These studies suggest that altered instructional practices in introductory STEM courses can substantially improve student outcomes, but they provide only limited information on how efficient these practices are when implemented at scale in more typical learning environments (such as lecture halls of two hundred or more) at a research university.

Furthermore, the existing literature provides limited information regarding the effects of promising instructional practices on students who are particularly at risk for attrition from STEM fields, including students who are the first in their families to attend college (Davis 2012; Nunez and Cuccaro-Alamin 1998). Only 20 percent of students from underrepresented groups who aspire to a STEM degree successfully graduate with one within five years; first-generation college students have lower undergraduate grade point averages (GPAs) and are less likely to persist in STEM than students of college-educated parents (Hurtado, Eagen, and Chang 2010; Vuong, Brown-Welty, and Tracz 2010; Ishitani 2006; Aspelmeier et al. 2012; Chen 2005; DeFreitas and Rinn 2013; Martinez et al. 2009). The first two years are crucial in narrowing the gap for these at-risk students; instructional practices may play a role (Chen 2005).

We evaluate three broad categories of promising instructional strategies implemented at scale in large lecture courses: teaching epistemology explicitly and coherently; using formative and summative assessments; and group-based or interactive learning. This work builds on a related study analyzing undergraduate survey data from the eight large University of California campuses, which found that cultures of engagement varied by major into two categories related to the purpose of the degree for upper division students (Brint, Cantwell, and Hanneman 2008). Our study uses data from course observations and syllabi to capture the extent to which instructors in lower division STEM courses implement these promising instructional practices and the impact they may have on student achievement.

The NAS identified "teaching epistemology explicitly and coherently" as a promising practice for undergraduate STEM instruction (Nielsen 2011, 24). We define epistemology as understanding the concepts, separating fact from opinion, and critically analyzing concepts (Goldman 1986). For example, instructors might teach epistemology by modeling problem-solving techniques during lecture and guiding analysis of concepts—sometimes referred to as "thinking aloud." In other cases, they might teach epistemology by describing

---

[1]. In the experimental section, 211 of 271 students attended the day of the test, versus 171 of 267 for the control section. All students were offered extra credit for their time.

a key concept's intellectual history and its relevance to their research or to the field more broadly (DeLuca and Lari 2013; Pace and Middendorf 2004). Explicit coherent teaching includes systematically rearranging course content according to students' epistemological awareness and metacognition and strategically addressing science misconceptions prevalent among undergraduates (Grant 2008). To illustrate, instructors can intentionally refer to prior course content and big ideas, provide reinforcement through exam content, and connect content with everyday experience, helping students reframe understanding.

The NAS report advocates use of structured evaluations to improve undergraduate STEM instruction "using formative assessment techniques and feedback loops to change practice" as well as "developing learning objectives and aligning assessments with those objectives" (Nielsen 2011, 24). Formative assessments offer immediate feedback to both student and instructor. This feedback allows instructors to modify their teaching based on current student understanding and allows students to modify their study strategies (Black 2013; Harlen and James 1997). Formative assessment occurs when instructors check for students' understanding (via clicker questions and in-class exercises) and modify the lecture accordingly (Han and Finkelstein 2013). Instances of effective summative assessment include repeated use of graded exams, quizzes, and homework (Black 2013; Harlen and James 1997). These allow the instructor to ensure that learning objectives and assessments are properly aligned. Summative assessments also provide feedback so that students can modify their study strategies.

Interactive lectures provide opportunities for students to interact with peers and instructors (Singer, Nielsen, and Schweingruber 2012). Promising practices designed to improve interaction in lectures include: "allowing students to 'do' science, such as learning in labs and problem solving," "providing structured group learning experiences," and "promoting active, engaged learning" (Nielsen 2011, 24). Student-centered approaches create opportunities for students to collaborate over a single problem, or for more extended periods in a "flipped format" (Garcia, Gasiewski, and Hurtado 2011; Stage and Kinzie 2009). In addition to instructional reform, course structure reform—such as the addition of a lab section—provides added opportunity for collaboration (Nasr and Ramadan 2008; Farrior et al. 2007; Khousmi and Hadjou 2005).

METHOD

Our study uses systematic observations of instructional practice in large introductory STEM lecture courses from the Schools of Biological and Physical Sciences at UCI during the Spring 2013, Fall 2013, and Winter 2014 quarters. UCI is a highly selective institution and these schools are among the fastest-growing units on campus. Together, they enroll 55 percent of UCI undergraduates and 95 percent of UCI undergraduates in STEM fields. Enrollment for these schools has increased by 20 percent between 2003 and 2012. Over the same period, UCI's student population has undergone substantial demographic changes. Currently, 55 percent of UCI students are first-generation college students and 30 percent are members of underrepresented minority groups (UC Irvine Office of Institutional Research 2013).

Although more than 95 percent of UCI undergraduates earn a bachelor's of arts (BA) within six years, many students who begin as STEM majors transfer to other disciplines. After six years, fewer than half of incoming freshmen in the School of Physical Sciences earn a baccalaureate degree from that school, while retention rates of majors in Biological Sciences hover at approximately 60 percent (UC Irvine Office of Institutional Research 2013). In an effort to improve STEM persistence, both schools are undertaking instructional reforms. However, considerable instructional variation exists at UCI both across courses and even across sections of the same course. Course instructors have considerable discretion over their pedagogical methods. In many cases, lecturers—a category of instructors that includes adjuncts as well as teaching professors with security of employment—are leaders in the adoption of promising instructional practices.

By linking data from our observations of instruction in large gateway lecture courses with student-level administrative data, we take advantage of variation in instruction across sections of the same course to conduct a nonexperimental, population-based evaluation of the extent to which promising instructional practices promote positive student outcomes during the first two years.

Sample and Procedure

We observed instruction in forty introductory STEM courses at UCI. Our study identified all courses in the School of Biological Sciences and Physical Sciences that were prerequisites for other mandatory courses in one or more STEM major, were offered in multiple sections during the course of the year, and enrolled two hundred or more students. Eight courses met these criteria: Biological Sciences, From DNA to Organisms (BioSci 93), General Chemistry (Chem 1A, 1B, and 1C), Organic Chemistry (Chem 51A and Chem 51B), Single-Variate Calculus (Math 2A), and Classical Physics (Phys 7C).[2] It is useful to note that the courses in our sample play somewhat different roles on campus. Introductory Biology (BioSci 93) is the first of several mandatory courses for the Biology major. Similarly, the general chemistry series and organic chemistry courses are required for several STEM majors. By contrast, a lower proportion of students are required to take the next course in the sequence for Mathematics 2A and Physics 7C. During the year of the study, the university offered forty-two sections of these courses; forty sections participated in the study. Trained research assistants observed one course session in the first three weeks and one course session in the last three weeks of regular instruction. An overview of the course sample is presented in table 1.

For each observation, research assistants videotape lectures and collect data on instructional strategies using a researcher-developed observation protocol known as Simple Protocol for Observing Undergraduate Teaching (SPROUT).[3] Observations include detailed field notes during the lecture that are subsequently transferred to the observation protocol and contain both dichotomous indicators and qualitative evidence. Two researchers overlapped on 20 percent of the course sessions with inter-rater reliability of Cohen's kappa = 0.80. Coding disagreements and ambiguities were discussed among the research team as they occurred during the data collection process. Course materials such as syllabi and key handouts are also collected to identify content related to epistemology, assessment, and interaction.

Student administrative data was collected from the Office of Institutional Research (OIR). Our sample is diverse—58 percent are first-generation college students, 26 percent are members of underrepresented minority groups, and 56 percent are female. In addition to demographic and academic data, OIR provides course enrollments and grades (both in observed courses and in courses that students take in subsequent terms), allowing us to track student progress toward STEM degrees. The sample consists of UCI freshmen and sophomores attending one or more focal (that is, observed) courses. As few transfer students enroll in these introductory courses, they are excluded from analysis. The total sample includes 4,801 students. Students can enroll in more than one of the observed courses; thus a single student can provide more than one case and the analysis file includes 11,803 distinct observations.

Measures

The present study considers the relation between instruction and three measures of student success: student grades in the observed course (measured on a four-point scale, where an A is 4.0 and an F is 0.0), student odds of enrolling in subsequent courses toward STEM degrees, and student grades in subsequent

---

2. Organic Chemistry is a three-course sequence. However, no specific course follows the third course in the sequence and so we included only the first two courses in our analyses, using the third only in our measures of course progression and subsequent course grades.

3. SPROUT adapted content from three well-known observation protocols: U-Teach Observation Protocol, or UTOP (Walkington et al. 2012); the Reformed Teaching Observation Protocol, or RTOP (Sawada et al. 2002); and Teaching Dimensions Observation Protocol, or TDOP (Hora and Ferrare 2014). SPROUT is available online at http://www.projectsprout.education.uci.edu (accessed February 23, 2016).

Table 1. Description of Full Sample

Variable	Total Observations	Total Students	Mean/Percent	Standard Deviation	Minimum	Maximum
Epistemology[a]	11,803	4,801	0.00	1.00	−1.62	1.70
Assessment[a]	11,803	4,801	0.08	0.96	−1.00	2.60
Interaction[a]	11,803	4,801	0.06	0.99	−1.07	2.36
Math SAT[a]	11,494	4,610	0.00	1.00	−3.77	2.16
Verbal SAT[a]	11,494	4,610	0.00	1.00	−3.49	2.72
High school GPA[a]	11,786	4,789	0.00	1.00	−5.50	2.39
Focal course AP	11,803	4,801	0.30	0.46	0.00	1.00
Male	11,791	4,792	0.42	0.49	0.00	1.00
Black	11,791	4,792	0.02	0.12	0.00	1.00
Hispanic	11,791	4,792	0.21	0.41	0.00	1.00
Nonresident	11,791	4,792	0.09	0.29	0.00	1.00
White	11,791	4,792	0.12	0.32	0.00	1.00
Other	11,803	4,801	0.03	0.18	0.00	1.00
Low-income status	11,791	4,792	0.40	0.49	0.00	1.00
First-generation college	11,791	4,792	0.55	0.50	0.00	1.00
Focal course in major	11,803	4,801	0.63	0.48	0.00	1.00
Full-time student	11,803	4,801	1.00	0.07	0.00	1.00
Freshman	11,791	4,792	0.96	0.19	0.00	1.00
Repeating course	11,803	4,801	0.02	0.13	0.00	1.00

Source: Author's calculations.

Note: Observations are repeated cases of students because students are enrolled in one or more observed courses.

[a]Denotes scores are standardized. Asians were used as the reference group, as the university is considered a minority majority university (nearly 50 percent Asian). All others are dummy variables.

STEM courses.[4] Course syllabi indicate that grades in these classes were not curved to the mean, but rather on a straight point scale (Carrell and West 2008). Each of the observed courses serves as a prerequisite for another course in the same field. For example, students are required to successfully complete BioSci 93 to enroll in BioSci 94. Our subsequent enrollment outcome is a dichotomous measure of whether the student completed the subsequent course during the next academic term.[5] Our third outcome is the student's grade in that subsequent course, conditional on enrollment in the subsequent course and measured on a four-point scale.

We create composites for three instructional variables of interest: epistemology, assessment, and interaction. Items from observed lectures at both time points are summed to create a course composite measure. In these analyses, we assume that instructional practices are consistent across sections taught by the same instructor.[6] Correlation tables for the variables between the first and second obser-

---

4. Although many studies on instructional practices use concept inventories or examinations, these were not available in this observational cross-disciplinary study.

5. The full sample was used to analyze whether students completed the subsequent course; the student fixed effects sample was used to analyze grade in observed and subsequent course.

6. We tested this assumption by observing multiple course sections taught by three instructors. These observations returned a high degree to consistency within instructors across classes, with observations of instructional practices correlating at the 0.93 level across sections.

vation are included in appendix C. Because of the limited number of observed courses, a confirmatory factor analysis on the measurement model was not possible. As a result, we conceptualize our measures as indices or composites rather than as latent variables. The three measures capture the degree to which instructors engage in each of the three broad categories of instructional practices rather than indicators of how well instructors implement these practices (instructional quality).

The *epistemology* scale measures the extent to which instructors taught epistemology explicitly and coherently. We use five items from SPROUT to assess whether the instructor: models problem-solving techniques; makes connections between the course material and everyday student experience; refers to what students learned in prior course content; explicitly refers to themes, major theories, or other "big ideas" in the course; and refers explicitly to content on an upcoming exam. Summed across time points, epistemology practices range from 3 to 8 with a mean of 5.76 and standard deviation of 1.84 (alpha = 0.54). The correlation of the measure across both time points is 0.33. While some instructors engage in these activities relatively consistently across the instructional quarter, others refer to prior course content more in the beginning and "big ideas" at the end.

To measure *assessment* practices within the course, we use four items from SPROUT and four items from coded course syllabi. Assessment items include whether students take a quiz during study observations; whether instructor measures student understanding; whether instructor modifies lecture content as a result of measuring student understanding; number of clicker questions during the observed lectures; whether course has online homework; whether course has traditional homework; number of weekly quizzes; and number of exams. Across both time points, assessment practices range from 3 to 23 with a mean of 7.46 and a standard deviation of 5.28 (alpha = 0.70). The correlation of observed assessment practices across both time points is 0.69.

To measure instructional practices related to *interaction*, we use four items from SPROUT and one item from the coded syllabi. These include whether the lecture is interactive inclusive of student-peer or student-instructor exchanges; whether the instructor asks students to work in groups; whether work is conducted during the lecture; whether the course uses a flipped format; and whether a laboratory section is associated with the lecture. Across both time points, group-based or interactive practices range from 0 to 6 with a mean of 1.70 and standard deviation of 1.57 (alpha = 0.61). The correlation of group-based or interactive practices observed across both time points is 0.74.

To ease interpretation, we standardize the instructional variables and create z-scores. Because alphas of the constructs were relatively low, we estimate additional models using the individual items which constitute each of the scales. We note the results of these models when they are significantly different from zero in appendix B.

Where appropriate, analyses use demographic data collected from OIR, including gender (male or female), ethnicity (Asian American, African American, Hispanic, white, and other), first generation to attend college, and income status. Student academic characteristics are measured using weighted high school grade point average, mathematics and verbal SAT scores, and whether or not students took an advanced placement exam corresponding with the observed course. To ease interpretation, we standardize all continuous variables and create z-scores.

ANALYSES

The first analytic step involves descriptive investigation regarding the extent to which instruction and student outcomes vary across course sections. Observable student characteristics are associated with student exposure to three broad instructional variables, which may be a concern for interpreting the relation between exposure to instruction and academic outcomes.

After considering the student factors that predict exposure to promising instructional practices, we consider the relation between these practices and student achievement. We conduct a series of logistic and ordinary least squares regressions of the following basic form:

(1) $Y_i = \beta_0 + \beta_1 Instruction + \beta_2 Covariates_i + \Sigma\beta_3 Course + \Sigma\beta_4 T + \varepsilon$

where Y_i is the outcome of interest (odds of taking next course in STEM sequence). *Instruction* is the composite score for the specific instructional practice. *Covariates* represents a vector of student-level controls described above, including college enrollment year, transfer status, high school grade point average, SAT scores, gender, first generation to attend college, low income status, whether or not the student is repeating the course, and ethnicity. *Course* includes a matrix of course-title fixed effects designed to control for aspects of content, instruction, and student behavior that do not vary across sections of the same course.

We use a student fixed-effects model to more reliably identify the causal effects of instruction on grade in observed and subsequent course. This includes a high school fixed-effect term controlling for characteristics of high schools attended before matriculation at UCI. It may be that students from the same high school have similar preparation or prior knowledge that affects their performance, and to the extent that students from the same high school enroll together in the same sections of introductory-level courses, and that high school characteristics could confound analysis of instructional practices. These analyses take advantage of the fact that many students are enrolled in multiple courses that we observe. For example, typical first-year biology majors at UCI might enroll in as many as four observed courses (introductory biology, general chemistry, organic chemistry, and calculus). Repeated observations make it possible to account for observed and unobserved student characteristics and behaviors that are constant within a student, and thus more reliably estimate the extent to which exposure to promising instructional practices influences student academic behavior in that course and the subsequent course, net of observed and unobserved student characteristics (for analyses using a very similar design in public high school settings, see Clotfelter, Ladd, and Vigdor 2007; Xu, Hannaway, and Taylor 2011). These models take the following general form:

(2) $Y_{ij} = \beta_0 + \beta_1 Instruction_j + \Sigma\beta_2 Course_j + \Sigma\beta_3 Covariates + \Sigma\beta_4 Student_i + \varepsilon$

In this equation, Y_{ij} is the outcome of interest: student grades in focal course j and student grades in which focal course j is a prerequisite. *Student* in this model is a matrix of student fixed effects, controlling for all characteristics of students that are fixed across courses, including observable characteristics such as student race, gender, and economic and academic background, as well as invariant student characteristics such as intelligence and motivation.[7] The parameter of interest in this model, *Instruction*, therefore estimates the extent to which exposure to a given instruction technique in a given course influences a student's achievement in that course (along with subsequent course) when compared with other observed courses also taken by that student.

Model 2 provides more internally valid estimates of the causal effects of exposure to instruction than model 1. To be included in the student fixed-effects model, students must take at least three observed courses, which ensures that students take courses in more than one discipline. For example, rather than just Chem 1A and Chem 1B, a student taking three or more courses might also take BioSci 93. Nearly half of the students meet this criterion and thus contribute to the student fixed-effects analyses. Although the students in the fixed-effects sample do not differ significantly from students in the whole sample on demographic characteristics, they do score higher on several measures of prior achievement and include more STEM majors than the full sample. Table

---

7. Because student characteristics such as race and family background do not vary across course observations, model 2 excludes many of the student-level controls that our multivariate models include. However, the model includes controls for student characteristics that do vary across courses, including indicators of whether students completed AP courses relevant to the focal course and whether they are repeating the course.

Table 2. Student Fixed-Effects Sample: Students in Three or More Observed Courses

Variable	Observations	Students	Mean/ Percent	Standard Deviation	Minimum	Maximum
Epistemology[a]	8,303	2,382	−0.01	1.00	−1.62	1.70
Assessment[a]	8,303	2,382	0.12	0.98	−1.00	2.60
Interaction[a]	8,303	2,382	0.07	1.03	−1.07	2.36
Math SAT[a]	8,216	2,353	0.02	0.96	−3.29	2.16
Verbal SAT[a]	8,216	2,353	0.05	0.97	−3.38	2.72
High school GPA[a]	8,297	2,379	0.10	0.90	−4.59	2.14
Focal course AP	8,303	2,382	0.32	0.46	0.00	1.00
Male	8,297	2,379	0.42	0.49	0.00	1.00
Gender unknown	8,297	2,379	0.00	0.05	0.00	1.00
Black	8,297	2,379	0.02	0.12	0.00	1.00
Hispanic	8,297	2,379	0.20	0.40	0.00	1.00
Nonresident	8,297	2,379	0.08	0.26	0.00	1.00
White	8,297	2,379	0.12	0.32	0.00	1.00
Other	8,303	2,382	0.03	0.18	0.00	1.00
Low-income status	8,297	2,379	0.41	0.49	0.00	1.00
First-generation college	8,297	2,379	0.55	0.50	0.00	1.00
Focal course in major	8,303	2,382	0.71	0.45	0.00	1.00
Full-time student	8,303	2,382	1.00	0.06	0.00	1.00
Freshman	8,297	2,379	0.99	0.12	0.00	1.00
Repeating course	8,303	2,382	0.02	0.14	0.00	1.00

Source: Author's calculations.
[a]Denotes scores are standardized. Asians were used as the reference group because the university is considered a minority majority university (nearly 50 percent Asian). All others are dummy variables. In the Mean/Percent column, decimals for dummy variables show the percentage of students in that category.

1 provides descriptive statistics for the full sample and table 2 provides descriptive statistics for the student fixed-effects sample.[8] It is possible that the student fixed-effects model does not fully address the selection issues, because students may be more or less highly motivated by specific classes. However, by isolating instructional effects for individual students, it is the best approach to reliably identify the causal effects of instruction on observed and subsequent course.

In supplementary analyses, we add a series of instruction*first-generation student interaction terms to our student fixed-effects models. These interactions estimate the extent to which the association between instruction and student outcomes is different for students who are the first in their families to enroll in college compared with their peers who have more extensive exposure to higher education settings.

RESULTS

We include descriptive data on courses and instructional practices, followed by associations between these practices and student outcomes.

Instructional Variation Across and Within Courses

Table 3 provides a description of sample size by course, along with percent of students in each course who progress to the next course.

---
8. All models use the Huber-White estimator to correct for clustering at the course section level.

Table 3. Students Enrolled in Focal Course and Subsequent Course

	Number of Course Sections	Number of Instructors	Number of Students	Enrolled in Subsequent Course	Number of Students with Subsequent Course Grade
Biological Sciences 93	6	6	1,931	72.14%	1,393
Chemistry 1A	7	5	2,488	67.73%	1,685
Chemistry 1B	5	4	1,765	72.69%	1,283
Chemistry 1C	4	2	1,377	72.11%	993
Chemistry 51A	4	4	1,186	75.21%	892
Chemistry 51B	3	3	847	80.40%	681
Mathematics 2A	7	5	1,253	49.48%	620
Physics 7C	4	4	956	43.62%	417
Total	40	31	11,803	67.48%	7,964

Source: Author's calculations.

Because these courses are effectively a program gateway, administrators and instructors meet regularly to discuss course syllabi, instructional materials, and content. These conversations limit instructor freedom to define course content, but instructors have considerable autonomy over instructional strategies.

Table 4 provides descriptive data for three instructional measures (epistemology, assessment, and interaction). Observed instruction varies in important ways across disciplines and courses. Because all biology and physics course sections use clickers, courses in these fields rate higher than courses in other disciplines on the assessment scale. Biology has the highest mean on the interaction index, whereas Chem 51A and Chem 1C generate the highest means on the epistemology scale. Chem 1B and Math 2A yield the lowest means for all three instructional measures.

Most instructional practices also vary substantially across sections within the same course. Although BioSci 93 course sections involve more interactive instruction on average than other courses, we observe considerable variation in the prevalence of interactive instruction among the six BioSci 93 sections. Indeed, the standard deviation for the interactive instruction among BioSci 93 students (1.41) is larger than that for interactive instruction in the overall sample (1.00). This variation across course sections is important for our identification strategy given that we include course fixed effects. Less variation is evident in the use of formative and summative assessments across course sections relative to the variation across course sections in interactive instruction and explicit instruction about epistemology. Indeed, for Chem 1C we observe no variation in the use of assessment across course sections. Such within-course homogeneity makes it particularly difficult to identify the effects of assessment on student outcomes.

Student Selection into Instructional Environments

Because we cannot randomly assign students to classes, values in table 5 show the extent to which observable student characteristics predict instructional strategies used in the classroom. These analyses include controls for course titles, which explain between 50 percent and 80 percent of the observed variation in instructional exposure.[9]

Exposure to explicit epistemological instruction and assessment do not seem to vary

---

9. Supplementary models using observable student characteristics to predict exposure to three instructional strategies (excluding course title controls) explain only 2 to 3 percent of the variance, but return similar relationships between student characteristics and instructional exposure.

Table 4. Instructional Variation Across and Within Courses

	Mean	Standard Deviation	Minimum	Maximum
Epistemology scale				
Biological Sciences 93	−0.78	0.31	−1.06	0.04
Chemistry 1A	0.53	1.03	−1.62	1.15
Chemistry 1B	−0.71	0.39	−1.06	0.60
Chemistry 1C	0.84	0.27	0.60	1.15
Chemistry 51A	1.02	0.77	0.04	1.70
Chemistry 51B	−0.08	1.36	−1.62	1.70
Mathematics 2A	−0.60	0.82	−1.62	0.60
Physics 7C	−0.11	0.25	−0.51	0.04
Assessment scale				
Biological Sciences 93	1.41	0.82	0.62	2.60
Chemistry 1A	0.30	0.64	−0.82	0.80
Chemistry 1B	−0.61	0.15	−0.64	0.08
Chemistry 1C	−0.64	0.00	−0.64	−0.64
Chemistry 51A	−0.68	0.25	−1.00	−0.46
Chemistry 51B	−0.68	0.14	−0.82	−0.46
Mathematics 2A	−0.33	0.44	−1.00	0.26
Physics 7C	1.31	0.54	0.98	2.60
Interaction scale				
Biological Sciences 93	0.88	1.43	−0.50	2.36
Chemistry 1A	0.51	0.83	−1.07	1.22
Chemistry 1B	−0.88	0.32	−1.07	0.74
Chemistry 1C	−0.57	0.57	−1.07	0.74
Chemistry 51A	0.15	0.53	−0.50	0.64
Chemistry 51B	−0.14	0.28	−0.50	0.07
Mathematics 2A	−0.34	0.43	−0.45	0.19
Physics 7C	0.42	0.74	−1.07	1.22

Source: Author's calculations.

substantially with observable student characteristics. However, we find that men, Hispanic students, nonresident international students, and students retaking a course (after failing it) are exposed to more interactive instruction than peers, conditional on other observable characteristics. Students' SAT math scores are negatively associated with exposure to interactive instruction after controlling for other student characteristics. This suggests that some at-risk students and students who previously failed tend to choose courses with relatively high levels of interactive instruction.

Associations Between Instruction and Student Outcomes

Figure 1 shows student rates of progression to the next course in the sequence after controlling for student characteristics. BioSci 93 has more than 85 percent of students successfully progressing to the next course in the program sequence, despite the fact that instructional practices vary considerably across biology sections. By contrast, we observe considerable variation in progression rates for students in Chem 1A and 1B (general chemistry) as well as Math 2A. In Math 2A, for example, we observe

Table 5. Selection by Observables with Course Fixed Effects

	Epistemology b/se	Assessment b/se	Interaction b/se
Male	0.002	0.018	0.038*
	(0.015)	(0.010)	(0.016)
Gender unknown	0.152	−0.008	0.124
	(0.115)	(0.112)	(0.153)
Standardized SAT math	−0.001	−0.009	−0.024*
	(0.009)	(0.006)	(0.010)
Standardized SAT verbal	0.009	0.009	0.012
	(0.008)	(0.005)	(0.009)
Standardized high school GPA	−0.004	0.001	−0.009
	(0.008)	(0.006)	(0.004)
Whether AP in focal course	−0.017	0.013	−0.024
	(0.015)	(0.011)	(0.017)
Black	0.019	−0.064	−0.111
	(0.060)	(0.042)	(0.066)
Hispanic	0.028	0.032*	0.058**
	(0.019)	(0.013)	(0.021)
Non-resident	0.061*	0.036	0.053
	(0.028)	(0.019)	(0.029)
White	−0.006	−0.018	−0.016
	(0.023)	(0.016)	(0.027)
Other ethnicity	0.026	0.011	0.004
	(0.037)	(0.025)	(0.041)
Whether focal course was a major requirement	0.036*	−0.008	−0.037*
	(0.015)	(0.011)	(0.017)
Whether student was fulltime	−0.065	−0.103	0.056
	(0.095)	(0.080)	(0.130)
Whether student was freshman	−0.159*	−0.044	0.021
	(0.070)	(0.046)	(0.075)
Whether student repeated the course	−0.020	−0.049*	0.487***
	(0.051)	(0.023)	(0.031)
Whether student was low-income status	0.047**	0.007	0.004
	(0.016)	(0.011)	(0.018)
Whether student was first to attend college	−0.031	−0.028*	−0.040*
	(0.016)	(0.011)	(0.018)
Constant	−0.585***	1.552***	0.823***
	(0.115)	(0.094)	(0.151)
N	11,493	11,493	11,493
R^2	0.462	0.726	0.375

Source: Author's calculations.
Note: Asians were used as the reference group, as the university is considered a minority majority university (nearly 50% Asian).
*$p < .05$; **$p < .01$; ***$p < .001$

Figure 1. Probability of Taking Next Course in Series

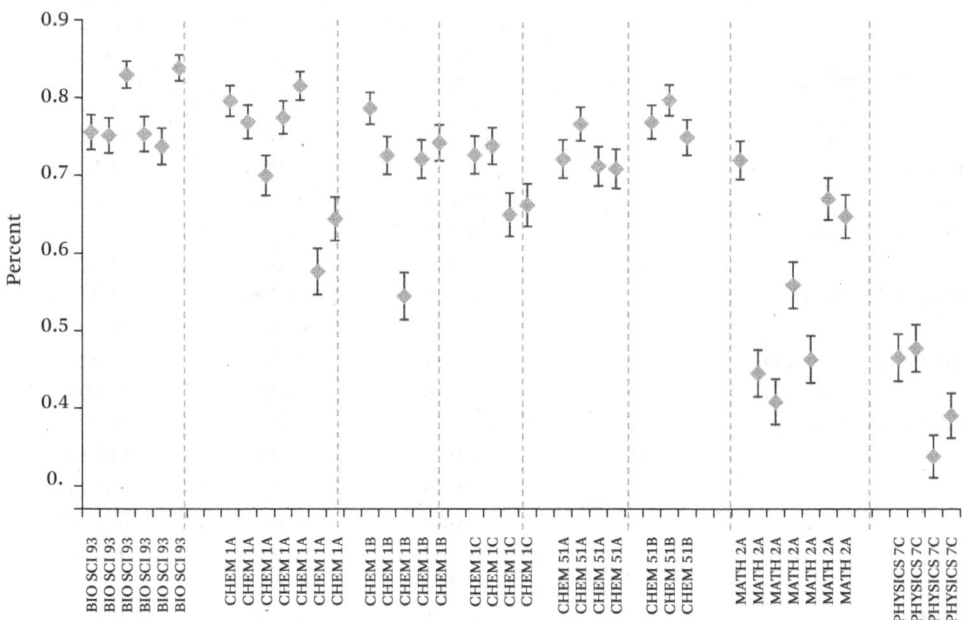

Source: Authors' calculations.

several course sections in which fewer than half of students progress to the next course in the sequence, as well as sections in which approximately 70 percent of the students progress to the next course in the sequence. However, many STEM majors are not required to take the subsequent course, Math 2B.

Figure 2 depicts the average grade earned in the subsequent course for those students who successfully progress, conditional on student characteristics. Grades prove to be relatively consistent in biology regardless of instructional practices for each section. This is not surprising as biology faculty standardized their grading. However, grades in chemistry and mathematics have larger standard deviations. Table 6 presents a series of analyses regressing student outcomes on instructional practices using the student fixed-effects sample (2,382 unique students; 4,762 observations). For external validity, we include analyses of the full sample in appendix C (4,801 students; 11,803 observations).

Grades in the observed course

The first panel considers the link between instructional practices and student grades in the observed course. Whereas the first two models indicate no significant link between epistemology or interaction and student grades, the third model (including all controls) suggests that students achieve higher grades in courses higher on epistemology (0.024, $p < 0.05$). In particular, subsequent analyses (see appendix B) of the five items comprising the epistemology scale point to positive effects on course grades for drawing connections to the real world (0.034, $p < 0.01$) and highlighting the "big picture" (0.073, $p < 0.05$). However, problem solving has a negative effect on observed course grade (−0.072, $p < 0.05$). The third model also suggests that students achieve higher grades in courses with increased interaction (0.031, $p < 0.01$). Of the five items making up this scale, subsequent analyses show that lectures inclusive of student-peer or student-instructor exchanges point to positive effects on course grades (0.067, $p < 0.001$). All three models suggest a similar positive effect on grades for courses that use more assessments (0.048, $p < 0.01$). In particular, subsequent analyses of the eight items this scale comprises point to a strong relation between the use of whole-class checks for understanding and

Figure 2. Average Student Grade in Subsequent Course

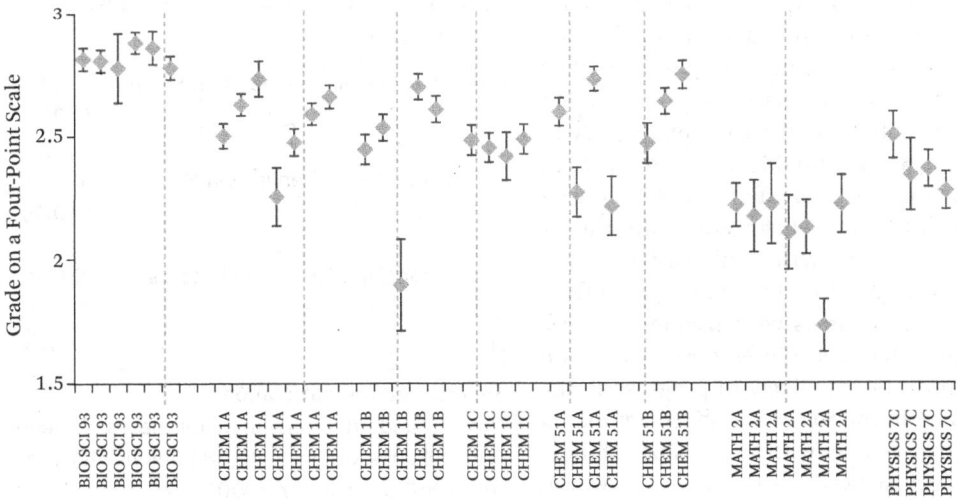

Source: Authors' calculations.

Table 6. Effects of Instruction on Student Grades in Observed and Subsequent Course

	Bivariate	+ Student Level Controls	+ High School Fixed Effects
Outcome: grade in observed course			
Epistemology	0.019	0.017	0.024*
	(0.011)	(0.011)	(0.012)
Assessment	0.036*	0.040*	0.048**
	(0.016)	(0.016)	(0.018)
Interaction	0.014	0.017	0.031**
	(0.011)	(0.010)	(0.012)
N	4,762	4,744	4,744
Outcome: grade in subsequent course			
Epistemology	−0.017	−0.017	−0.011
	(0.011)	(0.011)	(0.013)
Assessment	0.007	0.010	0.017
	(0.018)	(0.018)	(0.020)
Interaction	0.006	0.011	0.020
	(0.012)	(0.012)	(0.013)
N	4,762	4,744	4,744

Source: Authors' calculations.
Note: Standard errors in parentheses. N represents all observations for 2,382 unique students.
*$p < .05$; **$p < .01$; ***$p < .001$

grades (0.085, $p < 0.01$), such as a clicker question or asking all students to respond by raising their hands. Grade in current course may be problematic, however, because there may be a relationship between instructional practices and instructor grading policies.

Course Progression

To consider the relation between instructional practices and student odds of progressing to the next course in the STEM sequence, we used the full sample (see appendix A). Because the outcome for this analysis is dichotomous (in which students who enroll in the next course in the instructional sequence take a value of 1 and students who do not take a value of 0), we observe little variation among students who enroll at UCI from the same high school and even less variation applies to a single student. Therefore, we are unable to estimate high school or student fixed-effects models considering the link between instruction and student progression. However, the multivariate models reported in appendix A indicate that students who enroll in courses with frequent assessment and high levels of interactive instruction are significantly less likely to progress to the next course in the STEM sequence compared with peers in courses with lower values of these promising instructional practices. However, subsequent analyses point to a strong positive relation between problem solving and odds of progressing to the next course ($0.182, p < 0.01$) (see appendix B).

Grades in Subsequent Course

Perhaps the most powerful indicator of the extent to which instruction influences students' acquisition and retention is the association between instruction and grades in subsequent courses. These relations are presented in the second panel of table 6. The results from the third model indicate no relation between the three promising instructional practices and student achievement in subsequent courses. Supplemental analyses point to a positive association between problem solving in the current course and grade in the subsequent course ($0.097, p < 0.01$). Although suggestive, the multiple comparisons problem applies to these supplemental analyses, in which we test the effects of twelve instructional variables.

Table 7 provides some evidence to suggest that these instructional practices have differential effects for an important student subgroup—first-generation college students. We include an interaction term to allow the association between instruction and subsequent student achievement to vary between first-generation college students and peers with college-educated parents. We find that first-generation students experience significantly higher gains in subsequent course grades than their counterparts when exposed to frequent assessment ($0.065, p < 0.01$) and interactive instruction ($0.057, p < 0.01$), but not explicit instruction in epistemology.

Table 7. Effects of Instruction on First-Generation College Student and Grade in Subsequent Course

Epistemology*First Generation Status	0.002
	(0.018)
Assessment*First Generation Status	0.065**
	(0.024)
Interaction*First Generation Status	0.057**
	(0.021)
N	4,744

Source: Authors' calculations.
Note: Standard errors in parentheses. N represents all observations for 2,382 unique students.
*$p < .05$; **$p < .01$; ***$p < .001$

DISCUSSION

This study aims to evaluate the effects of three widely agreed-upon promising practices—explicit instruction in epistemology or "thinking like a scientist," formative and summative assessment, and group-based or interactive learning—as implemented at scale in large undergraduate introductory STEM courses (Nielsen 2011, 24). Small-scale studies and discipline-specific studies suggest these strategies have potential for improving student outcomes (Hake 1998; NAE 2005; Nielsen 2011; Wolter et al. 2011). However, in the current study, which investigates these practices in large undergraduate STEM courses typical of major research universities, we find little evidence to suggest that promising instructional practices improve student outcomes for the average UCI student. UCI is a single example and not generalizable to all undergraduate STEM universities. Yet the university is fairly typical of at least one important segment of the American higher education system—the large research university. Close examination of promising instructional strategies at this large, decentralized institution is capable of providing new insights regarding promising instructional strategies implemented at scale.

We use variation across sections of the same course to illustrate the effects of promising instructional practices on student grades in their current course, course progression, and subsequent grades. Our findings suggest that the relation between instructional practices and student outcomes is weak. Regardless of the extent to which instructors use promising instructional practices, student outcomes are fairly similar across course sections. Our most conservative student fixed-effects models suggest that students earn slightly higher grades in courses where instructors use explicit epistemological instruction, frequent assessment, and group-based or interactive learning. However, we find no evidence to suggest that these strategies have an effect on grades in subsequent courses for the average student. Furthermore, we find some evidence to suggest that first-generation college students benefit uniquely from exposure to frequent assessment and highly interactive instructional strategies.

Our findings also provide insights into the relation between instructional practices and students' odds of progressing to subsequent courses in the STEM sequence. Although we are unable to estimate fixed-effects models on course progress, our multivariate models indicate that students exposed to frequent assessment and group-based or interactive learning are less likely to progress to the next course in the series than their peers in more traditional lecture classes. This finding raises important questions regarding the implications of promising instructional practices, implemented at scale, for improving student persistence in STEM fields. Future analyses should address the consequences of instructional practices for student persistence more extensively. Our findings—that the same instructional practices that predict high grades in a given course do not predict enrollment and success in subsequent courses—somewhat parallel Carrell and West's findings (2008). This study, which randomly assigned students to core courses at the U.S. Air Force Academy, finds that students who performed well in their initial mathematics course performed significantly worse in the mandatory subsequent courses in math, science, and engineering. Furthermore, they find that teacher effects are quite different between current and subsequent courses. Although students get lower grades, on average, in courses with high-ranking, highly educated tenured instructors, these same instructor characteristics positively predict student performance in subsequent courses.

However, two important caveats apply to these general findings. First, we find some evidence that two of the promising practices—exposure to formative and summative assessment and group-based or interactive instructional strategies—do benefit first-generation college students. These practices have a positive impact on grade in the next course in the STEM series. Given that first-generation students disproportionately drop out of STEM, this finding can be valuable for mitigating this attrition rate. Because we found no evidence that promising practices have a negative impact on the general population but a positive one for first-generation students, this may be an important consideration in their adaptation.

Second, our observational data focus on the extent to which instructors use particular strategies and not how well they implement thems. We suspect that this distinction is crucial. At UCI and in many other higher education settings, instructors have a great deal of professional autonomy, receive little pedagogical training, and have few signals regarding the effectiveness of their instruction and few incentives to invest considerable time and energy to teaching. After observing each of this study's courses, we conducted brief, informal interviews with each of the instructors we observed. We learned that many dedicated instructors refrain from implementing the sorts of promising practices that we highlight in this paper, choosing to stick instead with tried and true instructional techniques. Meanwhile, other instructors struggle to implement highly touted "promising practices" in an effective manner. We believe that future research and instructional reform efforts should devote attention to the processes through which instructors encounter and adopt promising instructional practices. In particular, we hope that the sorts of observational data our project has collected can help instructors reflect on their practices and learn from one another.

Third, UCI is a selective institution. At the

time of this study, to enroll in introductory chemistry, biology, and mathematics courses, UCI students must either score above 600 on the mathematics portion of the SAT or complete a rigorous set of developmental math courses. Although our sample of UCI introductory STEM students is ethnically and economically diverse, these students are likely to be more motivated and academically engaged than their countparts nationwide. These characteristics may blunt the relation between instruction and student learning, insofar as UCI students' study skills and motivation can compensate for courses with ineffective instruction. If true, it is possible that promising instructional practices have a larger impact among heterogeneous students enrolled in STEM courses at community colleges and other less selective colleges and universities, especially given that these colleges typically include more first-generation students who were found to benefit from the practices we observed (Wolter et al. 2011). Future research needs to address the effects of these promising practices at scale in heterogeneous settings, such as community colleges.

APPENDIX A

Analyses of Full Sample

Table A1. Effects of Instruction for Full Sample

	Bivariate	+ Student Level Controls	+ High School Fixed Effects	Student Fixed Effects
Outcome: grade in observed course				
Epistemology	−0.006	−0.003	0.010	0.024*
	(0.014)	(0.013)	(0.012)	(0.011)
Assessment	−0.023	−0.018	−0.013	0.048**
	(0.02)	(0.017)	(0.018)	(0.017)
Interaction	−0.055***	−0.030**	−0.016	0.031**
	(0.013)	(0.011)	(0.011)	(0.011)
N	11,348	11,347	11,346	4,744
Outcome: odds of progressing to next course				
Epistemology	−0.037	−0.046	—	—
	(0.028)	(0.029)		
Assessment	−0.168***	−0.171***	—	—
	(0.041)	(0.042)		
Interaction	−0.113***	−0.092***	—	—
	(0.026)	(0.027)		
N	11,803	11,493	—	—
Outcome: grade in subsequent course				
Epistemology	−0.042**	−0.046***	−0.038**	−0.011
	(0.015)	(0.013)	(0.014)	(0.012)
Assessment	−0.016	−0.012	−0.006	0.017
	(0.021)	(0.019)	(0.021)	(0.020)
Interaction	−0.050***	−0.017	−0.001	0.020
	(0.013)	(0.012)	(0.013)	(0.013)
N	7,905	7,762	7,761	4,744

Source: Authors' calculations.

Note: Student fixed effects include only students who took three or more of the observed courses. Standard errors in parentheses.

*$p < .05$; **$p < .01$; ***$p < .001$

APPENDIX B

Results of Analyses of Individual Scale Items

Table B1. Effects of Statistically Significant Individual Items for Three Instructional Scales

	Student Fixed-Effects Sample
Grade in observed course	
Epistemology	
Problem solving	−0.072*
	(0.021)
Real world examples	0.034**
	(0.013)
Big picture/ideas	0.073***
	(0.021)
Assessment	
Checking for understanding	0.085***
	(0.019)
Interaction	
Interactive lecture	0.067***
	(0.015)
Grade in subsequent course	
Epistemology	
Problem solving	0.097**
	(0.031)
N	4,744

Source: Author's calculations.
Note: The items listed are individual components of the composite scales that were statistically significant. N represents all observations for 2,382 unique students. Standard errors in parentheses.
*$p < .05$; **$p < .01$; ***$p < .001$

Table B2. Effects of Statistically Significant Individual Items for Three Instructional Scales

	Bivariate	+ Student Level Controls
Outcome: Odds of progressing to next course		
Epistemology		
Problem solving	0.302***	0.182**
	(0.066)	(0.068)
N	11,494	11,493

Source: Author's calculations.
Note: The items listed are individual components of the composite scales that were statistically significant. Student fixed effects sample does not have enough variation to estimate odds of progressing. Standard errors in parentheses.
*$p < .05$; **$p < .01$; ***$p < .001$

APPENDIX C

Correlations of Pre- and Post- Scale Items

Table C1. Correlation Matrix for Epistemology Scale

	Problem Solving1	Problem Solving2	Real World1	Real World2	Prior Course1	Prior Course2	Big Picture1	Big Picture2	Test 1	Test 2
Problem solving1	1.00									
Problem solving2	0.51	1.00								
Real world1	−0.34	−0.32	1.00							
Real world2	−0.34	−0.28	0.67	1.00						
Prior course1	−0.06	−0.26	0.00	−0.03	1.00					
Prior course2	−0.04	0.36	0.15	0.09	−0.06	1.00				
Big picture1	0.06	0.11	0.03	0.06	0.33	0.01	1.00			
Big picture2	−0.05	0.21	0.04	0.12	−0.05	0.09	0.18	1.00		
Test1	0.04	0.27	0.07	0.06	0.03	0.20	0.21	0.14	1.00	
Test2	0.11	0.22	0.13	0.05	0.05	0.05	0.07	0.40	0.47	1.00

Source: Authors' calculations.
Note: Instructors seem to mention prior course content at the beginning of the term and big picture/ideas at the end of the term.

Table C2. Correlation Matrix for Assessment Scale

	Assessment1	Assessment2	Check Understanding1	Check Understanding2	Modify Lesson1	Modify Lesson2	Number Click Ques 1	Number Click Ques 2
Assessment1	1.00							
Assessment2	0.00	1.00						
Check understanding1	0.18	0.40	1.00					
Check understanding2	0.12	0.42	0.46	1.00				
Modify lesson1	−0.05	0.13	0.62	0.36	1.00			
Modify lesson2	0.19	0.28	0.38	0.72	0.28	1.00		
Number click ques1	0.17	0.17	0.58	0.27	0.41	0.26	1.00	
Number click ques2	0.05	0.51	0.63	0.67	0.37	0.67	0.57	1.00

Source: Authors' calculations.
Note: Assessments, such as quizzes, were rarely observed.

Table C3. Correlation Matrix for Interaction Scale

	Group 1	Group 2	Interactive 1	Interactive 2	Desk Work 1	Desk Work 2
Group1	1.00					
Group2	0.54	1.00				
Interactive1	0.09	0.26	1.00			
Interactive2	0.03	0.20	0.27	1.00		
Desk work1	0.30	0.27	0.29	0.37	1.00	
Desk work2	−0.07	−0.06	0.12	0.14	0.38	1.00

Source: Authors' calculations.
Note: The interactive variable is on a scale of 0 to 3, thus one would imagine variation in the interaction between pre and post.

REFERENCES

Antepohl, Wolfram, and Stefan Herzig. 1999. "Problem-Based Learning Versus Lecture-Based Learning in a Course of Basic Pharmacology: A Controlled, Randomized Study." *Medical Education* 33(2): 106–13.

Aspelmeier, Jeffery E., Michael M. Love, Lauren A. McGill, Ann N. Elliott, and Thomas W. Pierce. 2012. "Self-Esteem, Locus of Control, College Adjustment, and GPA Among First- and Continuing-Generation Students: A Moderator Model of Generational Status." *Research in Higher Education* 53(7): 755–81.

Baillie, Caroline, and Geraldine Fitzgerald. 2010. "Motivation and Attribution in Engineering Students." *European Journal of Engineering Education* 25(2): 145–55.

Black, Paul. 2013. "An Assessment Perezhivanie: Building an Assessment Pedagogy for, with and of Early Childhood Science Learning." In *Valuing Assessment in Science Education: Pedagogy, Curriculum, Policy*, edited by Deborah Corrigan, Richard Gunstone, and Alister Jones. New York: Springer.

Brint, Steven, Allison M. Cantwell, and Robert A. Hanneman. 2008. "The Two Cultures of Undergraduate Academic Engagement." *Research in Higher Education* 49(5): 383–402.

Carrell, Scott E., and James E. West. 2008. "Does Professor Quality Matter? Evidence from Random Assignment of Students to Professors." *NBER* working paper no. w14081. Cambridge, Mass.: National Bureau of Economic Re search.

Chaplin, Susan. 2009. "Assessment of the Impact of Case Studies on Student Learning Gains in an Introductory Biology Course." *Journal of College Science Teaching* 39(1): 72–79.

Chen, Xianglei. 2005. *First-Generation Students in Postsecondary Education: A Look at Their College Transcripts.* NCES 2005-171. Washington: U.S. Department of Education.

Clotfelter, Charles T., Helen F. Ladd, and Jacob L. Vigdor. 2007. "How and Why Do Teacher Credentials Matter for Student Achievement?" *NBER* working paper no. 12828. Cambridge, Mass.: National Bureau of Economic Research.

Colliver, Jerry A. 2000. "Effectiveness of Problem-Based Learning Curricular: Research and Theory." *Academic Medicine* 75(3): 259–66.

Crouch, Catherine H., and Eric Mazur. 2001. "Peer Instruction: Ten Years of Experience and Results." *American Journal of Physics* 69(9): 970–77.

Davis, Jeff. 2012. *The First Generation Student Experience: Implications for Campus Practice, and Strategies for Improving persistence and Success.* Sterling, Va.: Stylus Publishing.

DeFreitas, Stacie Craft, and Anne Rinn. 2013. "Academic Achievement in First Generation College Students: The Role of Academic Self-Concept." *Journal of the Scholarship of Teaching and Learning* 13(1): 57–67.

DeLuca, V. William, and Nasim Lari. 2013. "Developing Students' Metacognition Skills in a Data-Rich Environment." *Journal of STEM Education: Innovations and Research* 14(1): 45–55.

Deslauriers, Louis. Ellen Schelew, and Carl Wieman. 2011. "Improved Learning in Large-Enrollment Physics Class." *Science* 332(6031): 862–64.

Dochy, Filip, Mien Segers, Piet Van den Bossche, and David Gijbels. 2003. "Effects of Problem-Based Learning: A Meta-Analysis." *Learning and Instruction* 13(5): 533–68.

Dougherty, Ralph C., Graig W. Bowen, Terry A. Berger, William S. Rees, Edward K. Mellon, Elizabeth J. Pulliam. 1995. "Cooperative Learning and Enhanced Communication: Effects on Student Performance, Retention, and Attitudes in General Chemistry." *Journal of Chemical Education* 72(2): 793–97.

Farrior, Donna, William Hamill, Leslie Keiser, Michael Kessler, Peter LoPresti, Jerry McCoy, Shirley Barbara Pomeranz, William Potter, and Bryan Tapp. 2007. "Interdisciplinary Lively Application Projects in Calculus Courses." *Journal of STEM Education* 8(3): 1–13.

Felder, Richard M., Gary N. Felder, and E. Jacquelin Dietz. 1998. "A Longitudinal Study of Engineering Student Performance and Retention v. Comparisons with Traditionally-Taught Students." *Journal of Engineering Education* 87(4): 469–80.

Freeman, Scott, Sarah L. Eddy, Miles McDonough, Michelle K. Smith, Nnadozie Okoroafor, Hannah Jordt, and Mary Pat Wenderoth. 2014. "Active Learning Increases Student Performance in Science, Engineering, and Mathematics." *Proceedings of the National Academy of Sciences* 111(23): 8410–15.

Garcia, Gina A., Josephine A. Gasiewski, and Sylvia Hurtado. 2011. "Principle of Good Practice in Introductory STEM Courses: Listening to the Voices of Faculty and Students." *Association for* the Study of Higher Education. Accessed December 17, 2015. http://www.heri.ucla.edu/nih/downloads/ASHE2011GasiewskiIntroClassrooms.pdf.

Gijbels, David, Filip Dochy, Piet Van den Bossche, and Mien Segers. 2005. "Effects of Problem-Based Learning: A Meta-Analysis from the Angle of Assessment." *Review of Educational Research* 75(1): 27–61.

Goldin, Claudia, and Lawrence Katz. 2009. *The Race Between Education and Technology.* Boston, Mass.: Harvard University Press.

Goldman, Alvin I. 1986. *Epistemology and Cognition.* Boston, Mass.: Harvard University Press.

Grant, Bruce W. 2008. "Practitioner Research as a Way of Knowing: A Case Study of Teacher Learning in Improving Undergraduates' Concept Acquisition of Evolution by Natural Selection." NAS Reviewed Commissioned Paper from the National Research Council Board on Science Education Workshop "Linking Evidence and Promising Practices in STEM Undergraduate Education." Washington, D.C. (June 30, 2008).

Hake, Richard R. 1998. "Interactive-Engagement Versus Traditional Methods: A Six-Thousand Student Survey of Mechanics Test Data for Introductory Physics Courses." *American Journal of Physics* 66(1): 64–74.

Han, Jae Hoon, and Adam Finkelstein. 2013. "Understanding the Effects of Professors' Pedagogical Development with Clicker Assessment and Feedback Technologies and the Impact on Students' Engagement and Learning in Higher Education." *Computers & Education* 65(1): 64–76.

Harlen, Wynne, and Mary James. 1997. "Assessment and Learning: Differences and Relationships Between Formative and Summative Assessment." *Assessment in Education* 4(3): 365–79.

Hora, Matthew T., and Joseph J. Ferrare. 2014. "Re-measuring Postsecondary Teaching: How Singular Categories of Instruction Obscure the Multiple Dimensions of Classroom Practice." *Journal of College Science Teaching* 43(3): 36–41.

Hurtado, Sylvia, Kevin Eagen, and Mitchell Chang. 2010. "Degrees of Success: Bachelor's Degree Completion Rates Among Initial STEM Majors." Research brief. Los Angeles: University of California, Higher Education Research Institute. Accessed December 17, 2015. http://www.heri.ucla.edu/nih/downloads/2010%20-%20Hurtado,%20Eagan,%20Chang%20-%20Degrees%20of%20Success.pdf.

Ishitani, Terry T. 2006. "Studying Attrition and Degree Completion Behavior Among First-Generation College Students in the United States." *Journal of Higher Education* 77(5): 861–85.

Khousmi, Ahmed, and Brahim Hadjou. 2005. "Learning Probabilities in Computer Engineering by Using a Competency and Problem-Based Approach." *Journal of STEM Education* 6(3/4): 5–14.

Knight, Jennifer K., and William B. Wood. 2005. "Teaching More by Lecturing Less." *Cell Biology Education* 4(4): 298–310.

Kyle, William C. 1997. "The Imperative to Improve Undergraduate Education in Science, Mathematics, Engineering, and Technology." *Journal of Research in Science Teaching* 34(6): 547–49.

Lansiquot, Reneta D., Reginald A. Blake, Janet Liou-Mark, and A. E. Dreyfuss. 2011. "Interdisciplinary Problem-Solving to Advance STEM Success for All Students." *Peer Review: Association of American Colleges and Universities* 13(3): 19–22.

Levy, Frank, and Richard J. Murnane. 2012. *The New Division of Labor: How Computers Are Creating the Next Job Market.* Princeton, N.J.: Princeton University Press.

Martinez, Julia A., Kenneth J. Sher, Jennifer L. Krull, and Phillip K. Wood. 2009. "Blue-Collar Scholars?: Mediators and Moderators of University Attrition in First-Generation College Students." *Journal of College Student Development* 50(1): 87–103.

McGinn, Michelle K., and Wolff-Michael Roth. 1999. "Preparing Students for Competent Scientific Practice: Implications of Recent Research in Science and Technology Studies." *Educational Researcher* 28(3): 14–24.

Mervis, Jeffrey. 2010. "Better Intro Courses Seen as Key to Reducing Attrition of STEM Majors." *Science* 330(6002): 306.

Michael, Joel. 2006. "Where's the Evidence that Active Learning Works?" *Advances in Physiology Education* 30(4): 159–67.

Nasr, Karim J., and Bassem H. Ramadan. 2008. "Impact Assessment of Problem-Based Learning in an Engineering Course." *Journal of STEM Education* 9(3/4): 16–24.

National Academy of Engineering (NAE). 2005. *Educating the Engineer of 2020: Adapting Engineering Education to the New Century.* Washington, D.C.: National Academies Press.

National Science Board (NSB). 2010. "Projected

Growth of Employment in S&E Occupations, Chapter 3 Science and Engineering." Last modified January 2010. Accessed October 20, 2014. http://www.nsf.gov/statistics/seind10/c3/c3s.htm.

Newman, Mark J. 2005. "Problem-Based Learning: An Introduction and Overview of the Key Features of the Approach." *Journal of Veterinary Medical Education* 32(1): 12–20.

Nielsen, Natalie. 2011. *Promising Practices in Undergraduate Science, Technology, Engineering, and Mathematics Education: Summary of Two Workshops.* Washington, D.C.: National Academies Press.

Nunez, Anne-Marie, and Stephanie Cuccaro-Alamin. 1998. *First-Generation Students: Undergraduates Whose Parents Never Enrolled in Postsecondary Education.* NCES 98-082. Washington: U.S. Department of Education. Accessed December 17, 2015. http://nces.ed.gov/pubs98/98082.pdf.

Pace, David, and Joan Middendorf. 2004. "Decoding the Disciplines: Helping Students Learn Disciplinary Ways of Thinking." *New Directions for Teaching and Learning Special Issue* 2004(98):1–12.

Sawada, Daiyo, Michael D. Piburn, Eugene Judson, Jeff Turley, Kathleen Falconer, Russell Benford, and Irene Bloom. 2002. "Measuring Reform Practices in Science and Mathematics Classrooms: The Reformed Teaching Observation Protocol." *School Science and Mathematics* 102(6): 245–53.

Singer, Susan R., Natalie R. Nielsen, and Heidi A. Schweingruber. 2012. *Discipline-Based Education Research: Understanding and Improving Learning in Undergraduate Science and Engineering.* Washington, D.C.: National Academies Press.

Stage, Frances K., and Jillian Kinzie. 2009. "Reform in Undergraduate Science, Technology, Engineering, and Mathematics: The Classroom Context." *Journal of General Education* 58(2): 85–105.

Strobel, Johannes, and Angela van Barneveld. 2009. "When Is PBL More Effective? A Meta-Synthesis of Meta-Analyses Comparing PBL to Conventional Classroom." *Interdisciplinary Journal of Problem-Based Learning* 3(1): 44–58.

Tinto, Vincent. 2006. "Research and Practice of Student Retention: What Next?" *Journal of College Student Retention: Research, Theory and Practice* 8(1): 1–19.

University of California, Irvine Office of Institutional Research. 2013. Data provided under IRB# 2012-9277. Accessed December 17, 2015. http://www.oir.uci.edu.

Upcraft, M. Lee, John N. Gardner, and Betsy O. Barefoot, eds. 2005. *Challenge and Support: Creating Climates for First-Year Student Success.* San Francisco: Jossey-Bass.

Vergara, Claudie E., Mark Urban-Lurain, Cindee Dresen, Tammy Coxen, Taryn MacFarlane, Kysha Frazier, and Thomas F. Wolff. 2009. "Aligning Computing Education with Engineering Workforce Computational Needs: New Curricular Directions to Improve Computational Thinking in Engineering Graduates." Paper presented at the Frontiers in Education. San Antonio, Tex. (October 21, 2009).

Vuong, Mui, Sharon Brown-Welty, and Susan Tracz. 2010. "The Effects of Self-Efficacy on Academic Success of First-Generation College Sophomore Students." *Journal of College Student Development* 51(1): 50–64.

Walkington, Candice, Prerna Arora, Shasta Ihorn, Jessica Gordon, Mary Walker, Larry Abraham, and Mary Marder. 2012. "Development of the UTeach Observation Protocol: A Classroom Observation Instrument to Evaluate Mathematics and Science Teachers from the UTeach Preparation Program." Unpublished paper. Southern Methodist University.

Wolter, Bjørn H. K., Mary A. Lundeberg, Hosun Kang, and Clyde F. Herreld. 2011. "Students' Perceptions of Using Personal Response Systems ("Clicker") with Cases in Science." *Journal of College Science Teaching* 40(4): 14–19.

Xu, Zeyu, Jane Hannaway, and Colin Taylor. 2011. "Making a Difference? The Effects of Teach for America in High School." *Journal of Policy Analysis and Management* 30(3): 447–69.